T0319381

APOSTLES OF INEQUALITY

Rural Poverty, Political Economy, and the *Economist*, 1760–1860

JIM HANDY

Apostles of Inequality

Rural Poverty, Political Economy, and the *Economist*, 1760–1860

UNIVERSITY OF TORONTO PRESS
Toronto Buffalo London

ISBN 978-1-4875-6353-0 (cloth)   ISBN 978-1-4875-6355-4 (EPUB)
                                  ISBN 978-1-4875-6354-7 (PDF)

Library and Archives Canada Cataloguing in Publication

Title: Apostles of inequality : rural poverty, political economy, and the Economist, 1760–1860 / Jim Handy.
Names: Handy, Jim, 1952– author.
Description: Includes bibliographical references and index.
Identifiers: Canadiana (print) 2021038252X | Canadiana (ebook) 20210382627 | ISBN 9781487563530 (cloth) | ISBN 9781487563554 (EPUB) | ISBN 9781487563547 (PDF)
Subjects: LCSH: Rural poor – England – History – 18th century. | LCSH: Rural poor – England – History – 19th century. | LCSH: Agriculture and state – England – History – 18th century. | LCSH: Agriculture and state – England – History – 19th century. | LCSH: England – Economic conditions – 18th century. | LCSH: England – Economic conditions – 19th century. | LCSH: England – Rural conditions.
Classification: LCC HC79.P6 H36 2022 | DDC 362.5094209/033–dc23

We wish to acknowledge the land on which the University of Toronto Press operates. This land is the traditional territory of the Wendat, the Anishnaabeg, the Haudenosaunee, the Métis, and the Mississaugas of the Credit First Nation.

University of Toronto Press acknowledges the financial support of the Government of Canada, the Canada Council for the Arts, and the Ontario Arts Council, an agency of the Government of Ontario, for its publishing activities.

 Canada Council for the Arts   Conseil des Arts du Canada

 ONTARIO ARTS COUNCIL
CONSEIL DES ARTS DE L'ONTARIO
an Ontario government agency
un organisme du gouvernement de l'Ontario

Funded by the Government of Canada   Financé par le gouvernement du Canada    Canadä

Contents

Acknowledgments

It has taken a long time for this work to move from idea, to research, to words on the page, and then to publication. The debts I have incurred have multiplied as the years have gone by. I can never hope to acknowledge all of them here, let alone begin to repay them.

First, I would like to thank the many people in villages in highland Guatemala who more than forty years ago first taught me to look at peasant farming differently and who since then have provided me with lessons in perseverance and determination despite the many afflictions they have been forced to bear. The lessons they have taught me permeate the pages of this book.

I have had the great fortune for more than three decades to work in what must be, at least from my experience, the most convivial History Department in the world. It is hard to imagine colleagues more pleasant to work with, more insightful in their comments, more genuinely interested in one another's research, and readier to read carefully each other's work. Their insights, useful comments on, and kind criticisms of aspects of this work as it progressed from idea to somewhat confused chapters presented at research workshops to more polished ventures were always welcome. If space provided, I would list here each of them; a more generalized though deeply felt expression of my gratitude will need to suffice. I do wish to thank especially Andrew Watson, who carefully read the manuscript as it neared the end of its journey. I also wish to thank Rilla Friesen, who did a superb job in the original copyediting of the rough manuscript.

I have also had the pleasure of working with some remarkable students, many of whom have become respected scholars. Some of the ideas in the book first saw light as lectures and discussions presented over two decades in a course entitled "The Menace of Progress." I have benefited immensely from the engagement and encouragement (and sometimes scepticism) students have brought to these discussions every year. Their enthusiasm helped reinforce my own beliefs that the history presented here was important and had contemporary consequences, and their questions helped me refine my approach to that history. One of those students, Carla Fehr, should be singled out. She was persuaded, many years ago, that the most exciting project for summer employment might be to read old editions of the *Economist* newspaper. This was before the paper was digitized and, thus, a much more daunting task. Though I am not sure she did, in fact, find it to be an exciting summer's task, she continued on to do a very fine master's thesis on the topic. A good portion of my early appreciation for the importance of the *Economist* stemmed from our conversations. A number of other graduate students helped inspire or inform some of this work: Patrick Chasse, Matt Gravlin, and Michael Kirkpatrick should all be thanked.

Much earlier versions of some of the work in chapters 2, 9, and 10 appeared as articles in the *Journal of Agrarian Change, Studies in Political Economy*, and the *Canadian Journal of History*. I wish to thank the editors and anonymous reviewers of those journals for their comments.

I would also like to thank the team at the University of Toronto Press, especially Stephen Shapiro. Stephen has been exactly what one might hope for in an acquisitions editor: engaged, genuinely interested (apparently) in the book and its ideas, encouraging, and helpful. Three anonymous reviewers provided timely suggestions and useful criticisms; addressing many of them helped make this work stronger. I, of course, remain solely responsible for any errors that remain.

Finally, I would like to thank Annette Desmarais, who listened patiently much too often to discussions about Arthur Young, Robert Malthus, and James Wilson. She, nevertheless, found the time to read every word of this manuscript, often multiple times, to make useful and insightful comments, while being unfailingly supportive. I dedicate this to her.

Foreword

Sometimes writing a history takes you on a journey to unexpected places. This was one of those. This book started life envisioned as a relatively short work focused on what the *Economist* had to say about rural labour and, especially, about the dangers of allowing rural labourers access to land. It grew as I got deeper into the topic and, especially, as I sought answers to questions the *Economist* provoked. Thus, I worked backwards in time in researching this, starting with the paper and its writing, tracing my exploration back to the writings of the political economists who inspired many of the paper's ideas, and then digging deeper into changes in agriculture, rural labour, and poor law practice and legislation to the middle part of the eighteenth century.

Along the way I encountered lots of people who would accompany me for parts of this journey: the crew who wrote and published the *Economist*, the political economists of the late eighteenth and early nineteenth centuries whose work both interested and at times frustrated me so, and surprisingly an ultimately pleasant companion, Arthur Young. There were others who shared shorter portions of this journey, most notably William Cobbett. Mostly, I enjoyed their company and I tried in this work to provide at least glimpses into their lives and character, along with a discussion of their ideas and their impact.

That I should have enjoyed their company so much, despite my concerns about the nature and impact of their ideas, comes as a bit of surprise to me given my background. I consider myself to be, by training and inclination, a historian of peasants: aspects of peasant livelihoods, production, and their struggles. This work has been, until now, somewhat removed from the British historical experience, focusing primarily on Central America and the Caribbean. I have also spent more three decades offering classes on various aspects of the history of "development," covering its most obvious incarnation in the period from the termination of the Second World War to the end of the twentieth century and tracing the roots of these ideas to earlier concepts of progress, modernity, and civilization as practised both in Europe itself and in its colonies through the nineteenth and much of the twentieth centuries. I have long understood that much of the development economic literature was informed by a particular reading of English economic history, particularly English agricultural history.

Work in these two distinct but linked historical topics has often left me amazed at the way peasants have been misunderstood and, often, attacked both by those making policy in the various countries I have studied and, truth be told, by many historians and other academics who have written about them. Peasants have most often been treated as symptoms of a kind of social problem. Discussions of them abound with tropes depicting them as remnants of earlier, slowly disappearing social formations, as checks on economic and national development, as inefficient and impoverished, as tradition bound and resistant to improvement, and – still – as dangerous because of a tendency to have too many children.

Yet four decades of working with and writing about peasants in various locations has proven to me that none of these descriptions describes either contemporary or historical peasant lifestyles adequately. One cannot spend time with a Mayan family in highland Guatemala without being taken with the efficiency and sustainability of their agricultural production; the care and localized knowledge that goes into a successful poly-cropped *milpa*, utilizing one or more of several thousand types of maize, intercropped with frijole, squash, chilies, and a variety of other "weeds" used to replenish soil and provide nutritious garnishes, much of it shaded by permaculture of avocado and coffee. Rather than being bound by tradition, such *milpa* is almost always the site of constant innovation and evolution. Similarly, no one can stand in a Jamaican *conuco* and have a well-versed farmer explain how each plant feeds and cares for those around it in a multi-layered ecosystem integrating plants, it seems, from all corners of the world, without being impressed by the wonderful messiness of it all.

Equally impressive, at least to me, are the peasant lifestyles that grow up around this wonderfully productive agriculture. Complex, intricate, and sophisticated lives that, nonetheless, limit needs and, when not too stressed by policies that sought to change them, or take their land, or force on them wage labour, offered multiple satisfactions. Yet, too often peasants have been denigrated as barbaric, lazy, and ignorant and attacked as symbols of a past best left behind – or, in more sympathetic works, viewed as romantic vestiges of a past simplicity that, while attractive, has no place in the modern world; a stance that has always been perplexing to me given the productivity and efficiency of their production and the self-reliant nature of peasant lives and communities.

Searching to understand the roots of this long attack on peasants brought me to this study of agricultural change and accompanying ideas about political economy in Britain from the 1760s to the 1860s. I was struck by familiar aspects of this history. Despite the arguments of agricultural improvers, it seems clear from the accounts of contemporaries that small holders got more from the same amount of land than even the most "improved" capital-intensive large holding. Yet despite England's deepening food pressures and rural poverty, these small holders were continually attacked both in the political economy literature and in policy, at least until the mid-nineteenth century, when William Thomas Thornton and J.S. Mill began to champion peasant agriculture among political economists.

My own background meant that this study has a bit of an edge; a bit of, I hope, controlled anger. I wanted to explore this history with a purpose. I didn't want to occlude the complexities and nuances in the writings and the lives of the people I write about here. I did not want to present a caricature of them; but I also did not want to get lost in a finely detailed study of the work of any of the political economists I discuss here. Rather I wanted to demonstrate how, no matter how useful some of their "principles of political economy" might have been in explaining and inspiring increased trade, manufacturing, and economic growth, their obsession with the purported wonders of capital applied to agriculture and the benefits the rural poor would gain by relying solely on wage labour led to policies that helped impoverish rural labourers. In rural areas, for a hundred years, they kept prescribing the same medicine arguing that it would somehow this time, magically, lead to less poverty, though it never did.

Nor did I want to gloss over the immense complexities and regional differences that are part of the story of agriculture and rural poverty in England through the late eighteenth and early nineteenth centuries. I benefitted greatly and borrowed widely from many of the very impressive histories that have provided us with detailed and finely grained studies of regions and parishes through this period. I did, however, want to keep my focus on the broader trends in a way that would allow this history to make the process of impoverishment that accompanied these changes clear. In the end, I hope I have demonstrated how the belief that the rural poor would naturally be indolent if not driven by absolute necessity, that peasants (cottagers and those holding small common rights) were inefficient and capricious farmers, and that England and the rural poor themselves would benefit if they were forced to rely solely on wage labour with no access to land of their own to farm was as divorced from any serious attempt to understand peasant productivity and livelihoods as are the contemporary attacks on peasants in diverse locales around the world.

APOSTLES OF INEQUALITY

Chapter One

Introduction: "The Multiplication of Wretchedness"

In 1767, as he somewhat desperately tried to find something he was good at, having failed as a farmer, Arthur Young wrote an extended essay of advice to the English upper classes about agriculture and rural society. In his *Farmer's Letters to the People of England*, Young, who would in the next few decades earn a reputation as the most knowledgeable authority on agriculture in England, was most adamant that he was not trying to turn the gentry into farmers, but rather that he would have them be "improvers." Young was insistent that these improving gentry treat their estates as businesses. Especially, they needed to unleash capital through mortgaging their properties and putting the money thus raised "sacred to the intended purpose" of making their estates fit to be let at high rents and thus "attended with great and speedy profit."[1]

Young was also concerned about the need to reduce expenditure on relief for the poor and about how to make agricultural labourers more industrious. He cautioned that the number of those relying on the parish increased constantly and recommended that poor relief be eliminated for the able bodied. All of those receiving relief should be housed in 100 Houses of Industry; their children would also be enclosed there, "for nine out of ten of the worthless of the poor, were brought up by their parents in idleness and pilfering." To those who thought his remedy lacked humanity, he rejoined, "We are to have the burthen [*sic*] of maintaining you, we should do it where and in what manner we please."[2]

Almost a century later, the *Economist* newspaper also commented extensively on agriculture and rural life for the English upper and middle classes. The scene had changed dramatically, but many of the concerns remained constant. Like Young, the paper was intent on clearing the way for capital. The paper warned farmers: "Either land must be dealt with on commercial principles or it must go out of cultivation. ... The problem therefore, now to be solved is, how can capital be attracted to the soil?"[3] The *Economist* crowed triumphantly that changes to agriculture had "broken down the parochial and patriarchal barriers which made each spot of land a gaol, though a home, for a particular portion of the community, and the same progress will cause them to be entirely removed."[4] Still, the paper fretted about poor relief and expressed itself perplexed about how to address the "enormous evil" represented by those collecting relief.[5]

The ninety years between Young's *Letters* and the *Economist*'s congratulatory observation about the removal of the rural poor from their parish were marked by both dramatic changes in the English countryside and intense debate about the nature of those changes and their benefits. For many of the proponents of change, agricultural improvement through new crops, alterations in crop mixes and rotations, and – most especially – the enclosure of common land and the investment of capital in agriculture were said to increase agricultural productivity dramatically. Indeed, these changes were so widespread that many commentators then, and historians since, talked about an agricultural revolution, although there has been intense debate surrounding both the nature of these changes and when they had the most profound effects.

This fixation on capital was anything but beneficial for the majority of the population in rural England. Agricultural wages declined substantially throughout this period, especially in those areas of the country where such change was most pronounced. But falling wages were not the only problem. Through more than 5,000 enclosure acts involving seven million acres of land, thousands of people were deprived of access to common resources many had used to provide for an independent livelihood or to augment wages, whether they had enjoyed an official common right or not. Even more damage was done through the steady decline in the percentage of the rural population with access to cottage gardens. These tiny yet amazingly productive plots of land often made the difference between relative comfort and a measure of independence on the one hand, and complete dependence on precarious wage employment on the other.

The loss of nonwage supports meant increasing numbers of the rural poor needed to buy more of their necessities, though they could now least afford to do so. The result was a marked decline in the standard of living of the majority of the rural population of England at the very time the wonders of the agricultural revolution were said to be unfolding. By the middle of the nineteenth century, cottage housing for agricultural labourers was so diminished that on average they were crowded into less than a third of the space mandated as the bare minimum allowed per person in workhouses.[6] And by 1864, after a century of agricultural revolution, according to one report to the House of Commons, half of the agricultural labourers were chronically malnourished.[7]

Seeing progress in the midst of this increased poverty and dislocation required a purposefully obscured vision that blamed the poor for their own poverty and, despite the evidence, held firm to the promise of capital. This book focuses on the ways such blame was assigned, the sorts (and sources) of blueprints for prosperity that were proffered, and the steady resistance offered by the rural poor to such dispossession. It highlights three distinct yet linked geneses for this blinkered vision of poverty and dislocation masquerading as progress.

The first emerged from those most ardently pushing for changes to agriculture and rural society in the last few decades of the eighteenth and into the early nineteenth century. They constantly asserted the benefits of enclosure, counselled draconian measures to reduce poor relief, and attacked cottage gardens and any other elements of rural society that contributed to some form of independence for rural labourers. When they saw poverty, they blamed it on the commons, on the indolence of the poor, or on the purported evils of small-holder agriculture. Arthur Young, for example, suggested that such small-holder agriculture led to "a multiplication of wretchedness"[8] and worked assiduously to prevent the rural poor from getting access to land. In doing so, he contributed decisively to justifying the wretchedness that was surely multiplying in rural England.

But Young had a dramatic conversion. Once inclined either not to see poverty or to blame the poor for their situation, from the mid-1790s he devoted his energies to combatting increasing poverty by arguing for the benefits to be derived by providing the poor with land. Young's conversion provides us with important insights into the nature of change in rural England. His reports, and those of like-minded landlords in the Board of Agriculture and Internal Improvement and in the Society for Bettering the Condition and Increasing the Comforts of the Poor, provide us with convincing testimony both about spreading poverty and about the productivity of peasant agriculture. The very limited success of Young's campaign for land for the poor also tells us much about the nature of English society at the turn of the nineteenth century and the strength of the blinkered vision of society that Young had once been so successful in promulgating.

That vision, along with blaming the poor for their own poverty and dismissing the benefits to be derived from allowing the poor access to land of their own, reified capital as the source of all wealth and proclaimed it to be the elixir required to reduce poverty. An essential part of making that vision acceptable was the growing fascination with ideas surrounding political economy. Adam Smith's *An Inquiry into the Nature and Cause of the Wealth of Nations* published in 1776 cautioned against a society dominated by merchants and manufacturers and advocated for fair wages for workers. Nonetheless, by early in the nineteenth century, Smith's work was constantly referred to as the basis for what was increasingly proclaimed to be the "science" of political economy; his vision of "universal opulence" that stemmed from the division of labour and the investment of capital was the promise inherent in experiments that followed. Two of the scientists dabbling in this social laboratory stand out. The Reverend Thomas Robert Malthus's *An Essay on the Principle of Population* was important in identifying population increase as the root of continued and deepening poverty; Malthus, thus, ingeniously, was able to blame the poor both for their own poverty and for the failures of political economy to deliver on its promises. Nassau Senior was most adept at applying a particularly rigid interpretation of the lessons of political economy to the practical business of government policy, most importantly in spearheading the 1832–4 Poor Law Commission. Smith, Malthus, Senior, and the numerous others who flocked to the banner of political economy in the first half of the nineteenth century shared a vision of capital as the source of all wealth, the "occult principle of the system," as Piercy Ravenstone expressed it.[9]

Ravenstone, probably a pseudonym for Richard Puller Sr., was one of a series of critics who questioned the claims of political economy. Many of them disputed the benefits purported to derive from capital, and instead extolled the productivity and industriousness of small, "peasant" agriculturalists. As Ravenstone said, if capital eliminated poverty why was England "oppressed with capital even to plethory," while her labourers starved?[10] For these critics, political economy was not science but an alchemy hiding the depredations of capital.

Perhaps the most effective purveyor of the purported lessons of political economy was, from its inception in 1843, the *Economist* newspaper, the third source examined in this book. James Wilson, the founding editor, stated that the paper needed to reflect "nothing but pure principles."[11] But principles in the hands of Wilson and his crew of writers too easily became a toxic brew infused with a particularly brutal assertion of the need for self-reliance. This was felt in its steadfast opposition to the provision of land to the rural poor a half century after Arthur Young had argued that such measures were essential to relieve rural poverty. "Pure principles" also led the paper to oppose a shortened workday for women and children in textile factories, to condemn all relief during the Irish Potato Famine, and to cheer for a southern victory in the US Civil War. Increasingly, as the lessons of political economy failed time and again to turn poverty into prosperity and turmoil into steady progress, the paper employed a hardening racial explanation for such obstinance.

Throughout these one hundred years of calamity for the poor, those who championed capital chanted a continual refrain about the need to teach the rural poor self-reliance. Poor relief, it was said, had robbed the English peasantry and rural worker of both their self-respect and self-reliance. Allowing workers to go "on the parish" built a dependency that, according to the 1834 Poor Law Report, meant those receiving poor relief had "all a slave's security of subsistence, without his liability to punishment."[12] However, their vision of self-reliance was a peculiarly limited one. All of the various ways the rural poor demonstrated tenacious self-reliance were discounted, disregarded, and attacked. Those with access to little bits of land they turned into wonderfully productive gardens; those who scratched parts of a living from common "wastes"; those who gleaned the leftover grain in fields, raised a pig or two, and a hive or three, and chased after geese, and, when particularly fortunate, milked a cow and made cheese and sold milk; all those who pieced together modest livings out of little bits of land and meagre opportunity were told continually and repeatedly that their hard-won comfort was an illusion and that they should place their faith in the benefits of working for wages at the behest of those with capital: a siren song sung for over a hundred years.

Apostles of Inequality

This book argues that the proponents of the benefits of capital were apostles of inequality – though they may not have either perceived or intended this outcome. They helped make increasing poverty acceptable through arguments that the measures leading inexorably to such ends – depriving the rural poor of land, eliminating poor relief, paving the way for capital – were "ordained by providence" (as the *Economist* proclaimed) and the promise of their ultimate benefit could only be explained by political economy. This study explores the damage this caused primarily by examining the writings and words of these apostles themselves. This is not a new argument. Karl Marx most famously traced the links between policy and propaganda favouring capital, the dispossession of peasants and commoners, and the resultant distress. In the more than a century and a half since Marx wrote, many others have explored with great skill aspects of this transformation. In addition, there is a very large literature that examines in detail the nature of agricultural change during this period. While a large portion of this literature deals rather exclusively with questions of increases in yields and productivity, many studies also painstakingly and effectively outline the decline in rural wages and the impact on rural livelihoods.[13] A century or more of eloquent condemnations of enclosure and careful assessments of the impact of the loss of common resources has contributed to our understanding of what this particular agricultural revolution meant for commoners.[14]

By discussing the combination of forces that helped make the rural poor even poorer – that is, declining wages, enclosure and the elimination of common rights, and the dramatic reduction in the availability of cottage gardens – this work provides a stark image of the declining fortunes of the bulk of the rural labourers in England over this period. This book especially focuses on the loss of cottage gardens, a deprivation not as often explored in the historiography as the damage caused by enclosure, for example, but, if we can judge by the accounts of contemporaries, one that was equally devastating.[15] Our exploration of change in rural England at the end of the eighteenth and into the early nineteenth century provides detailed and convincing evidence of the productivity of cottage gardens: the result of diligent labour, long experience, and the "enchantment of property" as the reformed Arthur Young would express it. There are numerous examples of this productivity from the letters reprinted in the *Annals of Agriculture* in the early 1790s to the works of William Thomas Thornton and J.S. Mill in the 1840s. In one sense, then, this book is intended to reinforce arguments about the productivity of very small-scale agriculture against the pretensions of improved and "high" agriculture.

This study does not attempt a detailed discussion of the sophisticated arguments that contributed to the "science" of political economy near the end of the eighteenth century and the first few decades of the nineteenth. It does, however, add to this discussion by focusing on the way the "science" of political economy and its application failed the rural poor. By tracing the increasingly rigid application of ideas of self-reliance and the attractions of the self-serving notion that such ideas were somehow "natural law" from Smith to Malthus and Senior, this work also provides an insight into how they deepened, or were perverted, into virulent arguments about laissez faire. Useful in this discussion is the attention paid here to some of the critics of political economy: especially Piercy Ravenstone, Thomas Hodgskin, and William Thomas Thornton. Their criticisms help us identify the particular moments of myopia in the writings on political economy.

Finally, the clearest expression of popularization of notions of political economy and their application to policy comes from the *Economist* newspaper, especially during the long tenure of its founding editor, James Wilson. There have been a few studies of the newspaper.[16] The most notable of these have focused on an institutional history of the paper over more than a century and half. None has explored in depth, and critically, the paper's arguments about issues to do with agrarian capital, rural poverty and a host of other related issues – from slavery in the Caribbean and the southern United States to the Great Indian Rebellion – over the first couple of decades of the paper's existence. Through a careful reading of the first twenty years of the *Economist*, from 1843 to 1863, this book outlines how what Wilson argued were the "pure principles" of political economy provided justification for further dispossession both in rural England and around the world.

What ties all of this together, and the underlying theme of the book, is a focus on the writings and arguments of those who most ardently pressed the case for capital and championed measures to ensure its dominance and the resistance of the rural poor. These "apostles of inequality" often sincerely believed they were preparing the way for a more generalized prosperity. Some, like Arthur Young and Robert Malthus, often struggled to find ways their work could better accommodate the needs of the poor. But too often, "principles" became more important than people and millions suffered as a consequence.

This book explores the writings, and the impact, of these apostles of inequality in three sections divided into nine chapters. The first section deals with the impact of agricultural change. When Arthur Young set out to champion agricultural improvement in the 1760s, he was not clearing new fields. Important alterations in rural economies and social relations, many similar to those advocated by Young, had been working through rural England for at least a century before 1750. But clearly, in the mind of Young and his fellow "improvers," much was left to be done. Everywhere Young went he thought he encountered land crying out for enclosure and the investment of capital. He saw workers made indolent by access to commons, small farmers made wretched because they clung to property, and slothful rural poor dependent on relief and too readily frequenting the ale house. Spurred by the writings of those championing "improvement" like the early Young, buttressed by the supposed lessons of political economy, and egged on by the *Economist*, during this century more than seven million acres of common land were enclosed, the Poor Laws – after decades of debate – were finally altered to make receiving relief more difficult and more loathsome, and a war on cottages was waged. It was in this century between 1750 and 1850 that changes in rural economies and social structures were most clearly felt in dramatically falling living standards and increased wretchedness. For a century, accompanying the boasts about the marvellous developments in agriculture wrought by improvement, enclosure, high agriculture, and – most importantly – capital, were devastated rural households, increased poverty, and dramatic unrest.

The discussion of agricultural change during this century is primarily explored through a close examination of the contemporary literature. Chapter 2 focuses on Arthur Young's arguments for enclosure and agricultural improvement, along with his desire to court the favour of the rich and powerful. Young obtained many of his personal goals in 1793 when he was named Secretary to the Board of Agriculture and Internal Improvement. This post allowed him to rub shoulders with the richest and most powerful landowners in Britain and to help shape agricultural policy in the country. This chapter reads Young's many books and pamphlets along with his voluminous writing in the *Annals of Agriculture and Other Useful Arts* before 1795 as perhaps the clearest articulation of what informed observers thought best constituted agricultural improvement. His works also outline most clearly how little concerned Young and others were, initially, about the effects of such change on the rural poor.

Young's often strident condemnation of the poor changed dramatically after 1795. Personal tragedy contributed to his change of heart, but he was most convinced by his apprehension of growing poverty. His concerns were shared by a number of the landowners in the Board; many wrote glowing testimonials about the benefits to be derived from giving the poor access to land and of the wonderful productivity of their small plots of land at a time when England was struggling to feed its population. Those testimonials are the subject of chapter 3. Many of these reports were sent to the Board of Agriculture; they were all published in *Annals of Agriculture* or the Reports of the Society for Bettering the Condition and Improving the Comforts of the Poor, which started in London in 1797; many of the landlords in the Board of Agriculture were members of the Society as well. A close reading of these reports and Young's pamphlets opposing the poverty brought on by enclosure, contrasted with the surveys of agriculture in each county done at the behest of the Board on the urging of Young – many carried out by Young himself – continuing to promote enclosure, reveals the tensions inherent in the dreams of agricultural improvement amid the reality of deepening rural poverty caused partly by the manifestation of these dreams. Arthur Young's personal crisis of faith can be interpreted as part of a much broader societal contradiction.

The fourth chapter outlines the nature of the opposition to those appeals for land for the poor and the arguments from landowners, tenant farmers, and others in favour of keeping rural labourers entirely dependent on wages and at the beck and call of large farmers. This chapter also explores the not surprising outcomes in heightened poverty and increased unrest; unrest so widespread and so long-lasting that it is not an exaggeration to suggest that England, especially southern England, was the scene of a rural war, marked by riot and arson, for half a century beginning near the end of the 1700s. Though distinct periods of unrest have been widely studied – most significantly the Swing arsons in the early 1830s – viewing the wide arc of rural unrest from the 1790s to the 1840s and contrasting that with the refusal to ameliorate rural poverty by providing cottagers with land helps focus the source of the unrest in declining rural livelihoods and the causes of that decline in the insistence that rural labourers be solely dependent on wages.

The second section turns to major works on political economy, from Smith's 1776 *Inquiry* through the multiple versions of Malthus's *Essay on the Principle of Population* to the lectures and reports of Nassau Senior in the 1830s to 1850s. This book concentrates on specific elements of the writings of Smith and Malthus. In the case of Smith, it explores the striking difference in focus in his two major works: *The Theory of Moral Sentiments*, published in 1759, and his most famous work, *An Inquiry into the Nature and Causes of the Wealth of Nations*, from 1776. It also examines his attitude to capital and wages, the reception of his work, and the uses to which it was put. Chapter 5 also discusses the writings of Thomas Robert Malthus and their impact. Celebrated primarily for the arguments originally presented in his *Essay on the Principle of Population*, first published anonymously in 1798, Malthus was one of the most influential political economists of the early nineteenth century. He substantially revised and expanded the 1798 edition in 1803, and made mostly minor changes to this 1803 edition in new editions in 1806, 1807, 1817, and 1826. His work was the subject of intense debate and both derision and appreciation during his life and since. He appears to have changed his mind about many of the fundamental precepts outlined in 1798, but sought always to frame new arguments in ways that did not unduly diminish the power of his most noteworthy claim to fame. Though associated most often with an attack on the poor and their propensity to propagate, Malthus also sought to outline more clearly than most how wages for the poor could be increased. Nonetheless, his ideas were easily adapted to support the predilection to blame the poor for their own poverty, to caution against making the poor less poor by giving them access to land, and to argue about the inevitability of inequality. This chapter examines the struggles evident in Malthus's writing as he turned from the *Essay on the Principle of Population* to his *Principles of Political Economy* published late in 1820.

Nassau Senior and the Poor Laws are the twin anchors for chapter 6. First, however, the chapter examines some of the growing body of literature criticizing the core ideas of political economy as espoused by Malthus and taken up by Senior. I pay particular attention to Piercy Ravenstone's *A Few Doubts*, which not only attacked Malthus's assertions about population increase as the root of poverty but also articulated increasing hesitancies about the fascination with capital, "the deity of their idolatry which they have set up to worship in the high places of the Lord."[17] Though less celebrated than Smith and Malthus, Senior was a central figure in a range of government commissions dealing with factory legislation, Ireland, hand-weavers, and, most importantly, the Poor Laws. His views on political economy were explained in painfully dry lectures presented as the longtime Drummond Chair in Political Economy at the University of Oxford. He blamed the poor for their own poverty even more harshly than Malthus had done, and more energetically opposed any attempt to relieve that poverty. Senior's work marked a more ideologically rigid appeal to self-reliance. This attitude found fruition of sorts in the revisions to the Poor Laws passed in 1834. Nassau Senior dominated the Commission established to investigate these laws and to recommend revisions. These recommendations encapsulated a hardening attitude towards the poor and a determination to force on them an industrious self-reliance dependent on wage labour. Despite the substantial differences in their approaches to political economy, Smith, Malthus, and Senior all extolled the importance of capital and its necessary role in invigorating labour.

The need to foster diligent industry among labourers would take centre stage in the *Economist* as well. The *Economist*, from its inception in 1843 to shortly after the founding editor died in India in 1860, is the focus of the third section of this book. The founding editor, James Wilson, was a hat-maker and ardent anti–Corn Law crusader. He was funded partly by one of England's wealthiest men, William Pleydell-Bouverie, Lord Radnor. The paper assembled an interesting and, in some ways, disparate crew of writers to turn out a new edition every Saturday. Wilson rode herd over them and wrote most of the leading articles, even after Lord Radnor helped him get elected to the House of Commons in 1847. The *Economist* became an influential voice popularizing a particularly limited view of political economy obsessed with reducing government "interference" in the economy, preaching the "natural law" of supply and demand, and returning again and again to the necessity of self-reliance: self-reliance defined in a particular and limited way by the paper. Chapter 7 outlines the founding of the paper, its precepts, and the history of the writers most involved in its production. Chapter 8 explores the anti–Corn Law struggles, the *Economist*'s writings about agriculture, its championing of capital-intensive large farms, and its virulent opposition to peasant farming or any movement to provide small plots of land to labourers. The paper was most influential, and destructive, in its writings about Ireland during the famine years. Here it most vigorously opposed relief efforts and supported policies designed to remove cottiers from the land. It counselled increased coercion and repression when such policies led, inevitably, to unrest. As the *Economist* said, the Irish peasantry were, "like the Indians, doomed to extermination. ... They lie beyond the pale."[18] Chapter 9 explores the impact of the paper's writings on Ireland.

Chapter 10 details the *Economist*'s writings on cotton, slavery, and India. It also explores the paper's increasing use of arguments about race to explain the failures of political economy. Wilson and other writers for the *Economist* were closely tied to textile manufacturing interests in Manchester. This inevitably meant the paper was obsessed with the supply of cotton and, in turn, constantly exercised about the question of slavery. Both Wilson and the paper continually reiterated their opposition to slavery. But, the paper always opposed any actions that might endanger the supply of cotton or impede the ability to find labour to work cotton. Increasingly under the influence of its soon-to-be-next editor, Walter Bagehot, it came close to arguing that the only fitting role for West Africa in the world economy was to supply slaves. And it favoured a Southern victory and secession as the best outcome of the Civil War.

The *Economist*'s writings on cotton and slavery were the clearest expressions of a hardening attitude towards race from the middle of the century on. But, they were not the only such examples. Under Bagehot, as the paper became increasingly exasperated with the unwillingness of everyone to fall into line with its proffered solutions for society's ills – remedies that meant clearing the way for capital and forcing labourers to feel the "the beneficent whip of hunger and cold"[19] when they were not appropriately industrious – it found explanations for that opposition in the backwardness of other, mostly darker, races. In a chilling foretelling of an invigorated taste for empire and the brutality of late colonialism to come, by the 1860s the paper informed its readers:

> The one necessary essential to the development of ... new sources of prosperity is the arrangement of some industrial system under which very large bodies of dark labourers will work willingly under a very few European supervisors. It is not only individual labour which is required, but organised labour, labour so scientifically arranged that the maximum result shall be obtained at a minimum cost.[20]

Tracing the apparent contradictions in the paper, its convenient amnesia about some of its earlier positions, its attitudes to race, and its constant reiterations that the dictates of political economy somehow reflected only the laws of nature illustrates most clearly how an ideology meant to reveal the means to universal opulence could lead so often to arguments for dispossession and brutality.

For over a century these apostles of inequality justified dispossession and increasing poverty in the name of political economy and at the behest of capital. The victims of the misplaced faith in agricultural revolution and political economy were to be found in diverse places: from English commoners and cottagers, Irish cottiers, Southern US slaves and Jamaican ex-slaves, to Indian ryots. This is the story of how their impoverishment was justified.

PART ONE

Arthur Young, the Agricultural Revolution, and the Spread of Poverty

Chapter Two

"The Yoke of Improvement"

In his *Farmer's Letters to the People of England*, written in the 1760s, Arthur Young argued that, "The laboring poor, in general, earn now sufficient to live decently cloathed, and in good health."[1] But Young's *Farmer's Letters* was written on the cusp of dramatically falling living standards for rural workers, cottagers, and commoners; a decline brought on by population growth, declining real wages, a shift in woollen handicraft production from the south to the north (and eventually a movement from hand looms to power looms), increasingly rigid and miserly poor relief, the reduction of common rights through waves of enclosures, and attacks on cottagers and cottage gardens.

England's population increased dramatically during the century from 1750 to 1850, from just over 6 million people in England and Wales in 1751, to over 9 million by 1801, and just under 18 million by 1851. Changes to agriculture have been credited with allowing England for the most part to keep food production in line with this increased population.[2] Though England turned from being a substantial food exporter to being a net importer during this period, a number of scholars have argued that a dramatic increase in yields and rural labour productivity fostered by agricultural improvement during this century helped offset the population increase and allowed for the "redundant" rural population to spearhead the industrial revolution.[3]

Primarily through an examination of the writings of Arthur Young and his work with the Board of Agriculture and Internal Improvement, the semi-official instrument for large estate owners, this chapter explores what Young and others saw as the most essential elements of agricultural improvement in the second half of the eighteenth century and outlines how it can best be distinguished from the currents of change that had been swirling through rural England for more than a century before 1750. Arthur Young's life and writings provide us with important insights into the arguments about agriculture in the second half of the eighteenth century and into the first few decades of the nineteenth. He left behind a remarkable legacy of essays, books, reports, and pamphlets that encompass fifty years of dramatic change in English agriculture. Young's most

Portrait of Arthur Young by John Russell, pastel, 1794 (NPG 6253). © National Portrait Gallery, London

ambitious work was the *Annals of Agriculture and Other Useful Arts*, begun in 1784 and published into the first decade of the nineteenth century. But his writing also illustrates most clearly the selective myopia that such champions used to justify increasing inequality and poverty. And his crisis of conscience in the middle of the 1790s reveals most clearly the damage wrought by such changes.

Young was an integral part of the debates surrounding the agricultural revolution and its effects. One biographer described him as "the untiring and eloquent apostle for the Agricultural Revolution."[4] He was also, for a while, an apostle of inequality. Young was for much of the period between the publication of his *Farmer's Letters to the People of England* in 1767 and his death in 1820 one of the foremost proponents of agricultural improvement, which he felt entailed enclosure of common land, expansive growth in the size and capital intensiveness of agricultural enterprises, and increasing reliance on wage labour for the rural poor. He worried constantly about the increased costs to farmers and landowners of poor relief and championed eliminating such relief as quickly as possible. And he was vociferous in warning about the need for vigilance on the part of the owners of property in the face of potential unrest. Young's writings earned him an appreciative audience among the largest landowners and most aggressive farmers. Indeed, in 1793, one year after his call for the formation of a terrorizing yeoman militia, he was rewarded with the position of Secretary to the Board of Agriculture and Internal Improvement, a semi-public association to support the interests of large landowners, and he served in that position until his death in 1820.

But, Young, more than perhaps any other commentator in England in the late eighteenth century, travelled the countryside. He was not immune to the heightened poverty he saw around him. Late in the century, he became not just an apostle for agricultural improvement, but a dedicated proponent of a means to address the poverty he saw, everywhere, increasing around him; an ardent champion of ways to offset the harm he, and others, had wrought in their pursuit of agricultural revolution. For this reformed Young, the key to help reduce this poverty was to provide the rural poor with land, convinced as he was of their dramatic productivity and the multiple benefits rural families would derive from such holdings. Notably, he was joined in this call by many of the landowners involved in the Board of Agriculture.

This chapter uses Young's voluminous writing to illustrate what most thoughtful observers of English agriculture meant by agricultural improvement in the second half of the eighteenth century. It begins by exploring, briefly, the changes in agriculture and rural livelihoods before 1750.

Agricultural Change before 1750

Arthur Young was born in 1741. His father, also Arthur, was the rector of Bradfield church in Suffolk and the family had for over 200 years owned a reasonably sized estate there. Arthur Young Sr. married into a wealthy family; the dowry brought to the wedding was substantial enough that Arthur's mother (Anna Lucrecia Coussmaker) was given control over the estate on the marriage. The land was rented out to tenant farmers and appears to have provided Arthur Sr. and family a respectable, if modest, living. Young remembers his father "living genteelly and driving a coach and four" on the income from his estate. Perhaps he lived beyond his means; he died in 1759 leaving substantial debts. Young attributed this decline in circumstances to an increase in the poor rates and to the ease of obtaining mortgages on property, a (relatively) new innovation for estate owners and one that permitted his father to live without paying close attention to the proceeds from the estate.

Arthur Young's early life provides us with a window into mid-eighteenth-century rural England. When he urged the gentry to invest capital in their estates, increase rents, and thus turn their estates into the most efficient vehicles for "great and speedy" profit, he was joining a long line of authors who had urged such "improvement" on English landowners. He was not suggesting anything radically new. Nonetheless, he was soon considered to be "the prophet of an improved agriculture of such industry that it is wonderful to relate," or so claimed G.E. Fussell in 1943.[5]

What constituted the "improved agriculture" with which Fussell was so enamoured and how was it different from agricultural practices and rural life before 1750? English society was dominated by a small group of landed nobles and gentry. Statistics on landownership and control are scarce and not trustworthy for most of the eighteenth century. The best records we have available for the country as a whole stem from the *Return of Owners of the Land* in 1873, a century after Young began writing. The *Return* indicated that slightly less than one-half of the agricultural land in England and Wales was owned by fewer than 2,000 people; 710 people controlled over one-quarter of the land.[6] The nineteenth-century figures most likely reflect, in broad strokes, landownership through the period we discuss here.[7]

In the decades since Fussell wrote there has been significant exploration of what, exactly, agricultural change during the century from 1750 to 1850 entailed and how important it was. Many of the trends once thought to distinguish this period were common for a century or more before 1750: increased agricultural productivity, changes in crop mixes, enclosure, the elimination of many small landholders or tenant farmers, the commercialization of leases, and the dominance of the capitalist trifecta (large landowners – capitalist tenant farmer – wage dependent rural labourers) were all evident in parts of England well before Young urged such improvements. Important among these changes were the introduction of new crops and agricultural techniques – increased use of root crops for animal fodder, specialization in wheat production accompanied by pulses especially in the southeast, improved pastures for more intensive livestock production, and convertible husbandry – that increased yields substantially. Arthur Young would have us believe that such improvements were dependent on enclosure and large-scale, capital-intense farming; a function of late eighteenth century agricultural improvements. But it seems clear from the literature that many of these innovations were developed by very small-scale farmers, often associated with "garden" agriculture, and that much of this increase in yields occurred before 1750.[8]

Also important was a steady decline in those holding property through copyhold (that is, a traditional long lease arrangement consolidated through paying a "fine" on the commencement of the lease) and increased use of "commercial" leases. Landholders had traditionally obtained a significant amount of their capital through the payment of fines on the commencement of the copyhold. Though this often meant significantly lower rental payments for very long leases, landowners had few alternatives to raise capital. However, changes in mortgages after 1650 that limited liability and increased capital available in commercial banks provided landlords with options. Landlords' interest in maximizing their rents led to a higher percentage of farms being let on commercial leases. The momentum to turn copyhold to commercial leases gathered steam when rents increased in the second decade of the eighteenth century.[9] Accompanying such changes was a decline in the number of small holders and an increase in the average size of farm operations. Again, this was partly a function of the ability of landholders to access capital through mortgages permitting them to buy up land. But it was also the result of a tendency to let out land under new commercial leases in larger operations to farmers with capital to invest in the land. As Edward Lawrence observed in his 1727 "Duties of a Steward to his Lord," it was the steward's responsibility to attempt to "lay all the small farms, let to poor indigent tenants, to the great ones" and, thus to "turn several little ones into great ones."[10]

Arthur Young was particularly enthused by the promise offered by enclosure. But, enclosure was not restricted to the century between 1750 and 1850. There had been various waves of enclosure of common and "waste" land in England before 1750. Particularly aggressive enclosures following the Black Death in the late fourteenth and early fifteenth centuries, mostly to turn land to sheep, had inspired significant opposition. (Thomas More's *Utopia* was in many ways a protest at the changes wrought to rural society through such enclosures.) Royal protection for village populations and common lands followed but not before a long list of counties, especially in the southeast, were almost completely enclosed by the end of the 1500s.[11] From the late sixteenth through to the middle of the eighteenth century, most enclosures were by agreement, through which landlords needed to get the consent of copyholders and other tenants to enclose land. Nonetheless, about 70 per cent of all arable land in England was enclosed by 1700.[12] Detailed studies of different regions demonstrate how sporadic and limited much of this process was, however. And in much of England, especially in part of the Midlands, open fields were still common in 1750 and in others, though arable land had been enclosed, many people had access to common pastures and "wastes."[13] By the middle of that century, however, as landlords sought more aggressively to commercialize and maximize their operations, they became increasingly impatient at the slow pace required in enclosure by agreement. More often they turned to enclosure by acts: that is, separate acts of parliament to enclose property; occasional use of these in the first half of the eighteenth century were the forerunners to the great waves of "parliamentary" enclosures carried out through private acts of Parliament in the century between 1750 and 1850.[14]

Finally, one of the key ingredients in the decline of rural living standards was the increasing difficulty rural labourers had in renting cottages and getting access to cottage garden land either through rent or as part of the common right attached to the cottage. Buying up small farms to augment great estates or increasing the size of farming operations through leasing land to tenants in larger farm operations made numerous cottages and their gardens less necessary for the operations of an estate. An important incentive in the destruction of cottages was to reduce the number of people who could claim poor law relief in a parish. This trend gathered steam after 1750, especially as the numbers claiming poor relief grew from the 1790s on, but it was also evident in the decades before 1750. For example, Francis Guyton, the steward to Lord Fitzwilliam's estate in Northamptonshire, advised his Lord in 1702 to demolish the cottages on his estate to enhance the value of his land.[15]

A significant body of literature has argued, following Karl Marx and, more than a century later, Robert Brenner, that England was, by the end of the seventeenth century, dominated by the "classical landlord-capitalist tenant-wage labour structure" of agrarian capitalism. For Brenner this was essential in fostering both a "significant agrarian advance" and a "nearly uniquely symbiotic relationship between agriculture and industry" that permitted England's industrial development.[16] Many others, less sanguine about the real "development" Brenner claimed this permitted, have nonetheless agreed that much of this shift to agrarian capitalism had occurred well before 1750.[17]

Despite these changes – enclosure eliminating much common land, the reduction of the number of small farms and increase in both the sizes of estates and tenant farms, and decreased availability of cottages and cottage gardens – much of rural England was still in need of dramatic alteration if we are to believe the writing of Arthur Young and the accounts of the Board of Agriculture. An only slowing growing population and increased agricultural production led to steady deterioration in the price of agricultural products and a generalized agricultural depression for much of the late seventeenth and early decades of the eighteenth centuries. This curtailed some of the change and allowed many of the smallest peasant farmers to hold on to their land.[18]

Poorer sectors of rural society, relative to their situation half a century later, enjoyed reasonably secure livelihoods in the first half of the eighteenth century. Agricultural prices were low compared to wages. Many agricultural labourers still lived in cottages with access to garden plots and, increasingly throughout the century, land to grow potatoes. They were able to keep various types of livestock – geese, chickens, pigs, and, if they had access to pasture, an occasional cow – and to grow much of what they consumed in their garden plot. This cottage economy was often considered to be the most essential element of parish life and peasant well-being.

And, a significant percentage of the rural populace still enjoyed common-rights; both in arable land and common pasture or unimproved pasture in "wastes." Most cherished was the right to keep a cow or two on pasture, and enough hay land to keep them over winter. "Waste" land could be forest, rough pasture, or wetlands. Commoners (and frequently those without any official common right) used these lands for a variety of purposes: gathering wild fruit, herbs, and other nonfarmed produce, occasionally hunting wild game (where allowed by restrictive gaming laws), and most importantly foraging for fuel in the form of wood or peat. Some commons were stinted; that is, the number of animals someone could keep on the pasture limited. In these locations, it was not uncommon for wealthier members to purchase common rights, allowing them to pasture more animals and limiting access for others. In addition, open-field agriculture was not always equitably divided; in some communities, rights to open field strips were also purchased.[19] Still, many people in non-enclosed parishes who did not hold official common rights also enjoyed privileges sanctified by custom. These could include keeping geese or a pig, access to garden land through their occupancy of a cottage, and the "right" to glean left over grain missed in the harvest of open field land or the manor's and larger tenants' fields. Gleaning could provide grain for up to two months for a family.[20]

In addition, agricultural labourers and the smallest farmers were able to augment incomes through cottage handicraft production. This was immensely varied, but the most important such work was associated with woollen cloth production. Cottage handicraft production, especially lace making or straw plaiting, importantly, provided work and income for women and could be done at times when labour or the demands of their own farms were least onerous. Women were often responsible for caring for dairy cattle and the production of the milk and milk products, diversifying cottager incomes and improving the bargaining position of women in rural households.[21]

In the worst circumstances, there was an often-generous Poor Law that stipulated levels of relief for those temporarily needing assistance or for the old and infirm needing help on a longer term. The English Poor Law dated to the end of the sixteenth century. Assistance was provided to deserving residents and paid by poor rates assigned to landholders or those with sufficient other income. Poor rates and the regulations binding those receiving relief varied from parish to parish. As right to assistance was dependent on established residence (settlement) in a parish there were often attempts to prevent new settlement of those who might "go on the parish." Assistance was often miserly, especially to the able-bodied poor. In addition, there was a tendency at various times to favour relocation of the poor to dreaded workhouses. Nonetheless, through much of the first half of the eighteenth century, the Poor Laws functioned quite well. Poor rates were reasonable; the numbers on relief were modest in most parishes; and assistance was often both flexible and generous.[22]

All of these varied resources contributed to making the life of rural labourers and peasants relatively secure. Average life expectancy in rural England in the early 1700s was a very respectable forty-one years, indicating a population with at least a reasonably healthy living environment and adequate food. Importantly, the average height of prisoners and recruits for British and East India Company armies was highest in 1740; their height declined steadily over the next 120 years.[23]

"An Agricultural Revolution"?

What Arthur Young proposed, and most historians have agreed constituted "agricultural improvement" through to the first couple of decades of the nineteenth century, and "high" agriculture after that, was a complicated set of institutional, infrastructural, and farming changes. Along with enclosure to be discussed further below, this included a broad range of practices: escalating rents charged by landowners to improving tenant farmers on fully commercial leases; extensive capital investment in draining, fencing and preparing land; increased use of labour-saving equipment and increased animal power; the cultivation of a diverse set of relatively new crops used to stall feed more animals and the improvement of pasture through new forms of ground cover; extensive application of manure and other fertilizers to maintain soil fertility which, along with new crop rotations, allowed for the reduction of land held in fallow. E.A. Wrigley, most notably, has argued that the combination of new crops, especially perhaps clover, which improved pastures, and more intense fertilizing through increased numbers of livestock, combined to foster what he calls "advanced organic agriculture" and sparked significant productivity gains in agriculture.[24] While no longer considered to be exclusive to the century from 1750 to 1850, the pace of change increased dramatically through this century, especially, as it turned out, for those elements which most led to falling rural living standards.

There is substantial debate about what agricultural improvement meant in terms of farm size. It is generally agreed that over the course of the late seventeenth and early eighteenth centuries, landlords tended to rent out their land in larger units to more commercially oriented farmers. There is, however, disagreement over what happened to farm size during the period of the so-called agricultural revolution in the century following 1750. Much of the literature in the early twentieth century asserted a relationship between these more commercial farming practices, enclosure, and a dramatic increase in farm size and the elimination of small holders. Beginning around the middle of the twentieth century, historians using taxation records argued, instead, that the number of small farms actually increased with enclosure, sustained by high prices especially during the war with France at the end of the eighteenth and the first decade of the nineteenth centuries. This assertion has been strenuously contested by Jeannette Neeson and Jane Humphries.[25] While there is no clear agreement about this among historians, virtually all contemporary accounts of rural England, especially in the south, through this period – both those opposed to and in favour of such change – remarked repeatedly on the dramatic expansion of farm size and the destruction of both the smallholder and the yeoman farmer.

In summary, many of the changes once thought to be part of the "agricultural revolution" between 1750 and 1850 were evident in many parts of England in the century before 1750. Nonetheless, recent studies have sought, once again, to focus attention on the alterations to agriculture and rural society in that century and have argued that if we are to locate an "agricultural revolution," it lies there. Mark Overton, for example, has cited a dramatic increase in output per acre, and most importantly, an "unprecedented" spike in labour productivity. Other works have echoed some of this assessment. Even those authors who discount the idea of an agricultural revolution in this period have agreed that the period between 1750 and 1850 was marked by dramatic increase in labour productivity.[26]

"Hunger ... will sweeten the severest labour"

Whether a revolution or not, agricultural "improvement" in the latter half of the eighteenth century left rural labourers, cottagers, and commoners in the path of a perfect storm. Demands for agricultural improvement occurred along with intensified movements to invest capital in the land, to reshape control over the land, and to discipline rural labour. English landowners and large-scale tenant farmers were obsessed with ensuring an adequate supply of disciplined labourers. There were constant complaints over the centuries about the indolence and laziness of English labourers. Thomas Manley, writing in 1669, argued that English workers were "too proud to beg, too lazy to work, when 'tis either too hot or too cold, and will choose their own time and wages, or you may do your work yourself."[27] But these complaints escalated in the eighteenth and nineteenth century. Most often blamed for labourers' lack of sufficient vigour was anything that contributed to a perceived independence from wages; the three biggest culprits in eighteenth- and nineteenth-century England were common-rights, cottage land, and the poor laws. It is no surprise that each of them was under attack during the agricultural revolution.

Beginning after the mid-point of the eighteenth century, rural England and Wales were swept by wave after wave of enclosures – that is, extinguishing common-rights through the allocation of common resources to individual ownership. Closely associated with arguments about agricultural improvement, these enclosures are most often called the "parliamentary" enclosures, because each needed to be approved by a private act of parliament. In total, between 1750 and 1850, there were 5000 such acts affecting about seven million acres of land.[28]

There is substantial debate about the effects of the parliamentary enclosures. This debate is partly a function of regional differences, partly the result of differences in methodology, ideology or in the way the value of the commons was assessed. In the 1950s, Robert Chambers asserted that while common-right was important, it was only "a thin and squalid curtain" shielding "the growing army of labourers from utter proletarianization."[29] More recently, Leigh Shaw-Taylor argued that by the latter part of the eighteenth century, few people had access to significant common resources and the majority of the rural population would have been overwhelmingly dependent on wage labour. In contrast, many other authors have stressed the central role played in rural communities by common resources and their importance to the well-being of villagers. Many villagers would have combined resources; that is, both a small rented arable acreage, or worked in a trade, while depending on common right for pasture land or more arable land. Certainly, many of those advocating ways to make labourers work hard or for less pointed to the continued importance of common land as a barrier to those plans.[30]

In 1785, the Reverend and Chief Justice John Howlett, a friend of both Adam Smith and Arthur Young, claimed that without enclosure "we shall have remained as rude, as naked, as savage" as distant forefathers. Further, he said,

> Seldom have I passed over an extensive waste, but I have been shocked with the proportionate number of half-naked, and half-starved women and and children, with pale meagre faces, peeping out of their miserable huts, or lazing and lounging about after a few paltry geese, or scabby worthless sheep. [31]

Howlett echoed some common perceptions of the supposed indolence and poverty that accompanied commons, including the continual reference to unenclosed land as "waste." Less than a decade later, the Board of Agriculture fostered a series of reports on agricultural progress across the country, shepherded by Arthur Young. One common theme in many of them was the independence/indolence of those with access to common lands. John Bishton, who crafted the first report on the county of Shropshire in 1794, commented, "The use of common land by labourers operates upon the mind as a sort of independence. [With enclosure] the labourers will work every day in the year, their children will be put to labour early, that subordination of the lower ranks of society which in present times is so much wanted, would be thereby considerably secured."[32] John Billingsley, author of another of the county reports, was even more explicit. He said:

> the imaginary benefits of stocking a common, the possession of a cow or two, with a hog, and a few geese, naturally exalts the peasant ... It inspires some degree of confidence in a property inadequate to his support. In sauntering after his cattle, he acquires a habit of indolence. Quarter, half, and occasionally whole days are imperceptibly lost. Day-labour becomes disgusting.[33]

In addition, following enclosure, landlords constantly jacked up the rent to tenants, seemingly regardless of agricultural prices or profits. This was Young's most constant exhortation to landlords. It appears to have been well founded. David Chambers and G. E. Mingay estimated that enclosure provided net return as high as 20 per cent to landlords in the late eighteenth century.[34] All of these impulses contributed to the enclosures that swept through England between 1750 and 1850, especially during the most active periods during the 1770s and the two decades of high agricultural prices associated with the war with France from 1793 to 1815. We will examine the impact of these enclosures on the poor at some length below.

Relief provided to the poor was just as frequently blamed for the perceived laziness of workers. Along with Arthur Young's *Farmer's Letters* from the 1760s advocating for an increased reliance on workhouses and demanding the end of out-door relief (that is, assistance given to the poor in their cottages), especially for the able-bodied, many others commented on the way poor relief discouraged industriousness. Writing in 1786, Joseph Townsend railed against the existing laws for poor relief, arguing that "hunger, either felt or feared, … will sweeten the severest labours … tame the fiercest animals, it teaches decency and civility obedience and subjection, to the most brutish, the most obstinate, and the most perverse." But poor relief "tends to destroy the harmony and beauty, the symmetry and order of that system, which God and nature have established in the world."[35] Arthur Young was more succinct, but equally appalled by the Poor Laws. In 1771, he wrote "every one but an ideot [*sic*] knows. … that the lower classes must be kept poor, or they will never be industrious."[36] Or, as the Report of the Select Committee on the Poor Laws in 1817 said, "By diminishing this natural impulse by which men are instigated to industry and good conduct … this system is perpetually encouraging and increasing the amount of misery it was designed to alleviate." [37]

Goaded by these powerful spurs – the potential offered by new capital, and the perceived need to make labour more responsive and submissive – estate owners, large-scale tenant farmers, and others with capital engaged in wholesale assault on those very things that had helped foster the relative well-being of the bulk of the rural population. They were abetted by Parliament and counselled along the way by many apostles of inequality, most notably, perhaps, Arthur Young. The central element of this attack was enclosure and an accompanying movement against cottage lands.

"Golden Dreams of Improvement"

Arthur Young provided much of the ammunition. Young was, by late in the eighteenth century, as one of his biographers argued, "Without questions … the most famous authority on agriculture in the English-speaking world."[38] Young had taken a strange route to that station. The family estate had not proved sufficient to fund the education of Arthur and his elder brother at university. Arthur was instead apprenticed to a wine merchant to learn accounting; a position at the Tomlinson accounting house awaited (his sister had married John Tomlinson). The death of his sister disrupted this arrangement and rescued Young from that fate before he could enter employment. With little income and few prospects, Young attempted to publish a monthly magazine, *The Universal Museum: or, Gentlemen's and Ladies' Polite Magazine of History, Politicks, and Literature*. Young printed five editions before giving it up and returning to Bradfield to try farming.[39]

He took over an expiring lease on 80 acres in the estate.[40] Young had even less success as a farmer than as a magazine publisher. As Young himself said, "I had no more idea of farming than of physics or divinity." Elsewhere he admitted, "Young, eager, and totally ignorant ... it was not surprising that I squandered much money, under golden dreams of improvement."[41] After four years, he left Bradfield. There is some disagreement as to the reasons for his hasty departure. He married into a wealthy family in 1765. It was not a happy marriage for long and there is evidence that Young's wife, Martha Allen, and his mother did not get along.[42] Young himself said that he left Bradfield after the birth of his first daughter in 1766, "[f]inding a mixture of families inconsistent with comfortable living."[43] Others suggested that his attempt at farming lost so much money that his mother removed him from the lease.[44]

This set a pattern. During his life he purchased or leased three other farms, each one a failure in its own way. In 1767, he used the dowry from his marriage to contract for a 300-acre farm at Samford Hall. Young asserted that his inability to invest enough capital doomed his efforts there. In writing to his wife that year, he bemoaned, "I would give my right hand that I had never seen this place." He sold out the lease at substantial loss and contracted for a smaller farm at North Mimms, Hertfordshire. Though this was poor land without much prospect, Young's failure to make North Mimms profitable might have had much to do with the distraction of his regular job. He spent the week as the parliamentary reporter for the *Morning Post*, walking the seventeen miles to his farm and back each weekend. His journal entry for one of those years said: "What a year of incessant activity ... No carthorse ever laboured as I did ... spending like an idiot, always in debt, in spite of what I earned."[45]

After giving up North Mimms and following a brief tour of Ireland, he was hired as the agent for Lord Kingsborough in Ireland. Young's employment there did not last long either, the termination of his contract having to do with a suspicion, at least, of romantic entanglement between the Lord's wife and the handsome and vigorous Young.[46] He did gain a £72 annuity from the Lord. After this, his farming was mostly restricted to Bradfield. His mother's sister died in 1782, leaving him with a substantial annuity and land near Bradfield. In 1788 his mother died, leaving him free to manage the estate as he saw fit. Nevertheless, despite sufficient capital and a renewed interest in Bradfield later in his life – and even with his reputation as an agricultural expert – Bradfield never really impressed visitors. One last venture was also unsuccessful. During his travels for his growing body of agricultural books, he ran across a large amount of land in Yorkshire that had recently been made available through enclosure. In 1792 Young purchased the property, consisting of two different parcels of over 1,000 acres each and adjoining 1,613 acres of King's Land held on long-term lease. But the next year, when appointed as secretary to the Board of Agriculture, he sold the property for "much less profit than I had reason to expect."[47]

By this time, Young was much better known for his writing. He had tried his hand at writing before. Along with his adventures in magazine publishing, he penned a small number of pamphlets and four novels, none of these of particular import or renown. His *Farmer's Letters to the People of England* went to three editions and had some influence, but was originally published anonymously. In searching for the farm at North Mimms, however, Young did finally arrive at something he was good at. He published his observations about agricultural experimentation and change he had encountered as *Six Week's Tour through the Southern Counties of England and Wales* in 1768. Thus began Young's career as a cheerleader for agricultural improvement and a staunch ally of large landowners.

In 1770, he followed up with *A Six Month's Tour through the North of England* and the next year with *A Farmer's Tour through the East of England*. The tours provided very specific and detailed information about farming, soil, and crops in various districts. He paid particular attention to the course of crop rotation and habits of manuring, and highlighted agricultural experimentation. In the last few decades, there has been significant criticism of Young's tours. His knowledge of farming, his attention to changes in soils, and his estimates for crop improvements have all been questioned.[48] Young certainly followed a template in his tours and his observations were limited. The normal pattern was for him to advertise his upcoming tour in a particular region and invite landowners and tenant farmers to meet with him. As his reputation and his contacts grew, he took advantage of introductions provided by associates and invitations to view their farms and stay at their estates. Young's tours, thus, were heavily influenced by innovating landlords; he readily admits that most of his discussions were with wealthy estate owners as, in his view, these were the only ones with sufficient resources to experiment; that they provided better fare and accommodation for a sojourning Young also inclined Young to them.

Young also published a variety of pamphlets and more substantial studies on various other agricultural topics. Along with *The Farmer's Letters*, these included *The Farmer's Calendar* in 1771; *Observations on the Present State of the Waste Lands of Great Britain* in 1773; and *Political Arithmetic* in 1774. These were followed by *A Tour of Ireland* in 1780 and his most famous work, *Travels during the Years 1787, 1788 and 1789 in the Kingdom of France* in 1790. His most ambitious publishing work was the *Annals of Agriculture and Other Useful Arts*, begun in 1784. Published once or twice a year, each volume contained 400 to 600 pages; Young wrote one-third or more of each volume, and the rest consisted of letters and reports sent to him for publication. He published forty-six volumes in total, stopping in 1806, although an additional volume with left-over material appeared a decade later. The journal was full of specific advice for enterprising and improving farmers and landowners: the best course of crop rotation in specific soils, the most productive breed of sheep, how to build the most durable hedges. It had lots of articles about the best and most efficient use of fertilizer and the results of experiments with a wide range of crops – from turnips, to cabbages, potatoes, and carrots – as animal fodder. It never failed to applaud enclosures and to comment on the miraculous changes that resulted from them. *Annals* never sold in significant numbers; Young often complained about the lack of subscribers, which occasionally numbered only slightly more than 300 and averaged about 3,000.[49] Nonetheless, *Annals* acted as an important print community for those interested in agricultural improvement and was essential in spreading the gospel of the agricultural revolution.

It was to a certain extent the reputation gained through *Annals*, as well as the reaction to his warnings about rural unrest, that led to Young being named as Secretary to the Board of Agriculture and Internal Improvement in 1793. The Board of Agriculture was created through the work of Sir John Sinclair. Sinclair was an active and vigorous improving estate owner from the north of Scotland. He had convinced Prime Minister Pitt to fund the Board partly to repay Sinclair for his assistance in solving a currency crisis in 1792–3. The Board was provided with an annuity of £3000 from parliament and charged with improving agricultural production throughout Britain. From its inception in 1793, the Board focused most of its attention on two issues both strongly advocated by Young: fostering enclosure and an ambitious survey of agriculture in all the counties of the kingdom. Sinclair dominated the Board through most of its existence from 1793 to 1820, but not without controversy. He was voted out in 1798, succeeded briefly by Lord Sommerville, Lord Carrington, and then Lord Sheffield, before Sinclair became President again in 1806. He resigned again in 1814, plagued by ill health and financial difficulties. On his own estates in Scotland, he had worked diligently to turn his small tenant farmers and shepherds into agricultural workers on farms rented out in larger chunks. Sinclair turned aside criticisms of his tactics, arguing, "Improvement, in all senses of the word, had to mean compulsory reorganization." Through such measures he was able to increase the rent he received for his property by more than five times between 1790 and 1812. Nonetheless, multiple agricultural failures and extraordinary expenses in maintaining a home in London meant he was bankrupt by the time he stepped down from the Board.[50]

Young was Secretary to the Board until his death in 1820. At the Board, Young was in his element. He was remarkably attuned to the flattering attention of prominent and wealthy men. Appointment as Secretary to the Board allowed him to rub shoulders continuously with the mighty and powerful.

He was always aware of the class difference that separated him from the other members. But, fifty-one years old at the time of his appointment, handsome, and well travelled, he was a regular guest at Board members' dinners. He commented with great satisfaction in his memoirs that, "I dined out from twenty-five to thirty days in the month and had, in the time, forty invitations from people of the highest rank and consequence."[51] It also helped him meet one of his other constant concerns: how he would pay for his somewhat extravagant tastes. His position paid him £400 every eighteen months.[52]

"No Evil More Pernicious to the Public"

Young was most obsessed with enclosure. In *Political Arithmetic*, published in 1774, Arthur Young warned, "Without inclosures there can be no good husbandry; while a country is laid out in open fields, every good farmer tied down to the husbandry of his slovenly neighbours, it is simply impossible that agriculture should flourish."[53] In his *Month's Tour of Northamptonshire, Leicestershire, etc* in 1791, he argued, "The advantages of inclosing to every class of people are now so well understood, [and] combatted at present but by a few old women who dislike it for no other reason but a … hatred of novelty."[54] In 1807 in his report on agriculture in Oxfordshire, he was still warning that the "Goths and Vandals of the open fields touch the civilization of the enclosures" and lamenting the number of unenclosed estates in the county.[55] The editor of the 1950 edition of his *Travels in France* argued that, "Enclosure was indeed his panacea for every ill."[56]

While Young was at great pains to try to argue that there were increased yields and productivity after enclosure, most often he focused on the benefits to landlords coming from increased rents. The accounts of his tours are full of glowing reports about the increased rents landlords could charge after enclosure.[57] Young used heightened rents as a substitute for more detailed explorations of increased yields; in much of his writing there was an assumption that if rents increased it presupposed higher yields. But, Young had a kind of pre-Darwinian vision of the impact of rents on tenants. He expressed exasperation with landowners who let their land for low rents, arguing that "There is no evil more pernicious to the public. … There is no good husbandry without high rents."[58] While ideally enclosure would be accompanied by improvement in draining and fencing, Young argued that landlords should increase rents following enclosure even without improvements. Tenant farmers would thus find "it impossible … to live without going quickly to work with improvements; this raised the spirit of industry." Under such demands, tenants must find the most efficient means of farming or be forced from the land.[59] No wonder the landlords in the Board admired his writing so.

The Board was also dedicated to encouraging enclosure. At the inception of the Board, Sinclair linked enclosure to the war with France then just begun:

"Why should we not attempt a campaign against our domestic foe … let us subdue Finchley Common … let us compel Eppling Forest to submit to the yoke of improvement."[60] Reflecting some of the arguments then most common in Scottish Enlightenment thought, Sinclair argued land held in common was incompatible with agriculture. "The idea of having lands in common," he said "… is to be derived from that barbarous state of society, when men were strangers to any higher occupation than those of hunters or shepherds." Young and Sinclair convinced the Board to focus on a General Enclosure Bill that would end the need for a separate act of Parliament for each enclosure and simplify the process enormously. Sinclair, in presenting the proposed bill to Parliament, also dismissed any idea that such an act would harm the rural poor. While enclosure might force them from their cottages, Sinclair assured the House, "It is impossible to suppose that the Poor should be injured by that circumstance, which secures to them a good market for their labour (in which the real riches of a Cottager consists)."[61] Young had argued for an act that would provide "an unlimited power of enclosure" as early as the 1760s. He had supported a proposition for such an act in parliament in 1780 and again in 1790. The Board presented the most serious proposal for a General Enclosure Act to Parliament in 1796. Despite their efforts, the Bill did not pass. The Board proposed another in 1798 that did not get to a vote. Finally, in 1801, a much-reduced bill, simplifying the process but not removing the need for each individual act, was passed.[62]

Young was also a staunch opponent of small farming. Large farmers, he argued, with more capital to invest on their activities, would always farm better and employ more labour. The large farmer "can build, hedge, ditch, plant, plough, harrow, drain, manure, hoe, weed … execute every operation of his business better and more effectually than a little farmer."[63] But he was equally opposed to small farming because he worried that such farms led to misery and an unsustainable increase in population. He argued in his *Travels in France* that France was overpopulated and blamed this on the ability of French peasants to hang onto their land as "whatever promises the appearance of subsistence induces men to marry." The division of land into smallholdings led only to "a multiplication of wretchedness." Little properties "tempt the poor to have cattle – to have property – and, in consequence misery." In England, on the other hand, he argued that agricultural workers, not similarly tempted to own property at all, were "well clothed, well nourished, tolerably drunken with superfluity, well lodged and at ease; and amongst them, not one in a thousand has either land or cattle."[64] Thus, relieved of any fear about the detrimental effects that might accrue from the expansion of large farms and extinguishing common rights, Young could counsel enclosure without expressing much concern for its effects on the poor.

Yet, the poor rates continued to increase, quintupling between 1750 and 1803.[65] Young argued that relief provided to the poor was not only detrimental to landlords who needed to pay the poor rates, but disastrous for society as a whole. In his *Farmer's Letters* he asserted that any excess income the poor had "was constantly expended by the husband in … idleness and ale, and by the wife in that of tea."[66] Indeed, Young was obsessed with idleness and tea drinking. In his *Farmer's Tour through the East of England*, in 1771, he commented how in one district the poor rates had increased more than ten times in fifteen years. Rather than suggesting that such an increase might indeed reflect the devastating impact of some of the changes to agriculture then underway, he instead reported, "and this vast rise they attribute much to the excess of tea drinking; the lowest of the poor drink it twice a day while their children have not bread to eat."[67]

Consequently, the need for revisions to the poor laws was a common topic in *Annals*. In *The Farmer's Letters*, Young had recommended the complete elimination of poor relief for the able-bodied and had urged that all children of those receiving relief should be placed in workhouses. With this, Young tapped into a mounting tide of resentment of the poor; various harsh remedies were advocated and some implemented, intending to make going "on the parish" a terrifying prospect. In 1723, Parliament had authorized any parish to set up a workhouse to house the poor; by 1777 there were almost 2,000 of them in England. Those receiving relief were often required to "bind-out" or apprentice their children to reduce the costs to the parish. Still, there was significant opposition to workhouses by the parish overseers, often drawn from among small farmers or tradesmen and sympathetic to the poor, and by the end of the century less than 10 per cent of those receiving relief were in workhouses. Young and many of his correspondents in *Annals* argued most strongly for a dramatic expansion of workhouses. Young had proposed the creation of a hundred Houses of Industry to house all those on relief, centralizing workhouses and removing their operation from the often too sympathetic parish officers. This proposal was discussed at length in *Annals*. A Reverend Mills applauded the plan, arguing that the Houses would be of "considerable advantage to the landlord and tenant in particular … as from such institutions, the enormous and increasing expence [*sic*] of maintaining the poor may be much reduced and the young families of lazy and vicious parents be brought up in habits of industry, morality and religion." Mills followed with a full description of the operations of a workhouse he attended in Hitchom, Suffolk, created in 1779. The house had about 170 people. They were called to prayer every morning at 6:00 in summer and 7:00 in winter, then immediately after set to work, mostly spinning. All inhabitants, including the aged and children, worked for twelve hours a day. "The parents thus having leisure for amusement and conversation with one another, and their children for mirth and play." Their diet consisted of "broth or milk" for breakfast and bread and cheese for dinner and supper, broken up occasionally by "feed cake" or meat dumplings and "garden stuff." Every

Thursday, the committee of professionals running the house – that is, along with Mills, a surgeon, a matron, a house clerk, and a treasurer – met, at which "the idle and disorderly were reproved and punished, the industrious and good commended and rewarded."[68]

Mills' account was joined by a number of well-known commentators with arguments for workhouses and against the demands of the poor. Putting children to work was a particularly favoured topic in some of the discussion. One letter commented that local officials had decided that no person would get relief for a child above five years of age "who was not able to knit" or above the age of nine who was not able to "spin linen or woollen."[69] Young's friend Thomas Ruggles (with whom Young had spent a week inspecting his estate in Essex)[70] published a long series of letters in *Annals*, later collected into a separate volume, on the history of poor relief, emphasizing the rapid growth in the costs of poor relief and supporting the need for all poor to be sent to workhouses. Ruggles particularly thought children needed to be put to work early and for long hours. As Ruggles said, "Can it be supposed that a generation of industrious adults will arise from a race of idle children."[71] Jeremy Bentham also first published his plan for the creation of a profit-making company to put the poor to work, modelled along the lines of the East India Company, in the *Annals*. He asked for Young's and the readers' assistance in "forming a valuation of that part of the national livestock which has no feathers and walks upon two legs."[72] During these years, nowhere in the writing of Young or in the pages of the *Annals* does one find a suggestion that escalating numbers of people relying on relief might be an indication of a real increase in rural poverty. Most certainly, only most rarely can one find any hint of uncertainty about the benefits of the agricultural changes underway.

"Repressing the Democratic Mischief of Transferring Property"

There was, however, great concern about the potential for unrest. Arthur Young's most popular work was his *Travels in France*. Young had the great fortune to have completed his travels just before the beginning of the French Revolution. Despite suffering a serious fever upon his return, he hurried through the publication; the book came out at a time when the English public was greatly exercised about and interested in France. Young's observations about French agriculture and society converted him into something of a recognized expert on France at a particularly propitious time. Young took full advantage of this opportunity to prove his worth to the rich and powerful. In his *Travels* he proposed the need for a landed militia "formed of every man that possesses a certain degree of property, rank and file as well as officers … such a force would be amply sufficient for repressing those riots, whose object might be, immediately or ultimately, the democratic mischief of transferring property."[73]

In case anyone missed the significance of this argument, Young published a small pamphlet the next year entitled *The Example of France, a Warning to Britain*. Here, he doubled down on his argument. He asserted that the "quarrel" then occurring in France "is alone a question of property; it is a trial at arms, whether those who have nothing shall not seize and possess the property of those who have something … which can never end but in the equal and universal ruin of all." He warned that English landowners were wrong to trust in the army to safeguard their property.[74] Landed militias became somewhat of an obsession for Young. He continued his calls for their formation in the *Annals*, warning that "popular tyranny is a catching phrenzy that will surely spread." He returned again and again to this in the journal, asking on occasion, "Have you enrolled yourself in a patriotic corps?" and warning about the consequences if his readers did not. He was also quite involved in the formation of such a militia in his home county of Suffolk. As we will see in chapter 4, the Yeoman cavalry were essential, and brutal, in putting down rural unrest during the next four decades.[75] Young's central role at the forefront of this movement did much to curry the favour of large landowners.

Changes to English agriculture through the second half of the eighteenth century and continuing through the early decades of the nineteenth may or may not have fostered increased agricultural production. The costs to the majority of those living in the countryside were dismissed as a necessary price to pay for improvement – like the "forced relocation" Sir John Sinclair imposed on his former tenants and shepherds in the name of progress. From the 1760s to 1790s, Arthur Young used his growing reputation as the most knowledgeable observer of English agriculture to push the very changes that were most disadvantageous to commoners, cottagers, and labourers in the countryside: enclosure, policies against small farmers, a draconian reduction in poor relief, and horrendous institutionalization for any who persisted in claiming such relief. Finally, to ensure there would be no popular challenges to the resultant growing inequality, Young insistently called for an armed force of landowners sufficient to quell any such unrest. Through all of this, Young was not simply an "untiring and eloquent apostle for the agricultural revolution" but also an apostle for inequality and increased wretchedness.

But something happened on the way to the revolution. By the mid-point of the 1790s, at the height of his fame and influence, Arthur Young noticed that the very changes he advocated for so strongly were spreading poverty and misery in rural England. Importantly, Young was joined in this discovery by a substantial group of the most powerful estate owners; together they began to call for ways of mitigating that poverty. We turn to Young's change of heart and the lessons we can draw from estate owners' concerns in our next chapter.

Chapter Three

"The Enchantment of Property"

Nearing the end of an eventful and influential life, Arthur Young expressed mostly regret. Looking back, he believed his most important work had been his failed attempt, decades earlier, to ensure that cottagers harmed by enclosure would be provided with land for a garden, a potato plot, and to keep a cow. "[O]f all the essays and papers I have produced, none I think so pardonable as this, so convincing by facts, and so satisfactory to any candid reader. ... It will, I trust, remain a proof of what ought to have been done."[1]

Young was by this time living a very different life than that discussed in chapter 2. Once one of the most celebrated authors on English agriculture and secretary to the influential Board of Agriculture and Internal Improvement, he had revelled in the company and attention of the rich and powerful. But by the end of the first decade of the nineteenth century, going blind, having embraced religious dissent after the death of his youngest daughter in 1797, he spent most of his time at his modest estate in Bradfield, Suffolk, where, he said, no matter the weather, he would wake at 4:00 and "walk up to my neck in the garden pond, pray, and then read till breakfast; read, walk, and farm till dinner, and so on till it is dark."[2] He died in 1820, remembered primarily by his secretary and the parishioners of the small church at Bradfield.

Arthur Young's later writings tell us much about the ugly side of late eighteenth- and early nineteenth-century agricultural change. Young became convinced that enclosure and "an open war against cottages" were leading to deepening poverty in England. He thus dedicated much of his attention to providing remedies for the damage caused by the ideas he had once advocated so strongly. Many commentators have suggested that the death of his daughter and his religious conversion prompted Young's about-face. But a careful reading of Young's works and attention paid to the public opinions of some of the most powerful landowners in England, many of whom were members of the Board of Agriculture, suggest that the explanation for his change of heart is more complicated and linked to increasing levels of poverty in rural England.

Young was joined in the call for the need for garden plots for cottagers, both to reduce poverty and the poor rates and to increase agricultural production, by many of the most powerful landed gentry.

This chapter details the impact of late eighteenth- and early nineteenth-century change on commoners, cottagers, and agricultural labourers. It uses the testimony of Young and the other members of the powerful Board of Agriculture, once the most vocal proponents of enclosure, to highlight the negative consequences of these experiments.

Despite the spirited defence of cottage gardens by Young and many influential members of the Board of Agriculture, and a belated recognition that those with only small amounts of land were the most productive farmers and most careful stewards of the land, their arguments had little impact on policies towards the rural poor. As we will explore in the next chapter, such inequality helped foster class resentment and increased violence in rural England in the early decades of the nineteenth century. Far from leading to rural prosperity, the eighteenth- and nineteenth-century agricultural revolution fostered a countryside marked by increased returns to capital, an impoverished agricultural workforce, and a rural society seething with conflict.

"Precarious Condition of Hirelings"

While G.E. Fussell could extoll "an improved agriculture of such industry that it is wonderful to relate" and Mark Overton could wonder at the "unprecedented increase in labour productivity" that marked agricultural change during this period, many other commentators, closer to the scene, had a very different impression of what was going on in rural England in the late eighteenth century. Arthur Young and others who preached enclosure argued that both agriculture and the rural population itself would be best served if labourers had no property; that is, if they were simply labourers in a thoroughly capitalist agricultural system marked by large-scale tenant farmers investing capital on the land, paying high rents to landowners, and employing labourers dependent on wages. It was a continuous refrain, sung by agricultural improvers beginning in the 1760s, echoed by political economists like Thomas Robert Malthus and Nassau Senior through the first few decades of the nineteenth century, and reiterated constantly by the *Economist* newspaper until the 1860s: almost a century of promises of prosperity that instead took a devastating toll on rural labourers, commoners, and cottagers.

Most people living in the countryside depended, to some extent, on wages. Real agricultural wages fell substantially beginning in the 1770s and continued to be depressed until the 1850s in the south and east. In 1955 Phelps Brown and Hopkins provided an estimate of real wages in England and Wales. According to their calculations, rural wages fell by 30 per cent between 1730 and 1800 and did not reach their 1730 levels again until the 1840s. Subsequent research has done little to change this basic argument except to make the decline more dramatic and more extended.[3] Keith Snell's careful comparison of agricultural wages and food prices indicated that real wages for fully employed men and women fell by about 20 per cent between 1750 and 1833; in southern England agricultural wages fell further to 79 per cent of the 1833 average by 1851. This understates the decline; especially in the south and the east, where the triad of agrarian progress – high rents, capitalist tenant farmers, and wage dependent labourers – was most dominant, precarious employment (seasonal, weekly, daily or even hourly) replaced more dependable employment, particularly for women.[4]

War with France from 1793 to 1815, with a short break in 1802, and a series of bad harvests in the 1790s made the situation worse. Food prices rose dramatically in the 1790s; costs of basic grains in 1801 were three times those in 1794. Nominal wages increased slightly, but not nearly enough to compensate for dramatic price increases for labourers now dependent on more purchased goods. Roger Wells has argued that agricultural wages for the vast majority of rural labourers throughout England during the 1790s and the first few years of the nineteenth century did not cover the cost of even the most basic and insufficient diet. As a result, he says, mortality rates "spiraled upwards" in the years after the turn of the century as "echoes of famine."[5] Even by the 1860s, a survey by Dr. E. Smith presented to the House of Commons reported that close to half the people in agricultural districts in England were chronically malnourished.[6]

While the famine years reported on by Wells soon ended and agricultural prices fell in the new century, especially after the war with France ended, this benefitted rural workers little. Landlords had increased rents dramatically during the war and did not reduce them subsequently despite falling agricultural prices, putting pressure on new large-scale tenant farmers who had often invested substantial amounts of capital in improvements during the high-price years. Tenant farmers, hard-pressed, sought to reduce costs by paring down the number and wages of workers. William Cobbett, in his account of his rides through the English countryside in 1822–6, argued that farmers had devised a "scheme for squeezing rents out of the bones of the labourer." They had reduced labourers' wages "so low as to make the labourer a walking skeleton."[7]

Other changes contributed to increasing poverty in rural areas through this century. Despite questions about the impact of enclosure on the rural poor, discussed in chapter 2, Jane Humphries, Jeanette Neeson, and others argued convincingly that, at least for the Midlands region, common-rights were still important in the late eighteenth century and that enclosure had a devastating impact on smallholders. Neeson asserted that in Northamptonshire, within ten years of enclosure, 49 per cent of the original small-owners no longer held land, or at least enough land to appear on tax records.[8] Much of the most recent historiography has suggested that the avalanche of contemporary writings from the late eighteenth through the early nineteenth centuries that expressed dismay over the loss of common lands and the collapse of small farm agriculture was not overly pessimistic. Certainly, contemporaries were under few illusions about the devastating impact of such changes.

The loss of common land and declining wages were only part of the story. Equally complicit in contemporary accounts of declining living standards for the rural poor were a decline in the number of small farms as large farmers spread their acreages (engrossing) and an accompanying collapse in the amount of land available as cottage gardens. Ardent champions of improvement, like Young, advocated most strongly for a shift from customary leasing agreements, often assigned for many years or even a number of lives, to more thoroughly commercial leases, very often on a year-to-year basis. Such leases made it easier for landlords to consolidate their holdings and let them to larger tenant farmers. The result, most widespread in the south, was the steady erosion of the position of relatively small farmers. One telling anecdote was provided in a letter to the *Brighton Gazette* in 1787 by a reader identified only as "A Lady." She recounts coming upon a man about eighty years old who was disconsolate, sitting on a stone fence in a Shoreham church yard. She says he had lost his farm of some seventy acres that he had rented for forty-one years. The fellow said:

> It was a bad hour for the happiness of Old England, when the Lords of the country took it into their heads to make one farm out of ten – the evils of such a measure can never be sufficiently lamented – the poor cottagers wander about the villages with broken hearts, and sorrowfully predict the time when Great Britain … shall have but two sets of inhabitants – the proud wealthy, and the spiritless poor.[9]

Around the same time, the Reverend David Davies commented on the condition of the agricultural populace in his community, Barkham in Berkshire, where he had been Rector since 1782: "For a long time past their condition has been going from bad to worse continually." Full employment was scarce and wages kept falling. He attributed this shocking decline in the security of the poor to a number of changes. Rich farmers were taking advantage of enclosure and in other ways engrossing their estates. While this "elevated the body of farmers above their proper level," it brought poverty and ruin to the less prosperous. Not only had real wages declined dramatically, but rich farmers had turned cottages into crowded and squalid shared tenements, denying cottagers access to garden plots or land to maintain a cow. With less income, labourers were forced, nonetheless, to purchase more of their needs. The result was a downward spiral of poverty. As Davies said:

> The depriving of the peasantry of all landed property has beggared multitudes. …
> Formerly many of the lower sort of people occupied tenements of their own, with parcels of land about them, or they rented such of others. On these they raised

for themselves a considerable part of their subsistence without being obliged as now to buy all they want at shops. ... But since these small parcels of land have been swallowed up in the contiguous farms and inclosures ... the families which used to occupy them are crowded together in decayed farm-houses, with hardly enough to keep a cabbage garden; and being reduced to mere hirelings, they are, of course, very liable to come to want. ... Thus an amazing number of people have been reduced from a comfortable state of partial independence to the precarious condition of hirelings, who, when out of work, must immediately come to their parish.

Davies called for new regulations that restricted the increase in large farms. He insisted that cottagers must be allowed some land for garden produce, for potatoes, a cow, some flax and hemp. "[T]he fatal consequence of that policy which deprives labouring people of the expectation of possessing any property in the soil, must be the extinction of every generous principle in their minds." Moreover, the "destruction of small farms, and of cottages having land about them, has so greatly contributed to bring the lower peasantry into the starving condition in which we now see them ... [T]his practice has been reducing the generality of small-farmers into day labourers, and the great body of day-labourers into beggars, and has been multiplying and impoverishing even beggars themselves."[10]

Three decades later, William Cobbett was particularly struck by how much more depressed agricultural workers were in the southeast, where improved grain agriculture had more fully flourished than in other parts of England, resulting in less land available for cottage gardens. Labouring people, he argued, "invariably do best in the *woodland* and *forest* and *wild* countries. Where the mighty grasper has *all under his eye*, they can get little." Later in his journeys, on the Isle of Thanet, he observed, "It is a country of corn ... All was corn around me." As a consequence, the labourers were poor, dirty, and ragged. "Invariably I have observed that the richer the soil and the more destitute of wood; that is to say, the more purely a corn country, the more miserable the labourers."[11]

Of course, part of the decline in living standards was due to enclosure. Enclosure acts were occasionally brought forward and agreed to as a simple expedient for agriculturalists with dispersed strips of lands to consolidate their holdings. However, most often, enclosure was requested by the largest and wealthiest in a community. Enclosure was often strenuously opposed by others with rights in the commons, and on occasion they were successful in preventing the approval of an enclosure bill. On balance, though, it seems clear that even when the majority of the poor in a parish opposed enclosure, they were unable to prevent it. Commons rights were not always equally distributed; in locations where common rights had been purchased and accumulated, people had votes according to the number of such rights they held. Often when there was significant opposition the request to enclose would be withdrawn until those pushing for enclosure could consolidate support; the Bill would be brought forward again some years later. In the meantime, wealthier neighbours and outside investors bought up leases and rights and reduced the number of those who might oppose the Bill.

All those with recognized commons rights were to be accommodated with plots of land in proportion to their rights in the commons, but there were numerous obstacles in their way. The amount of land to be allocated was reduced to compensate tithe holders on the land, often pinching the size of the small individual plots below that necessary to maintain any livestock. The loss of commons pasture, often designated wastelands, was devastating for those who received only small plots of land through enclosure. Enclosure was an expensive proposition; legal fees, improvements, and fencing meant the total cost of enclosure might have been as high as £12 per acre. Part of the common and wasteland was often sold to finance these costs, further reducing the amount of land each rights holder would receive.[12] Fencing, particularly, was an expensive proposition for the smallest landholders, and yet was required within a very short time after the enclosure bill. Those receiving small amounts of land were commonly forced to sell because of their inability to sustain such costs.

There were, as well, usually large numbers of people – often the poorest in the community – who did not have any recognized common rights and received nothing but misery from enclosure. Many cottagers, for example, rented their cottage and had no common right and simply lost access to attached garden land after enclosure. In addition, virtually all communities held many people who had no common rights but had often enjoyed access to unimproved pasture or common resources in woodlands and fens; all lost through enclosure. Even those with common rights who received some land were impoverished through new restrictions on their ability to collect wood or peat for fuel on what had been common forestland or waste before enclosure. Many commentators linked the decline in cottage bread- and beer-making to difficulties in obtaining fuel.

Enclosure was accompanied often by mean-spirited denial of long-held customary practices not officially recognized as common rights. One good example of this was gleaning. Long held to be a right of commoners (and others) in a community, gleaning could contribute substantially to the needs of a family and was particularly important as part of women's contribution to the household economy. Gentry and tenant farmers increasingly sought to curtail access to recently harvested land for gleaning in the 1780s. In one well-known case, the overseer of the estate for Lord Cornwallis sought to deny gleaning to a poor widowed cottager, Mary Houghton. Through the assistance of Capel Lofft, a progressive landowner and lawyer, Houghton's case was taken to court twice. The court found in 1788 that no right of gleaning existed, at least in this case.[13]

The celebrated chronicler of England's rural worlds, George Sturt, wrote in his 1912 *Change in the Village*:

> To the enclosure of the common more than any other cause may be traced all of the changes which have subsequently passed over the village. It was like knocking the keystone out of the arch ... So the once self-supporting cottager turned into a spender of money at the baker's, the coal-merchants, the provision-dealers; and, of course needing to spend money he needed first to get it.[14]

The most influential of these early works on enclosure was J.L. and Barbara Hammond's *The Village Labourer, 1760–1832*, published in 1913. This careful and impassioned study of the impact of late eighteenth- and early nineteenth-century change on the village remains one of the classics of English social history. They argued that with enclosure the "anchor of the poor was gone."[15]

"An Open War against Cottages"

An equally devastating, but less well-documented, process during these years was what Arthur Young called "an open war against cottages."[16] This war had many fronts. On the one hand, enclosure had often entailed tearing down cottages as land was consolidated. A more important front in this war was associated with growing resentment against the Poor Laws. As mentioned earlier, English Poor Laws had functioned reasonably well into the 1770s. But in the following decades, the increasing costs and the supposed deleterious effects poor relief had on the work ethic of the poor led to strenuous arguments for either changes to or the elimination of poor relief. The Settlement Act of 1662 had ruled that the poor were only eligible for relief in the parish of their settlement. How, exactly, people could establish settlement changed from time to time, and was interpreted differently from parish to parish. Outside of living in the parish of one's birth, settlement could sometimes be obtained by full time employment over a full year; in the early eighteenth century, settlement in a new parish had often been granted to young men or women who were employed for a year or more as live-in servants. There were complicated rulings concerning the right of settlement for children born out of wedlock, for squatters and others without official access to land, and for those employed for less than a full year.

Even many people not particularly sympathetic to the poor opposed the settlement regulations. Young called the act "the most false, mischievous, and pernicious system that ever barbarism devised."[17] Adam Smith also railed against it, suggesting in his 1776 *Inquiry into the Wealth of Nations* that, "There is scarce a poor man in England …who has not in some part of his life felt himself cruelly oppressed by this ill-contrived law of settlements."[18] The 1662 act had provided for the legal removal of any person "liable to become a charge on the parish and to convey such a person or persons to such a parish where he or they were last legally settled." The result was an often complicated and costly process of removal whereby poor people who applied for relief or, in some cases, only appeared as if they might apply for relief were removed from parishes and transferred to the last official parish of settlement. In 1840, for example, there were 11,000 removal orders involving 32,000 paupers in England and Wales. Alternatively, arrangements were often made for the parish of settlement to pay relief costs for those "settled" but not resident in a parish rather than engage in the costly process of receiving returning paupers in a parish where they would, most likely, end up on the relief roles as well. Quite obviously parishes were loath to do this; the costs of nonresident relief further induced parishes to make it increasingly hard to obtain settlement.[19]

As poverty deepened and enclosure left more people without means of support, opposition to poor relief increased. In many parishes, especially in so-called close (or closed) parishes – that is, parishes where virtually all of the land was owned by very few people – landowners and parish officials forbade building new cottages or tore down existing ones as a means to reduce the numbers of those who might go on the parish and drive up the poor rates paid by landowners or large tenants. Young scolded such landlords, saying "to prohibit cottages, which when built, would be filled with industrious inhabitants, is a violent and mischievous system."[20] On the one hand, landowners believed, perhaps correctly, that high poor rates assigned to their lands reduced the rents they could charge their large tenants. On the other, as the complaint from David Davies suggests, to increase rents landlords also began to pack people into their cottages, doubling or tripling the families living in the cottages and ensuring that they would have little or no garden land. Very often labourers living in these warrens needed to travel significant distances each day to work in a "close" parish. Two decades after Young condemned the war on cottages, William Cobbett recounted the effects of its continuation; he described how "the villages are wasting away … there is a *shocking decay*, a great dilapidation and constant pulling down or falling down of houses."[21] Another half century after Cobbett, the *Economist* reported, "In nearly every rural district, the landowners pull down the existing cottages when opportunity offers, and prevent, where they can, the erection of new ones"[22] – nearly a century of war on cottages.

Indeed, rents for cottages probably doubled between the 1790s and the 1830s as the spaces available for families diminished.[23] One study in 1864 determined that in the areas surveyed, in 5,375 cottages there were 8,805 bedrooms for 25,000 people. Space per person was 156 cu. feet, or less than a third of the minimum mandated in the workhouses created under the 1834 Poor Law.[24]

As a result of this war, cottagers, who previously could rely on some garden land and perhaps a potato field, the opportunity to raise chickens, a pig, and perhaps access to enough pasture to keep a cow, were now entirely dependent on increasingly sporadic wages.

By the last couple of decades of the eighteenth century, the Poor Law, which had worked reasonably well for two centuries, began to unravel because of increasing poverty and landlord opposition. In the face of rising prices for grains, in 1795 poor relief was set in some parishes on a scale reflecting prices. Eventually, many parishes adopted this scale. While this helped offset rising prices for some of the poor, it did not address the fundamental problems. Over time, as the cost of the poor rose, the scale was often reduced or ignored. More problematically, with increasing unemployment, less opportunity for full employment, and more people without access to land to provide for themselves, the system all but collapsed. The poor rates charged to landowners increased dramatically, especially in some parishes in the south and east.[25] As migration to other districts was restricted, poor labourers often found themselves virtual prisoners in their parish, unwilling to move where they did not have settlement, but refused permission to build a cottage or start a family. Contracts for live-in servants now often stipulated employment terms of less than a year to avoid granting residence to these labourers; parishes sometimes fined farmers who broke these new regulations and allowed people to obtain settlement. In some "pauperised parishes," poor relief became a kind of de facto wage and those receiving relief were sent "on the rounds" working in teams where the parish assigned them, their wages paid mostly by the parish. Or, poor relief was used to top up inadequate wages; farmers' wage costs were thus subsidized by other ratepayers. As the Hammonds remarked, "The Poor Law which had once been the hospital became now the prison for the poor."[26]

By 1832, the total sum of poor relief provided in England and Wales was just over £7 million, about five times what it had been in 1770. From the late eighteenth century on, there were various attempts to amend or eliminate the Poor Laws. As we will see, virtually all of the practitioners of the new "science" of political economy called for the elimination of poor relief in the early years of the nineteenth century. There were dozens of reports and commissions regarding the poor laws through these years. In 1817, the House of Commons Committee on the Poor Laws, though it could propose no acceptable substitute, warned that if the rates were allowed to increase as they were the poor rates would absorb all of the potential rent leading to "neglect and ruin of the land." Finally, in 1832 a Poor Law Commission was established and its report led to the most substantial revisions to the Poor Laws in the form of the New Poor Laws of 1834. This report was largely the work of Nassau Senior; its focus was on reducing dramatically the costs of relief through the elimination of "out-door" relief and reliance on purposefully dreadful workhouses. It kept intact, however, the Law of Settlement.

Any examination of the functioning of the Poor Laws in the early nineteenth century leads to the conclusion that the labour market was in complete disarray. In some ways, this was clearly the convulsions of an incomplete transition from a rural society in which agricultural labour was only one important component in the survival strategies of a population that also enjoyed significant other resources (many of which they believed to be more important than wage labour) to one in which, deprived of these resources, the rural poor needed to depend on wages in an agricultural system that did not always need them and was not willing to pay adequately for their labour when it did. It was also, however, the natural outcome of a system in which landowners and large farmers fretted constantly about the need to reduce the independence of labourers and conspired to pursue policies that would do just that, while at the same time reducing wages and fostering an increase in labour "productivity" that reduced further the demand for labour. The victims in that transition – those who could no longer depend on the commons or rely partly on cottage gardens and small plots of land – became even poorer as the agricultural revolution unfolded.

"To Heal a Soul Too Careless in its Duty"

Despite his desire to curry the favour of the rich and powerful, and his determined attempts to ignore the poor – or notice only their supposed idleness – in his travels Arthur Young was not entirely blind to the evidence of growing distress in the countryside. Nor was he immune to a heightened level of concern about such distress among a number of the powerful landowners he courted. By the 1790s, Arthur Young's writing – and the pages of the *Annals* – reflected a growing obsession with the state of the poor and a belief that the best way to remedy their situation was to provide all labourers with cottage gardens. As we will see, Young was most definitely not alone in this. Young's concern for the poor became most apparent at roughly the same time as the death of his daughter, which affected him deeply.

By the 1790s, Young had succeeded in many of his dreams. He had fashioned for himself a career as a celebrated author on all things agricultural. By somewhat happy coincidence, he was considered to be a knowledgeable commentator on France. He communicated and conversed with important political and literary figures in England and around the world: visiting Edmund Burke, carrying out a correspondence with George Washington, answering entreaties from Jeremy Bentham, and being inducted into Royal and Agricultural Societies in Britain and their equivalent on the continent. Most importantly to him, his position as Secretary to the Board of Agriculture and Internal Improvement put him in the company of the most important landed gentry in Britain. While he continued to feel the slight of both his lack of title and his only very modest landholding, he was often sought both as a dinner companion and for his farming advice. He was, however, continually troubled by difficulties over money and despite his success, it appears, not particularly happy. His memoirs provide a portrait of a troubled man who felt constantly overworked and underappreciated. In his "Memoirs of the Last Thirty Years of a Farming Life," published in *Annals* in 1791 and meant to act as an advertisement for his *Travels in France*, Young complained, "And here ends my narrative of thirty years … I may say with confidence … that during that period I have hardly known what an idle hour has been. I have worked more like a coalheaver (though without his reward) … And, for what?"[27] Young was just recovering from a fever that may have affected his mood at that time, but he was never far from bouts of melancholy and self-pity.

Young had four children: a son, Arthur, and three daughters, Marie, Elizabeth, and Martha Ann. Elizabeth died of tuberculosis in 1794 at the age of twenty-six. In 1797, still struggling with finances despite his appointment to the Board of Agriculture, he lived in unhealthy rented accommodations in London. His youngest daughter, Martha Ann, nicknamed Bobbin, then fourteen, was staying with him while attending school. She came down with tuberculosis and despite Young's desperate ministrations, she eventually died of the illness.

Her death affected him deeply. Young removed himself to Bradfield, where he refused company and read incessantly, mostly religious tracks. He was most taken with William Wilberforce's newly published *Practical View of the Prevailing System of Professed Christians in the Higher and Middle Ranks of this Country, Contrasted with Real Christianity.*[28] He clearly blamed himself for Bobbin's death, compounding his grief. He lost himself in a sorrow which he declared to be "the best physician to heal a soul that has been too careless in its duty to God."

According to Henry Higgs, "Young was a broken man" after the death of Martha Ann. "He carried his bereavement ever within him. A settled gloom deepened into religious fanaticism."[29] He was certainly in many ways a changed man. Though he continued to work for the Board, he more often found solace in solitude at Bradfield. When he was in London, he avoided the lavish dinners he used to enjoy so much and sought out the company of Methodists and other religious dissenters. But he continued to publish *Annals* and to produce pamphlets on various subjects. It is in this period that Young produced his most interesting and important works on social conditions in the English countryside.

The dramatic change in the tone and substance of Young's writing, beginning around this time, has attracted some discussion and speculation. Most often the traumatic death of Martha Ann is highlighted. Patricia James perhaps most clearly espouses this view: "Poor Young," she says, "was unhappily married and inconsolable after the death of his favourite child, overworked and afflicted with religious near-mania."[30] There is no doubt that Young was strongly affected by her death, but such an explanation discounts the impact of the deepening poverty in England on Young, who perhaps more than any other writer travelled the countryside in these years. Redcliffe Salaman might have caught the inspiration a little more accurately when he said that the "crisis of 1795 and the distress which ensued, reawakened his dormant humanitarianism."[31] Young was not alone in his response to this distress and his growing concern should be considered along with the public statements and reports of a number of powerful landowners all deeply disturbed by what they saw happening in the countryside.

The evidence for a "dormant humanitarianism" in Young's writing before the mid-1790s is, admittedly, limited. But, even in the early writings of this young apostle for inequality desperate to be admired by the landed gentry one can find hints of what would eventually be his full-blown opposition to the ugly side of the agricultural revolution. Some of Young's early work demonstrated a sensitivity to the poor and a certain hesitancy about the outcome of enclosure. In 1773, in his *Observations on the Present State of Waste Lands of Great Britain*, he had cautioned against the continued monopolization of land through enclosure and very large farms. This practice was encouraging emigration by making it more difficult for young farmers to start out. He suggested the state buy land (or that it be purchased through public subscription) and this land be sold on easy terms to poor farmers in lots of twenty to thirty acres.[32] This was a remarkable proposal from someone who the next year would go on at some length about the dangers of small farms and the benefits of large ones. His contradictions didn't end there. A decade before commenting on English peasants "drunken with superfluity" in *Travels in France*, Young published his *Tour of Ireland*. Here he contrasted the "pinched bellies" in English cottages with the full stomachs of Irish cottiers fed well on potatoes. This tour also prompted in Young a controversial appreciation for the potato as food for humans; he had previously thought of it primarily as animal fodder. He says, "I will not assert that potatoes are better food than bread and cheese; but I have no doubt a bellyful of one being much better than half a bellyful of the other."[33]

Young's *Travels in France* has most often been read, correctly, as an attack on the poverty he believed inherent in small farms. Nonetheless, he occasionally let his powers of observation overcome his bias. Young commented that the region around Bearn was all "in the hands of little proprietors, with the farms being so small as to occasion a vicious and miserable population." And yet, here, "[a]n air of neatness, warmth and comfort breathes over the whole." The farmers lived in "a succession of many well-built, tight and comfortable farming cottages, built of stone, and covered with tiles, each having its little garden … with plenty of peach and other fruit-trees, nursed with so much care, that nothing but the fostering attention of the owner could effect anything like it. To every house belongs a farm, perfectly enclosed, with grass borders mown and neatly kept around the corn fields."[34] This passage is noteworthy not simply because it illustrates an often-buried appreciation of the pleasures of small farmer domesticity and the painstaking care which they brought to their little farms, but also because this description so closely resembles arguments made by Young and many members of the Board of Agriculture about the benefits of cottage gardens a decade later. Elsewhere in *Travels*, he commented on how peasant farmers "turn rocks into scenes of fertility, because I suppose their own," and later, "The magic of property turns sand into gold."[35]

Though Young championed enclosure as a means for increasing production all his life, he did allow himself a glimpse of the evils lurking for the poor in the process. An enclosure act named commissioners to allocate compensation in land to those who held common-right and to determine the distribution of land in the newly enclosed area. Such powers were open to abuse, especially as the commissioners were often tied through patronage to the large estate owners in the district being enclosed or had interest in the enclosure themselves. As early as the 1780s, Young warned about the abuse of commissioners and cautioned that they too often disregarded the interests of the poor. It was partly to systematize the powers of commissioners, as well as to simplify the process of enclosure, that Young had for years pushed the idea of a General Enclosure Bill replacing the need for separate parliamentary acts. Very quickly after its formation the Board took on this task as well. In 1796, the president of the Board proposed such a bill to Parliament, the first of a number of failed attempts by Sinclair to get one passed. Importantly, this proposal included a demand that each enclosure include land for cottagers; it also sought to alleviate the costs of fencing land for the poorest recipients.[36]

That same year the Earl of Winchilsea, on the urging of Sinclair, sent an extraordinary commentary to the Board of Agriculture; Young printed the commentary in the *Annals* as well. The Earl of Winchilsea was a prominent member of the Board of Agriculture, a well-known agricultural improver with an estate of over 13,000 acres. Winchilsea said that on his estates labourers were guaranteed the rental of small plots of land for gardens and for keeping cows. According to Winchilsea, not only did the land benefit the families, but the workers were also "more fit to endure labour." The land "gives them a sort of independence, which makes them set a higher value on their character." The provision of even a *rood* (1/4 acre) of land would allow the family to grow what they needed to consume, would improve their character, and reduce the poor rates by removing them from the parish rolls. This was especially important as a means to allow widows and the elderly to maintain their independence. Moreover, they would gladly pay the same rent for the land as large tenant farmers. Young added a note of his own to Winchilsea's account. "As land cultivated as a garden," he said, "will produce a greater quantity of food for man than in any other way, and as four-fifths of the labour bestowed upon their gardens will be done by labourers at extra hours and when they and their children would be otherwise unemployed, it may not be too much to say, that 100,000 acres allotted cottagers as garden ground, will produce equal to what 150,000 acres cultivated in the ordinary way would give."[37]

In this one short description, it would seem that much of what Young had advocated through most of his adult life and many of the precepts of the agricultural revolution were being challenged. Not only was Winchilsea arguing that workers would be much better off if they did not need to depend solely on wages but rather would benefit if they could grow and raise much of what they needed, he was also suggesting that estate owners need not favour large tenants in the renting of the land; they could get equal rents from cottagers. Perhaps even more extraordinary were Young's comments: cottagers working tiny plots of land could get 50 per cent more food on the same amount of land as large capital-intensive tenant farmers could.

Winchilsea's comments did not stand alone. Indeed, from this point on one can detect a very decided shift in the tone and subject matter of the *Annals*. Though the journal was still very much concerned with agricultural experimentation, now along with such articles as "The Value of the Cluster Potatoe [*sic*] and of Carrots Ascertained in Feeding Hogs"[38] were numerous reports like Winchilsea's and extended commentary about the poor. Though Young's subsequent personal tragedies no doubt deepened his embrace of these discussions, the shift clearly began well before the death of Martha Ann.

The same year as Winchilsea's commentary, in the next edition of the *Annals*, a series of letters commented further on the conditions of the poor. The author of one letter entitled "Management of the Poor in Leeds" not only agreed wholeheartedly with Winchilsea's proposal but suggested that its adoption would "introduce a new system in the management of the poor. Instead of their going with unblushing countenance to demand relief ... they would be ashamed of being accounted paupers." In what may have been a slight on Young's fascination with a militia of landed property, this author also suggested, "There must be something radically wrong in every system of laws that cannot be executed in peaceable time without the assistance of soldiers."[39]

Conditions in the country continued to deteriorate and the change in focus of the *Annals* – and to some extent the most active members of the Board – became even more noticeable. In 1798, Sir Thomas Bernard sent a note that was published in *Annals*. Bernard was a large landowner and reformer, a member of the Board of Agriculture, and one of the driving forces behind the Society for Bettering the Condition and Increasing the Comforts of the Poor formed in 1797.[40] Bernard described a cottage and garden near Tadcaster that he had often admired when passing on the road. One day, Bernard stopped to enquire about the land and its occupant. It was farmed by sixty-seven-year-old Brinton Abbot and his wife. Abbot had a rood (1/4 acre) of land "inclosed by a cut quick hedge, and containing the cottage, fifteen apple trees, one green gage, three winesour plum trees, two apricot trees, several gooseberry and currant bushes, abundance of common vegetables, and three hives of bees." Abbot got about forty bushels of potatoes from his land and worked a little for Squire Fairfax hoeing turnips. Abbot and his wife of forty-five years (unnamed in Bernard's account) and seven children "lived very happily together on the land." Abbot had lost a cottage and land through an earlier enclosure. Bernard says, "At the time of the inclosure of Poppleton, when he had six young children living, and his wife preparing to lie in of a seventh, his whole system of economy and arrangements were at once destroyed: his house, his garden, his field taken from him." Only the fortuitous arrangement of the rood of land from Squire Fairfax had allowed Abbot to rebuild his life and avoid depending on poor relief.[41]

The next year, Young convinced Lord Carrington, the new president of the Board of Agriculture, to extend a general call to its members to comment on the question of scarcity and the effect of providing cottagers with land. The Board was inundated with responses, most published in the *Annals*. Among them, Joseph Scott argued:

> In my humble opinion, if industrious labourers were only supplied with a rood of land each, even if they paid a fair rent for it, it would be of more real lasting advantage to them than anything that has been done for them this century; inasmuch as it would … attract him to labour in his garden, morning, evenings and all leisure days, which are often wasted in ale houses; enable him to keep a pig … and to secure plenty of onions, turnips, herbs, and potatoes for the barren winter.[42]

Sir Henry Vavasour cited the example of one man, among many, in his estate in Yorkshire: Thomas Rook had less than three acres that were cultivated by Rook, his wife, and their twelve-year-old daughter "In their *spare* hours from the daily hired work, seldom a whole day off, except in harvest." Rook kept two cows and two pigs and made the entire cost of rent in butter he sold. Vavasour concluded, "It is very evident that this man clears for his three acres more than a farmer can possibly lay by from more than eighty acres of land in the common husbandry of the country … and it must be obvious to every one how great the advantages must be to society of cultivating land in this manner."[43] John Parkinson responded that for twenty-five years, cottagers on his estate had been provided with the right to rent a small portion of land. "The difference betwixt the situation of the poor as possess or occupy land and such as have none is very wide … instead of going to the market to *buy* provision, he frequently has to there to *sell* his abundance, and consequently, has seldom or never occasion to call upon the parish for relief."[44]

The glowing reports on the beneficial effects of providing the rural poor with land continued for some years. In 1806, Sir William Pulteney, one of the wealthiest members of the Board of Agriculture, sent in a most interesting note. He described the garden of one of the cottagers on his estate. The couple were unnamed in his report, but the husband was a collier, and the wife did most of the work on the garden. It had started out as very poor soil, which she had improved immensely over the years through constant care. She paid three shillings' rent for the land and had it for three "lives"; they had been there for 38 years. They had six living children; five had died. She planted land in corn, potatoes, and garden stuff. She raised a pig, purchased young in February, fattened from kitchen scraps and garden waste and sold in January. She kept no land in fallow and got better yields than the larger farmers around her. Pulteney attributed her success to routine honed through constant care: weeds were dispatched instantly, she had developed a routine for seeding the wheat along with digging up the potatoes, and she manured whenever she could, even collecting manure from the road for the garden.[45]

In another note, T. Babington stressed that the cottagers with land on his estate were "among the most respectable and useful of farmers' labourers." The returns from their land, he said, "adds prodigiously to the comforts of the cottagers or village-trademan's family." Moreover, they were the best stewards of his land. Babington said, "My land, in the hands of the labouring classes, has improved faster than that occupied by the generality of my more wealthy tenants. The former have always plans on foot for increasing the fertility of their little spots." Babington argued that through such a system, "An important addition is made to the useful class of men, the labour of whose hands fully supplies them with necessaries and decent comforts, and whose well-employed capital and good habits render them a robust and flourishing peasantry, above dependence on a parish, but not above regular labour." The only evil Babington could report from such a system is that they sometimes spent time on Sunday working their land when they should be in "pious contemplation."[46]

Sir John Sinclair also added his observations. He recommended providing all cottagers with enough land to keep a cow. He suggested that 3¼ acres would be ideal. This amount of land would preclude ploughing as "spade culture is infinitely preferable." He suggested that such an arrangement would leave the cottager free for paid labour 285 days of the year, but that the proceeds from the plot of land would equal all his wages. He continued:

> I shall conclude with asking if anyone can figure for himself a more delightful spectacle than an industrious cottager, his busy wife, and healthy family living in a comfortable house, rented by himself, cultivating his little territory with his own hands, and enjoying the profits arising from his own labour and industry; or whether it is possible for a generous landholder to employ his property with more satisfaction or in a manner more likely to promote not only his own but the public interest.[47]

Young was not content simply to reprint these accounts in his *Annals*; he added his own strong arguments for providing land for cottagers. Young became increasingly concerned about scarcity and the situation of the poor. In a report in 1799, "On the Price of Corn: and the Situation of the Poor in the Ensuing Winter," he called on the wealthy to reduce their consumption of oats for dogs and horses, "Their horses may subsist on hay, but the poor cannot." He also demonstrated a vastly different approach to poor relief. The advocate of one hundred Houses of Industry a decade earlier was now convinced that, "All of this wretchedness (is) wrought into a system of oppression, by the horrible abuse of keeping workhouses a mere terror to prevent the application of relief."[48] This was not the only shift in reporting on the Poor Laws that can be discerned in the journal. While earlier editions had favoured harsh treatments in workhouses as a way to make them a less tolerable option for the poor, by 1798, the journal was reporting more regularly on the abuse of the poor in the houses. That year, a report from a local paper, the *Lewes Journal,* was reprinted in the *Annals* and commented on by Young. In this story, a seven-year-old girl fled an abusive workhouse and got lost in the woods trying to return home. Young used this story as an opportunity to chastise those responsible for poor relief. Both the local paper and *Annals* were most angered by the practice of "farming" the poor, that is, sending inmates of workhouses out to work for others. Young commented that the horrors of workhouses were notorious, especially when their inmates were farmed, and it was not fitting that large families were denied relief simply because they would not "go into a (perhaps) crowded workhouse." Young called on the readers of the journal to send him any other such information they might have about the abuses in workhouses.[49] In his 1799 report he returned to this theme, arguing that a poor man and his family should have a right to relief "without going into a work house to receive it."[50]

Arthur Young, who had so steadfastly worked to ignore the poor in his travels or who had been disgusted by their idleness and tea-drinking, now noticed them almost everywhere and protested their treatment often. In 1800, he wrote in *Annals,* "I know families in my neighbourhood in Suffolk, eight and even nine sleeping in two beds ... Is this the way that English families live, while England is annually boasted as the most prosperous country upon earth? ... It is disgraceful to a Christian country to house our poor in the situation I have described. With the commerce and wealth of the world in our hands, our cottagers are miserable."[51]

Hovering over all of this discussion of land for cottagers was the malignant shadow of enclosure and the loss of cottage land. Enclosure had been the central tenet of the agricultural revolution. Both the Board and Young himself had been dedicated to its maximum application. Young continued to support aspects of enclosure all of his life. Yet, there was no denying the harm it had wrought. A series of letters to the Board near the end of the century had pointed out the negative consequences of enclosure in many parts of the country. Sir O.G. Paul had written to the Board when it had proposed a General Enclosure

Bill in 1796. He believed that enclosure had led to a severe decline in the number of people with access to land, "Without entering into the very doubtful question of the good or evil tendency of large farms," he argued, "it may be admitted without contest, that in proportion to the population, the number of those persons who cultivate at all for themselves is grievously diminished: of those who cultivate sufficiently for the supply of the family and *a little* more the class is nearly annihilated."[52] A few years later, J. L'Oster provided a generalized condemnation of the effects of enclosure. Though enclosures "may be a necessary step to carrying the agriculture of a country to the highest possible pitch of perfection, as some assert, it is counterbalanced by many serious evils." Among these evils was the rise of "opulent farmers" who converted cottages that had formerly housed families with their plots of land into tenements with numerous families with no access to land. The little farmer was thus "sinking into the mass of labourers." He called this "the diseased enlargement of one member (of the public body) from the wasting of another" and pointed out how this eliminated opportunities for the useful employ of small capital resulting from the stifling of demand for "small occupations." Finally, he warned, "The only radical remedy for the evils that press hard upon the lower orders will be found in land, by a judicious distribution of which, adapted to local situation and circumstances, means will be afforded to the industrious of feeding and clothing themselves."[53]

Finally, in 1800, Young produced his best-known condemnation of the impacts of enclosure: *An Inquiry into the Propriety of Applying Wastes to the Better Maintenance and Support of the Poor.* In this work, Young argued that though he continued to support enclosure, "instead of giving property to the poor, or preserving it, or enabling them to acquire it, the very contrary effect has taken place: and this evil was by no means *necessarily* connected with the measure of enclosing, it was a mischief that might easily have been avoided, and ought most carefully be avoided in future." Nevertheless, Young argued, "The fact is, that in nineteen enclosure bills in twenty they are injured ... The poor in these parishes may say, and with truth, *Parliament may be tender of property: all I know is, I had a cow, and an act of Parliament has taken it from me.* And thousands may make this speech with truth." Young argued that, instead, enclosure should focus on providing the poor with land. It was clear that the "great engine wherewith the poor may be governed and provided for the most easily and the most cheaply is property." The "enchantment of property" if offered to the poor would lead to great exertions: "To become independent, to marry a girl and fix her in a spot they can call their own, instigates a conduct, not a trace of which would be seen with the motive never in view. With this powerful impulse they ... will call into life and vigour every principle of industry." Young thus called for all enclosures to set land aside that was inalienably attached to each cottage, sufficient for a garden, a potato plot, and to keep a cow. Where not enough land still existed in common to do this, parishes would be required to purchase such land, with the costs to be repaid through rent charged to the cottagers. Parishes would be more than adequately compensated through a reduction in the money going to the poor.

Young was, from this point, clearly conflicted. He continued to support enclosure and to argue that it was necessary to promote agricultural efficiency and rescue farming from the constraints of both commoners and small farmers. In his *Inquiry*, for example, he ends by reaffirming, "There is not a man in England more urgent than I am for a general enclosure, but I contend that the felicity of the poor should be fixed by means of enclosure."[54] In one of the last county surveys prepared for the Board in 1807 in Oxfordshire, Young still argued that the county was one of the most prosperous precisely because enclosure had affected more of this county than anywhere else in England. Consequently, a "vast amelioration has been wrought." He warned that "a great deal of ignorance and barbarity remains. The Goths and Vandals of open fields touch the civilization of enclosures."[55] Yet he was continually confronted by the damage wrought by enclosure. In 1804, in reporting on the County of Bedford, he engaged in conversation with one cottager who said, "inclosing would ruin England: it was worse than ten wars." Young asked, "Why, my friend, what have you lost by it?" The cottager answered: "*I kept four cows before the parish was inclosed, and now I do not keep so much as a goose. And you ask me what I lost?*" Though Young continued to support enclosure, he reiterated that the poor must be made "rightly not to see enclosure as a terror."[56] In 1808, the Board published a *General Report on Enclosures* written by Young. Here Young not only admitted that enclosure had hurt most profoundly the "little farmers" but counsels their demise; it "is an evil to them which is to be regretted" he said, "but ... these little arable occupiers must give way to the progressive improvement of the kingdom." Nonetheless, his summary provides a litany of the effects on the poor of enclosures: In Souldrop, Bedford, "The condition of the labouring poor much worse now than before enclosure ..." In Letcomb, Berkshire, "The poor seem the greatest sufferers; they can no longer keep a cow, which before many of them did ..." In Stafford, Ashford, "All their cows gone and much wretchedness." The list goes on; it was a particularly melancholy assessment of the damage done.[57]

The confusion and uncertainty demonstrated by Young in the last two decades of his life reflect a growing disillusionment with the impacts of the agricultural revolution of the late eighteenth and early nineteenth centuries. There were severe limits to the arguments by Young and many powerful members of the Board in favour of the poor. Neither Young nor most of these other writers envisioned cottagers living from the returns of their land. Indeed, one of their most important arguments was that such self-provisioning would make them better, more dependable labourers. That such land would also dramatically reduce the poor rates landholders needed to pay was, of course, an added benefit. Still, Young's writings and the wide range of letters sent into the Board provide us with contradictory views of late eighteenth and early nineteenth century agricultural change. Young's views shift from a self-confident assertion of the profound and widespread benefits to be obtained from enclosure to one equally concerned with its effects on the poor and dismayed at many of the changes he perceived in rural England. Young was joined in expressing these concerns by many of the most powerful and wealthy estate owners and members of the Board of Agriculture, all apparently no longer quite so assured about the benefits of the agricultural revolution. They spoke eloquently about the benefits to be gained by the poor and by society in general if rural labourers were given access to cottage land; they also described in intimate detail the quite wonderful productivity of these small plots of land.

Late in his life, Young expressed disappointment that his work did not lead to legislation modifying enclosures. He remarked in his memoirs, "[M]y enquiry into the cottage system for poor people will have no more effect … than if I had whistled Alley Croker."[58] Indeed, despite ample evidence of the devastating effects of changes to agriculture, there was significant opposition to Young's later views within the Board of Agriculture and among estate owners in general. This opposition helped ensure that the poverty and inequality associated with the agricultural revolution would deepen and resentment of it harden. Violence, conflict, and opposition would turn parts of rural England into a battleground in the decades to come.

Chapter Four

"A Rooted Hatred Between the Rich and the Poor"

On a cold morning in November 1830, a meeting of the magistrates at Hailsham was interrupted when seven hundred rural labourers entered town and insisted on seeing Lord Gage. They refused to disperse until they could personally present their demands in the form of a letter, which read in part:

> We the labourers of Ringmer and surrounding villages, having for a long period suffered the greatest privations and endured the most debasing treatment with the greatest resignation and forbearance, in the hope that time and circumstance would bring about an amelioration of our condition, till, worn out by hope deferred...we have taken this method...for the purpose of making known our grievances.

They requested an increase of wages to 2s 3d per day for a married man, along with the dismissal of the overseer of parochial relief. "This is what we ask at your hands – this is what we expect, and we sincerely trust this is what we shall not be under painful necessity of demanding."[1]

The veiled threat in the last line of the letter was to be taken seriously in southern England in 1830. The region was caught up in the throes of what has become known as the "Captain Swing" disturbances. Haystacks, wheat ricks, barns, houses, and – most pointedly – thrashing machines were set on fire or destroyed on an almost nightly basis through 1830 to 1832 as workers protested low wages, more stringent relief measures, and the introduction of machines meant to reduce the demand for labour even further. As disturbing as the actual fires were the threatening letters often signed by "Swing" respectfully warning farmers of an imminent fire if they didn't mend their ways.

The Captain Swing disturbances are the best known of the early nineteenth-century rural protests. They were joined by a host of other expressions of outrage. Riots against the high cost of food, attacks on parish overseers, demands for higher pay, protests against further enclosures, the "Bread or Blood" riots in 1816, protests against the New Poor Laws passed in 1834, the Rebecca

Portrait of William Cobbett by F. Croall, after unknown artist, line engraving, 1840s–1850s (NPG D7609). © National Portrait Gallery, London

Riots in Wales in the 1840s, and a further spate of fires in the 1840s all made the "Peaceable Kingdom" anything but in the early nineteenth century. Along with these outbreaks of violence – moments when the "greatest resignation and forbearance" had reached its limits – was a long-simmering hostility that etched itself into life across rural England. Much more numerous than riots and fires were the moments, like that cold November morning in Hailsham, when workers' despair led them to find the courage to make demands en masse of their masters, employers, and tormentors. English rural labourers did not suddenly turn into a surly mob handy with a torch and ready to run the parish overseer out of town. As numerous commentators attested, rural workers were driven by desperate poverty that, by the third decade of the century, seemed unrelenting and insufferable. As a *Times* editorial said in commenting on another spate of fires in the 1840s, "Of a truth there is something rotten in our state of England."[2] That rot was the predictable outcome of the agricultural revolution and the logical consequence of measures taken to make agricultural workers wholly dependent on wages and deprive the peasantry of land.

In 1792, Arthur Young warned of threats to the rights of property and the prospect of rural unrest. "The idea of the division of property" he said, "is so sweet a medicine to the great mass of mankind, that it will find enthusiastic followers in every country." He cautioned that the "catching phrenzy" of "popular tyranny" would find adherents even among soldiers in the army and, consequently, he called on all men of substantial property in England to enroll in an armed militia.[3] Within a very few years, Young's call would seem prescient; yeoman cavalry were often used as shock troops in brutally confronting rural unrest between the 1790s and 1830s.

Young's strident warnings about popular unrest and the threat to property were understandable, coming as they did with France in the throes of the revolution. But there was plenty of reason for unrest, and portents for more to come, in England itself. Rural workers' wages had been declining for some decades by the 1790s; common lands were being enclosed and the poorest of the poor denied access to those resources; cottage gardens were harder to come by, and the worst was yet to come. A few short years after Young's warnings, many of the rural poor suffered severe deprivation as harvests failed and fewer of them could rely on self-provisioning through common lands or cottage gardens.

Eventually, Young had, belatedly perhaps, tried to temper the worst effects of that revolution by advocating for garden land for cottagers. He was joined in that call by many of the most powerful estate owners in the country, all touting the benefits to be derived from providing labourers with land: not only would labourers and their families be better off, but the land would make them more industrious, sober, and dependable workers. It was also, they argued, the only way to reduce the costs of poor relief. In addition, Young had most ardently argued that providing agricultural labourers with land would be the best means for governing them. "[T]he man will love his country better even for a pig," Young implored.[4] Though others would express similar sentiments in the next few decades, and Young would continue to reiterate this appeal until his death in 1820, these proposals were, for the most part, ignored. As the eighteenth century ended and through the first half of the nineteenth, rural England seethed as increasing numbers lost access to land and labourers became dependent on a wage that would not allow them to survive and work that, even at starving wages, was seldom regular or dependable.

This chapter outlines the multiple points of opposition to the call for land for cottagers. It then explores the nature of rural unrest through the first few decades of the nineteenth century, and landowner, farmer, and government response to that unrest.

"All the Sweat of their Brow"

Arthur Young's appeal for land for cottagers as a means for ameliorating spreading misery had both been inspired by and helped spur a remarkable range of testimony about the benefits of cottage lands from a wide array of influential members of the Board of Agriculture. Nonetheless, his newly professed concern for the poor also prompted much opposition. Appeals for land for cottagers in the *Annals* were often enthusiastic; indeed, many of them provided moving and compelling stories of what cottagers had been able to do on their land. But they were not uniformly positive. John Boys of Kent responded that though there was little doubt that labourers could get an adequate living from a few acres of land, growing vegetables and selling them in the markets, such land made them too independent. As he said, "When a labourer in this part of Kent is put into possession of three or four acres of land, his labour is, in great measure, lost to the community."[5] Given how convulsed by protest Kent would become in a few short years, this was a telling comment; its sentiment, that farmers (presumably the "community" to which Boys was referring) wanted labourers to be wholly dependent on wage labour would echo throughout reports on rural labour for the next four decades. Even Thomas Ruggles, once a good friend of Young and obsessed, like Young, with the rise in poor rates, opposed Young's suggestions. He commented in a letter to Young, "As to your idea of giving the poor property in land *to ease their minds and provide a permanent relief,* I conceive it to be Quixotic in the extreme."[6]

Young soon ran into trouble with the Board as well. Sir John Sinclair was voted out of the President's position in 1798, largely because of his inability to handle the finances of the Board. He was briefly replaced by Lord Somerville and then Lord Carrington. Young was not pleased with either selection, but it was with Carrington he experienced most difficulty. Young's focus on the poor had prompted significant opposition among members of the Board and in the House of Lords; there was a danger that the annual subvention for the Board would be removed. This was particularly so after the Board, on Young's urging, had convinced the government to import rice from India through the East India Company to deal with an expected shortage of grain in 1800. There was certainly a devastating shortage of grain that year, but the rice did not arrive until after the better 1801 harvest, and the government was on the hook for the money it had guaranteed importers. But most opposition came as a result of Young's increased advocacy for the poor. Carrington complained in his 1803 speech as President, "I can truly say, that much the most painful and difficult part of my duty, has arisen from prejudices excited by some of the early publications of the Board. … It must be admitted that some of them were suffered to be printed without due examination, and that it will be our duty to expunge every exceptional passage from future editions." While this was partly directed at Sinclair, it was clear that the most egregious "exceptional passages" had come from the pen of Young. Young complained that Carrington was "fretting and worrying and upon the full fidget about … the criticisms in the House of Lords upon the publications of the Board" and considered abandoning the Board.[7]

Some of the most powerful members of the Board also opposed Young's proposals for land to alleviate rural poverty. In 1801, one diary entry said simply, "Friday to London, Saturday, Farmers' Club. An argument with Lord Egremont and company on land for the poor: everybody against it. What infatuation!"[8] This would have been a noteworthy disagreement. The Earl of Egremont (George Wyndham III) was a very powerful member of the Board with a large estate and significant influence in the House of Lords. Described by William Cobbett as that "great swaggering fellow in Sussex," he was also an absentee landlord of substantial estates in Ireland. Egremont was considered an avid agricultural improver, and he and Young had once been on good terms. Egremont had been Young's first recommendation for President of the Board to replace Sinclair.[9] Others in the Board opposed these ideas as well. Young's 1801 appeal for land for cottagers, *An Inquiry into the Propriety of Apply Wastes to the Better Maintenance and Support of the Poor*, was not published by the Board, though it had sponsored many of his earlier writings. In the appendix to the publication, Young criticized the Board's unwillingness to support the proposal: "I must deem it a circumstance to be lamented; that this plan does not come recommended by some respectable establishment, whose sanction would secure attention."[10]

The opposition of the Board and other powerful landowners was justified using two arguments: concerns over increased population and the need to make labourers dependent on wages. Though few doubted the benefits of a bit of land to relieve the most pressing distress of rural households, landowners and farmers fretted about the independence such land would give to labourers. Though largely unstated, it was understood that independence would also lead to higher wages. Sir John Sinclair had argued that cottagers provided with three acres of land would make as much from their land as they would from the whole 285 days of the year left free to work for wages. It did not take much of a stretch of imagination for farmers to believe that such a system could well mean that labourers would be less eager for wage work.[11]

A similar concern drove thinking about leaving pasture in commons for poor labourers. John Billingsley, along with observing that reliance on the commons led to indolence, also remarked that with access to the commons, "day labour becomes disgusting." Enclosures, he argued, had in every circumstance benefited the cottager "by exciting a spirit of activity and industry, whereby habits of sloth have been by degrees overcome, and supineness and inactivity have been exchanged for vigour and exertion."[12]

To guarantee that sloth would be overcome by exertion, many farmers and landowners opposed the provision of land to cottagers even though, amid food scarcity and famine, it was generally understood that they produced more food per acre than even the best 'regular' husbandry. The Earl of Winchilsea felt compelled to express the hope that his proposal for allotments for labourers would be found acceptable because, "as the quantity of land required for gardens is very small, it will not excite the jealousy of farmers."[13] William Cobbett recounted how when farming at Botley, he had tried to get the Bishop of Winchester, who was the lord of the manor in a neighbouring parish, to:

> give titles to ... poor parishioners, who were willing to make, on the skirts of the wastes, enclosures not exceeding an acre each. ... Not a single man [that is, farmers in the parish] would agree to my proposal! One bull-frog farmer said it would make them *saucy!* And one true disciple of Malthus said that to facilitate their rearing of children was a harm! This man had ... land that had formerly been six farms and...ten or a dozen children. Never was there a greater mistake than to suppose that men are made saucy and idle by just and kind treatment.[14]

Even three decades after Young's *Inquiry*, through years of extreme distress in the countryside, the commissioners appointed in 1832 to make recommendations for a New Poor Law commented on how, in many districts, farmers opposed allotments; "We can do little or nothing to prevent pauperism; the farmers will have it." Elsewhere, the commissioners reported, employers preferred "paupers" (that is, those without any means of subsistence except labour) because such a system "enables them to dismiss and resume their labourers according to their daily or even hourly want of them, to reduce wages to the minimum, or even below the minimum of what will support an unmarried man."[15] A decade later when a newly minted evangelist for political economy, the *Economist* newspaper, argued against a new allotment movement, suggesting that it somehow demeaned workers, the *Examiner* newspaper retorted, "The true dread is that the labourer will reserve some of his strength for cultivation of his allotment ... and that his employer will not ... have all the sweat of his brow."[16]

Even those in favour of the provision of a little land to cottagers argued farmers needed to be vigilant to ensure workers never believed such land could allow them to neglect wage labour, and to ensure that allotments be kept tiny. George Culley, in his response to the Board's survey of estate owners, argued that cottagers should never get more than one-eighth of an acre for a garden plot as, if they receive more, they begin to believe that their plots will support them. "It takes them from off of everything else ... and instead of being benefited live, or rather barely exist, in poverty, and a degree of wretchedness, compared with those who have nothing to depend upon but their labour." Providing agricultural labourers with land, he said, was "the way to render a set of industrious people not industrious."[17] This argument against anything which might conspire to provide labourers with the means to decide if they wished to labour for the proffered wages or not was central to the basic structure of the new agricultural economy that was being crafted. Young always couched his argument about cottage lands as a means for making labourers more responsible and responsive, not less. In his celebrated dispute with the Reverend Thomas Robert Malthus this was one of the few things the two could agree on. In the Appendix to his 1806 edition of his constantly re-edited *Essay on the Principle of Population*, Malthus reluctantly embraced some aspects of cottage allotments but warned, "It would be absolutely essential to its ultimate success to prevent them from making it their principal dependence."[18] The Poor Law Commissioners in 1832 also warned that plots of land for labourers needed to be tiny: between one-sixteenth and one-quarter of an acre. If the labourer attempted to cultivate a larger piece of land, "he over-forces his strength and brings to his employers' labour a body exhausted by his struggle."[19]

In Thomas Thompson's report on cottagers in Lord Carrington's estate, which encompassed the whole parish of Humberston, Lincoln, Thompson warned: "The cottager who rents arable land, will seldom labour for other people; but will waste a great deal of time to little benefit to himself."[20] Assistant Commissioner Okedon, who had provided the warning to the Poor Law Commission that labourers should not be given more than one-sixteenth of an acre else he exhaust his body also provided a more striking warning against small farms: "But, let us consider a still more enlarged allotment, one which will occupy the *whole* time of the man and his family. ... The labourer then becomes a petty farmer, without capital, working land inadequately manured and half-cultivated, and yielding, of course insufficient crops as the return of fruitless exertions."[21]

This prejudice is striking and one that continued to work its malevolent magic on rural England for close to a century through the agricultural revolution. Despite being occasionally forced to recognize the industry and sober prosperity of small farmers in some locations, Young clung to this prejudice until his death. Perhaps inspired by his own failure to make Samford Hall pay because, he argued, he had insufficient capital, Young and many of the other heralds of the agricultural revolution professed to believe wholeheartedly in the need for capital to make farming industrious; this suggested that large farmers with ready access to capital would be more productive and would employ more labour. The purported magic of capital was a central tenet of the fairy dust of political economy more generally.

For anyone willing to see it, there was ample evidence of the productivity and efficiency of very small-scale farming. There was also plenty of evidence that it could provide a comfortable, if simple, life for a family. Joan Thirsk's discussion of intensive farming in the south Midlands demonstrated that small holdings of land – less than seven acres in many cases – employed in labour-intensive agriculture produced remarkable results, whether in open-field commons or individual plots. These "peasant" farmers grew a wide variety of crops in the seventeenth and eighteenth centuries: along with numerous types of vegetables, they produced industrial crops such as hemp, flax, and woad. Many families made mustard from wild mustard seeds collected in "wastes." As early as the third decade of the 1700s, a number of commentators had asserted that small farms of one acre or less produced as much foodstuff when planted in turnips, carrots, and cabbages as fifty acres of the general husbandry. Malcolm Thick has detailed how market gardeners with fewer than ten acres were easily able to maintain their families on the sale and produce of their land. One acre of market garden around London employed ten people full-time, and an additional twenty-five workers at harvest. These gardens were bursting with harvests of parsnips, carrots, turnips, cabbages, peas, beans, cucumbers, radishes, lettuces, asparagus, celery, and small fruit bushes and trees. Thirsk argues that it was commonplace for those writing on agriculture in the first half of the 1700s to argue that such gardeners "produced ten times more food than farmers from the same ground."[22]

Assertions about the productivity of peasant farming continued into the late eighteenth and early nineteenth centuries. Along with glowing reports of the efficiency of those farming garden land, such as Brinton Abbot and the collier's wife discussed above, we have numerous others who expressed wonderment at the diversity and productivity of such farms. William Cobbett provides us with an account of his own moment of recognition of such efficiency. In the early 1800s, while searching for a farm to purchase, he came across the small 150 acres of commons in Horton Heath. The commons was used to pasture the animals of large farmers, who had purchased stints. But on the periphery were thirty cottages. The cottagers, with no common right, on tiny plots of land scratched together around the edges of the common, raised more than one hundred beehives, sixty pigs, fifteen cows, five hundred poultry, and grew a multitude of crops on their garden plots. As Cobbett said, "My calculation was that the cottagers produced from their little bits in food for themselves and in things to be sold at the market more than any neighbouring farm of 200 acres."[23] Even Arthur Young, as always conflicted between the evidence from his own observations and his desire to be a prophet for improvement and large farming, provides us with evidence of their efficiency. In 1801 he published a "Cottager's Garden Calendar" in *Annals*. It is noteworthy for the remarkable range of crops and activities Young suggested went into a successful cottage garden. He provides dates for planting radishes, parsley, beans, cabbages, shallots, chives, leeks, carrots, potatoes, turnips, onions, parsnips, and kidney beans. He advises keeping bees – "three hives being often worth as much as your rent" – and pigs and manuring and fertilizing with almost everything that came from the kitchen.[24] While the agricultural revolution might have led to "an unprecedented rise in labour productivity" as Overton argued, this is mostly irrelevant. In an environment of food shortage, increasing imports and prices of foods, land scarcity, and abundant labour, which typified the eighty years from 1780 to 1860, peasant farming used the scarce factors of production most fully and its encouragement would have relieved almost a century of crushing poverty for the rural poor.

"Worn Out by Hope Deferred"

The agricultural labourers who confronted Lord Gage that cold November morning pronounced themselves "worn out by hope deferred." It is a fitting description of the rural poor in these terrible decades. We discussed above declining wage rates at the same time as prices rose precipitously and the rural poor were forced to purchase more of those things necessary for subsistence as they lost access to common resources and garden land. Here we explore the reaction to these changes among the rural poor.

In 1830, the *Kent Herald* reported that the peasantry were:

> in a state of reckless insubordination ... Bodies of men almost nightly and of late even by day, assemble and proceed from one farm to another destroying in the most open and daring manner the agricultural machinery on the premises. ... No man who possesses and dwells amid property of this description can lay his head on his pillow without the frightful anticipation of being roused to witness its destruction and endeavour to rescue his dwelling and his family from the flames.[25]

Fourteen years later, Sir Augustus Henniker warned the county quarter sessions in Suffolk of the unrest in the county. He described what he called "a frightful state of things" and pointed to a "wide-spread spirit of discontent."[26] The examples go on.

William Cobbett, in his exploration in the south and east of England during the years 1822 to 1826, cited "a rooted hatred between the rich and poor." In 1824, Cobbett, perhaps the national figure who best understood the concerns of rural labourers in the south, warned farmers (who he called bullfrogs because of their tendency to swallow up small farms in one gulp):

> It is well known that, generally speaking, your labourers hate you as they hate toads and adders. They regard you as their deadly enemies; as those who robbed them of their food and raiment and who trample on them and insult them ... and they detest you accordingly. ... force and force alone, keeps them in subjection to you.[27]

He went on to predict the Captain Swing uprising, leading to many declarations that he was, somehow, the mastermind behind it.

Rural England was in an almost constant state of upheaval from the last decade of the eighteenth century through the first half of the nineteenth.

Commentators at the time (and later historians) sometimes attempted to explain away that unrest as a temporary explosion brought on by food shortages caused by war and bad harvests, or short-lived unemployment caused by soldiers' return from the war. The panorama of unrest, of almost ceaseless riot, fires, and disturbances and often brutal response makes it clear that something more fundamental was at work during these decades. Not all of these riots were by agricultural labourers, but almost all were linked to the changes unleashed by the agricultural revolution.

There were periodic protests about the price or availability of food historically in England. They increased in frequency and intensity after the 1750s; no decade in the second half of the eighteenth century escaped substantial unrest. Protests became even more frequent near the end of the century. John Bohstedt estimated that there were forty-three food riots in one county in 1795 and 1800–1 alone.[28] Many of these riots were caused simply by rising costs for necessities and falling wages for many people increasingly reliant on purchases in the market. They also reflected a popular perception about what was acceptable in terms of buying and selling necessities. According to E.P. Thompson, "many of these grievances operated within a popular consensus of what were legitimate and what were illegitimate practices in marketing, milling, baking, etc." and he cautions against using the terms "mobs" or "riots" to describe these actions.[29] Roger Wells similarly argued that workers understood that the law of supply and demand determined price, but also viewed deviations from a broadly accepted moral economy as crimes. This included general condemnation of hoarding or selling out of the local market when food was scarce.[30] Bohstedt has expanded that argument to describe a "politics of provisions" that at times resembled a "national battle over food supplies."[31]

In the 1790s there were a series of arsons and other attacks on those hoarding grain. One warning from Oldham workers said, "we *know* Every Stack of Corn about the Country and Every Barn that have Corn concealed."[32] In the context of the devastating harvest of 1799–1800, riots against increased food prices spread throughout the country. In Nottingham, "a mob" attacked the bakers and distributed bread and flour to the poor. They then looted barges on the Trent River full of wheat, handing out sacks of wheat to the women and children among them. Though the supposed leaders of the riots were arrested they were soon "rescued by the mob." Yeoman Calvary were quickly brought in to restore order. However, the *Times* correspondent reported that the "poor inhabitants (especially women who were the principal agitators) ... absolutely defy them." The newspaper reported that the "vengeance of the Rioters is directed entirely against the Bakers, Millers, and Farmers," who they accused of hoarding grain. Similar riots occurred in nearby towns.[33] In Plymouth, rioters seized meat in butcher shops and bread in the bakeries, "paying anything or nothing for it just as they thought proper" according to one horrified witness.[34]

In Devonshire, about 700 people demanded a reduction in the price of corn, butter, and potatoes and threatened to hang the magistrate. The witness to the *Times* warned, "If something is not done this part of Devonshire will be as unsafe as Ireland."[35] In Exeter, the protestors were more organized; about 1000 workers gathered there and divided into groups "visited ... the farmers for miles around, and obliged them to sign an agreement to bring their wheat to market and sell it at 10s per bushel; and potatoes and other articles in proportion. They also obliged the bakers to sell the quartern loaf at 9d or 10d."[36] Similar riots in Oxford and many other towns were all put down with great difficulty, usually by the Yeoman cavalry so beloved by Young.

In 1816, news of an even more threatening series of events reached London. War with France ended in 1815 and hundreds of thousands of soldiers returned to the countryside. Work was hard to find and wages paltry. To guard against any reduction in the price of corn, and thus presumably farmers' profits and landowners' rents, Parliament passed new Corn Laws in 1815 that applied a sliding scale duty on imported grain, driving up the price. In Suffolk in May 1816, about 1,500 people gathered and attacked farmers, breaking thrashing machines and burning barns. According to one report, "They were armed with long heavy sticks, the ends of which ... were studded with short iron spikes ... Their flag was inscribed, 'Bread or Blood' and they threatened to march on London." A few days later, a similar crowd gathered at Bideford, Devon, and armed with bludgeons they prevented a cargo of potatoes from being sent. The presumed leaders were arrested but then were released by "an immense crowd of shipwrights and others." The best known of these 1816 riots began in Little-port, Cambridgshire. There had been a series of disturbances in the immediate vicinity in the preceding days; including a confrontation between workers and Yeoman Calvary in nearby Downham market. In Littleport, workers angered by low wages and high prices first attacked the home of a former overseer of the poor and then accosted other citizens before attacking the local vicar and magistrate. The protestors then moved on to the larger town of Ely, where they attacked a miller. The authorities attempted to placate the protestors with promises of higher wages and increased relief rates. But the next day fighting broke out between the protestors on one side and volunteer cavalry and the Royal Dragoons on the other. In the aftermath of the riot, seventy-five people were charged, five people were hanged, ten were imprisoned for twelve years, and twenty-two people were transported to Australia. The verdict was meant, in the words of J.L. and Barbara Hammond, "to strike terror in the hard part of the inhabitants." They might have been briefly successful. According to A.J. Peacock, the region "for several months seemed stunned by the vengeance taken by the authorities."[37] But the quiet did not last long. By 1818, new riots broke out.

While much of English society was shocked by this unrest, some expressed sympathy for the rioters. William Cobbett attacked those who were too harsh in their condemnation of the rioters. In the aftermath of the Bread or Blood riots he wrote: "It may be proper to call the offending persons '*insurgents, savages, villains, monsters & c'*... But, then, there are a great number of *Englishmen* who are insurgents, savages, villains, and monsters. ... The fact is, they are people in *want*. They are people who have *nothing to lose*, except their lives. ... it is *want*; it is *sheer hunger.*"[38] Cobbett later defended them by attacking – in a very funny and scathing letter – the Reverend Malthus who argued in his 1803 edition of the *Essay on Population* that there was no place at nature's banquet for those who could not support themselves and called for an end to poor relief. Cobbett responded saying:

> Your muddled Parson's head has led you into confusion here. The *law of* nature binds a man not *starve* in a land of plenty, and forbids his being punished for taking food, wherever he can find it. Your law of nature is sitting in Westminster ... and when (the labourer) is poor and hungry, to cast him to starve, or, to hang him if he takes food to save his life! That is your law of nature; that is a Parson's law of nature.[39]

Elsewhere, Cobbett attacked the whole mania for Malthus that prevailed among the gentry, farmers, and intellectuals: "You have no objection to a surplus population of parsons, of dead-weight of soldiers, or sailors," he said. "You have but one eyesore in this world; and that is the labouring man; who, while he is half starved and half naked himself, has his life wasting away in toiling by which you and your family are enriched. Farewell, Bull-Frogs."[40] Cobbett was an exceptional commentator on nineteenth century rural England, but he was not alone. The *Times* argued that those involved in the riot in Nottingham had acted because, "The poor are in utmost distress and cannot obtain flour."[41]

One might expect that, given a decade or more to recover from the war with France and to integrate returning soldiers into agriculture, the 1830s would be more peaceful. They were not. Inadequate wages, intermittent employment, high prices, and measures to reduce relief costs by cutting relief rates and appointing permanent assistant overseers, who were expected to be less sympathetic to the poor, all combined to make life a torment for agricultural workers, particularly in the south, where less land was available in pasture and waste and where there was less cottage employment in handloom weaving. In 1825 Cobbett described labourers in this region as "thin, ragged, shivering, dejected mortals, such as never were seen in any country upon earth."[42]

In 1830, a terrifying unrest spread across a broad sweep of the southeast of England, the area that had been most transformed into pure corn country through agricultural revolution in the last seventy years. Beginning in Kent, farmers who were introducing the labour-saving mechanical thrashing machines were warned to get rid of them. If not, the machines would be destroyed, and the farmers would be punished by fire. The warnings were sometimes signed "Swing" or "Captain Swing," a reference to the lead hand on a wheat-harvesting crew. The fires soon spread to Sussex and Surrey, north along the coast to Suffolk and Norfolk, and then encompassed most of southern England. At first, there was an attempt to blame the fires on the work of a single mysterious miscreant or a crew of vandals. Reports following the fires often mentioned a lone man in black on horseback or in a carriage seen shortly before the fires were lit. In December 1830 there were reports that the fires had spread to the counties of Shropshire and Cheshire. The *Times* correspondent informed the paper, "We have heard that a strange man was seen in the village on Friday last, and that he enquired of some children where any machines were used … Since the above was written we have heard that several persons of property … have received … threatening letters signed 'Swing.'"[43] As this explanation became increasingly untenable, it was argued that the fires were the work of only a small minority of labourers. As the *Norwich Mercury* prayed in 1831, "Would to God we could associate the whole community of labourers against the few, the atrocious perpetrators of these deeds of darkness and destruction."[44] But as the fires spread and the unrest among agriculturalists deepened, it became clear that these movements were homegrown and widespread expressions of outrage.

The alarm among landowners, farmers, authorities, and politicians is obvious in all reports: from Kent in October 1830 talking about a peasantry "in a state of reckless insubordination," to the chillingly banal report from Canterbury a month later saying, "We have not had burnings last night – the first interval of tranquility for some days past," to the account more than two years later in the *Brighton Herald* almost resignedly announcing, "The fiendish spirit of incendiarism is again devastating our county." As alarming as the fires was the unwillingness of the poor to assist parish authorities in extinguishing them. The *Brighton Herald* report, for instance, continued: "The fire was looked upon with the greatest apathy by the assembled labourers, many of whom refused to assist in extinguishing it."[45] At other fires, onlookers cheered at moments when the fire caused parts of the structures to collapse. Soon the protests targeted not just thrashing machines, but all farmers who refused to pay higher wages.

But the fires were really the illuminating and frightening tip of a much deeper peasant unrest. A report from the *Maidstone Journal* in Kent argued that the "resident peasantry" were generally not considered to be perpetrators of local fires but then discussed the "riotous" meetings of labourers kept peaceable only by the presence of Royal Dragoon Guards. This story ends, "for the most part the assembled labourers have generally obtained their demand – an increase in wages. It is evident however that if something be not done for farmers, this cannot last."[46] This incident fits a pattern. Rural workers organized into often peaceful but still threatening crowds to press their demands for higher wages.

The "midnight incendiaries" were mostly responsible for them being taken seriously. So, from the *Maidstone Journal* again in Hawkhurst:

> The poor and ill-disposed of this and several adjoining parishes rose en masse on Tuesday last to demand higher wages and a proportionate rise in the scale of parish relief. ... Their mode of assembling was riotous and alarming to the timid, and their invitations to the gentlemen and farmers to meet them were not of the most courteous description.[47]

As in the case of the meeting with Lord Gage mentioned above, very often the masses of workers took it upon themselves to interrupt the quarter sessions or the meeting of magistrates. In November 1830 in North Walsham, Norfolk, the *Times* correspondent reported, "Friday a body of about 70 men marched into this town while the magistrates were sitting and sent in a message that they wanted to speak to them ... the men persisted in entering the room in a body and informed the Bench they were resolved no thrashing machines should be used in their parishes. ... They then adjourned to a cheap beer-house to refresh themselves and marched back in the same order in which they came – the magistrates not thinking it advisable to interfere with them." There is no hiding the alarm, only hinted at in that last sentence, that permeates the reports of such mass protests. A letter from Southampton to the *Times* reported, "The town is in great fear of the mob entering it at night. ... Several fires last night."[48] In Salisbury, as a crowd of 2000 people gathered outside of town, "all the neighbourhood is in great consternation ... All the shops are shut in ... town."[49]

Often farmers said they could not afford to raise wages unless their rents and tithes were lowered. The rural poor then turned their anger on the church and other tithe holders, perhaps helped along by the writing and speeches of William Cobbett.[50] In December 1830, the *Dorsett Chronicle* reprinted a letter received by the Reverend Dr. Rudge, rector of Hawkchurch. It read, "Sir – Wrote this to you to tell you if you don't loer your tithes you and all you prmises shall be burned on the 20th so som month in a short time, for we poor destress solls will not suffer no longer ... and land-holders and Mr. Barnes shall be destroyed likewise in a short time, from your friend, 'Swing."[51] A more peaceable protest by "300 working men" in Hurstgreen, Sussex, surrounded the rector of the parish. "We do not want to create a disturbance," they said, "we want the tithes to be lowered and then the farmers can give us better wages. ... They disowned all connexion with the incendiaries, and said they only wanted to live."[52]

Just as often their anger was turned to the parish overseer. This was often the outcome of a move to hire permanent assistant overseers in parishes; the intent was that a nonelected overseer would be less sympathetic to the poor and more determined to reduce relief rates. Cobbett described this process in his inimitable way:

> The whole history of this horrid plague lies in a very few words. ... labourers have. ... been treated with the greatest possible harshness and insolence; ... hired overseers have been set over them to make them draw carts and wagons, and otherwise treat them as beasts of burden; that old men and little boys, and women, have been harnessed and worked in this way; that men have been put up for auction and sold for a length of time to labour for the highest bidder; that husbands and wives have been forcibly separated, as the males and females of livestock are, in order to prevent the natural consequences of cohabitation.[53]

Thus, after an assembly of labourers in the parish of Bride, Kent, determined to send representatives to all the neighbouring farmers to demand a wage of 2s 3d, they attacked the assistant overseer of the poor. They escorted him out of the parish on a carriage drawn by a team of twelve women while some five hundred men, women, and children cheered. The story from the *Globe* newspaper said this was "a truly ludicrous sight, but a just caution to all arbitrary overseers."[54] When the peasantry met with Lord Gage to request higher wages they also demanded that the governor of the Ringmer poor house be discharged so "that in case we are obliged, through misfortune or affliction to seek parochial relief, we may apply to one of our neighbouring farmers or tradesmen, who would naturally feel some sympathy for our situation and who would be much better acquainted with our characters and our claims."[55]

The *Times* was, in general, sympathetic to the rural poor and – like Cobbett – walked a line between expressing such sympathy, explaining the reasons for their unrest, while necessarily condemning the fires. Many of the correspondents writing for rural papers and many of the letters to the editor were equally sympathetic. In one of its first reports about fires in Kent, the *Times* went on to argue,

> The fact is that the labouring classes have been long borne down, oppressed in every way by their superiors, and by the political system upheld by their superiors. They have been gradually thrust down, and trampled on, despised, driven to starvation, misery and despair. The tendency of the whole social arrangement in England for many years has been to foster and protect the great properties at the expense of the poor and industrious. ... The labourer has been literally ground down to the very dust. ... The consolidation of estates, the destruction of the small farms, the enclosures of common lands, the heavy impositions on the necessaries of life. ... The master has become a gentleman, and the servant sunk into a brutal slave.[56]

It was not just the *Times* that expressed such sentiments. The *Morning Chronicle* reported from Berkshire: "The state of the poor ... is miserable beyond description." This reporter said the root of the misery lay in the enclosure of Windsor Forest during the war, when prices were high: "A number of farmers sunk capital on the lands at that time, and abandoned cultivation when prices fell, leaving the unemployed poor a burden on the parishes."[57] Numerous letters to the editors also expressed concern for the condition of the workers. One from a farmer and landlord in Suffolk blamed mostly the operations of the Poor Laws, "which made poverty a crime, and transportation from parish to parish the punishment. ... The labourer of the present day is too wretched to fear death, and too oppressed to heed punishment."[58]

If the letters to the newspaper evinced some sympathy for the workers driven to unrest by despair, the same could not be said for the authorities. Most of the assemblies of the labouring poor were confronted by Young's Yeoman Calvary. Their response, on occasion, was so brutal that it prompted debate in the House of Commons about whether their use should be prohibited.[59] Cobbett warned farmers that when their labourers see them armed and "swaggering about with hairy caps on your heads" they naturally become more opposed to them; this provoked more fires.[60]

When these forces were not sufficient, ready use was made of the Royal Dragoon Guards. It appears that farmers in many districts relied on military force to prevent having to accede to any of the workers' requests. A report from Reading, Berkshire, in 1830 recounted a serious uprising by workers. Nonetheless, this correspondent said, "The most alarming part of the case is that the landowners and I fear the magistracy are not disposed to concession, but calculate upon putting down the tumults by force – and by military force." The correspondent suggested that the interests of magistrates, landowners, and tithe-holders were all linked in their desire not to feel the effects of acceding to any of the workers' requests.[61] The Radical Henry Hunt argued in the House that farmers welcomed the destruction of thrashing machines as an excuse to call in the cavalry for "wherever the yeomanry was called out, the wages were kept down."[62] While in the early stages of the uprisings there was some complaint about the leniency of the magistrates, there was little such criticism about the trials held later. In total, more than a thousand people were charged because of this unrest; 19 people were hanged, 481 people transported, and 600 people jailed.[63]

The outcome of peasant and rural worker protest in the 1830s was not inspiring. The violence helped focus national and political attention on the plight of the poor, especially in the south. It also helped the cause of some of those who argued for reform as the only possible antidote to more unrest. William Cobbett, particularly, argued that the Reform Bill passed in 1832 was due more to the protests of "country labourers than all the rest of the nation put together," and highlighted that debt by celebrating its passage with Hampshire farmworkers.[64] The widespread use of thrashing machines was delayed by the uprising, but with wages so low large farmers had little need of the labour-saving machines. Agricultural wages in the south rose briefly during and immediately after the revolt but were soon reduced.[65]

The most immediate effects of these protests were the creation of a more efficient police force as a means to strengthen the repressive response to rural worker protests, and the determination to restructure the Poor Laws to reduce their costs and help discipline labour. The central figure in the crafting of the New Poor Laws was Nassau Senior, who figures prominently in our discussion of political economy in the next section. We will leave a careful examination of these changes till then. It is worth pointing out, however, that the New Poor Laws did not respond to the concerns of rural workers or demands of protestors. Protestors and petitioners continuously asked for two things: that relief rates provide enough for a family to live on, and that decisions about relief be made not by permanent assistant overseers but by committees composed of neighbours and parishioners. Instead, the New Poor Laws centralized decision-making even further and focused on eliminating "out-door" relief to able-bodied workers as completely as possible, forcing workers and families into workhouses made purposefully repulsive to reduce the costs of poor relief and reinforce diligence.

"I ask what you must expect but fire"

Especially in the south, conditions for rural labourers hardly improved in the decades that followed the Swing unrest. Protest and violence continued as well. There was significant conflict over game laws and gleaning. An increasing number of large landowners, many of them new owners who invested commercial or imperial fortunes in the land, took to using their estates as sites for leisure. This included expanding parks, occasionally by destroying whole communities of cottages, and stocking their forests for hunting and shooting. It also occasionally included (perhaps ironically as they worked so hard to expel commoners from these forests) hiring resident "hermits" to inhabit their forests to give them the air of authenticity.[66] Taking game in forests was reserved for those with rents worth over £100 a year – a figure raised in the early nineteenth century to £150. According to some estimates, this would include about one in 800 people in most parishes. During the year 1791, a quarter of the prisoners in the Oxford County jail were there for poaching or other game or wood offences.[67] Into the nineteenth century, the rural poor became ever more dependent on eking out survival however they could and estate gamekeepers worked to keep poachers at bay. Conflict between the two became increasingly frequent and increasingly violent. Responding to Lord John Russell's enquiry into the Poor Law in 1824, Cobbett pointed out how paltry poor relief was, "while the wretched labourer … is to be punished with transportation if he pursue a wild animal by night; and one third of the prisoners in all the gaols of England, consist of men whose crime is that of seeking to allay the craving of hunger by pursing those animals which God has given to all mankind."[68] Restrictions on taking game were not simply about preventing the poor from hunting. More onerous were proscriptions that prevented farmers and cottagers from attacking predators that damaged their fields in the name of keeping game for landowners' pleasure; rabbits were the most notorious pest.

Conflict over gleaning was also frequent. Despite the ruling in the Mary Houghton case described above, labourers and commoners continued to treat gleaning as a right and to protest when it was denied. Through the nineteenth century chairmen of quarter session courts continued to feel the need to re-iterate the ruling that "gleaning itself is a trespass" without the consent of the owner or occupier of a field.[69] Most often, though, the cases that found their way to the newspapers concerned poor labourers taking farmers to court for injuries sustained when they were prevented from gleaning. In 1832, a poor Mrs. Bubb received compensation of £60 from the court after the wife of "an opulent farmer" struck her and broke her thigh bone when Mrs. Bubb tried to reclaim her gleaning. The next year Mary Theer received compensation of £50 from the county of Hertford Quarter Sessions after she had been brutally struck by a farmer's servant. In both these cases, though the courts reiterated the right to deny gleaning, compensation was ordered because of too violent an exercise of that right. As an indication of the popular interest in such cases, the latter trial was said to last more than seven hours "with an excessively crowded court."[70]

Even more popular outrage accompanied the case of Lord Radnor's estate manager forcibly preventing two women, one well advanced in a pregnancy, from gleaning in a field the Lord reserved for his prize pigs. Numerous letters to the editor of the *Times* were indignant that the Lord would try these two women "for the atrocity of picking up that which the pigs had left!" They were also upset that Lord Radnor had sat in as magistrate in Salisbury when the case against his manager was brought to the court. Another letter complained, "The privilege which the poor once enjoyed is now leased for the pigs. Well this is at least consistent. No better exemplification could have been found of that swinish destruction of amiable and generous feeling. … Where once were venerable humane, genial and good producing customs – customs which tended to knit … the social bond – are now Lord Radnor's pigs!" One letter was in the form of a poem, entitled "The Peer, the Poor and the Pigs" and another sought to rewrite scripture according to Lord Radnor with one commandment being, "Thou shalt leave for thine own hogs the gleaning of thy fields."[71]

There was also much interest in renewing the campaign for garden land and cottages for rural workers. Following each period of major rural unrest various attempts were made to prompt the allocation of land. Young continued to appeal for such measures, writing opinion pieces and letters to the editor in favour of such land for most of his life; doing so most particularly in the immediate aftermath of the Bread or Blood Riots in 1816. Letters from others arguing in favour of cottage garden land were also common in newspapers. In 1819 there was a spate of such letters as the House debated a bill permitting the allocation of small plots of land as part of each enclosure (that is, permitting such action, not requiring it as Young had hoped). Thomas Bernard sent a letter to the *Times* making an argument similar to that he had made two decades earlier. Estate owners, parish rectors and others also added their voices in favour of such a bill.[72] The *Times* joined in the campaign, publishing an editorial denouncing enclosures in general and especially asserting that contrary to the arguments in their favour, the amount of food produced in the country had decreased because of them. They cited a "Gentleman … (who) has within the last three or four years visited most parts of England" who described the effect of enclosures this way:

> An enclosure takes place and … the cottage encroachments are thrown down and the peasantry dive for refuge to the workhouse … Dormant, abstract, and unprofitable rights and interests have been converted into substantial and profitable estates, but these estates have been taken from those who cultivated them to greater advantage for the country though they had no legal right to the enjoyment of them.[73]

Thomas Wright, particularly, spearheaded a campaign for the creation of a "Cottage Society" through public subscription that would provide rural labourers with four to twelve acres of land for rent on moderate terms.[74]

In the context of the 1830 Captain Swing riots, there were regular assertions that the fires did not affect those parishes in which the gentry provided cottage lands for their workers. The *Kentish Gazette*, for example, argued that on Winchilsea's land in Westwell the poor had land for their own use. "The consequence of this attention to the wants of the poor has been that not a single act of incendiarism or riot has occurred within the limits of the extensive parish."[75] A quick series of acts in parliament following the outbreak of the Swing riots allowed for the provision of very small allotments for spade agriculture and for fuel, but they resulted in few substantial changes. The Labourers' Friend Society was created and following the Swing riots tried to push the issue of allotments.[76]

In the context of another outbreak of fires in the 1840s, a new movement was launched to try to provide garden allotments for the rural poor. At a meeting of the "Society for the Improvement of the Condition of the Labouring Classes" held in London in May 1844, there was a general agreement among the gentry and others present about the value of allotments. James Colquhoun, the MP for Dunbartonshire, argued that the allotments provided near Birmingham "had induced habits of order, thrift and sobriety among the poor." Such allotments might also "be the means of correcting those feelings of alienation and estrangement which now prevailed between the two classes of society, separating the rich from the poor and making the poor regard the rich … as their opponents." The Society dedicated itself to extending the allotment system following this meeting and worked diligently for the next few decades at convincing land-owners to provide such allotments.[77]

Widespread protest continued through the 1840s throughout Britain and the United Kingdom. In Ireland, monster rallies for repeal of the Union led by Daniel O'Connell worried officials and seemed to capture the sense of rural unrest. In Scotland, non-intrusionists from the Free Church were perceived to be prone to riot and for many represented the ideals of a more equitable, Gaelic, rural society. Perhaps most worrying in the early 1840s were the Rebecca Riots in Wales. Begun principally as protests over continual demands for payments on turnpikes, the riots soon spread and clearly reflected a dissatisfaction with the continued poverty of rural labourers. The Royal Commission of Inquiry into the riots reported that, though first limited to turnpike charges, the root causes of the complaints were not so easily met. The commissioners pointed to "general and increasing poverty – a poverty so great that the people can with difficulty subsist."[78] At one of the commission's public meetings with nearly a thousand workers in attendance, one labourer said,

> Ah! They want to catch 'Becca and yet at the same time they do not know who she is; they are looking for 'Becca, they do not know where to find her, and yet she may be seen everywhere … Where then is 'Becca? Everywhere. Who then is 'Becca? Everyone is 'Becca. She is getting stronger and stouter and more bold every day, for the things on which she thrives are our grievances. … If you want to kill 'Becca, I can tell you a way to do it – give bread to the poor, and give them enough of it.[79]

Though the *Economist* quipped that the constant movement of troops to these various disturbances "will help improve railway dividends,"[80] the continuing unrest was not to be taken lightly, especially as another spate of fires spread terror in Berkshire, Suffolk, and Norfolk. The *Times* reported that between September 1843 and June 1844 in one county, 131 agricultural fires had been reported to one insurance company alone. As they had in the 1830s, some of the elite wanted to believe that the fires were the act of a very small element who simply needed to be punished with greater severity. Lord Stradbroke from Suffolk, for example, assured the House of Lords that the fires were "traceable to private spite or individual maliciousness" and could easily be controlled.[81]

Reports from the countryside suggested otherwise. At an 1844 meeting of labourers at Brehmill, Wiltshire, Mary Ferris told the crowd that the men were often afraid to speak up because of the fear they would lose their wages – a voice from the crowd replied, they were living on potatoes and water and "had not the spirit to speak." She lamented, "Her children were often crying round her for food, and she did not know how to get any. She said the men knew nothing of their hardships in comparison to women, they brought the 8s home on Saturday night, but the management was left to the women, who could not supply the wants of their families from it."[82] When haystacks were set on fire at a farm in Rampston, Cambridge-shire, in October, 1844, the fire quickly spread to farm buildings. Fire engines got there promptly, but according to one report, "they were entirely useless, as there were not hands sufficient to work them, the labourers of the village refused to assist … Some of the Rampton people during the progress of the fires amused themselves with roasting apples, which had been stolen from a neighbouring or-chard; whilst others were eating fowls which they roasted with the feathers on."[83]

A sympathetic *Times* correspondent, Campbell Foster, filed a series of stories on the fires in 1844. Like Young a half century before, he argued persuasively for the value of garden ground and a snug cottage. He reported that a clear pattern existed: where agricultural labourers were well paid and had the use of cottage allotments there were no fires. Even in those districts with low wages and half-employment, cottage allotments "were little oases in their deserts. … There grew his rent." He continued, "It was delightful to see the pride and sat-isfaction and cheerfulness with which the cottagers having allotments viewed their little crops of corn, and potatoes, and peas." But, in the districts where fires predominate, the workers had irregular employment at bad wages and few allotments. "The farmer looks at them as he does his horses – as animals out of whom he must get so much work at as little cost as possible." This corre-spondent summed up the cause of the fires as the combination of the practice of hiring labourers by the day instead of by the year, the implementation of the New Poor Laws, and the enclosure of the commons and vacant lands and engrossing of farms. All of this had led "many of the peasantry to that degraded and reckless state, that they can contemplate with indifference the burning of property." Or, as one threatening letter sent to farmers near Stowmarket asked, "Gentlemen, I have thought it proper of wrighting these few words just to show and let you know how pore are oppressed in this place. … I ask what you must expect but fire."[84]

"The Peasant's Friend"

Perhaps it would be fitting to end this chapter with an eloquent denunciation of the changes wrought in England in the first few decades of the nineteenth century. It is from a letter to the Editor of the *Times* signed by "The Peasant's Friend"; almost certainly it is from the pen of William Cobbett. It is worth quoting at length for its romantic vision of the past and condemnation of the present. Clearly in this and many of the other works that denounced condi-tions in the countryside in these decades, this past was more imagined than remembered. But the Cottage Economy recommended by Cobbett was not based simply on romanticizing. For many, the independent cottage family with purposefully limited needs and which produced much of what it consumed formed the real basis of parish life and welfare. Remembering its best attributes was important, both as a way to foster opposition to the present degradations and as a means to imagine a more just rural society.

On behalf of the ill paid, three parts starved and utterly degraded agricultural labourers of England. [Suffering from] the breaking up of the small farms, ... the ruinous and demoralizing maladministration of the poor laws; the abominable, tyrannical, and unjust game laws; and the total destruction of all the home comforts of the labouring poor. When farms consisted of from 30 to 100 acres, they were tenanted by the honest, sterling, old-fashioned, English yeomen. ... The labourers of one of this class were his humble friends, attached to him by the strongest ties that can attach man to man ... At that period, the peasant, when the ... labours of the day were closed, ... if married, wended his way to his own snug tidy little cottage, and partook of an ample though frugal meal in the company of his wife and children ... he would then hie to his patch of garden ground, and after working there for an hour or two, you might see him lounging over his pig-sty and talking to his wife concerning the number of extra bushels of barleymeal which old Bess would require before her thriving sides would be fat enough to adorn the cottage rafters. ... O, it was a beautiful picture of contented toil, steady loyalty, parental affection, and faithful love. ... Then a peasant had something to live for ... But, alas, the scene is sadly changed now. When the rage for large farms began to prevail, the peasant's friend, the petty farmer, as he was called, was swept away, and in his place sprung up a proud and bloated mass of rank unwieldy flesh, with no feeling but for himself, with no capacity save a bibulous one ... On they went "helter-skelter" the landlord and the tenant cheered to the shout of "forward, forward, forward"! The landlord more than doubled his establishment. The farmer ... more than quadrupled his expenses. Then sounded the knell of the English peasant's comforts ... Then first began the grinding system which has since crushed the peasantry, to even the marrow and the bones, and from that time to the present those who ought to have been his benefactors and protectors have, vampire like, sucked his best blood and have gorged on the unholy banquet. ... his piggery, his little patch of garden ground, and his right of common, were wrenched from him by the strong grip of avarice in power, and were added to the acres of the gentleman farmer.[85]

For most of the century between 1750 and 1850, England had embarked on a grand experiment. Putting their faith in increased productivity they presumed would result from the application of enlightenment ideas of progress to agriculture, landowners, farmers, and politicians facilitated fundamental changes in rural society. New crops, different crop rotations, convertible husbandry, extensive draining of wetlands, stall feeding livestock, the application of heaps of manure, and capital all contributed to modest increases in yields. Although the benefits in terms of productivity from this "agricultural revolution" were minimal, there is little doubt about the social consequences. Enclosure, the elimination of common rights, the destruction of cottages and – perhaps most important – the erosion of the cottage economy all contributed to a dramatic decline in the living standards of the majority of the population: the rural poor. Politicians, farmers, and landowners justified these changes as necessary to feed an increased population and touted the benefits the rural poor would derive from being forced to rely solely on wage labour. But a steady stream of commentators, many of them deeply enmeshed in the agricultural revolution, made it clear that cottagers were the most productive and efficient, producing the most food (and as importantly, a more diverse range of nutritious food) from a given piece of land than large-scale farmers were capable of doing. Cottagers themselves eloquently and constantly argued for the comforts of a cottage, the independence of the garden plot, the benefits of a cow, and the occasional luxury of a pig.

The agricultural revolution might have led to more labour productivity, as some historians have argued. But increased labour productivity in an environment of surplus labour and artificially created land shortage (that is, the denial of land to those who would work it through heightened inequality) was of little practical value except to increase the profits of farmers and the rent for landowners. The result, as the *Times* opined in 1832, was the creation "of a race of farming capitalists" and the steady deterioration of the position of the rural poor from small farmer, commoner, or cottager to day labourer.[86] Social relations in rural areas deteriorated, conflict deepened, and violence escalated. The rich and powerful and those who aspired to such positions desperately sought solutions to the growing unrest that did not entail redistributing land or reducing profits to farmers or rents to landlords. Increasingly, they found comfort in repression and solace in the arguments of political economists who sold the snake oil of "natural law" as a pretended response to the immiserization of the rural majority and the violent conflicts it engendered. As J.L. and Barbara Hammond observed, their work "robbed poverty of its sting for the rich by presenting it as Nature's medicine."[87]

PART TWO

Political Economy and "the Great
Lottery of Life"

Chapter Five

Political Economy and the Rural Poor

In 1804, Arthur Young and the Reverend Thomas Robert Malthus engaged in a heated dispute. Malthus, in the much-expanded 1803 second edition of his *Essay on the Principle of Population*, had criticized Young's call for land for the poor, arguing that this would lead to dramatic population increase and invoking the spectre of Ireland as the expected result. He was particularly worried that provision of cottages for the poor would lead to early marriage. Young responded to Malthus in an appeal not to allow theories to override real actions to benefit the poor.

Young argued that Malthus's central proposition that people should remain celibate until they could provide for a family "runs counter to the strongest passions in the heart of a man" and insisted:

> [T]o tell such a man in health and vigour that *he is not to marry but to burn*; remaining chaste is a cruel insult – to be chaste until what happens: until he has saved enough to support a family without a house to put them in, or land to feed them?. ... chastity without the hope of a wife – prudence to save for the possession of what can never be possessed – to wait ten years for a wife without a bed, and children without a house, land, or cow? Any idea more visionary never issued from the heated imagination of a poet. ... The question between Mr. Malthus and myself is, shall their [cottages'] inhabitants be in a comfortable state, cut off from parish relief, or shall they remain miserably poor ... will any man contend that you shall not render 500,000 families comfortable because they will increase? – seeming to assume the false assumption that if they are not comfortable they will not increase; though the proofs to the contrary are seen in the millions?[1]

There was more to this dispute than simply a difference of opinion between two men of privilege, one somewhat marginalized but still influential, the other soon to be the single most important voice shaping an understanding of political economy. Young had on occasion predicted many of the elements in

Portrait of Adam Smith by Mackenzie, after James Tassie, stipple engraving, published 1809 (NPG D6775). © National Portrait Gallery, London

Portrait of Thomas Robert Malthus probably by Amable Nicolas Fournier, printed by Drouart, after John Linnell, stipple engraving, before 1861 (NPG D13689). © National Portrait Gallery, London

Malthus's writings well before Malthus's 1798 edition of *Essay on the Principle of Population*. Young had warned, for example, in his discussion of France, that providing small amounts of land to the poor led to unsustainable population increase because "whatever promises the appearance of subsistence induces men to marry."[2] And as we have seen, he expressed concerns about the effects of the Poor Law thirty years before Malthus's 1798 work. By 1804, Young's views had changed, driven by his understanding of the extent of poverty in rural England and the rural poor's capacity to provide for themselves if given the opportunity.

Young sought to address the roots of poverty by providing the rural poor with what they most ardently desired. Though he faced significant criticism for these ideas, he enjoyed the support of a substantial number of influential and powerful estate owners. Malthus's *Essay on the Principle of Population* was, conversely, a call to address poverty by depriving the poor of land and a stark warning about the consequences of providing it to them. To understand this distinction does not mean we need see Malthus as a purposefully malevolent force, as he has often been portrayed. But it does require us to appreciate the consequences of his arguments as they shaped ideas of political economy through the first half of the nineteenth century. In early nineteenth-century England, theory, ostensibly informed by some understanding of political economy, too often provided ammunition for policies that deepened poverty in the name of some imagined future benefit.

Malthus wrote in the giant shadow of Adam Smith. Like Malthus's various works, which inspired almost equal parts admiration, confusion, and consternation, Smith's *An Inquiry into the Nature and Causes of the Wealth of Nations*, published first in 1776, had a decidedly mixed legacy. Initially viewed as a progressive appeal to reshaping economic relations and embraced by some notable radicals – or essentially ignored for two decades and not of particular importance, if we are to believe other accounts – by the early 1800s, shorn of its more progressive elements, it had become a central plank of a political economy used to reify capital and promote particularly destructive policies towards the rural poor.

By the beginning of the nineteenth century, it seemed that anyone who wanted to be taken seriously as an intellectual had produced their own "principles" of political economy, and all, at least symbolically, referred to *Wealth of Nations*. Though the most prominent of them sometimes contradicted each other on important points, almost all agreed on fundamental principles: the "market," by which they meant a supposed law of supply and demand, should be left most often to function with little regulation; the supply of labour was just one other commodity that would regulate itself through the market if it were not perverted by poor relief, restrictions on mobility, or attempts to "artificially" supplement wages; and most importantly, the key to economic growth and increased wealth was to be found in the elixir of what Smith sometimes called stock and sometimes capital.

Political economy often became an exposition about the magic of capital, in the service of which all else needed to make way. Increasingly political economists argued not that an unregulated free market dominated by capital was one possible way of organizing society, but rather that it was the law of nature, "ordained by providence" as the *Economist* newspaper would assert, and its religious application guaranteed progress. The members of the London Political Economy Club (including Malthus, David Ricardo, and James Mill) were urged, at its second and formative meeting in April 1821, to be on constant guard for any legislation "particularly at variance with the principles of Political Economy" and to put forward "means of over-ruling such evils." Further, they were to find ways to "access the public mind" to counteract the spread of ideas not in line with "reasonable truths" about political economy.[3]

This chapter explores the writings and influence of Adam Smith and Thomas Robert Malthus, focusing on those aspects of their writing that were most easily turned to constructing "reasonable truths": truths that would turn into policies and arguments that helped deepen poverty in rural England.

The Impartial Spectator

Adam Smith was part of a remarkable group of philosophers, scientists, and agriculturalists clustered around the universities at Glasgow and Edinburgh in the late eighteenth and early nineteenth centuries. Smith was born in 1723 in the small port and linen town of Kirkcaldy, about twelve miles north of Edinburgh. His father was the Commissioner of Customs in Kirkcaldy but died before Smith was born. Smith lived with his mother, who was from a local landowning family, in their home in Kirkcaldy for much of his life. He studied moral philosophy at the University of Glasgow under the noted philosopher Frances Hutcheson and later attended Oxford for six apparently unpleasant years before returning to Scotland. He was appointed to a position at the University of Glasgow in 1751 and then took over his mentor's chair in Moral Philosophy.

In 1759, Smith published *The Theory of Moral Sentiments*, an extended discussion of what prompts feelings of sympathy and benevolence in people and how this affects society. The book was well received and partly due to its renown he was offered a position as the private tutor for the young Duke of Buccleugh as he toured France and Switzerland in 1764–6. Smith benefited from the arrangement immensely; the short period as tutor earned Smith a pension of £300 a year for life, nearly double his salary at Glasgow.[4]

Free to pursue his own work, Smith retired to his mother's home in Kirkcaldy, where he wrote most of *An Inquiry into the Nature and Causes of the Wealth of Nations*. While Smith communicated with a range of intellectual notables in Britain and France and spent the last couple of years of this period in London, he wrote most of this work in splendid isolation, often dictating the book to his mother and, later, his secretary while he rubbed his head on the mantle in the study of the house. Following its publication, Smith was named a Commissioner of Customs at Edinburgh. Although he continued to write, producing new editions of *Moral Sentiments* and *Wealth* and supposedly working on a volume on jurisprudence that linked the two, Smith mostly lived "the rest of his life as a celebrity, visited by cultural tourists," according to Nicholas Phillipson.[5]

While most of Smith's unpublished works were destroyed, two sets of students' notes from Smith's lectures at the University of Glasgow were uncovered in the late nineteenth century and mid-twentieth century respectively. These notes, the first set more detailed but truncated from classes in 1762 and 1763 and the second set somewhat more concise (presumably from the following academic year), have been combined and published as the *Lectures on Jurisprudence*.[6]

In *The Theory of Moral Sentiments* published in 1759, Adam Smith wrote:

All members of human society stand in need of each other's assistance and are likewise exposed to mutual injuries. Where the necessary assistance is reciprocally afforded from love, from gratitude, from friendship, and esteem, the society flourishes and is happy. All the different members of it are bound together by the agreeable bonds of love and affection.[7]

Less than twenty years later, in his best-known work, Smith argued:

[M]an has almost constant occasion for the help of his brethren, and it is in vain for him to expect it from their benevolence only. He will be more likely to prevail if he can interest their self-love in his favour and shew them that it is for their own advantage to do for him what he requires of them. ... It is not from benevolence of the butcher, the brewer, or the baker that we expect our dinner, but from their regard for their own interest. We must address ourselves not to their humanity, but their self-love.[8]

How much distance is there between the love and affection commended in 1759 and the self-love and self-interest so prevalent in 1776? A number of authors have argued forcefully that there is no contradiction between the two statements, and that they address similar tendencies to cooperate in society.[9] It is true that in both works the outcome is a somewhat surprising social harmony. Nonetheless, most readers would find that the books demonstrate, at least, strikingly different approaches to society. The first dealt with how moral considerations lead to sympathy and benevolence and prompt people to deal kindly with each other. It barely mentioned the economy. The second dealt with political economy and argued that individuals pursuing their own self-interests (self-love) would lead unexpectedly to general well-being. Smith had planned a further book that was meant to provide a bridge between moral sentiments and political economy through an examination of the fundamental bases of law. The student notes gathered in *Lectures on Jurisprudence*, however, reveal mostly rehearsals for arguments found later in *Wealth of Nations*.

Let's deal first with *Moral Sentiments*. Smith starts the book with a statement of its primary topic: "How selfish soever man may be supposed, there are evidently some principles in his nature, which interest him in the fortune of others and render their happiness necessary to him, though he derives nothing from it, except the pleasures of seeing it." Thus, by "acting according to the dictates of our moral faculties we necessarily pursue the most effectual means for promoting the happiness of mankind."[10]

Smith then set out to explain why this should be so. In this Smith was not treading new ground; a long line of writers had addressed this topic: Smith's mentor, Frances Hutcheson; his friend David Hume; and, perhaps most notably, Bernard Mandeville. Mandeville had also predicted some of Smith's points about the benefits of allowing people to pursue their own self-interest. In 1705 Mandeville published a kind of short poem entitled *The Grumbling Hive*, which was reprinted as a pirated pamphlet and received some fame. In 1714 he sought to explain further the poem's meaning in the form of an essay on the origin of moral virtue entitled *The Fable of the Bees: or, Private Vices, Publick Benefits*. In 1729, he produced an expanded version under the same title.

Grumbling Hive predicted a harmonious society – "the whole Mass a Paradise" – from everyone following their own vices. Thus, even at the beginning of the eighteenth century, ideas about the beneficial results of allowing people to pursue their own self-interests were commonplace enough that Mandeville could present them in his humorous doggerel; that self-interest was perceived to be a complicated mix of moral virtue, vice, and the desire to meet increased wants. In language that was somewhat more engaging than Smith's much-cited "Invisible Hand," Mandeville argued, "Felicity, ... would flow spontaneously from the Nature of every large Society, if none were to divert or interrupt the Stream."[11]

Most contemporary writers dismissed Mandeville's work. Part of the difficulty was Mandeville's use of the terms "vice" and "virtue." But Mandeville also suggested complex motives for industriousness. He argued that the motives that inspire men to industry "all center on Self-Love." The need to "gratify" the "multiplicity of his Desires" leads men to undertake tasks that no "Tyrant ... should exact ... from his innocent slaves."[12] Wants (what Mandeville called Appetites and Passions) could continually increase and, thus, inspire industry though dire poverty was left behind. Thus, according to Mandeville, "man" would be spurred to industry through "the multiplicity of his Desires, and the continual Opposition he meets with in his Endeavours to gratify them."[13]

In the *Moral Sentiments*, Smith dismissed Mandeville's ideas, arguing that "the notions of the author are in almost every respect erroneous." Nonetheless, he admitted that the "lively, humourous ... course and rustic eloquence" of

Mandeville's work has lent it some unwarranted attention.[14] Smith's dismissal was not surprising given the humour Mandeville brought to topics Smith considered to be immensely serious, and there were many other ways in which Smith objected to Mandeville's arguments in favour of vice, luxury, opulence, and inequality.

In seeking to explain why we were driven to be so interested in the happiness of others and how that compulsion affected society, Smith introduced the idea of the "impartial spectator." He argued that people felt the need not only to be thought to be acting kindly to others but, more importantly, they wanted to believe themselves to be acting kindly. As Smith says:

> Man naturally desires, not only to be loved, but to be lovely; or to be that thing which is the natural and proper object of love. He naturally dreads, not only to be hated, but to be hateful; or to be that thing which is the natural and proper object of hatred. He desires not only praise, but praise-worthiness ... But in order to attain this satisfaction, we must become the impartial spectators of our character and conduct.[15]

Smith returns to this idea again and again in *Moral Sentiments*. The key to being not just thought to be lovely but thinking oneself to be lovely lies in the "impartial spectator": an inner voice that seeks to confirm to everyone that they are worthy of love and respect and ties the idea of self-love to general well-being. In seeking their own happiness, individuals need to live morally. Conversely, in the only use of the term "invisible hand" in this work he argued that the rich:

> in spite of their natural selfishness and rapacity, though they mean only their own convenience, though the sole end which they propose from the labours of all thousands they employ be the gratification of their own vain and insatiable desires, they divide with the poor the produce of their improvements. They are led by an invisible hand to make nearly the same distribution of necessaries of life which would have been made had the earth been divided into equal portions among all its inhabitants.[16]

Broader questions of poverty, labour, and economic arrangements were mostly absent in the work. There was very little about the ways such moral sentiments generated economic activities or desires for growth. When he did talk about the economy, the message was strangely mixed. Early in the work, Smith asserted that "all the toil and bustle of this world" could not possibly be caused by the desire for the necessities of life as "the wages of meanest labourer" could supply them. Smith argued instead that it was the need for the approbation of others, and especially the belief that one truly deserved that approbation, that prompted people to strive to better their condition.[17]

The Invisible Hand of Capital

In 1776, after close to a decade dedicated to writing enabled by his handsome pension from the Duke of Buccleugh, Smith published *The Wealth of Nations*. It is on the basis of this work that Smith has been hailed as the "Father of Modern Economics" and was extolled, along with Thomas Robert Malthus, as one of the two "masters" of political economy through the nineteenth century by the *Economist*.

An Inquiry into the Nature and Causes of the Wealth of Nations was originally presented in close to a thousand pages organized into five "books": on the division of labour and the composition of price, capital or stock, the history of economic growth (opulence) in various societies, mercantilism and trade, and revenue and taxation. Smith began *The Wealth of Nations* with a discussion of the benefits to be derived from the division of labour and his famous example of a pin factory. He argued that with each man performing specific functions in the manufacture of a pin, production would rise dramatically. Working independently, a craftsman might make little more than a pin a day, and certainly no more than twenty. Working in a factory through the division of labour, 10 workers could make 48,000 pins, each one making some 240 times the original number.[18] Such productivity would come from the increased dexterity gained by each worker, by the time saved through not having to shift from task to task, and from the technological improvements and inventions that would be facilitated through the simplification of tasks. This increased productivity spread through society was the source of "that universal opulence which extends itself to the lowest ranks of the people."[19] But the full effect of the division of labour can only occur when people's natural tendency to "truck and barter" through trade was not inhibited.

Smith argued that the key to prosperity was "[t]he uniform, constant, and uninterrupted effort of every man to better his condition [and this is] the principle from which publick and national, as well as private opulence is originally derived."[20] It is in this connection that Smith used the idea of the "invisible hand" (which appears only once in *Wealth* as it does in *Moral Sentiments*). He argued that in looking out for their own self-interests,

> every individual necessarily labours to render the annual revenue of society as great as he can. He generally, indeed, neither intends to promote the publick interest, nor knows how much he is promoting it. ... he intends only his own gain, and he is in this, as in many other cases, led by an invisible hand to promote an end which was no part of it. By pursuing his own interests he frequently promotes that of the society more effectively than when he really intends to promote it.[21]

(We will return to this statement again below.)

For Smith, it was this natural harmony of self-interests that led to the beneficial effects of liberty. In attempting to regulate a society based on such natural harmony, government "must always be exposed to innumerable delusions and for the proper performance of which no human wisdom or knowledge could ever be sufficient." Thus, as Smith said, "All systems, either of preference or of restraint, therefore, being thus completely taken away, the obvious and simple system of natural liberty establishes itself of its own accord."[22]

Smith also highlighted the importance of capital. In his *Lectures on Jurisprudence*, he argued that the benefits of the division of labour are so obvious that one wonders why "every nation should continue so long in a poor and indigent state as we find it does." The chief cause is the difficulty of accumulating capital: "This is one great cause of the slow progress of opulence in every country; till some stock be produced there can be no division of labour, and before a division of labour take place there can be very little accumulation of stock."[23]

He continued to extoll the importance of capital in *Wealth of Nations*. For example, the quote that contains the mention of the invisible hand (cited above) is preceded by this sentence: "As every individual, therefore, endeavours as much as he can both *to employ his capital* in support of domestic industry, and so to direct that industry that its produce may be of the greatest value; every individual necessarily labours. … [emphasis added]." Thus, the invisible hand used as a metaphor for a harmonious system is used in *Wealth of Nations* primarily as an argument for freedom for capital.

One could continue to cite examples of Smith's emphasis on the beneficial effects of the investment of capital: "The general industry of the country, being always in proportion to the capital which employs it."[24] Or, in restating of the invisible hand argument: "Every individual is continually exerting himself to find out the most advantageous *employment for whatever capital* he can command [emphasis added]. It is his own advantage, indeed, and not that of society, which he has in view. But the study of his own advantage naturally, or rather necessarily, leads him to prefer that employment which is most advantageous to the society."[25]

Smith, unlike some of the more ardent proponents of laissez-faire in the early nineteenth century, conceived of an active and involved government in some spheres, but one that would leave the economy to function on its own. The major purpose of government was to guarantee the protection of private property. He began his *Lectures on Jurisprudence* with the argument that the chief design of every government was to guarantee the "secure and peaceable possession of property."[26] In *Wealth*, he recited a more direct warning about the need for government's protection of private property:

> For one very rich man, there must be at least five hundred poor, and the affluence of the few supposes the indigence of the many. The affluence of the rich excites the indignation of the poor, who are often driven by want, and prompted by envy, to

invade his possessions. It is only under the shelter of the civil magistrate that the owner of that valuable property, which is acquired by the labour of many years, or perhaps many successive generations, can sleep a night in security. He is at all times surrounded by unknown enemies, whom, though he never provoked, he can never appease, and from whose injustice he can be protected only by the powerful arm of the civil magistrate continually held up to chastise it.[27]

"As Stupid and as Ignorant as Possible"

Smith hoped his "universal opulence" would percolate to the poorest of society. He argued: "No Society can surely be flourishing and happy, of which the far greater part of the members are poor and miserable. It is but equity, besides, that they who feed, cloath, and lodge the whole body of the people should have such a share of the produce of their own labour as to be themselves tolerably well fed, cloathed and lodged."[28] He believed that employers naturally combined to reduce wages[29] and cautioned that governments should treat with the greatest suspicion suggestions for legislation that came from manufacturers.

Smith embraced arguments about expanding needs and dismissed the idea, expressed by many others at the time, that poverty was the necessary spur to industry. Instead, Smith followed the lead of Mandeville and James Steuart. In his *Inquiry into the Principles of Political Economy*, published in 1767, Steuart had proposed that increased desires would multiply needs: "Let any man make an experiment of this nature upon himself by entering into a shop. He will nowhere so quickly discover his wants as there. Everything he sees appears … necessary …" Thus, for Steuart, men would now be forced to labour "because they are slaves to their own wants."[30] While Smith would not state the case so plainly, and did not cite Steuart, he embraced the idea that expanding needs would prompt continued labour even as goods became cheaper.

Smith asserted that wages in Britain in the 1770s were more than adequate for a comfortable living. Generally, however, he favoured "liberal" wages[31] and advocated for the "freedom" of labour to choose their own employment. He was opposed to the Law of Settlement, which he felt restricted labour mobility in the countryside, and restrictions imposed by apprenticeship and guilds. As he argued, "The property which every man has in his own labour, as it is the original foundation of all property, so it is the most sacred and inviolable."[32] Smith also maintained that agriculture benefited society more than manufacturing and, like Cobbett (but without his flair) he approved of the relations between the small farmer and his labourers, whom he "considers as almost an equal," and compared this favourably to those between nobles and their servants. He even asserted that no man should hold more land than they could cultivate.[33]

Smith's arguments in favour of increasing wages and freedom for workers and his warnings about the "mean avarice" of merchants led to many of his ideas being embraced by those defending the rights of labourers, including some well-known radicals. Thomas Paine, for example, was an admirer for a while.[34]

Despite these generally positive arguments, Smith's ideas concerning labour and wages, stuck solidly in the framework of supply and demand, offered little concrete promise of deliverance from poverty. He argued that labour, like every other commodity, needed to be determined by supply and demand:

> [I]t is only among the inferior ranks of people that the scantiness of subsistence can set limits to the further multiplication of the human species; and it can do so in no other way than by destroying a great part of the children which their fruitful marriages produce. ... It is in this manner that demand for men, like that for any other commodity, necessarily regulates the production of men, quickens when it goes on too slowly, and stops when it advances too fast.[35]

Though the division of labour was the key to the opulence that would entail from the frenzied investment of capital, it carried with it some dreadful consequences. One of the contradictions in *Wealth of Nations* was Smith's early account of the division of labour in which he confidently expressed a vision of workers, confronted by simplistic and repetitive tasks, developing technology to make their work more efficient. Later, though, Smith came to a more dismal assessment of the effect of such work. Smith said:

> In the progress of the division of labour, the employment of the far greater of those who live by labour, that is, of the great body of people, comes to be confined to a few very simple operations. ... The man whose life is spent performing a few simple operations ... generally becomes as stupid and ignorant as it is possible for a human creature to become. The torpor of his mind renders him not only incapable of relishing or bearing any part in any rational conversation, but of conceiving of any generous, noble, or tender sentiment, and consequently of forming any just judgement concerning many even of the ordinary duties of private life ...[36]

Smith proposed some vague remedies through education, but, overall, seemed not overly concerned with how his "system of perfect liberty" would regulate the supply of humans through destroying children or make workers "as stupid and ignorant" as possible.

Embracing Smith

It has been common to assert that *Wealth of Nations* was the single most important work on political economy in the eighteenth century and that, consequently, Smith was almost immediately fêted for the accomplishment. D.D. Raphael's introduction to the 1991 edition began: "*The Wealth of Nations* is the first of the great classics of economic theory. One can go further and say that, historically speaking, it is the greatest classical work of the social sciences."[37] Knud Haakonssen asserted that when it appeared in 1776 "it soon overshadowed Smith's name as a moral philosopher; from then on, he was the great political economist."[38] Nonetheless, there is some question about what was original in *The Wealth of Nations*, and how readily and what parts of the work were embraced.

Ideas of supply and demand and a general understanding about the freedom to trade were widespread and prevalent through society. Most people had long naturally understood the self-interest of the butcher and baker and others and did not need to be reminded of those by Smith. Many other aspects of Smith's arguments had been well rehearsed before the publication of *Wealth of Nations*.

Indeed, a full century before *Wealth of Nations*, William Petty, the physician-general for Cromwell's army in Ireland and the surveyor-general of Ireland following its subjugation, had both argued about the need for limited government interference in the economy (employing, appropriately, a medical metaphor) and detailed in a more convincing fashion than Smith the benefits to be gained through a division of labour. Petty demonstrated how this process was naturally applied in Dutch shipbuilding and in cloth manufacturing.[39] And Smith's rather strange choice of a pin factory to demonstrate this might have been based on a similar discussion of a needle factory described by the French writer Noël-Antoine Pluche decades earlier.[40]

Thus, much of what Smith presented in *Wealth* was not new. Joyce Appleby, in surveying the economic literature of the seventeenth and eighteenth centuries, sums up the argument: "When Adam Smith freighted the full burden of automatic, self-sustaining economic laws upon the basic human qualities of a love to 'truck and barter' and a ceaseless urge to 'self-improvement,' he was standing in a long line of thinkers who had rested their theories upon these tendencies in human behaviour."[41] Salim Rashid goes further; he argues that, "A careful comparison of *Wealth of Nations* with the literature of the seventeenth and eighteenth centuries shows that what is true is not original and what is original is not true."[42]

The dispute about the originality and even the value of Smith's *Wealth of Nations* is mirrored by disagreement about its reception and Smith's renown. Commentators like Raphael and Haakonssen mentioned above, who stress a ready renown for *Wealth of Nations* and immediate celebration of its author, often cite references to Smith in debates in the House of Commons or the multiple editions of his work.[43] These seem overstated. Kirk Willis has argued that while there were about forty references to Smith in debates in the House between 1776 and 1800, he was not uppermost in the minds of legislators. Many other economists were mentioned more often; hundreds of references were made to Arthur Young.[44] While both *Wealth of Nations* and *Moral Sentiments* went through several editions, this was not uncommon in British publishing circles, and there is some debate about their success. In a letter to his publisher in 1780 asking for copies of the book, Smith quipped that he appears to have been the publisher's only customer for it. Smith complained, as well, that a small review he wrote of a different author had received more notice than his book.[45] Michael Perelman has pointed out that when Thomas Robert Malthus checked the 1784 edition of the book out of his school library in 1789, he was only the third person to have done so.[46]

How do we square the apparent disregard for *Wealth of Nations* for at least two decades after its release with the constant references to its impact on political economy in the nineteenth and twentieth centuries? What does this say about how *Wealth* was used? One reference to Smith's work in Parliament perhaps holds a clue. In 1795, both Samuel Whitbread, a vigorous reformer arguing for a minimum wage for rural labourers, and William Pitt, arguing against such an action, used Smith's arguments as justification for their approach. Soon, Smith's works would be used primarily to support Pitt's side of this and similar arguments. According to Emma Rothschild, *Wealth* was written at a time of "an unfrightened mind" before the French Revolution, when Smith could borrow freely from a host of French writers. Very soon after the publication of *Wealth*, however, the French Revolution made discussions of "systems of natural liberty" somewhat problematic in Britain.[47]

Smith's few comments about the benefits of adequate wages and cautions about misery were easily forgotten. In the context not just of the French Revolution, but also of increasing enclosure, the attack on cottages, and heightened rural poverty and unrest in the last years of the eighteenth and first decades of the nineteenth centuries, what Adam Shapiro called "the depoliticization impetus of Smith's narrative" proved most useful.[48] Or, as David McNally has argued, "defenders of the status quo stripped Smith's economic theory of its commitment to rising employment and wages ... in order to justify the ill fortunes of labourers as necessary and inevitable."[49] Concerns about poverty could be shunted aside while the unregulated economy was left to its natural instincts and capital given freedom to roam.

Thomas Robert Malthus and "the Great Lottery of Life"

One evening in 1797 a young man and his father engaged in a cordial debate about a recent publication – a simple event that happened over dinners innumerable times all over the world through the centuries. This one was to have significant consequences.

The father, Daniel Malthus, was a moderately well-off member of the English gentry with a country home in Surrey. His son, Thomas Robert Malthus, was less settled in life. In 1797 he was in his 30s, a bachelor and living at his parents' home, making do on a tiny income as the Anglican curate of the small parish of Okewood, Surrey. The debate was about the merits of an essay in *The Enquirer: Reflections on Education, Manners and Literature in a Series of Essays* published in instalments through 1797 by William Godwin. The father approved of Godwin's ideas; the son most decidedly did not. The father, perhaps tiring of the discussion, suggested that his son put his argument in writing. The result was *An Essay on the Principle of Population* published in 1798.

Malthus's *Essay* was a relatively short pamphlet, which was expanded dramatically in 1803 and reissued with mostly minor revisions in 1806, 1807, 1817, and 1826. The "principle of population" espoused in the *Essay* became an important tenet of political economy soon after its publication. Its influence was such that Malthus became one of the central figures in political economy through the first half of the nineteenth century, the other most noteworthy being David Ricardo. Malthus and Ricardo were good friends, communicated frequently, commented on each other's work, and were, briefly, among the pillars of the Political Economy Club.[50]

Gertrude Himmelfarb has argued that Malthus's view of political economy "supplanted that of Adam Smith" through the early part of the nineteenth century.[51] This overstates the case; instead, a simplified understanding of Malthus's assertions was grafted on to a sanitized version of Smith's views to further arguments against any relief for the poor that might be perceived to increase population. By the 1840s, the *Economist* newspaper declared Adam Smith and Malthus to be the two "masters of economic science." Here we outline Malthus's arguments about the rural poor and the legacy of his writings.

Thomas Robert Malthus (always known as Robert) was born in 1766, the second son of Daniel Malthus and Henrietta Graham. Daniel enjoyed a comfortable, if restless, life as a minor member of the gentry. Two years after Robert Malthus was born, Daniel and Henrietta sold the family estate and went travelling. They did so for most of the next eighteen years. Robert studied at boarding schools and with various tutors, including Gilbert Wakefield (the controversial author and religious dissenter), and then went to Jesus College, Cambridge, where he studied mostly mathematics. Upon graduation in 1788, he took orders in the Anglican church and became the curate at his poor parish. Daniel and Henrietta returned to a country home in nearby Albury, Surrey. Robert moved in. Daniel died in 1800; Henrietta followed him a few months later.

Despite having a cleft lip and palate that often made his speech difficult to understand, Malthus made the best of his opportunities. After the publication of his *Essay*, he took a fellowship at Cambridge. In 1804, his family connections allowed him to be assigned the Rectory at the village of Walesby on the death of the rector, Reverend Whitcomb. This provided him with an income of £300 a year, and Malthus received that income for the rest of his life.[52] In 1803, he published a much-expanded edition of *An Essay on the Principle of Population,* and in 1805, largely on the basis of its reception, he was appointed as the first Professor of General History, Politics, Commerce and Finance at the newly established British East India Company College at Haileybury in Hertfordshire. Malthus taught there and lived in college housing until his death in 1834.

In 1802 Malthus accompanied some extended family members on a trip to Switzerland and France. He and his first cousin once removed, Harriet Eckersall, fell in love, but Malthus's fellowship at Cambridge required him to be a bachelor. The appointment as Rector of Walesby removed these constraints and in April 1804, Robert, then thirty-eight, and Harriet, twenty-six, were married. Their first child, Henry, was born eight months later. The two, by all accounts, lived happily together and had two more children, both daughters, before Malthus died of a heart attack at age sixty-eight.

Godwin and the Injustice of Property

The discussion between Daniel and Robert Malthus that evening in 1797 concerned an essay in William Godwin's *The Enquirer*, and Malthus's subsequent *Essay on Population* was explicitly directed at Godwin's 1793 publication, *An Enquiry Concerning Political Justice and its influence on general virtue and happiness*. Godwin, a well-known radical essayist and author, was near the height of his fame in 1797. He was a religious dissenter and had been a nonconformist minister before moving to London to write in 1782. He was soon immersed in radical literary circles. In 1793, Godwin had written *An Inquiry Concerning Political Justice* and an equally popular novel depicting inequities in the English justice system, *Things as they Are; or the Adventures of Caleb Williams*. In 1797, he followed this up with the series of essays entitled *The Enquirer* that so inspired Daniel and infuriated Robert.

The essays in *The Enquirer* addressed a diverse range of topics, including inequality, poverty, avarice, and trade. Malthus identified Godwin's essay "Avarice and Profusion" as the topic of the fateful conversation.[53] In this essay, Godwin took aim at Steuart's and Smith's assertions about the value of expanded needs. Godwin argued that every new commodity, because it requires more labour, robs the poor of leisure. Further, Godwin said, "It is a gross and ridiculous error to suppose that the rich pay for anything. There is no wealth in this world except ... the labour of man. ... What is misnamed wealth, is merely a power vested in certain individuals by the institutions of society, to compel others to labour for their benefit."[54]

Godwin referred constantly back to his 1793 *Political Justice* throughout *The Enquirer*, and it was to this book, more than any other, that Malthus addressed his *Essay*. In *Political Justice*, Godwin had attacked private property and the political and judicial systems that protected and reproduced inequities. He argued that throughout Europe the inequality of property deprived most people of "almost every accommodation that can render life tolerable or secure." Moreover, support for such inequality meant:

> the poor man will be induced to regard the state of society as a state of war, an unjust combination, not for protecting every man in his rights and securing to him the means of his existence, but for engrossing all its advantages to a few favoured individuals and reserving for ... the rest want, dependence, and misery.

The rich, he argued, controlled the state and "are perpetually reducing oppression into a system, and depriving the poor of that little commonage of nature ... which might otherwise have remained to them."[55] Godwin asserted:

> [In] the present state of human society ... the peasant and labourer work, till their understandings are benumbed with toil, their sinews contracted and made callous ... their bodies invaded with infirmities and surrendered to an untimely grave. ... At evening they return to a family, famished with hunger, exposed half naked to the inclemencies of the sky, hardly sheltered.[56]

In contrast, Godwin argued, without the injustice of property, "the narrow principle of selfishness would vanish. ... No man would be an enemy to his neighbour, for they would have nothing for which to contend. ... [and] each man would be united to his neighbour in love and mutual kindness."[57] Such a system would lead to a welcome end to industriousness undertaken to accumulate goods brought on by self-love. Instead, "The true remedy is for men to reduce their wants to the fewest possible, and as much as possible simplify the mode of supplying them."[58]

In the least accomplished section of this work, Godwin also addressed the question of population. The inequitable system of private property was keeping the increase of population at a minimum by "strangling a considerable portion of our children in their cradle." But he asserted that without the injustice of property, a few hours of serious labour a day would provide for five times the current population of Europe. Moreover, as men and women became more enlightened, they would be drawn to each other for intellectual rather than sensual stimulation and thus limit population increase.[59]

The Essay on Population

It is not difficult to understand how in 1798, after a decade as curate to a poor parish in Surrey, Malthus might balk at Godwin's rosy view of a more equitable future society obtained through human perfectibility. In Okewood, Malthus was used to seeing impoverished families desperately trying to make do. Though most of the common fields in Surrey had been enclosed before

1750, the area was subject to a new round of enclosure of common pasture and "waste" land after the beginning of the war with France and the accompanying dramatic increase in agricultural prices.[60] By 1800, about 13 per cent of the population of Okewood relied on parish relief, slightly more than the national average.[61]

Malthus's books, the various editions of the *Essay on the Principle of Population* and his *Principles of Political Economy* published in 1820, have been severely criticized, both at the time of writing and in the years since. Robert Southey, the Romantic and briefly radical poet, called Malthus a "mischievous reptile,"[62] while Godwin deemed him to be a "dark and terrible genius." Cobbett continually made fun of Malthus's "Parson's Mind."[63] Karl Marx, who, perhaps surprisingly, appreciated much of the work of early political economists, savaged Malthus. In a note, Marx argued that the *Essay* was:

> nothing more than a schoolboyish, superficial plagiary. … 'the principle of population,' in the midst of a great social crisis … was greeted with jubilance by the English oligarchy as the great destroyer of all hankerings after human development. Malthus, hugely astonished by his success, gave himself to stuffing into his book materials superficially compiled.[64]

But criticisms of Malthus's arguments were not limited to those opposing liberal political economy. Malthus was regularly critiqued by leading proponents of political economy through the decades when he enjoyed his most influence. One of the founders of the Political Economy Club, Robert Torrens, commented in 1815 that "in the leading questions of economical science, Mr. Malthus scarcely ever embraced a principle which he did not subsequently abandon."[65] The celebrated French economist Jean-Baptiste Say was puzzled by the differences between the *Essay* and Malthus's *Principles of Political Economy*, suggesting, "Either the author of the *Essay on the Principle of Population* or the author of *Principles of Political Economy* is wrong."[66] Thomas De Quincy as well asserted that apart from the obvious value of his arguments on population, Malthus "stumbled at every step" in all other aspects of his work.[67] Walter Bagehot, the editor of the *Economist* from 1861 to 1878, once observed, "There is a mist of speculation over his facts, and a vapour of fact over his theories."[68] Even some of Malthus's admirers were forced to admit that the initial *Essay on the Principle of Population* "made an author of Mr. Malthus … rather before his time."[69] It is also undoubtedly true that Malthus was surprised by the reception of the *Essay*. He admitted he wrote it initially to marshal his thoughts after the discussion with his father, but determined that even "the least light, on a topic so generally interesting, might be received with candour" and he sought its publication.[70] Malthus himself lamented in a letter shortly before his death, "It is astonishing how many express a horror of my book who have never read it."[71]

More recently, especially since the bicentennial anniversary of the first edition of the *Essay* in 1998, a greater appreciation for Malthus's contributions to political economy has been expressed. Focusing on his arguments for economic growth and rising wages, many have attempted to move the discussion of Malthus beyond his initial dire arguments about population increase and make him into an advocate for the poor.[72] It is not clear that a careful reading of the various editions of the *Essay on the Principle of Population* along with Malthus's other major work, *Principles of Political Economy*, diminishes the "horror." It does, however, provide a picture of the humanity and humility that marked Malthus's attempts to understand political economy and find ways political economy could usefully suggest arguments to reduce poverty. The confusion in his work, as marked by Say and Torrens, was caused partly by a willingness to question his own arguments and explore new avenues in political economy. Nonetheless, burdened with the need to keep his arguments within what he referred to as "the impregnable fortress" of his initial assertions about the principles of population, his writings could never liberate themselves entirely from his initial attack on the poor.

In the first edition of *The Essay on the Principle of Population*, Malthus sought to correct what he considered to be dangerous assertions about the potential for improvements in the human condition and inequality. These assertions were dangerous, he argued, because they ignored the underlying causes of human misery, what he called the fixed laws of nature: food is necessary to existence and "passion between the sexes is necessary and will remain in its present state." Further he warned, "The power of population is infinitely greater than the power in the earth to produce subsistence for man."[73] Malthus concluded, "I see no way by which man can escape from the weight of this law which pervades all animated nature. No fancied equality, no agrarian regulations in their utmost extent, could remove the pressure of it even for a single century."[74]

His central and simplistic argument that population would increase geometrically while the provision of food could only possibly increase arithmetically is well known. Malthus outlined more fully how the vague assertion put forth by Smith that labourers, like any commodity, would (re)produce themselves according to demand might function. Malthus described a pendulum-like effect beginning when subsistence was adequate and the "power of population" would function to increase population levels. This would necessarily reduce the availability of subsistence and produce a "season of distress" during which "the discouragement to marriage and the difficulty of rearing a family are so great, that population is at a stand."[75] Cultivators would increase production through the use of cheaper labour until population and subsistence were in another equilibrium. Distress being relieved, population would increase again, and the cycle would continue. Like Godwin and Smith, Malthus was prepared to recognize that the rich and capitalists "contribute frequently to prolong the season of distress among the poor," but he argued that no possible form of society "could prevent the almost constant action of misery" on the majority of the population.[76]

Malthus found some relief from the depressing scenario of constant misery in a series of preventative checks that he argued prompted people to delay marriage and, thus, children. For the poor, this entailed a constant apprehension of the potential for privation and suffering sufficient to counteract the "passion between the sexes." In England, the beneficial impact of such checks was muted by the Poor Laws. According to Malthus, though they provided some minimal immediate support for the poor, "they have spread the general evil over a much larger surface."[77] For Malthus, this was so for a variety of reasons. Poor relief increased the demand for food without increasing its supply, raising the price of food for those not on relief and spreading misery. Anything that prevented the poor from needing to rely on their own industry led them to indolence.[78] Moreover, by providing a false security, parish relief induced the poor to spend at the alehouse that which they should save, content to leave wife and family to the care of the parish upon death. Malthus argued that such a man "might yet hesitate in thus dissipating his earnings, if he were assured that … his family might starve or be left to the support of casual bounty."[79] Most importantly, the poor laws removed the restraints that prevented a man from marrying before he could afford having a family. With the relief provided by the Poor Laws, "A poor man may marry with little or no prospect of being able to support a family in independence. They may be said therefore in some measure to create the poor which they maintain."[80] Indeed, the effects of early marriage were so pernicious that, "A labourer who marries without being able to support a family, may in some respects be considered as an enemy to all his fellow-labourers."[81]

It was Malthus's defence of inequality that was most striking, perhaps. Malthus returned constantly to the argument that poverty and misery were not caused by inequality, but rather by the principle of population that ensured the constant reemergence of periods of distress. He criticized Godwin for suggesting that many of the evils of the world were caused by institutions that perpetuated inequality. Malthus argued instead that institutions were "mere feathers that float on the surface" of the inevitable laws of nature.[82] Indeed, for Malthus, inequality was both inevitable and necessary. In response to Godwin's view that inequality in property led to conflict and selfishness, Malthus warned instead: "Man cannot live in the midst of plenty … Were there no established administration of property, every man would be obliged to guard with force his little store. Selfishness would be triumphant."[83]

Along with proving to himself that private ownership somehow ended selfishness, Malthus asserted:

> When these two fundamental laws of society, the security of property, and the institution of marriage, were once established, inequality of conditions must

necessarily follow. Those who were born after the division of property, would come into a world already possessed. If their parents, from having too large a family, could not give them sufficient for their support, what are they to do in a world where every thing is appropriated? ... It has appeared that from the inevitable laws of nature, some human beings must suffer from want. These are the unhappy persons who, in the great lottery of life, have drawn a blank.[84]

Malthus was most adamant that such inequality was both natural and, in many ways beneficial. In one single drawn out sentence, he dismissed all attempts at reducing inequality. He argued:

It thus appears that a society constituted according to the most beautiful form that imagination can conceive, with benevolence for its moving principle, instead of self-love, ... would, from the inevitable laws of nature, ... degenerate into a society, constructed upon a plan not essentially different from that which prevails in every known State at present: I mean a society divided into a class of proprietors, and a class of labourers, and self-love for the main-spring of the great machine.[85]

Blaming the Poor for Their Poverty

Malthus published a much-expanded version of the *Essay* in 1803 and it was primarily on the basis of this edition that his reputation was solidified. The 1803 edition was triple the length of the original and set out in two volumes. Malthus himself said that the new edition was intended both to broaden his discussion of the checks to population increase and "to soften some of the harshest conclusions of the first essay."[86]

A large portion of the additional material in the 1803 and subsequent editions was concerned with population histories of various places in the world at various times, from classical Europe to North America to India. Malthus had a dual purpose in providing this history. The first was to prove his central argument that in most places population tended to expand until it reached the carrying capacity of the land, at which point it was held in check primarily through famine. But that general assertion was contrasted with his histories of parts of modern Europe where, through moral restraint that delayed marriage, population increase was curtailed. The first volume, with the histories of the ancient world and societies outside of Europe, was necessarily based on some scanty historical evidence. Much of that history we would now understand to be incomplete or simply wrong.

The second volume was meant to provide evidence for a new emphasis in the 1803 edition: the role of moral restraint in delaying marriage and avoiding the worst aspects of population increase. The emphasis placed on this in the 1803 and subsequent editions was both a significant qualifier to the dismal vision of the first edition, and a partial embrace of the ideas of the improvement in the human condition suggested by Godwin and others. Malthus also focused more heavily on the importance of chastity before marriage and of restraint within it. As Malthus argued, "The law of chastity cannot be violated without producing evil." He also further emphasized the importance of unfulfilled desires in prompting industriousness. Thus, chastity before marriage needed to cause some discomfort in order to compel people to work to better their situations so they could marry. (One suspects that this played such a prominent role in the 1803 edition of the *Essay* because it was an important issue in his own life with regard to Harriet Eckersall and the restrictions imposed by his Cambridge fellowship.) It was also the loss of this spur to industry that Malthus pointed to when rejecting birth control. In an appendix to the 1806 edition, Malthus argued that even within marriage, restraint, rather than any other form of birth control, was required to avoid indolence. To force themselves to industry, people needed to feel constantly the tension between the "attraction between the sexes" and the threat of diminished circumstances caused by too many children.[87]

The 1803 edition also focused more heavily on outlining the detrimental effects of the Poor Laws, expounding on the threat represented by the poor, and making frequent assertions that the poor were responsible for their own poverty. What had been a short discussion of the Poor Laws in the 1798 edition became two chapters in 1803. Malthus stressed that the real causes of the misery of the poor were to be found neither in corrupt institutions nor unequal distribution of property. Instead, he suggested, all discussion of these issues threatened to throw "a veil of obscurity" over the true cause of poverty:

> When the wages of labour are hardly sufficient to maintain two children, a man marries and has five or six. He, of course, finds himself miserably distressed. He accuses his parish for their tardy and sparing fulfillment of its obligation to assist him. He accuses the avarice of the rich … He accuses the partial and unjust institutions of society. … In searching for objects of accusation he never adverts to the quarter from which all his misfortunes originate. The last person he would think of accusing is himself, on whom, the whole of the blame lies.[88]

Malthus concluded his discussion of the Poor Laws with a call for the elimination of parish relief, proposing that no child born a year after its repeal should "ever be entitled to parish assistance."[89]

A significant portion of Malthus's work was devoted to meeting the threat represented by the discontent of the poor. For the multiple subsequent editions after 1803, Malthus mostly tinkered; replacing this word with that, making some small additions, and removing those bits that had provoked the most virulent response. The quote below was one of those he removed after 1803, but there is little doubt it captured well Malthus's view of the poor at the time. It is worth reciting fully here:

> A man who is born into a world already possessed, if he cannot get subsistence from his parents on whom he has a just demand, and if the society do not want his labour, has no claim of *right* to the smallest portion of food and, in fact, has no business to be where he is. At nature's mighty feast there is no vacant cover for him. She tells him to be gone, and will quickly execute her own orders, if he do not work upon the compassion of some of her guests. If these guests get up and make room for him, other intruders immediately appear demanding the same favour. The report of a provision for all that come fills the hall with numerous claimants. The order and harmony of the feast is disturbed, the plenty that before reigned is changed into scarcity; and the happiness of the guests is destroyed by the spectacle of misery and dependence in every part of the hall. … If the great truths on these subjects were more generally circulated, and the lower classes of people could be convinced that, by the laws of nature, independently of any particular institutions, except the great one of property, which is absolutely necessary in order to attain any considerable produce, no person has any claim of any right on society for subsistence, if his labour will not purchase it, the greatest part of the mischievous declamation on the unjust institutions of society would fall powerless to the ground.[90]

No wonder, Robert Southey, in a review of the 1803 edition, suggested, "He writes advice for the poor for the rich to read; they of course will approve his opinions."[91]

Malthus's Principles

And yet, Malthus at times demonstrated a keen compassion for the lot of the poor and struggled to understand how the principles of political economy might be employed to better their position in life. Malthus, clearly, had a heightened appreciation for the power of political economy, coupled with a belief that it was a science with underlying, steadfast principles. In 1803 he had argued that "Political economy is perhaps the only science of which it may be said that the ignorance of it is not merely a deprivation of good, but produces great evil."[92]

But as he worked to understand and articulate how political economy might provide insights into ways to reduce poverty, he was often drawn to conclusions that came close to contradicting his one real claim to fame: the principle of population. This included his recognition that the Poor Laws had not increased the English population as much as suggested they would. Nonetheless, he continued to attack the Poor Laws without much change until the 1817 edition of the *Essay*.[93]

By subsequent editions as well, Malthus focused less heavily on the original assertion that it was an absolute inability to produce enough food that limited population growth. Rather he first argued that it was a lack of cottage accommodation and later embraced a more familiar argument about wants. Instead of limits to food, he increasingly referred to "something like a standard of wretchedness, a point below which they will not continue to marry and propagate their species." He argued that the goal of political economists should be "to raise this standard as high as possible by cultivating a spirit of independence, a decent pride, and a taste for cleanliness and comfort among the poor."[94] Nonetheless, in an exchange of letters with Nassau Senior in the 1820s, when Senior tried to make an argument similar to Malthus's "standard of wretchedness" as part of a general assertion that it was no longer this Malthusian dilemma that confronted European societies, Malthus disagreed and reiterated, "as far as we can judge from history, there has never been a period of any considerable length, when premature mortality and vice, specifically arising from the pressure of population against food, has not prevailed to a considerable extent."[95]

Apart from a few small pamphlets and the minor revisions to the *Essay* in 1806, 1807, and 1817, Malthus produced little between his major opus in 1803 and 1820. That year, he published his long-delayed *Principles of Political Economy*. In *Principles*, Malthus stuck fairly closely to the arguments of Adam Smith – not surprising given that his lectures on political economy to the students at the East India Company college at Haileybury apparently followed Smith's *Wealth of Nations* faithfully.[96] He reiterated his opinion about the need for the recognition of ownership in private property and returned to his "lottery of life" explanation for inequality. In *Principles* he argued, "Some persons or other must necessarily be the proprietors." Malthus was prepared to admit that for the labourer, it would be better if he possessed the land and the labour. But this "matters not to society." Furthermore, this "by no means implies that the labourer, who in the lottery of human life has not drawn a prize of land, suffers any hardship or injustice in being obliged to give something in exchange for the use of what belongs to another."[97]

He also highlighted the key role played by capital. For Malthus, the key to prosperity lay in the employment of capital, and the "accumulation of capital, and its efficiency in the increase of wealth and population, depends almost entirely upon its power of setting labour to work, or, in other words upon its power of commanding labour."[98] And he recited Smith's argument that labour was a commodity that commanded its own price in the market. According to Malthus, therefore, the only safe way to increase wages was to reduce the supply of labourers. Encouraging the poor to have families resulted in "overstocking the market with a commodity which we still say that we wish to be dear." He asserted, instead, that "withholding the supplies of labour is the only possible way of really raising its price; and that they themselves, being the possessors of this commodity, have alone the power to do this."[99]

Malthus expressed disagreement with many of the ideas of his good friend David Ricardo and his disciples. One of these revolved around Malthus's contention of the extra benefits resulting from the investment of capital in agriculture as opposed to manufacturing. For Malthus, investment in agriculture had the dual advantage of both increasing production and wages while increasing the supply and reducing the cost of food. This emphasis helped explain Malthus's support for reduced taxation of estates and, especially, the Corn Laws, the latter position placing him in opposition to the majority of political economists. Malthus also took a different view of the nature of rent than Ricardo and his followers.

Another view that distinguished Malthus from most of the other political economists at the time concerned the question of effective demand. Ricardo, following Jean-Baptiste Say, had argued that production created its own demand and thus there could never be a general glut of commodities. It was to some extent Malthus's preoccupation with this possibility that led him in *Principles* to a dual focus on the role of increased demand and the necessity to continually spur industriousness through unfulfilled wants.[100] As he said, "It is unquestionable that wealth produces wants; but it is a still more important truth, that wants produces wealth."[101] The need to spur consumption of commodities was one of his justifications for supporting inequality. But, more importantly, for Malthus this meant: "The greatest of all difficulties in converting uncivilized and *thinly peopled* countries into civilized and *populous* ones, is to inspire them with the wants best calculated to excite their exertions in the production of wealth [emphasis added]."[102]

Marx argued in *Capital* that Malthus had come full circle and had by this point discovered "the beautiful trinity of capitalist production: over-production, over-population, over-consumption – three very delicate monsters."[103] The nature of these delicate monsters meant Malthus continually felt the need to urge measures to force industriousness in the pursuit of expanded needs. On the one hand, he hoped that a "taste for the comforts and conveniences of life" would prompt people to delay marriage.[104] On the other, he constantly fretted that people could come by the necessities of life too easily. Malthus found the evidence for this most readily in Ireland. There he asserted that the potato made living too easy for the Irish cottiers and thus prevented them from being compelled to further industry. Malthus and Ricardo engaged in some correspondence concerning this immediately after Malthus's trip to Ireland in 1817. Ricardo responded to a letter from Malthus on the subject with a note: "Humboldt in his account of New Spain points out the very same evils you do in Ireland, proceeding from the same cause. The land there yields a great abundance of Bananas, Manioc, Potatoes and Wheat with very little labour, and the people having no taste for luxuries, having abundance of food, have the privilege of being idle." But Ricardo warned that the goal of political economy should be happiness and perhaps being idle was its own reward.[105] Nonetheless, Malthus recycled this argument in *Principles*, equating the banana to the potato and asserting that "the natural and necessary effect of this state of things, is the very general prevalence of habits of indolence."[106] Ricardo again cautioned against Malthus's tendency to enforce industriousness. In his unpublished notes of criticism of the work, Ricardo cited Jean-Baptiste Say's warning that, "it is not the province of the Political Economist to advise: – he is to tell you how you may become richer, but he is not to advise you to prefer riches to indolence, or indolence to riches."[107]

Malthus had enormous influence over ideas of political economy in the first half of the nineteenth century. David Ricardo, though disagreeing with Malthus on many points, had urged Malthus to write more, saying, "The public pay a most flattering attention to anything from your pen."[108] Nassau Senior described Malthus in 1828 as "our most imminent living philosopher" and Humphrey House argued that by early in the century Malthus's arguments became "the fixed, axiomatic belief of the educated world."[109] What they believed in was not the more nuanced explorations of effective demand, but rather the cruder and more easily understood arguments about the poor, what Donald Winch has somewhat exaggeratedly called "the caricature called Malthusianism."[110]

In his 1807 *Letter to Samuel Whitbread*, Malthus asserted:

> To those who know me personally, I feel that I have no occasion to defend my character from the imputation of hardness of heart; and to those who do not, I can only express my confidence that when they have attended to the subject as much as I have, they will be convinced that I have not admitted a single proposition which appears to detract from the present comforts and gratifications of the poor, without very strong grounds for believing that this would be more than compensated to them by the general and permanent improvement of their condition.[111]

There may be no good reason to believe that Malthus was not sincere in this expression of his good wishes for the poor. But his recipes for an improvement in their condition all revolved around denying them what they most desired: land for a garden and perhaps even a cow; a cottage to live in and raise a family; and poor relief when this was not available. Moreover, he recited arguments about their natural tendency to indolence and blamed the poor themselves for their poverty. In the hands of political economists to follow, these arguments became further reasons for even harsher policies towards the rural poor.

Chapter Six

Nassau Senior and the New Poor Laws

Robert Malthus died in 1834, just as the government passed changes to the Poor Laws he so ardently, if somewhat erratically, blamed for much of Britain's ills. After decades of debate and numerous Parliamentary Commissions, dramatic alterations to the way relief was to be provided for the rural (and urban) poor were recommended by a Select Committee in 1834 and quickly made into law.

There was much opposition to the new Poor Law regime. The *Brighton Patriot* described the new law as a:

> Bill that covers the land with child murders and incendiary fires ... that separates a man from his wife ... that tears children from the embrace of their parents ... that starves the widow and sends the aged in sorrow to their graves. A Bill which covered the country with huge battle prisons, for the incarceration of every man, woman, child who may ... be reduced to poverty.[1]

Conversely, the Annual Reports of the Poor Law Commissioners in the years immediately following the passage of the new laws included almost euphoric assessments of the impact of the law, from landlords, farmers, and Poor Law officials. One farmer reported "Since the introduction of the new system of Poor Laws, a most beneficial change has taken place in our parish. Before, we had a heavy surplus of population; this has nearly disappeared; the labourers will not accept relief in the workhouse; and will strain every nerve to keep out."[2]

Despite the striking difference in tone, these two assessments of the effects of the New Poor Laws are not contradictory. The New Poor Laws envisioned a reliance on consolidated workhouses – not unlike Arthur Young's 100 Houses of Industry recommended half a century earlier – made so unpleasant that the poor would "strain every nerve" to avoid them. Expenditure on the poor was reduced dramatically: between 1834 and 1836, the cost of poor relief fell by £1,559,625.[3] Less clear was whether the New Poor Laws reduced poverty or simply made the poor more desperate by mandating against the provision of

Portrait of Nassau William Senior after Henry Wyndham Phillips, stipple engraving, (1855) (NPG D5014). © National Portrait Gallery, London

relief except in workhouses. All accounts seem to point to the latter. Indeed, in many ways it was a reaction to the intended, institutional brutality of the New Poor Laws that insured they would never be fully implemented.

The most important architect of the New Poor Laws was Nassau Senior, who was labelled the "Prophet of Modern Capitalism" by his biographer, S. Leon Levy, in 1943.[4] He might have meant it as a compliment. A lawyer and political economist, Senior was less renowned than many of his contemporaries. Though Senior spent many years writing for the *Economist*, the newspaper provided an understated obituary on his death in 1864. It admitted that Senior was "scarcely to be described as a prominent political or social character." Nonetheless, it assured readers, Senior had "rendered in his day and generation more important and various services to his country than many whose names are far more widely known" and remarked on "an intellect singularly cool and clear."[5] Senior was indeed perhaps the political economist in the early decades of the nineteenth century most influential in directly shaping government legislation. He spearheaded the report of the Poor Law Commission leading to the passage of the New Poor Laws in 1834. But he was also involved in numerous other reports to government in which he argued against workers' attempts to create viable unions, opposed laws restricting hours of work, and counselled against the extension of poor laws and relief to Ireland.

This chapter discusses Senior's various roles in shaping specific policy reflecting the "science of political economy" in the first half of the nineteenth century.

It focuses primarily on his contribution to the 1834 New Poor Laws. The New Poor Laws and their impact – revealed partly through a series of scandals that helped lead to opposition to them – will also be detailed. Before engaging in that discussion, however, we will briefly outline some of the increasing opposition to the "science of political economy" and its fascination with capital.

"The Occult Principle of the System"

Marc Blaug has argued that by the first few decades of the nineteenth century, "a generation drunk on Malthusian wine" had imbibed many of the edicts of political economy, particularly the association of the old Poor Law with an undesired increase in the population of rural poor.[6] But there were many who refused to indulge. If Malthus (and Senior) sought to blame poverty on the poor's indolence and their proclivity to breed too often, and to combat that indolence through more effectively chaining them to capital, others continued to see inequality and oppression as the culprits. Most often their answer to such poverty, like the reformed Young, was to provide the rural poor with land. They were important in articulating opposition to the dominance of capital, questioned the "principles of population," and had a significant influence on Karl Marx as he worked out his ideas in *Capital* decades later.

Two of the most interesting of these were Piercy Ravenstone and Thomas Hodgskin. We will talk more about Hodgskin later, as he almost inexplicably became a writer for the *Economist* newspaper. Ravenstone is interesting partly because he never existed. Writing under a pseudonym, a mystery never completely solved, Ravenstone produced a fascinating attack on Malthus and his fellow political economists in the 1820s.

In 1821, one of London's most active publishers of material on political economy, John Murray, put out an essay entitled *A Few Doubts as to the Correctness of Some Opinions Generally Entertained on the Subjects of Population and Political Economy*, which was authored by Piercy Ravenstone. In his "advertisement" to begin the book, writing from a place named as Ravensdale Cottage, the author reported, "At my time of life, and in my retirement, I do not seek fame."[7] Unlike Malthus, who first published *An Essay on the Principle of Population* anonymously but quickly made himself known when the work began to receive critical attention, Ravenstone lived up to his claim that fame could do him no good. Though he published another booklet three years later, we do not know with certainty Ravenstone's identity.

Who was Ravenstone? There has been some speculation. The most likely culprits seem to have been reduced to a choice of three. Joseph Dorfman, who edited a copy of *Doubts* in the 1960s, believed him to be the Reverend Edward Edwards; Piero Sraffa, who wrote extensively on Ricardo, suggested the author was Richard Puller Junior. This latter interpretation seems to be most accepted, repeated, for example, by Patricia James and Michael Perelman. However, there is strong evidence that the author was Richard Puller Senior, not his son.[8] The Richard Pullers in question were wealthy bankers. It is unfortunate we do not know more about Ravenstone, for his work is most interesting and too often ignored.

Ravenstone focused much of his attention on a thorough and at times devastating critique of both the evidence and assumptions provided by Malthus. Ravenstone asked his readers to judge the soundness of his arguments, not the eloquence of its presentation for, as he said, "I have no practice in writing; I cannot contend in fascination of styles with the supporters of the geometrical ratio."[9] Ravenstone protested too much. His work stands as a thoroughly engaging refutation of much of the writing of Malthus and other political economists. That it did not contend with them for influence says more about the ready embrace of justifications for inequality than the merits of the argument or its presentation.[10]

Ravenstone sought to explain the increasing poverty of the rural labourer despite the growth of the economy. In his introduction, he briefly summarized the links between the principles of population and the principles of political economy. Malthus's work was premised on the idea that the ordinary condition of the labourer was that of "mitigated famine" that could only be countered through industriousness. But, according to the new science of political economy, the hard work of the labourer would do little to correct this. "All exertions of industry [labour] would be vain, ... unless regularly put in motion by capital, the occult principle of the system."[11]

Tracing population histories in a manner reminiscent of Malthus's expanded 1803 *Essay*, Ravenstone argued that in no spot in the world had population increased as quickly as Malthus suggested it would. Malthus had not only seriously overstated the rate of *potential* population increase by exaggerating the natural fecundity of women through childbearing age, but he had missed many of the reasons for a much lower *actual* population increase. According to Ravenstone, the enthusiastic embrace of the flawed arguments about the geometric ratio of population increase was prompted by its appeal to the wealthy. He argued, "so the geometrical ratio entirely owes it successes to its falling in with the prejudices of the rich and powerful; its celebrity proceeds from the aid it lent to them, in their encroachments on the rights of the poor."[12]

But Malthus erred even more egregiously in his discussion of the limits to the means of sustenance; that is, the arithmetic side of the ratio. Here, Ravenstone suggested, Malthus had performed his illusionary tricks through a "studied watchfulness ... in always contriving to keep clear of details," particular a certain "slipperiness" in never providing a beginning date for the commencement of the arithmetic increase of sustenance. If, however, one supposed this to have begun at the beginning, with Adam and Eve and their offspring, then "we shall be compelled to admit that the actual inhabitants of the world must be suffering habitually and unknowingly all the horrors of famine. One thousand millions of people must according to his theory be living on a quantity of food which is only sufficient for 1,328 persons."[13] This unperceived famine had not, of course, afflicted mankind. As Ravenstone said, "Unless any country can be adduced in which men have been able to live without food, we are irresistibly compelled to believe that for the last 3,500 years the geometrical and arithmetical ratios have jogged on quietly, side by side. … We find we have been frightened by a bugbear, who … has for the last thirty-five centuries been, and is very likely to continue, a harmless and manageable devil."[14]

The reason for this agreeable jog is that the production of sustenance is dependent on human industry, not on the absence of humans. It is labour that brings forth sustenance; cultivation abets further cultivation. "The more the earth is tormented, the more it is clothed with vegetation …" Quite the opposite to Malthus's argument about the dangers of too many people, Ravenstone asserted, "Plenty has everywhere followed numbers; a scanty subsistence has been the lot of every thinly-scattered people."[15] Though Malthus mostly ignored Ricardo's suggestion that there were useful insights from Ravenstone, Malthus himself came close to making these connections in his *Principles of Political Economy* – of course, within the "impregnable fortress" of the constant menace represented by the hungry poor.

Having dismissed Malthus's arguments about the dangers of too many people, Ravenstone set for himself the task of explaining, in the absence of the easy scapegoat of population increase, why the poor had become more miserable. The answer lay in the way each labourer was now required to support more idle men, and that fact could only be explained by the deformed growth of the rights of property, taxes on the poor, and the workings of capital.[16]

Unlike Godwin, Ravenstone was not opposed to individual property. He cautioned, "Property acts on nations as wine does on individuals: when taken in small quantities it excites and invigorates the system; its excess only brings on disease and prostration of strength." The drunken growth of the rights of property ensured that the labourer was prevented from making "use of his limbs without sharing the produce of his labour with those who contribute nothing to the success of his exertions."[17] Moreover, as the rights of property were further monopolized, the wealthy became the most powerful element of society; "their interests will be considered as the interests of the whole community; they will frame its laws, which of course will sanction all their usurpations." This led to the "dry-rot eating into the heart of … society": the proliferation of idle men sucking from the teat of the labourers' industry.[18]

Increased taxes on basic necessities to pay for the idle and the political apparatus that supported them constituted an attack on the labourer's wages. For example, Ravenstone argued that every item that went into brewing beer at cottages was taxed heavily. Beer effectively paid a tax of 300 per cent. The trade in tea made healthy profits and increased "wealth" through its multiple exchanges, while the worker was denied his beer. This was just one of the great consequences that "resulted from the attempt to supply the wants of the state out of the breakfast of the labourer."[19]

The great glue meant to hold this system together, he suggested, was capital. Ravenstone provided one of the most delightful critiques of the fascination with capital; it is worth quoting at some length:

> It is not an easy matter, however, to acquire an accurate idea of the nature of capital ... It has none but a metaphysical existence. ... it is around us, it is about us, it mixes in everything we do. Though itself invisible, its effects are but too apparent ... It serves to account for whatever cannot be accounted for in any other way. Where reason fails, where argument is insufficient, it operates like a talisman to silence all doubts. ... It is the great mother of all things, it is the cause of every event that happens in the world. Capital, according to them, is the parent of industry, the forerunner of all improvements. It builds our towns, cultivates our fields, it restrains the vagrant waters of our rivers, it covers our barren mountains with timber, it converts our deserts into gardens, it bids fertility arise where all before was desolation. It is the deity of their idolatry which they have set up to worship in the high places of the Lord; and were its power what they imagine, it would not be unworthy of their adoration.[20]

But, he observed, if capital was the elixir required to raise wages, as Malthus argued, why was Britain "oppressed with capital even to plethory" and yet her labourers were starving? Or, as he stated, "England is the Elysium of the capitalist, the purgatory of the labourer."[21]

Ravenstone argued that poor relief was required because the labourer had been made to carry the weight of all these idle men. Still, some protested that relief promoted idleness among the poor; these men "see public good in individual misery." Ravenstone suggested that for the "lover of a system, ... a true political economist ... self-interest is a treacherous counsellor, it knows how to disguise under specious names the most flagitious acts." The most villainous of these were the attempts to eliminate poor relief. He left no doubt he was referring both to Malthus specifically and to a set of nested ideas resting in political economy when he protested the pretensions to natural law and condemned those who professed it: "Human institutions are the real cause of all the misery with which we are surrounded, and he who in arrogance of his folly would trace them to any other source ... is equally an enemy to man whom he oppresses, and to God whom he maligns."[22]

Nassau Senior: "Governed by Fear"

Despite such critiques, it is not hard to understand why it was a much more comfortable proposition to blame the poor for their poverty, to find the explanation for increased misery in easy arguments about population increase, and to find solutions not in radical ideas meant to reduce inequities but in the need to increase capital and, most especially, to eliminate the purported impetus to population and impediment to industry provided by the Poor Laws. There was no more staunch defender of the promises of political economy for the rich and its threats to the poor than Nassau Senior.

Senior's ancestors were Jewish merchants who had originally fled Spain to the Netherlands and then arrived in England. His family's wealth and that of his wife's stemmed primarily from slavery, with extensive interests in the West Indies and the Royal African Company. Senior graduated from Oxford and was admitted to the bar in 1819. He continued to practise law through most of his life despite his many other interests. Indeed, he was probably best known to the public for his actions in some well-publicized lawsuits. The most famous of these were two negotiations he undertook for Jenny Lind, one of the most celebrated opera stars of the era. Senior was first involved in an unsuccessful negotiation surrounding the broken engagement between Lind and another Swedish opera star of the era, Julius Gunther. Subsequently, Senior also negotiated Lind's huge contract with P.T. Barnum for an American tour in 1850.

Senior was appointed a Master of Chancery in 1836 and received a government salary in that position for much of the rest of his life.[23] He was also appointed the first Drummond Chair of Political Economy at Oxford University, a position he held for ten years. In addition, he was employed on five different government commissions. He died in 1864.

Senior's position as the Drummond Chair offered him an unparalleled opportunity to shape debate around political economy. The position required him to produce a series of public lectures on slightly different themes each year; each set of public lectures was guaranteed publication. For the most part though, Senior failed to take advantage of this opportunity. The published lectures seldom reveal any innovative approaches to political economy. In addition, they are inordinately dull, with leaden prose and few catchy phrases.[24] Nonetheless, Senior doggedly fulfilled the duties of the chair, each year presenting a different series of lectures, and he was recognized among the increasingly crowded field of political economists. Based primarily on a pamphlet he had written opposing the Corn Laws in 1821, he was invited to join the Political Economy Club in 1823.

Senior outlined his approach to political economy in his first set of lectures to Oxford entitled "An Introductory Lecture on Political Economy" and again in an only slightly revised version more than twenty years later in 1847 in "Four Introductory Lectures on Political Economy." In the latter, he suggested that "no study ever attracted, during an equal period of time, so much attention from so many minds, as has been bestowed, during the last sixty years, on Political Economy." Despite this, he argued in both 1826 and 1847, political economy was "in a state of imperfect development." One of the reasons for this imperfect state was the result of the immense complication of the subject: "The machinery of civilized society is worked by so many antagonist springs, the dislike of labour, the desire for immediate enjoyment, and the love of accumulation are so perpetually counteracting one another." What stands out in these lectures is the determination that society revolved around these very limited, economic concerns. Smith and Malthus located their arguments about political economy in a somewhat broader understanding of society, morality, philosophy, and, in the case of Malthus, faith. There was little evidence of that in Senior's work. Indeed, he argued, that "the pursuit of wealth ... is the great source of moral improvement." While Smith might have come to the same conclusion, at least he worked hard to explain why, in his estimation, that might be so. Senior demonstrated no such need to explain this argument.[25]

Senior sometimes disagreed with Malthus, but always praised his work. In his pamphlet on the Corn Laws – in which, in opposition to Malthus, he joined the chorus of political economists opposed to the laws – he began with an appreciation of Malthus, suggesting that, "Perhaps the most valuable present which any living author has made to the world is Mr. Malthus's work on population."[26] The publication of his *Two Lectures on Population* delivered in 1828 included correspondence Senior had with Malthus. In his advertisement for the publication, Senior warned, "I feel the disadvantageous contrast to which I expose my own compositions by their juxta-position to those of our most imminent living philosophical writer."[27] But by the 1830s, Senior had, like many political economists, questioned the central and original premise of the principle of population: that the constant tension between the multiplying hungry poor and the limited capacity to feed them was the underlying determinant of population or economic growth.[28] He was, however, most assuredly on-side with Malthus on the question of the disastrous effects of the Poor Law in promoting the indolence of labour.

Senior's approach was distinguished by an even harder line towards questions of how to make the poor industrious, more akin to the arguments of Joseph Townsend four decades earlier than those of Malthus. He professed to believe, "The labouring population of every country is condemned by nature to a life which is one of struggle and want. ... Hunger and cold are the punishments by which she represses improvidence and sloth. If we remove those punishments we must substitute other means of repression."[29] Both Malthus and Senior shared a disdain for the Irish. But Malthus had tempered his criticism of Irish cottiers after a visit in 1817. Though as we will see in chapter 9 Senior was very involved in shaping policy and opinion on Ireland, he evidenced no softening in his approach: indeed, in the late 1840s, he was still countenancing draconian punishments for the Irish as part of a more general hardening of racial attitudes. He argued, "Races which like the Celts, have neither docility nor intelligence, must be governed by fear."[30]

Like Malthus, Senior was an ardent supporter of large landed proprietors, worried constantly about the costs of parish relief and its effect on rent, and was equally enthralled with the magic of capital. Senior occasionally expressed concerns for the poor. In his 1826 lecture, he allowed that a significant number of people in England survived "vibrating between the possession and the want of mere food."[31] However, unlike Malthus, who struggled to suggest ways political economy could be used to address that poverty (without compromising the fundamental ideas of the Principle of Population), Senior rarely demonstrated any such misgivings, restating constantly his belief that any restrictions on capital and any measure which blunted the lessons of self-reliance and industriousness were not only unwarranted but dangerous.

He was particularly close to the Whig administrations in power through much of the 1830s and in 1832 he provided a report to the government on unions. Unions had been allowed, with numerous restrictions, in 1825. Employers complained about attempts by working men to strike, picket, and prevent the hiring of replacement labour. Senior recognized that worker agitation grew out of long-held grievances but provided a report that painted union activists as an evil that threatened the very existence of the nation:

> if the manufacturer is to employ his capital, and the mechanist or chemist his ingenuity, only at the dictation of his short-sighted and rapacious workmen ...; if a few agitators are to be allowed to command a strike which first paralyses the industry of the peculiar class of workmen over whom they tyrannize, and then extends itself in an increasing circle ... and if all of this is to be unpunished. ... it is in vain to hope that we shall long retain the industry, the skill, or the capital on which our manufacturing superiority, and with the superiority or power, and almost our existence as a nation depends.

Senior recommended giving special powers to factory owners to allow them to "arrest" workers without warrant and making it a crime to solicit union membership.[32] This was a typical argument from Senior. He constantly expressed alarm at the potential consequences of any action that inhibited capital, predicting disastrous consequences.

In 1837, he was a member of a government commission to consider hours of work in manufacturing. Senior made two arguments against regulating maximum hours of work. In the first, he asserted that the fixed capital costs of manufacturing were so high that only the last hour of labour insured the capitalist's profit. Secondly, "the exceeding easiness of cotton-manufacturing labour renders long hours of work *practicable*" and, thus, there was no need to limit such work. Even for the times, Senior's arguments against reducing working hours for children were remarkably harsh. He opposed education instead of labour for children under thirteen, asserting that, "Instead of the vast and airy apartments of a well-regulated factory, they are kept in a small close room; and instead of the light work ... of a factory, which is really not more exercise than a child voluntarily takes, they have to sit on a form, supposed to be studying a spelling book." At a time when children and women normally worked twelve-hour days, he warned that any legislation that "should reduce the present comparatively short hours, must either destroy profit, or reduce wages to the Irish standards." The only other alternative was to increase prices. Here Senior was at his apocalyptic best: if such legislation was passed, he said, "I see as in a map, the succession of causes which will render the cotton manufactures of England mere matter of history."[33] It was another ten years before the government of Lord John Russell would pass a bill limiting the employment of women and children to eleven hours a day.

Senior demonstrated a remarkably harsh approach to any disruption of labour. He called the relationship between the worker and employer "the most important of all political relations" but then argued that the relationship was not "political" at all, but natural; the wage inevitably set by the value of that labour to the employer. As he warned: "[T]he instant the labourer is paid, not according to his *value*, but his *wants*, he ceases to be a freeman. He acquires the indolence, the improvidence, the rapacity, and the malignity, but not the subordination of the slave." Every time worker disturbances led to increased wages such victories only fuelled heightened unrest that would further unbalance this natural bargain: "[W]ho can doubt that he will measure his rights by his wishes, or that his wishes will extend with prospect of gratification? ... A breach has been made in the sea-wall, and with every succeeding irruption they will swell higher and spread more widely."[34]

In commenting on the Captain Swing disturbances among rural workers in the south in the early 1830s, he carried his criticism to ridiculous lengths. We have seen (in chapter 4) that this unrest was the result of numerous long-running grievances among rural workers; the use of thrashing machines was only the most obvious (and perhaps least important). Senior ignored all of the multiple grievances that had led to the outbreaks, focusing exclusively on the protest concerning the displacement of labour. He said, "Thrashing-machines are the present objects of hostility; flails will be next; then ploughs; and afterwards spades, will be found to diminish employment; and when it has been made penal to give advantage to labour by any tool or instrument whatever, the last step must be to prohibit the use of the right-hand."[35]

It was about the Poor Laws and population that Senior was most exercised and where he had his biggest impact. Senior had long been a vehement opponent of the Poor Laws, and, like Malthus, linked their destructive impact to population increase. In his first year of lectures as the Drummond Chair he argued that if the present conditions continued, "the poor rates will annually eat away a larger and larger surplus which otherwise would have gone to the landlord." Soon this would mean the complete destruction of rent. Thus was borne the mostly mythical "pauperized" parish in which estates would be abandoned because the poor rates were so high, a spectre that would haunt discussion of the Poor Laws for the next decade. When one such apparently afflicted parish was eventually found – Cholesbury, Buckinghamshire – out of the over 15,000 parishes in England and Wales, it was continually trotted out as a show horse demonstrating the real menace of the poor rates.[36]

In his 1830 lectures, he proposed that the only immediate palliative would be to encourage emigration but warned there was no indication that poor rural labourers were ready to leave. He suggested this was not surprising "if they are allowed to fix the labour they are to give, and the wages they are to receive; if they are to help themselves, while it lasts, from the whole property of the country, it is too much to expect that they will not prefer idleness, riot, and plunder at home, to subsistence, however ample, to be earned by toil and hardship abroad."[37] As he had when reporting on unions, he painted the implications of parish relief in dramatic colours; predicting the inevitable dissolution of society if it continued. In reporting to Lord Howick on proposals for the establishment of the Poor Laws in Ireland, Senior warned, "The experiment in England has produced a state of things which, if not immediately remedied, threatens the destruction of society." He predicted, "the destruction of industry, providence, and natural affection; the indefinite multiplication of a servile population; fires, riots, and noon-day robbery; the dissolution, in short, of the bonds of civilized society, are the natural, and if not abandoned in time, inevitable consequences."[38]

It appears that Senior's response to Lord Howick, along with the larger impetus caused by the Captain Swing protests, helped push the government to form another commission to examine the Poor Laws; it is not surprising, then, that Senior would be appointed as one of the commissioners. The commission was formed in 1832, the final report was sent to the government in 1834, and the New Poor Law passed later that year.

The New Poor Law and "Moral Plague"

Though ostensibly authored by all seven commissioners, the report was largely written by Nassau Senior and Edwin Chadwick, the latter an ardent follower of, and once private secretary to, Jeremy Bentham. The Poor Law Commissioners Report and Minutes of Evidence of 1834 is for historians a marvellous document. It provides close to 6,000 pages of information and opinion about the condition of the poor in England and Wales; the operations of the Poor Laws; and the opinions of parish poor law officials, farmers, landowners, and others about relief for the poor, the rate of wages, and the industry or indolence of workers. There are thousands of pages of responses from queries sent to officials in thousands of parishes, and more extensive reports from the various Assistant Commissioners sent out to districts throughout the country. It is an immense and valuable source concerning conditions in rural England and Wales in the 1830s.

But the rural poor had no voice at all in the report, and the thousands of pages of appendices that constitute the "evidence" makes distilling that evidence problematic. The responses from the Assistant Commissioners command attention, but these are condensed reports from brief meetings with those involved in supervising relief in some parishes. Many of the Assistant Commissioners complained that they had little time to complete their duties and visited parishes in their districts only briefly or not at all.[39]

More seriously, the Report of the Commissioners seems at times strangely divorced from any serious attempt to assess the evidence. It is hard not to see the report as a compendium of Nassau Senior's beliefs supported by evidence whose collection was skilfully managed and whose presentation was carefully curated to reflect those beliefs. Indeed, it is difficult to find any aspect of the final report, or the 1834 New Poor Law which followed, that differs in any significant way from ideas about the operation of the Poor Laws or their remedy expressed by Nassau Senior before the Commission was begun. As R.H. Tawney once said, the 1834 Report of the Poor Law Commission was a "brilliant, influential, and wildly unhistorical document."[40]

The 1832 Royal Commission into the Operation of the Poor Laws was, of course, not the first commission charged with recommending changes to the Poor Law. In 1817, a House of Commons committee was struck with that intention. Despite extensive consultation with a range of interested parties and reports from parish officers from many parts of the country, the committee provided no recommendations for changing the laws. In their own words, they "could not feel themselves justified in offering suggestions hastily to the House, on questions of acknowledged difficulty ... and on which ... the remedial efforts of the most able and enlightened men have practically failed."[41] This did not prevent them from essentially paraphrasing Malthus's arguments in their summary of the dangers presented by the operations of the Poor Laws. Poor relief, they argued, "with the increase of population which it was calculated to foster" and by suppressing the "natural impulse by which men are instigated to industry and good conduct ... is perpetually encouraging and increasing the amount of misery it was designed to alleviate."[42] The 1817 Committee warned that the poor rates were in danger of soon overwhelming parts of the country, burdening parishes with rates that reduced rents to minimal amounts or prevented landlords from renting their farms at all. But those presenting evidence to the committee offered no clear remedy. The most consistent complaint was against the costs and expenses of the settlement laws; workhouses as a remedy were both encouraged and opposed by parish officials.[43] In the appendices, two presentations made strong recommendations that the most viable means for reducing the poor rates was to provide the poor with land: T.G. Estcourt (who was also a member of the committee) provided evidence that renting one-fourth to one-half of an acre of land to the poor in Wiltshire had moved thirty-two families from the relief rolls; other evidence provided the accounts for a family with a "single cow cottage" in Lincolnshire, suggesting that any prudent inhabitant would receive a net return of over £11 a year and "rarely become chargeable to the parish."[44] Further commissions into the poor laws and rural labourers in the 1820s similarly failed to result in legislation.

It is quite remarkable that the 1834 report was completed and led to legislation, the Poor Law Amendment Act, in record time. The report was commissioned in 1832. Queries were sent to parishes late in that year. Assistant Commissioners were sent out to gather testimony in late 1832 and early 1833; they were meant to report by November of that year, though none did until early in 1834. Nonetheless, a preliminary report was sent to the Lord Chancellor by Senior early in 1833 and the final report was sent to the government in 1834. The new Poor Law Amendment Act was passed in August 1834.

Senior shepherded the report from beginning to end and ensured that its final form would reflect his well-established ideas about the dangers of poor relief. He drafted the queries sent out to parishes and the issues to be examined by the Assistant Commissioners. Senior's instructions to these Assistant Commissioners were designed to shape their reports in ways that reflected his set beliefs. For example, they were to address the question of whether parish officers were diligent in performing their duties. But the instructions already stated his opinion that such local officials did not have the time, experience, or skill necessary to perform their duties well. Senior informed the Assistant Commissioners that the existing parish officials would, most likely, demonstrate "partiality and favouritism to relations, friends, dependants, customers, or debtors of the overseer, or through the desire of general popularity, or through the fear of general unpopularity, or of the hostility of particular individuals." The Assistant Commissioners might have already been prepared to find fault in local parish administration of poor relief; with instructions like these before they set off to conduct their inquiries, they were almost certain to find the results Senior expected.[45]

Recent research has indicated that by far the most important expenditure for poor relief throughout the country was to the aged or those otherwise incapable of work. Relief given to the able-bodied in most parishes was minimal and temporary.[46] Nonetheless, the instructions to the Assistant Commissioners reflected Senior's near obsession with the supposed dangers of relief provided to the able-bodied poor, especially if this were provided outside of workhouses. The Assistant Commissioners were instructed to investigate the operation of existing work or poor houses, especially charged to "ascertain whether any means are adopted to prevent residence in the house from being an object of desire or indifference to the able-bodied poor." The instructions went on to detail the measures that Senior felt would make them less inviting places for the poor.

Not surprisingly, these become the measures the report recommended to the government and were an essential part of the New Poor Laws, all quite clearly determined to be part of the answer before the Assistant Commissioners left to engage in their work. Most importantly, as it turns out, the Assistant Commissioners were instructed to "collect facts and opinions as to the practicality and expediency of an enactment prohibiting, with any and what exceptions, relief to the able-bodied out of the workhouse or poor house in any parish possessing, of having the use of, such an establishment."

Finally, in summing up the instructions to the Assistant Commissioners, Senior detailed what he expected them to find. The "idleness, profligacy, and improvidence, which now debase the character" of labourers in the south was caused either by the changes made to the original intent of the Poor Law or because all attempts at public charity are a "very bad substitute" for private charity. Moreover, he warned that substantial changes to the Poor Law "must be attended with immediate local suffering." But if the Assistant Commissioners find that the "progress of the evil ... may be traced in the diminished cultivation and value of the land; the diminution of industry, forethought and natural affection among labourers ... in the accelerated increase of every form of profligacy; in fires, riots, and organised and almost treasonably robbery and devastation" than they needed to report to the Commissioners that such suffering was necessary.[47] It would be a very obtuse Assistant Commissioner who would not understand that he was expected to return with specific types of evidence.

The Commissioners asserted that they considered the responses to queries sent out to parishes as the "most valuable part of our evidence." They did not, however, attempt a systematic summary of those responses, appending them all to the report as Appendix B. The Commission abstracted responses from a selected set of the questions sent out to parishes – that is, nine of the more than fifty questions – for (alphabetically) the first seven counties in the country. The Commissioners argued that this selection effectively represented the country as a whole, though it was clearly dominated by southern agricultural counties with high relief rates – Bedfordshire, Berkshire, Buckinghamshire, Cambridgeshire being the first four – and the selection of nine questions of interest was, of course, not random. Even so, it is not clear the Commissioners' interpretation of these responses often fit the varied evidence provided even in these seven counties.[48]

Among the nine questions selected were queries about how many people were receiving relief and how they received it. Respondents were asked if workers were more or less obedient and efficient than they had been in the past, did they change employment more frequently, and could they comment on the causes of the "agricultural riots and burnings of 1830 and 1831." Senior argued that these responses showed that operations of the poor law had made labourers less keen and diligent. Yet the responses contained in the supplement were hardly unanimous on this point. W. Hopkins, the overseer in Upwell, Cambridge, for example, said, "I have no reason to complain of their habits of industry. There is, unfortunately, more often a want of work than there should be" and he attributed this to an unwillingness on the part of farmers to invest capital to employ labourers. If there was any clear pattern formed from these responses it was that in the southern districts there was little work to be had. In the other three counties in the supplement there was often little complaint about the industry of labourers. John Whits, the overseer in Alston, Cumberland, reported, "The labourers here are obliged to use much greater exertions than formerly, and indeed much more than is consistent with health, but in doing this, they are quite unable to provide for their families, and they seem altogether in a most deplorable state." Or, as William Steele, the Vestry clerk, in Walton, Cumberland, reported, while they worked very hard, "the hilarity of mind" evidenced by rural labourers in the past was "exchanged for distrust and gloom."[49]

Similarly questionable interpretations from the responses to question 53 were given concerning the causes of the unrest in 1830 and 1831. Senior argued that a large percentage of the responses identified the Poor Laws as the "reason" for the unrest. In fact, while a number of responses indicated that problems around poor relief contributed, other answers included more complex assessment of problems in the distribution of poor relief. And just as often, those who responded to this question stated there had been no unrest in their parish or highlighted worker distress. R. Alinot, the overseer in Turville, Buckinghamshire, said the unrest resulted from "distress so severe in character that drove the rioters to desperation." Even Lord Radnor reported that the causes of the unrest were "the low rates of wages, the harsh treatment of labourers, the desire to depress them; the general feeling of distrust and animosity between agricultural labourers and their employers." Or, as T.W. Hall in St. Mary, Reading, in Berkshire said, "From the best information I could procure, it is my belief that the riotous proceedings of 1830 and 1831 were the acts of the peasantry bowed down to the lowest possible amount of wages on which they could exist ..."[50] In the end only 10 per cent of the parishes in England and Wales presented any evidence to the Commission itself.

In response to a request from the Lord Chancellor in 1833, Senior wrote a letter summarizing what were to be the main recommendations of the Commission. As the Assistant Commissioners had not yet reported, this was ostensibly based on the responses to his queries. Senior reported, "I was prepared to find the System most injurious to the skill and diligence of the labourers, the profits of the farmers, and the rental of the landlords; but on these points also the results of the inquiry are worse than I had anticipated." This preliminary letter recommended the extensive use of well-regulated workhouses because the "dissolute poor hate its cleanliness, its regulations, its confinement, its classification; its labour and its absence of stimulants." Senior also recommended a "more effectual system of rural police."[51]

Reflecting the instructions given them, the reports from the Assistant Commissioners most often warned about the rising costs of poor relief and argued that in many instances such costs were reducing profits for farmers and rents for landowners. They reiterated arguments that such payments, especially supplements for children, prompted early marriage and too many children – an argument perhaps most vividly described by Cameron and Wrottesley:

> the Poor Laws have solved the political problem of how to call into existence the greatest possible number of people with the least amount of employment. ... The parish is a dam whose breast is, or seems to be inexhaustible. Each individual mouth indeed can only draw a slender stream of her unwholesome milk, but every mouth belonging to the litter, no matter how many they be, finds a teat on which it can fasten.[52]

The Assistant Commissioners echoed concerns about the local administration of relief. Most importantly, they reaffirmed Senior's arguments that relief needed to be offered only in centralized workhouses intentionally made abhorrent for those forced to depend on them. All of this, as one would expect, was dutifully included in the final report.

Perhaps most interesting, however, are the findings of the Assistant Commissioners that did not fit with Senior's predilections and thus were not reflected in the final report. Assistant Commissioners were instructed to investigate the provision of small plots of land to the rural poor but were cautioned constantly to keep in mind the need to avoid the creation of subpopulation of poor cottagers similar to Irish cottiers. Remarkably, almost all the reports from the Assistant Commissioners and many of the responses to queries in the parishes provided glowing accounts of the benefits to be derived from providing land to the poor, though a number of them included warnings about not allowing such land to take too much of the sweat of the labourer that should rightly be reserved for the farmers who might employ him. There also appeared to be a general agreement among the Assistant Commissioners that many of farmers opposed the provision of land to labourers. Pringle, whose territory included Southampton and parts of Hampshire, Cumberland, and Westmoreland, reported that farmers feared this "interfered" with their access to labour. There were also a number of witnesses who testified that farmers refused to hire labourers who had taken advantage of opportunities to rent land.[53]

Nonetheless, Okedon, the Assistant Commissioner for Oxfordshire and part of Dorsetshire, reported that in the southeastern part of the latter, some farmers still let cottages with garden land to workers. This, he said, had "done more to preserve the spirit of independence than anything else I have met with"; each cottage coming free had ten to fifteen applicants "all eager and contending for a preference." Okedon suggested such land could be rented at £8 an acre, a significant premium over rents charged to large occupiers.[54]

Majendie, the Assistant Commissioner for East Surrey, East Sussex, Kent, and most of Essex, was even more enthusiastic, and clearer about the detrimental effects on labourers when deprived of land. He said:

> Of the acquisition of land by labourers the effect is invariably beneficial; the character and conduct seem immediately raised, by having means of exerting themselves in some other mode in addition to the uncertain demand for labour. … it can be no secret to them that the crops which may be raised by their exertions on small plots of land are infinitely greater than those produced by ordinary cultivation. The denial of land to them will constantly produce an increase of ill-feeling on their part. … Extraordinary instances of accumulation of capital from small beginnings are reported, and the mere circumstance of enabling a labourer to sell so many days' labour to himself, diminishes the demand either on the farmer's or the parish purse.[55]

Similarly, Power in Cambridge provided the example of the provision of small allotments of a half-acre each to "some of the worst characters" in the parish beginning in 1823. Though the population in the parish had increased by 25 per cent since 1821, the poor rates had fallen by 15 per cent.[56] Moylan, the Assistant Commissioner in Stafford and Chester commented on how the harvests from small allotments near Lichfield were "quite astonishing."[57]

Some of the Assistant Commissioners expressed reservations about the amount of land labourers should get and echoed Senior's concerns about recreating the dreaded Irish model. Okedon warned that any allotment needed to be kept inordinately small – one-sixteenth of an acre – or the labourer "overforces his strength and brings to his employer's labour a body exhausted by his struggle." Dutifully following Senior's admonishments, he followed with an imagined portrait of a country full of hovels, a cottier population like Ireland, and "misery and pauperism everywhere" if more land than this was given to rural labourers.[58] Walcott in North Wales expressed similar concerns about the amount of land labourers should hold.[59] Perhaps Henry Stuart, the Assistant Commissioner for Suffolk and Norfolk, expressed the argument in the way most likely to reinforce Senior's tendencies. He warned:

> It is remarkable, that while many of the evils which afflict society in England arise from the Poor Laws, and in Ireland from a cottier population, it should seem to many benevolent and well-meaning persons that the remedy for each country is to give Poor Laws to Ireland and introduce the cottier system into England; that what is one great cause of mischief in one country, would prove the cure, if transplanted, to the other.[60]

But others downplayed these concerns and explicitly rejected Senior's warnings about increasing a poor cottier population. Majendie argued, to the contrary, the "tendency to reckless improvidence in marriage seems rather to be checked by placing before the labourer something to look forward to beyond the resource of daily labour for a master."[61] Moylan was equally adamant that only good could come from providing the rural poor with land:

> I look upon the acquisition of a freehold in land by the labouring man, to be an object worthy of the highest encouragement. ... I confess I do not apprehend from it the danger of creating a cottier population *resembling that of Ireland*. The division of land in small farms at *exorbitant rents* is an indisputable evil. ... Encouraging the labourer of this country to become the owner of an inheritance (I care not how small) which he may transmit to his children, is quite another question, and one which, in my humble judgement, has not received the notice it deserves. Let us rather hope to create a cottier population resembling that of Protestant Switzerland, of those parts of the South of France, where proprietors possess often *less* than an acre of ground, and where contentment and morality are apparent even to a passing stranger like myself.[62]

Senior, Chadwick, and the other Commissioners were free to interpret and present all of this information however they wished in their final report. Not surprisingly the final version differed little from Senior's already well-known views or from his preliminary recommendations to the Lord Chancellor composed before the Assistant Commissioners had testified. The report argued that the Poor Laws "educated a new generation in idleness, ignorance and dishonesty." Further:

> It appears to the pauper that the Government has undertaken to repeal, in his favour, the ordinary laws of nature; to enact that the children shall not suffer for the misconduct of the parents—the wife for that of the husband, or the husband for that of the wife: that no one shall lose the means of a comfortable subsistence, whatever his indolence, prodigality, or vice; in short, that the penalty which, after all, must be paid by someone for idleness and improvidence, is to fall, not on the guilty person or his family but on the proprietors of the lands and the houses encumbered by his settlement. Can we wonder if the uneducated are seduced into approving a system which aims its allurements at all the weakest parts of our nature – which offers marriage to the young, security to the anxious, ease to the lazy, and impunity to the profligate?[63]

Not surprisingly, the central focus of the Commission's report was to prevent the provision of relief to the able-bodied. While the report referred to many aspects of the Poor Laws as "evil"; the provision of assistance to the able-bodied was variously described as the "master evil," the "vital evil," the "greatest evil," the "central evil," and the "most pressing evil" of that system.[64] Thus, their first recommendation was that with some minor exceptions "all relief whatever to able-bodied persons or to their families otherwise than in well-regulated work-houses ... shall be deemed unlawful, and shall cease." In justifying this the re-port repeated Young's harsh arguments from almost seventy years earlier: "The express or implied ground of his application is, that he is in danger of perishing from want. Requesting to be rescued from that danger out of the property of others, he must accept assistance on the terms, whatever they may be, which the common welfare requires."[65]

Local Poor Law officials were too easily intimidated into "mal-adminis-tration" of the existing laws. Thus, the second recommendation was for the creation of a Central Board to administer the Poor Laws, naming Assistant Commissioners as necessary. This Board and the Commissioners would be "empowered and directed to frame and enforce the regulations for the govern-ment of workhouses ... such regulations shall, as far as may be practicable, be uniform throughout the country." Parishes were to be required to "incorpo-rate with others for the purposes of workhouse management" sending their own poor to centralized workhouses and paying a proportionate amount of the expenses.[66] This centralization of authority for parish relief was a major change. Though legislation in the 1700s had made it possible for parishes to create unions for the purposes of supporting workhouses, this had not had a wide impact and relief remained primarily a parish concern. As we have seen, workers protested even when the parish hired paid assistant overseers rather than having Poor Law decisions made by parish vestries or by unpaid neigh-bours placed temporarily in the position of overseers.

The Board would "fix a maximum consumption per head" for residents of the workhouses but would leave it to local officers to reduce costs below this amount "if they can safely do so." Those in workhouses would be separated into the old and really impotent, children, and the able-bodied. Men and women would be separated, even married couples. The Board would have the power to "apprentice" children where they saw fit. Any funds given in relief to the able-bodied should be considered a loan, to be repaid through "attachment to subsequent wages."[67] This was indeed a draconian re-invention of the poor re-lief, and it bears the imprint of Senior at every step.

Though the most consistent recommendation from the Assistant Com-missioners and from the responses to queries about what might help reduce poverty was the provision of land to the rural poor, the Commission did not recommend this. Instead, it argued that since it had been shown that labourers would pay more for small plots of land than larger occupiers any such provision could be left to free operation of the market and "the necessity for any public inquiry on these points seem [sic] to be at an end."[68]

The Poor Law Amendment Act was passed in August 1834, barely two weeks after the report was completed. Though Parliament did not accept all the recommendations from the report, the act bore its imprint and followed its rationale. Edwin Chadwick described it as an experiment in government administration for the treatment of a "moral plague."[69] Instead of a Central Board, it created a Poor Law Commission with three commissioners. Edwin Chadwick was named Secretary to the Commission. The central item in the new law was the denial of out-door relief and a reliance on centralized workhouses, deliberately made repugnant to those forced to enter them; or, in the words of the Second Annual Report of the Poor Law Commissioners, where they could be assured those in the workhouse were "not advanced to a condition above those who maintain themselves by the fruits of their own independent labour."[70] Only those over sixty were to receive tea; there was to be no fraternizing between the sexes, even husband and wives in the same house, and, of course, inhabitants of the workhouses were not free to come and go. Over 15,000 parishes were now organized into 531 unions. Instead of applying to a neighbour or the local parish curate and local farmers for relief, the destitute now needed to apply to a Union Relieving Officer, who after the law, might be responsible for 15–20 parishes. Keith Snell reported that one such officer took one minute for each case that came before him.[71]

Senior's role in shepherding the Commission's report into legislation was outlined in the *Economist*'s obituary: "[I]t was Mr. Senior principally who, when the Ministers shrank aghast from the completeness and consistently logical principle of the measure recommended ... gradually screwed their courage to the sticking point, and by his pertinacity and persuasiveness succeeded at once in convincing their loose understandings and their timid nerves."[72]

"Confined like a Felon without any Crime"

Felix Driver has argued the union workhouse "was designed to accomplish ... a revolution in the moral arithmetic of pauperism."[73] As Norman Longmate has suggested, "a visitor new to England might have supposed that the whole of the English countryside had been swept up by some gigantic crime-wave and that these were vast jails, run up hastily to accommodate a whole army of prisoners."[74] In some ways this was indeed the case. The workhouses were only the most obvious representation of a system which increasingly sought to criminalize poverty and the poor and to use that criminalization to enforce industry. As James Reynolds, who was in a workhouse in the 1840s, wrote:

> I sometimes look up to the bit of blue sky
> High over my head, with a tear in my eye.
> Surrounded by walls that are too high to climb
> Confined like a felon without any crime.[75]

The self-congratulatory reports from the Poor Law Commissioners in the first few years after the passage of the law reflect the relationship between the brutality of the law and disciplining labour. Assistant Commissioner Hall reported in 1836 that in response to the law, "There is a very general increase in the habits of industry among the labouring classes. Persons who could never be made to work before have become good labourers. ... the workhouse is held in great dread." Assistant Commissioner Stevens suggested that the labourers were "a very different race of people from what they were, altogether more obliging in manner."[76] Following the terrible winter of 1836–7, during which early snows had ended farming operations and thrown many rural labourers out of work, the Poor Law Commissioners warned it was precisely during such times of "general distress" that poor law officials needed to be most vigorous in their application of the new principles, "Tales of distress will be believed, not because they are verified, but because they are highly probable." They were cheered, however, by the fact that they knew of no instance in which any union workhouse had been filled "by an influx of able-bodied paupers" though the Assistant Commissioners could point to numerous examples of supposedly destitute workers who had applied for relief but refused to accept entry to the workhouse.[77]

The *Times* asserted that to get into a workhouse, labourers needed to have local farmers sign off to prove there was no work to be had. According to the *Times* correspondent, farmers would hold this as a threat over the labourers. "Some farmers would offer very low wages and refuse to sign off if the labourer refused to work for wages he could not subsist on."[78] Other reports from the countryside indicate the scale of opposition to the workhouses and the brutal consequences of the new law: children eating grass and living in holes dug in hay ricks to avoid entering the workhouse; the poor falling to their knees and offering prayers when, not infrequently, poor houses under construction burned down; old couples starving themselves to the point of death to avoid separation in a workhouse. Nonetheless, to a certain extent, the system had less effect than one might expect simply because it proved to be too brutal. Though the Commission could disallow expenditures, parishes consistently refused to send all those seeking relief to the workhouse and nowhere in England did the majority of the able-bodied receiving relief do so in workhouses, though the percentage came close in some parts of southern England in the 1840s. Confinement in a workhouse proved, in the long run, to be inordinately expensive compared to bits of relief provided to those at home.

The brutality of the workhouses, and especially the misery of the rations provided to those confined in them, led to a series of well-publicized scandals that meant even some of those who had most ardently supported them no longer did so. The language of Poor Law Commissioner Reports and not infrequent special inquiries into workhouse abuse turned from praising the changes in the law to expressing concerns over the effects of its application. Newspapers, particularly the *Times*, provided regular coverage of atrocities associated with the poor laws.

The most notorious of these scandals was in the union house at Andover. Workhouses had been provided with a series of six "Dietaries" (or minimal meal plans) to choose from when supplying food to the inhabitants of the houses. Even after the original ones were supplemented in subsequent years, the amount and quality of the food provided to the poor in the houses was still staggeringly insufficient. All workhouse inmates were expected to work; one of the jobs in a number of workhouses was to crush bones to create bone meal for fertilizer. In the Andover Union House, conditions culminated in what might have been the expected result. Men forced to work in crushing bones were so hungry on the rations provided that they were reduced to gnawing on the old bones. There had been reports of similar practices elsewhere for some years, but no clear public testimony. In the case of the Andover Union, however, a Select Committee of Inquiry had been called to look into allegations of dishonesty and excessive cruelty that had been lodged against the Master of the Workhouse, a Mr. McDougall. In the course of the enquiry there was testimony not only that the poor had been eating the gristle and marrow from the bones they were to break, but that others had been reduced to eating food that had been "thrown to the hogs and fowls." A *Times* reporter had been attending the hearings and reported on the atrocities. One of the witnesses to the committee said he doubted the public would have heard of the practice had it not been for the newspapers' reports.[79]

The Report of the Select Committee into the Andover Union marks a change in the approach to the New Poor Law. While the Committee pointed to misconduct on the part of the Master of the Workhouse and a lack of attention by the Guardians in contributing to the conditions at Andover, many of the Select Committee's complaints reflected misgivings about the intent of the law itself, criticizing harsh treatment and rigid approaches to applications for relief that forced people to accept lower wages rather than enter the workhouse. They also cited degrading conditions and work in the houses themselves that "prevent the really destitute from entering the Union house, and is not consistent with a mild and considerate administration of the law."[80] Partly as a result of these scandals, revision to the Poor Law Act in 1847 replaced the Poor Law Commission with a Poor Law Board and some of the most hated aspects of the law were removed, especially that which separated married couples in the houses. Nonetheless, the workhouses remained and the attacks on the "moral plague" represented by the destitute poor continued into the twentieth century.

At the beginning of its coverage of the Andover Union inquiry, the *Times* editorialized:

We have noticed on Saturday another secret inquiry by an Assistant Poor Law Commissioner into one of those deaths from destitution and neglect which are becoming so frequent in this country. Such events and such inquiries would, but a comparatively short time since, have been considered ... alien to the national character; but the operation of the Malthusian law has rendered these occurrences too familiar to occasion surprise or astonishment. The rapidity with which these Poor Law horrors press upon one another renders it somewhat difficult to deal in detail with cases as they arise.[81]

By then, however, a new and energetic purveyor of the science of political economy had emerged: the *Economist* newspaper. For the next twenty years, it applied a simplified distillation of Smith and Malthus as a salve on the open sores of early capitalism and empire. Not surprisingly, Nassau Senior figured prominently in the mix.

PART THREE

The *Economist* and a Political Economy "Ordained by Providence"

Chapter Seven

The *Economist*: "The Most Elementary Truths"

On 1 August 1843, a new paper was announced to the British public. The prospectus for *The Economist: The Political, Commercial, Agricultural and Free Trade Journal* promised a weekly paper appearing every Saturday in a morning and expanded afternoon edition. The paper celebrated the fact that "wealth and capital have been rapidly increasing … science and art have been working the most surprising miracles in aid of the human family." Nonetheless, it worried that despite this progress people seemed trapped in "unprecedented depression, anxiety, and uneasiness." The *Economist* argued that the only means for relieving this despair was to "emancipate commerce and industry from those trummels and restrictions with which short-sighted jealousies and unwise legislation have fettered them." The paper dedicated itself to popularizing the truths of political economy. Its most immediate goal was to support popular movements for free trade and, particularly, to end the Corn Laws, which restricted the import of grain. The prospectus declared that "FREE TRADE … will do more than any other visible agent to extend civilisation and morality throughout the world." In promoting the ideas of political economy and the advantages of free trade, the *Economist* declared that they were not driven by party interest; indeed they said, "we are of no class, or rather of every class."[1]

Since then, the *Economist* has had a surprising run and been tremendously influential. The contemporary weekly likes to extol its long history. It might be less ready to acknowledge its spotty record on issues to do with labour, race, and slavery. It did have an almost immediate impact when launched in 1843. By October 1845, the paper had doubled in size; the editor arguing that this was due to the dramatic increase in circulation and the demands of its readers for more information.[2] By 1847, its circulation had reached 4,000, a more than respectable number for a specialized weekly.[3] It changed a bit along the way in these first few years: at the beginning of 1845 the title was changed to *The Economist, Weekly Commercial Times, and Bankers' Gazette. A Political, Literary and General Newspaper.* As if this title was not clumsy enough, in October

Portrait of Hon. James Wilson by Frederick Stacpoole, after Sir John Watson-Gordon, mezzotint, published 1860 (NPG D37025). © National Portrait Gallery, London

of that year a separate section on railways was added. Thus, the full title of the paper from October 1845 to the end of the period we will discuss here was *The Economist, Weekly Commercial Times, Bankers' Gazette and Railway Monitor. A Political, Literary, and General Newspaper.*

Some things did not change. The founding editor, James Wilson, kept a close watch on the content of the paper from its inception until a few years before his death in 1860. The paper always published its material anonymously – not uncommon at the time – and despite the contribution of a range of authors, Wilson worked hard to maintain a consistent tone and approach. One constant focus was on the use of statistics as a buttress for arguments. As the paper suggested on the occasion of the publication of its first Monthly Statistical Supplement in November 1843: "Many have an impression that Statistics are dull and uninteresting; but such can only exist with those who are contented to look on long arrays of figures without reading them and learning the results, or the truths they teach ... what old prejudices and errors they dissipate."[4] The paper also worked hard to maintain the impression that their opinions and arguments were the result of calm and rational consideration of various sides of disputes. That an array of statistics and such dispassionate consideration always led to an argument favouring the interests of capital, touting the benefits of free trade, and warning against any restrictions on capital and the employment of labour only proved to the paper and, presumably, many of its readers the inherent truths of such approaches.

The *Economist* thus provides us with interesting and useful insights into the arguments used by those who would further the interests of capital. Its writers sought to use their interpretation of political economy, at times carried to almost caricatural heights, to argue for complete freedom for capital – freedom from government restrictions, from tariffs and duties, from the drag of custom and tradition, from any unwarranted demands by labour except those that the iron law of supply and demand entailed, and, as Wilson made clear in his leaders, from any of the demands of morality. For while the *Economist* might promise in its prospectus that free trade would "extend civilisation and morality around the world," the paper would time and again dismiss calls for moral decisions about society and the economy with arguments that, "As political economists … we do not lecture on morals here."[5] Or, again, "If the great principle of self-love may be relied on in business, it will surely not be found defective in morals."[6] One is reminded of Ravenstone's warnings about the dangers of such an easy path to the temple of virtue.

The *Economist* directed much of its attention to the changes this new liberalism demanded in the countryside; its raison d'être after all was the elimination of the Corn Laws, mostly accomplished by 1846. But it extended these concerns to include attacks on traditional landowners over what they considered vestiges of feudal practices. It campaigned for longer, more favourable leases for capitalist tenant farmers and championed agricultural improvement, now often called "high" farming. It most vigorously denied any suggestion that peasant farming could be productive or benefit the rural poor and ardently opposed providing rural labourers with land. Rural labourers needed to place their faith in heightened demand for their labour; a demand that would somehow materialize despite the labour-savings inherent in high farming. Or, rural labourers needed to abandon their romantic attachment to place and migrate to those areas needing their services. For the *Economist*, impressions of heightened poverty and distress in rural England were either erroneous or the result of yet imperfect applications of unrestricted trade and the freedom for capital. Increased inequality thus became a necessary stage toward greater prosperity which would, eventually – trust them – encompass all; for had not Smith promised "universal opulence" as the reward for the division of labour?

The paper did not restrict itself to arguments about England. It necessarily, in its view, sought to pave the way for freedom for capital in agriculture in all the far-flung corners of the world in which British capitalists were increasingly involved. It was an influential voice in proposing legislation for and fostering attitudes towards Ireland, especially in and around the years of famine and unrest associated with the collapse of the potato harvest in the second half of the 1840s. Wilson and William Rathbone Greg's deep connections to cotton manufacturers in Manchester meant the supply of cotton from the American South and the expanded slavery that accompanied its cultivation were important and recurring topics in the paper; the *Economist* always professed to detest slavery but this never seemed to interfere with a stance consistently favouring the break-up of the United States and the independence of the Confederate states. It was partly its ties to cotton that prompted the *Economist*'s close association with British interests in India, as well. Indeed, James Wilson died in India in 1860 while serving as the Financial Minister for the Council of India after the Great Indian Rebellion of 1857.

This next section details in four chapters the impact of this most influential apostle of inequality from its founding in 1843 to just after the death of Wilson. This chapter discusses the founding of the *Economist* and the writers involved in its production in the first two decades, and outlines the *Economist*'s approach to political economy, capital, government regulation, and progress. The second chapter in this section explores the paper's arguments about agriculture and agricultural labour. Despite increasing support for the efficiency of peasant agriculture among some important elements of English society, the *Economist* steadfastly opposed the allocation of land to peasant cultivators and argued strongly for the benefits of a purely capitalist agricultural regime. When faced with evidence of continued distress among agricultural labourers, the paper blamed the lingering effects of the Corn Laws, the continued dangers of the Poor Laws, and the myopia of traditional landlords. Remedies for such distress were always best to be found in a dependence on wage labour or abandoning the countryside. Chapter 9 analyses the paper's writing on Ireland and the *Economist*'s influential campaigns to restrict relief, unencumber estates, foster increased repression of rural unrest, and free Ireland to the discipline of the market. Chapter 10 discusses the *Economist*'s writing on cotton, slavery, and India. Over time, the failure of the market to foster the changes desired by the *Economist* led increasingly to arguments blaming the inability of "backward" races and cultures to succumb appropriately to the discipline of the market.

The Motley Crew

Currently, the publishing empire surrounding the *Economist* has a significant global reach. According to the company's website the paper has a circulation of close to 1.7 million and "is read by more of the world's political and business leaders than any other magazine." The paper has never been shy about trumpeting its own success or claiming influence. Nonetheless, despite its somewhat grandiose early title, it had limited circulation until almost a century after its first publication. It met with some immediate success and by 1847, its circulation had reached just over 4,000. But it soon fell below that and remained there until near the end of the century. Indeed, after the founding editor left the position in 1857 to concentrate on political office and government positions, the paper steadily lost influence. By the 1860s, it was much less compelling, despite the prestige of its editor, Walter Bagehot, not finding its footing comfortably again until the early twentieth century.[7]

Its early success was a function of its stance on some important political questions and its ties to the Anti-Corn Law League, but that success was also partly the result of lively and compelling writing by an interesting and diverse set of characters. The motley crew of writers was occasionally difficult for Wilson to herd, to make them reflect the coherent tone on which he insisted; but their writing was often engaging and occasionally one or two of them were able to slip something radical by the careful eye of Wilson. The crew included, among others, the sometimes-activist financer Lord Radnor; the founding editor, James Wilson; the sub-editor for some of this period, Herbert Spencer; and the writers – W. Rathbone Greg, Thomas Hodgskin, and Nassau Senior.

The paper was bankrolled by Lord Radnor, and he intended it to be primarily engaged in pushing for the end of the Corn Laws. The Earl of Radnor, William Pleydell-Bouverie, represented Salisbury in the House and was Vice-Lieutenant of the County of Wiltshire in south England. Radnor, whose attempts to restrict the gleaning of his fields for his prized pigs caused such an uproar in 1839 (described in chapter 4), was in the minority of large landowners in England in opposing the Corn Laws. The Corn Laws had been amended in 1815 to provide for a sliding scale of import duties on grain depending on the internal price. The duties protected domestic producers and helped landlords charge higher rents to tenant farmers, while increasing the costs for workers and other consumers.

Radnor was also somewhat distinct in that he opposed many other aspects of rural life he considered to be remnants of feudalism and privilege. He regularly lectured his tenants about the need to vote independently, not just follow his lead. He was an advocate for improved agriculture and modern leases and against provisions preventing tenants from eliminating troublesome game. He was also staunchly opposed to garden allotments for agricultural labourers and the provision of minimum wages. Radnor regularly wrote letters to the *Economist*, always, of course, reprinted with much demonstrated respect. It was clear, especially in the early years, that the paper carefully reflected Radnor's position on many issues.

James Wilson was not an obvious choice as founder and editor of a paper dedicated to the ideas of political economy. His father, a Quaker, was a woollen manufacturer in Hawick, Scotland. James Wilson was apprenticed while young to a hat manufacturer in the town. The business was soon purchased by Wilson's father for James and his brother. They transferred the business to London and James bought out his brother, but by 1837, due to the loss of most of his capital through speculating in indigo futures, he was near bankruptcy. The business struggled on. In 1839, though, he wrote his first pamphlet on political issues, this one attacking the Corn Laws. After two further pamphlets, Wilson sought a career as a writer, first approaching the *Examiner* newspaper about special editions. On being rejected, he established the *Economist* with the backing of Lord Radnor. In 1844, he sold what was left of his hat-making business and invested the money in the new venture. Success was such that he was soon able to repay Lord Radnor's loans.

Lord Radnor also paved Wilson's entry into politics. In 1847, Wilson was elected (barely) as a Whig/Liberal in Westbury, Wiltshire, which was Radnor's county. He was soon appointed as a Secretary to the Board of Control that oversaw East India Company business along with the Court of Directors of the company by Lord John Russell's government. He held his seat in the elections of 1852, though Russell's government was voted out. Later that decade, with Liberals back in power, he was appointed Financial Secretary of the Treasury. In 1858, the government asked him to take on the new position of the Financial Member of the Council of India as the government took direct control of the region from the East India Company following the rebellion. In 1859, he left for India with his wife and three of his daughters. He died there on 11 August 1860 of dysentery, partly because of his refusal to leave the heat of Calcutta as he battled to save his proposed income tax for India in the face of opposition.[8]

Wilson lived a life of prim Victorian respectability. He worked hard, responsibly carrying out a multiplicity of duties and endeavours with little fanfare. This was an attitude he expected the paper also to reflect. Wilson left the Quakers in 1832, joining the Anglican Church under the influence of his devout wife, Elizabeth Preston. They had six daughters, two of whom, Eliza and Julia, married writers associated with the paper. Eliza married Walter Bagehot and Julia married William Rathbone Greg.

Wilson was the dominant force in the paper, writing most of the major articles through the *Economist*'s first few years. Even after taking public office he continued to write the leaders and supervise the whole paper.[9] But he relied on a rather mismatched group of writers and associate editors to bring out the paper each week: Greg was born into one of the wealthiest cotton manufacturing families in Britain; Hodgskin had been a fairly well-known anarchist writer; Herbert Spencer was an almost destitute and disgraced railway engineer who would later be seen as the father of Social Darwinism. Senior, whom we have already met, was the only one who might be called an economist. What tied these men together (and to Wilson and Radnor) was a political philosophy of radical self-reliance and steadfast opposition to the Corn Laws. Most of them also came from religious nonconformist families.

For a decade, Greg was the workhorse of the paper along with Wilson. Greg's father, Samuel, owned a number of large cotton mills, most notably Quarry Bank Mill in Cheshire. By the 1820s, his five mills employed more than 2,000 people, making him one of the biggest textile manufacturers in the country. The Greg mills relied principally on child labour, most farmed out from local poor houses. In 1816, 70 per cent of the workforce were children; remarkably, they made up 55 per cent of the labour force in the Greg family's mills as late as 1855, long after other mills had stopped using children.[10] Along with child labour, Greg's mills – like most British cotton mills – relied on American slavery. Much of the capital for the early mills came from plantations the family owned in the West Indies. The Gregs were also closely connected to the Rathbone family out of Liverpool (W.R.'s sister, Elizabeth, married William Rathbone V, and, of course, W.R. was named after the family). Though Quaker, reformist, and anti-slavery activists, the Rathbones were also the first Liverpool merchants to begin importing cotton from America.[11]

The family fortunes began to decline with the death of Samuel in 1834, when the mills were divided among his four sons. Those of William Rathbone Greg and his closest brother, Samuel Jr., were in particular difficulty by the 1840s. William Rathbone blamed his trouble on labour agitation and he and his brothers were vehemently anti-labour and anti-democratic. In 1850, he sold the Bury mill he inherited for a fraction of what his father paid for it.

According to most sources, Wilson asked Greg to write for the *Economist* after discussions they had around Ireland at the beginning of the potato famine in 1846.[12] But it is almost certain that Wilson had communicated with Greg previously around the question of the Corn Laws. In 1842, Greg had written a prize-winning pamphlet on the Corn Laws, detailing the harm high grain prices inflicted on manufacturers. The Greg family were important in the anti–Corn Law meetings in Manchester; the elder brother Robert Hyde Greg was particularly involved.[13] Before 1846, the *Economist* was obsessed with reporting on these meetings. The Greg family had also been prominent in their opposition to legislation on factory labour, a subject dear to the *Economist* as well. Samuel Greg Jr. had been an important informant for Nassau Senior when he was part of the Royal Commission on Factory Regulation Act in which Senior opposed limiting the hours of the of labour for women and children in the 1830s. The eldest brother, Robert Hyde Greg, had been particularly important in agitation against the legislation.[14] And, as early as 1844, Wilson wrote in glowing terms about a pamphlet Greg had written on free trade with the colonies.[15] Greg, like Wilson, also wrote often about the dangers of expanding the franchise.[16] Greg's vehement anti-labour and anti-democratic ideas frequently found their way into the paper. Though perhaps more harshly expressed than those of Wilson, Greg's ideas probably differed little from Wilson's. Walter Bagehot argued that Greg was adept at turning Wilson's ideas into articles.[17] It seems clear that Wilson was drawn to Greg as a writer for the paper because of multiple points of agreement.

Greg wrote for the paper until 1856. After that, Wilson, from his position in the Treasury, arranged a sinecure for Greg as a Commissioner of Customs. Greg continued to work for the Civil Service until his retirement in 1877. Along with being a close professional associate of James Wilson, Greg was a frequent guest at the Wilson house. Greg, whose wife, Lucy Henry, was eventually committed to a mental asylum and with whom he spent little time, developed a long relationship with Wilson's daughter, Julia, marrying her after his wife's death in 1873.[18]

"Delightful characteristics ... contradicted by every page of history"

Perhaps the most surprising writer for the *Economist* was Thomas Hodgskin. Hodgskin was born and lived in poverty. His father worked in the naval yards and Hodgskin shipped out to sea as a cabin boy when he was twelve years old. He sailed for twelve years and "retired" as a half-pay officer when he was twenty-five. After a brief stint at the University of Edinburgh and some flirtation with utilitarianism, Hodgskin helped found the Mechanics' Institute, a popular adult school at which he gave regular lectures. He was drawn to ideas of political economy, but soon expanded on those to present arguments similar to those of Piercy Ravenstone about the way capital could distort societal balance and command more and more labour. Throughout his life, he was most concerned about the way such distortion led to laws that criminalized workers' struggles. A combination of utilitarianism, concern for the rights of labour, and suspicion of the institutions of government and society, led him to embrace a form of self-reliant anarchism.[19]

Hodgskin wrote three works of some importance before he began his stint with the *Economist*: *Labour Defended Against the Claims of Capital* in 1825, *Popular Political Economy* in 1827, and *The Natural and Artificial Rights of Property Contrasted* in 1832. Though these works were largely ignored, they had some lasting – and perhaps appropriately contradictory – impact: his ideas profoundly influenced both Karl Marx and Herbert Spencer.

In *Labour Defended*, Hodgskin, like Ravenstone, sought to unveil the sleight of hand that promised magic from capital and demonstrate that even fairy dust could not make the dominance of capital beneficial to the worker. Hodgskin argued, "All that we are compelled to suffer, all that we have inflicted on us, has been done for the advantage of capital." Hodgskin asserted that according to the arguments of the time, the absence of capital was purported to be the cause of poverty and suffering. For Hodgskin, "Under the influence of such notions, no laws for the protection of capital are thought too severe."[20] And, yet, let the workers begin to hint at combining to force higher wages or better working conditions and the full weight of the law would fall on them. Channelling Ravenstone, Hodgskin said, "One is almost tempted to believe that capital is a sort of cabalistic word, like Church or State, or any of those general terms which are invented by those who fleece the rest of mankind to conceal the hand that shears them. It is a sort of idol before which men must prostate themselves."[21]

Hodgskin also attacked Malthus's *Principles of Population*, arguing instead that an increase in population led to increased ingenuity and energy. It is this exertion and this ingenuity that increased food production and the promotion of happiness. Moreover, increased population also reduced social tensions as "collision rubs down and tames passions."[22]

Hodgskin's great project was to demonstrate how criminal law was an invention to protect the interests of capital. He worked on this most of his life, like Smith did with his promised volume on laws, never producing the final product. But Hodgskin, like Smith and his *Lectures in Jurisprudence*, provided a foretaste in a series of letters published as *The Natural and Artificial Right of Property Contrasted*. Like Ravenstone he warned that the "right of property … is now arming the land-owner and the capitalist against the peasant and the artisan" and warned that the struggle by workers made criminal by laws that prevented them from providing for their families would be the great dispute of the next two generations. He took issue with other philosophers – such as Bentham and James Mill – who argued that laws were a necessary evil "which curbs our naturally evil passions and desires (they adopting the doctrine of the priests, that the desires and passions of man are naturally evil) – which checks ambition, sees justice done, and encourages virtue. Delightful characteristics! which have the single fault of being contradicted by every page of history."[23]

Hodgskin had seven children and needed to write for a diverse set of newspapers to try to make ends meet, but his background does not immediately suggest that he would be a good fit for the *Economist*. He might have come to Wilson's attention through some of his various writing exploits, such as his regular articles for the *Morning Chronicle*. Wilson also occasionally wrote for the *Chronicle*, and they may well have crossed paths there. Hodgskin also gave lectures at the Mechanic's Institute and elsewhere opposing the Corn Laws; one of those lectures was published as a pamphlet in 1843. Hodgskin's opposition to "idle capitalists" and his defence of workers' rights caused him some trouble with both Greg and Wilson, and he was eventually let go after a split with Wilson. Nonetheless, his stance against the Corn Laws and an anarchist sentiment that championed individualism, self-reliance, and an abhorrence of government intervention did fit well with many of Wilson's predilections. He wrote for the paper from 1844 until 1857.

Though Hodgskin continued to work on his intended study of jurisprudence and occasionally contributed pieces on law to the paper, after leaving the

Economist he did not prosper. His work on law attracted little attention. The French writer Elie Halèvy says that a lecture entitled "Our Chief Crime" meant to outline many of his most important arguments attracted few people. He died in 1869 at 82. Halèvy remarked that not one London newspaper published a notice of his life and death on the occasion;[24] certainly not the *Economist*, then under the direction of the former banker Walter Bagehot.

Hodgskin did have a major impact on one other member of the crew. Herbert Spencer eventually became by far the most famous and the most influential of them. Before joining the paper, however, Spencer was perhaps the least accomplished of the writers and had the smallest impact on the paper while there. Unlike the other writers recruited to the paper in its early days, the young Spencer did not come to Wilson's attention primarily through publications opposing the Corn Laws (though he did produce a small pamphlet entitled *The Proper Sphere of Government* in 1843) – but rather from family connections. Spencer's father founded a nonconformist religious school but lost much of the family fortune in the lace industry when Herbert was quite young. Herbert was raised mostly by his uncle, Thomas Spencer, who was an ardent Anti–Corn Law League member. Through his uncle Spencer got started as civil engineer in railway construction; by 1844, though, he was working to provide technical "cover" for a railway huckster, W.B. Pritchard. Spencer advised his family not to invest in Pritchard's fanciful schemes but stayed in his employ until Pritchard was forced into bankruptcy in 1846. By 1848, Spencer was in rather desperate financial straits. Through the intervention of his uncle, Wilson offered him the position of subeditor at the paper. Spencer also took advantage of Wilson's offer of lodgings on the top floor of the paper's building on Wellington Street in London. In 1853, his uncle died, leaving him an estate of some size, and Spencer left the paper. Through his writings adapting Darwin's ideas of evolution to human society and fashioning a kind of heartless code of "survival of the fittest" he became perhaps the most popular philosopher of the later nineteenth century, influential in everything from poor law reform to the eugenics movement.

If we are to believe Spencer's own account, he did little real work while at the *Economist* and was particularly pleased that he was seldom overseen by Wilson, though in his autobiography he mentions dining with Wilson and Greg on more than one occasion. It was Hodgskin, though, who was his closest friend and confidante at the paper, often holding long conversations in the evening in Spencer's lodgings. Spencer had published a couple of pamphlets about the need to restrict the scope of government before beginning at the paper. While there, however, he finished his first major work, *Social Statics: or, the conditions essential to human happiness specified, and the first of them developed.* There were multiple influences evident in this work. It relied most heavily on a rather crude understanding of Malthus's arguments, carried to extremes even the Reverend would find disturbing. It argued vehemently against government intervention, and it ranted against the Poor Law and any assistance to the poor. Spencer's most insistent point, one he would pursue again and again in further writings, was that nature's punishments of the poor were the necessary corrections of a "universal system":

> Pervading all of Nature we may see at work a stern discipline which is a little cruel that it may be very kind ... when regarded in connexion with the interests of universal humanity, these harsh fatalities are seen to be full of beneficence ... Spurious philanthropists ... to prevent misery, would entail greater misery on future generations. ... Blind to the fact that under the natural law of things society is constantly excreting its unhealthy, imbecile, slow, vacillating, faithless members, these unthinking well-meaning men advocate an interference which not only stops the purifying process, but even increases the vitiation – absolutely encouraging the multiplication of the reckless and incompetent by offering them unfailing provision and ... bequeath to posterity a continually increasing curse.[25]

While much of Spencer's argument is carried to an extreme, many of the ideas in this work, especially those surrounding strict limits to the government, the need for a form of radical self-reliance, and concepts about the way individuals were adapting, slowly and with some pain, to a new industrial society, fit well with the ideas of Wilson and, especially, Hodgskin. David Wiltshire has argued that Hodgskin was "the greatest single influence on Spencer's thought" and "almost the whole of *Social Statics* could be interpreted as an elaboration of the theories of Thomas Hodgskin."[26] While some biographers inexplicably do not mention either Hodgskin or the *Economist* in the formation of Spencer's ideas,[27] Spencer himself attests otherwise. He says, "I think I may say that the character of my later career was mainly determined by the conceptions which were initiated, and the friendships which were formed, between the times at which my connexion with *The Economist* began and ended."[28]

With Nassau Senior, David Mitchell Aird as manager and sometimes writer on financial issues, Richard Holt Hutton and Walter Bagehot, and Sir George Cornewall Lewis, this was mostly the cast of characters that published the paper out of its busy office on the Strand in London. But what did they write and how did it influence the dispossession of the poor in England in the middle of the nineteenth century at the tail end of the 'agricultural revolution'?

"Political Economy Won't Do ... Try it in Siberia"

As indicated in the prospectus, the *Economist* dedicated itself to popularizing ideas of political economy. Every week, it promised leading articles "in which free trade principles will be most rigidly applied to all important questions of the day," along with "an article on the elementary principles of political economy, applied in a familiar and popular manner to practical experience." In these pursuits it necessarily both simplified and distilled complex ideas about political economy, seeking to fit such arguments to a multitude of issues. While it mentioned many political economists, it most often referred back to Smith and Malthus as "the masters of economic science." The paper extolled Malthus's arguments about the dangers of population increase. To argue otherwise, it said, "appears calling on us to unlearn the rules of arithmetic, and do our sums by the assertion that two and two make five."[29] By the 1850s, though – along with most political economists – the paper seems to have abandoned the central argument of the principle of population, much as Malthus had done in the 1820s.[30]

The *Economist* did more, perhaps, than any other journal to foster the idea that the "laws" of political economy were not simply the result of specific forms of legislation but, instead, were both "natural" and irrefutable. In 1846 it argued, "The laws of nature – of which the principles of social and political economy form an inalienable portion – can never be violated or neglected with impunity."[31] It referred constantly to the "natural law of political economy" and argued that these laws were also "ordained by providence." In this regard, of course, the *Economist* was following the example of many political economists, but the paper was, if anything, more rigid about what constituted those laws and more insistent on the dangers of deviating from them. Perhaps this was because, as Wilson said in a letter to his wife, the paper needed to reflect "nothing but pure principles."[32]

The *Economist* distilled the arguments about political economy into three fundamental doctrines: free, unrestricted trade would lead to economic growth through expanded production afforded through the division of labour; the poor could only benefit from increased wages, and these could only be achieved through the law of supply and demand; all government legislation was an unwarranted restriction on business and was to be opposed. While it occasionally needed to engage in some imaginative linguistic gymnastics to make the evidence fit the argument, the paper's writers usually managed to convince themselves, at least, that they had done so. Along the way, the paper also crafted a celebratory discourse about civilization and progress that reached particular heights around the 1851 Great Exhibition.

One of the paper's early leaders in January 1844, entitled "Civilisation: Commerce and Free Trade," captured the argument on the first of these issues well. It began:

> The most striking evidence of the progress of civilisation – of an advance towards a perfect social economy ... is to be found in the nearest approach to a perfect subdivision of labour. ... Every step has this distinctive stamp; from the savage state. ... to that of the highest civilisation, where subdivision and exchanges are

wrought into such a labyrinth of distant and remote actions, that the great bulk of men know not the source of supply, or the mode of production, of things which constitute their daily consumption.[33]

The wonders provided by increased demand, production, and a division of labour required only relief from government restriction: that is, free trade. The paper argued, "[T]here can be no increased demand without increased markets; and we cannot secure larger markets without an unrestricted power of exchange ... With free trade we might go on increasing our production without limit ... There is no other remedy."[34]

The paper's primary target in the campaign for free trade was the elimination of the Corn Laws. Indeed, until 1846, when the government of Robert Peel passed legislation progressively eliminating the sliding scale of tariffs for three years before they were to be completely removed, the paper was obsessed with the Corn Laws. Much of the paper was dedicated to accounts of Anti–Corn Law League meetings and the arguments made there. It sought, successfully, to build the impression that there was a great groundswell of popular and political opposition to the Corn Laws. Everything – increased production, prosperity, workers' wages, political change, civilization, progress, and society – depended on the elimination of the Corn Laws. With Lord Radnor's encouragement, the paper painted opposition to the elimination of the Corn Laws as a perversion by the great landowners in the House of Lords who sought only – and mistakenly – to augment their rents through such protection. In this it was remarkably, if exaggeratedly, consistent. On all occasions, it counselled those who could vote to put aside all other considerations and vote for free trade and the elimination of the Corn Laws. "Clear the decks by giving us Free Trade, and then prepare action on any other question interesting to the community."[35] The paper also turned every issue it could into an argument for the elimination of the Corn Laws; this included the poor pay of needlewomen in London and the potato famine in Ireland, along, of course, with the argument that this was the necessary prerequisite to relieving the distress of agricultural workers.[36] When, in 1849, the final duties eventually petered out, the *Economist* described a great banquet held in Manchester: "They could celebrate a great victory, while there was nobody vanquished. Their conquest was over evil."[37]

The *Economist* also argued that free trade was the best, indeed the only, way to benefit the poor by raising the demand for, and thus the wages of, workers. The paper was somewhat less successful in keeping steadfast about whether political economy need concern itself with the well-being of workers and the poor. The paper carried on a more-or-less constant feud with the *Times* newspaper. This was partly because Lord Radnor and the proprietor of the *Times* had fought since the *Times* had so gleefully skewered Radnor over his pigs. Radnor argued in a letter printed in the *Economist* that labourers should only be paid what the market demanded: "If the employer can get his work done for 7s a week, he is no more called upon to give 10s, than he would be called upon to give 30*L* for a cart-horse if could buy one that suited him for 21*L*." The *Times* responded:

> Lord Radnor and his brother economists have the whip-hand of the labourer, and are able to coerce him. ... [D]id Lord Radnor get his peerage in the open market? ... To cast him (the labourer) upon the open market is first to strip him, and then shut him out to the North-East wind, with the assurance that he is now in a state of nature, and with sufficient practice, can easily acquire an aptitude for it. Read him a lecture on the powers of adaptation possessed by the human hide.[38]

In January 1845, the *Times* wrote an editorial directed partly at the *Economist* arguing:

> Confess the plain fact, political economy won't do. ... It has had a fairish trial, both in talk and legislation these dozen years; the result is the ... agricultural labourers, the chief victims of the experiment, are considerably worse off than ever. Your system requires a much clearer ground than England now affords. Try it in Siberia.

The response from the *Economist* was decidedly weak: along with asserting that it had not been given a "fairish trial," the paper remarked, "It is a maudling way of meeting us to say that political economy does not teach us kindness to the poor. Why, neither does astronomy nor navigation."[39] The paper was attempting to argue that political economy was a science bound by laws that were not subject to concerns of morality or intent, but it was a decidedly lame retort: astronomy did not purport to reveal ways of governing society that would lead to "universal opulence" as political economy did.

"Tawdry Balderdash About the Poor"

The *Economist* also disputed with the *Times* and the *Morning Post* around the issue of the urban poor. A poor widow had pawned some of the sewing she had been given to fix in order to feed her children. When she was brought to trial, both the *Times* and the *Morning Post* sprang to her defence. The *Morning Post* attacked the "money-swelled, heartless wretches, the advocates of free trade and cheapness (who) have the shocking effrontery to pretend they are the friends of the working people." The *Economist* protested, echoing the arguments of Smith and Malthus, saying that any attempt to set minimum wages would fail; the only way the working class can be relieved is through higher wages caused by increased demand for or a diminishing supply of labour and commenting further: "Those laws which restrict trade are the true cause of all that combat and strife and contest for a miserable existence which, beginning with the poor needle women on Tower hill, and ascending through every rank, piercing every manufacturer, shopkeeper, and dealer in passing."[40]

The *Economist* presented itself as both an empathetic supporter of the poor, and a sober, cautious voice concerning laws or regulations meant to favour them. It is, perhaps, in this area we can see the most inconsistency in the paper. At times, it seemed almost desperately aware of the wretchedness of a large proportion of the population; at other times it could crow about progress and cavalierly dismiss claims of increasing poverty. For example, in May 1850 the paper's leaders had warned:

> It is utterly incompatible, we admit, with the safety of society, and with the well-being of the people, that they should remain as they are. We scarcely need revolutions abroad, and abortive attempt at riot and revolution, at home, to convince us that society is continually endangered by the mass of people being immersed in comparative poverty and misery.[41]

In August of the same year, though, when William Gladstone in Parliament had warned that the rich were getting richer and the poor were getting poorer, the paper felt the need to dismiss this argument, saying, "Mr. Gladstone's phrase was a mere phrase, and not the representation of a fact."[42]

The paper occasionally felt it necessary to defend itself against arguments that it was cold-hearted and unsympathetic to poor labourers. When shop workers began a movement to reduce working hours in London, the *Economist* responded, "That we wish well to efforts like these, we need hardly say." It then went on to indicate that the paper, in fact, did not wish them well. "A political economist when viewed through certain spectacles is the type of cold, callous, calculating, selfish, labour-grinding wretch, without heart or bowels ... We must put in our claim to a participation in the common sympathy of humanity." Still, they asked, "with the race that is run to retain possession of foreign markets – with profits cut down – how is it possible generally to shorten all hours of employment without the loss, in some shape or other, falling on salaries and wages."[43]

The paper's arguments about labour became most serious around any issue that might affect cotton manufacturers, with whom Wilson and the paper were closely tied. Various movements intent on limiting the hours of employment for women and children below the 12 hours then allowed, which had begun in the previous decade, were resuscitated in the 1840s. We have already seen how Nassau Senior responded in apocalyptic language to such propositions in the 1830s; it is not surprising that the *Economist* would take a similar stance. When Lord Ashley's first attempt to do so was met with some initial support in the House, the paper commented, "we can only express our surprise that enlightened men in the House of Commons ... should be found to give encouragement to such tawdry balderdash about the poor."[44] The next week, the lead story repeated closely Senior's arguments about the fixed costs of capital and the loss of markets, and it did so in almost equally alarmist tones: "Indeed, it would be difficult to contemplate the amount of confusion and danger which such interference between capital and labour would inflict on the country."[45]

The paper continued with its opposition to this and other legislation about factory labour for years to come. It expanded its denunciations to include any "interference" between labour and capital. Thus, in April 1844, it argued, "the more it is investigated the more we are compelled to acknowledge that in any interference with industry and capital, the law is powerful only for evil, but utterly powerless for good." The next week it warned against laws which would separate the interests of workers and capital "which rightly understood are perfectly inseparable."[46] When one member of the House indicated in a speech that he was preparing to make a motion regulating hourly wages, the *Economist* responded sarcastically, "And why not another to regulate the number of coats a man must wear, the number and sort of buttons he shall have on it."[47]

The paper continued in this vein throughout its campaign against the Ten Hour Bill. In February 1846, it tried to argue that a compulsory bill limiting hours of work meant "treating the working man like a *slave or serf*." While asserting that the *Economist* would happily see the reduction of hours for all labourers at some point in the future, it warned that given the current condition of the working class they would not use such time wisely: "Leisure, by itself, will be no blessing to the people."[48]

As Senior had in his own writings, the paper dismissed claims about the ill effects on health and morality of long working hours, even for children and women. It reprinted an article from the *Manchester Guardian*, for whom Wilson also wrote, that disputed claims about increased mortality rates in the city. The article argued, instead, that the city "affords an asylum to those unfortunate labourers and their families for whom the landlords cannot furnish employment" and sought to prove that reducing such movements would increase the mortality rates remarkably. The article also made completely erroneous arguments that mortality rates were much higher in the country in general than they were in the industrial cities.[49] In fact, life expectancy in the industrial cities of northern England was for most of the nineteenth century substantially lower than those that had prevailed in rural England 150 years earlier: Liverpool and Manchester had a life expectancy of 25 years in 1850, compared to over 40 in rural England in 1700. The height of recruits for the British and East India Company armies and of prisoners in jails also declined steadily from 1740 for the next 120 years, most notably in the industrial cities. Indeed, all indications are that, despite what the *Guardian* and the *Economist* argued, the health of inhabitants of Manchester and other industrial cities was significantly worse than rural inhabitants. It would continue to be so until near the end of the century.[50]

In 1850, when Lord Ashley argued in the House that a reduction in hours of work had led to workers being healthier, living longer, and being better educated the paper did not even try to answer his assertions. Instead, they responded by warning:

> The operations of capital, which Adam Smith thought no legislator should meddle with, are by this measure strictly repressed. To deprive land of half its fertility, … would not be a greater folly than to limit the productive power of machinery. At the same time, it would be less unjust, for the limitation cannot be placed on capital without making a direct attack on the rights of property.[51]

The paper had a conveniently short memory. A little over a decade later in commenting favourably on an attempt to extend the Children's Factory Act from cotton mills to other industries, it commented, "No one who knows how the Children's Factories [*sic*] Acts have worked in Lancashire and Yorkshire has any doubt *now* of the wisdom of those measures … It was one of the greatest blunders economists made to prejudice people against a true science by pushing it beyond its natural limits."[52] This partly reflected a movement away from a radical liberal stance on the part of the paper in the years immediately following the death of Wilson. But it was an argument that the paper would use on other topics, especially as we will see below around the issue of slavery: they warned that some arguments about the 'science' of political economy were pushed so far that they endangered belief in the science itself. It was an easy warning for the *Economist* to make only if one conveniently forgot that its writers, and the paper itself, were the primary culprits in pushing political economy beyond "its natural limits."

The More Perfect Laws of Providence

The third obsession of the paper was with the purported evils of government regulation. The paper almost always made a simple and powerful argument, which both echoed and extended Smith's work: the pursuit of self-interest (self-love) was natural and universal; it would lead both to prosperity and happiness; government interference could only inhibit the expression of self-love and thus, reduce both prosperity and happiness. These ideas were expressed in the paper through both warnings about government regulation and celebrations of individual freedoms. In 1845, for example, it suggested, "Unless it be for the prevention of crime, we know not for what purpose governments subsist." And went on to assert, "All history teaches that civilisation has been the result of individual freedom and exertion. … The work that lies before legislatures, for the most part, is to *undo their own errors*."[53] Or, as it continued in the same vein in 1848, "The more we give or allow scope to the free exercise of self-love, the more complete will be the social order."[54]

In a series attempting to allocate blame for the "wretchedness of the lower classes," the paper defended capitalists against complaints that their greed was causing distress. The article said, "It is amazingly easy to thunder forth tirades ... against selfishness and greediness, which after all, are nothing more than each man providing for and doing the best he can for himself." The article summed up the relationship between the capitalist and the worker by asserting that they "meet in the markets of the world to make their mutual exchanges, their bargains are voluntary, and if the labourer suffers from the exchange the fault lies in him ... not in the capitalist."[55] Continuing the series in the following weeks, the paper laid the blame for wretchedness squarely on the shoulders of government: "The vast and obvious difficulty of ascertaining true, and sound, and good principles, should impress on us great caution in erecting new systems when those that have been time honoured are crumbling to pieces. Among us *Laissez-faire* is comparatively a modern doctrine, but every day's experience commands governments more and more to throw individuals on their own resources."[56] The next week, echoing Malthus's argument about the inability for governments to effectively address poverty, it argued:

> We consider the mental degradation of the masses ... to be one of the most disastrous though collateral, effects of the legislation which intended to benefit the people. ... [T]he State ... is very much to blame for the condition of the people. The desire for happiness, or what is called self-interest, is universal ... It is the law of nature, and if the pursuit of self-interest, left equally free for all, do not lead to general welfare, no system of government can accomplish it.[57]

Ireland, as we will see, served as a constant foil to illuminate the dangers of government intervention. Most often, for the paper, the famine that devastated Ireland in the second half of the 1840s was not the result of the blight that attacked the potato plant, nor even the result of the monopolization of land by English landowners; rather, it lay in too-frequent government intervention. Thus, in discussing remedies for Ireland in 1847, the paper argued:

> The progress of civilisation is marked chiefly by the repeal of regulations ... The true secret of the failure of all acts of legislation which seek to promote the prosperity of commerce, the feeding of the people, or the advancement of private interests, is that they are not only miserably inefficient for the subjects they have in view but principally that they interfere with and artificially supersede the far more perfect laws which Providence ordained for the natural government of the world.[58]

The paper found evidence for this argument everywhere it looked. For example, in the context of a series of scandals in British railways in 1847 and 1848, some people called for an audit of railway accounts; this prompted the paper to leap to the defence of railways and oppose any such legislation: "We have had latterly a great deal too much legislation; the hundreds of bills of all kinds that are every session brought forward, and the many that are passed one year to be repealed the next, make legislation no better than a mockery and a nuisance."

The paper viewed this as more than a nuisance, and it went on to make clear the dire consequences of such legislation. In the midst of the revolutions that had occurred in Europe beginning in 1848, it asserted that the cause of that unrest was government regulation: "The Evils of 1848 should be … a memorable lesson. Then all the regulating Governments of the continent were, with one exception – shattered to pieces, while the little regulating Governments of England and the United States, which left individuals free to manage their own business … have stood erect and increased in strength."[59] But what constituted freedom on one side and tyranny on the other was clearly, partly, in the eye of the beholder. The riotous spring of 1848 provided the writers of the paper with some other obvious lessons. Among the most important of these: "The true interests of freedom are more endangered by the government falling into the hands of … the working classes, than by falling into the hands of even a military despot. … it is not in their hands that the reins of power can be safely held nor to them that the administration of freedom can be safely entrusted." Nevertheless, they argued that 1848 had also demonstrated to English workers that they enjoyed the greatest possible freedom "compatible with the existence of social order and wellbeing."[60]

Hats Off to the Nineteenth Century

Despite its constant complaints about government interference with natural proclivities, one of the most striking themes of the paper was a celebration of progress. This reached its heights around the 1851 Great Exhibition at the Crystal Palace. In January of that year, the paper began a series entitled "The First Half of the Nineteenth Century – Progress of the Nation and Race." The article celebrated "a leap forward in all the elements of material well-being such as neither scientific nor poetic fancy every pictured. … It has witnessed a more rapid and astonishing progress than *all* the centuries which preceded it."[61] In the other articles in the series, they argued that wealth had diffused throughout the middle classes, and that there was a greater public attention to the plight of the poor than at any time in history. Most assuredly, they argued, all people were now engaged in the pursuit of wealth: "[W]ealth is valued less as an exemption from toil, than as a call to effort, and an instrument of influence and power … if the poor do not work less, the rich certainly work more." This sober pursuit of wealth meant that "except in Ireland, and at the Universities, a drunken gentleman is one of the rarest sights in society."[62]

By the time of the opening of the Great Exhibition in May that year, the *Economist* was in full flight:

> The Queen of the mightiest empire of the globe – the empire in which industry is the most successfully cultivated, and in which its triumphs have been greatest – was fittingly occupied in consecrating the temple erected to its honour ... The Great Exhibition, as a sign of present peace throughout the civilised world, is a subject of great satisfaction; but as a sign of future and permanent peace ... and of a more glorious humanity than even poets imagined – is for reflecting minds a source of delight. ... The first of May, 1851, will, for a long period, be described in our books as one of the most memorable days in the history of Great Britain, and of the whole human race.[63]

The paper was particularly taken with the democratic aspects of the exhibition: commoners would soon get to walk on the same ground as the Queen and see the same sights she will see, "Where she treds, they will tred."[64] The paper did not comment on how this democratizing lesson was muted by the fact that admittance to the hall was regulated, with noble patrons to be followed first by season ticket holders, then five-shilling customers, then guinea visitors, only then to be followed at the end of the month by "shilling days." Perhaps the lesson was less obvious to all. Disappointingly, the first of the shilling days had very low attendance; as the paper explained it, "The multitude seems to have been afraid of one another, and comparatively very few went."[65] Elsewhere, the *Economist* cited a work by Samuel Taylor Coleridge, who commented on a man who "in involuntary homage to his own greatness" always took off his hat when talking about himself. Robert Kemp Philip compared this to the way people talked about the first half of the nineteenth century.[66]

Chapter Eight

Bad Farming – The Ghost of a Dead Monopoly

In a review of various books on agriculture in the second edition of the *Economist* in September 1843, the paper celebrated the new attitudes to farming demonstrated in these publications. "Here we may discern," the paper said, "how the active and intelligent landlords joined with the higher class of occupying farmers, are now at work, breaking up the hard clods of ignorance, prejudice, sloth, and indifference ... the *art* of husbandry, is rapidly changing into the *science* of agriculture."[1]

If these publications promised a transformation of English agriculture, in the opinion of the writers for the *Economist*, much needed to be done. Clearing the way for capital in agriculture was one of the central tenets of the paper's vision of the future. But it was in this area that the paper found itself battling the most formidable foes. Traditional landlords clung to protection and when such protection was removed in stages with the ending of the Corn Laws in 1846, they remained tied to "remnants of feudalism," demanding low rents from generation after generation of the same family in lifelong tenancies in a mistaken "sentimental hankering after a system which belonged to a different state of society."[2] Or, they continued to assert aristocratic privileges, kept game that destroyed tenants' crops, and sought high rents while clinging to "the ghost of a dead monopoly."[3] But tenant farmers, too, demonstrated congenital flaws: they refused to invest enough capital or to improve their farms sufficiently. They foolishly contracted leases they could not afford, or they took advantage of long-term leases without improving the land. The third leg on which English agriculture rested was no less disturbing. The *Economist* professed much sympathy for the plight of the agricultural labourer, "neglected and degraded, morally and physically" and bemoaned the "great absence of healthy, *masculine*, rational opinion [emphasis added]" on the best means to address this degradation.[4] But it continually opposed proposals for ameliorating those conditions that did not rely on wage labour and it demonstrated continual confusion over whether improved agriculture, now generally labelled "high" agriculture, would increase or reduce the demand for labour. It attacked particularly the few remaining commons and opposed any scheme to provide land to agricultural labourers. The paper dismissed any claim that peasant farming or small farming in general could prove beneficial.

But despite its frequent exhortations to landlords, farmers, and politicians to put agriculture on a firmer footing and to advance the science of agriculture through the embrace of high farming and the investment of capital, the *Economist* and its writers continued to be disappointed in the countryside. Despite the end of the Corn Laws, English agriculture was depressed through the end of the 1840s and into the 1850s; it temporarily revived during the Crimean War. By late in 1860s, however, it went into a deep decline not relieved until the twentieth century. Twenty years after the *Economist* celebrated the breaking up of "the hard clods of ignorance," English agriculture was increasingly uncompetitive, agricultural labourers remained restive, distressed, and hungry, and misguided people persisted in talking about the benefits and bounty associated with peasant agriculture.

"Sadly in want of The Economist"

The *Economist* was born out of the struggle to end the Corn Laws. The campaign to do so linked the manufacturers of England, especially Manchester, with reformers who sought to reduce food costs for factory labourers, and a few aristocratic landowners such as Lord Radnor and Lord Clarendon. The decisive support of the Anti–Corn Law League permitted the *Economist* to survive as a business through its first couple of years of financial losses. And it was shared opposition to the Corn Laws that united the various writers who worked for the paper in the early years. The campaign to end the Corn Laws, therefore, dominated writing in the paper in the first few years.

The paper had the support of some prominent landlords in its campaign to end the Corn Laws. The *Economist* argued time and again that the "best farmers" and the "wealthiest peers … do not fear it." Instead, they were "banded together in a league sworn to effect it."[5] Nonetheless, the campaign put the paper solidly in opposition to the majority of estate owners and many tenant farmers who believed that the price supports provided by the Corn Laws were essential to their rent or profits. It also meant that the *Economist* found itself in disagreement with one of its proclaimed "masters of political economy": Malthus. Malthus was unusual among early nineteenth century political economists in supporting the Corn Laws, arguing that they were necessary bulwarks against threatened food scarcity.

Defense of the Corn Laws was most often led by Agricultural Protection Societies. At their meetings the elimination of the Corn Laws was portrayed as an attack on all the sectors of society involved in agriculture. As the Duke of Northumberland stated in a letter defending the Agricultural Protection Societies:

> When I see a formidable body of influential persons combining together as a league for the destruction of the agriculturalists, sending itinerant orators to every part of the country for the dissemination of false statements – raising a plausible cry of "cheap bread" and endeavouring to set the labourers against the farmers, and the farmers against their landlords, ... which ... must prove ruinous to the country, it is then high time for the agriculturalists through the whole kingdom to unite as one body in self-defence.[6]

Indeed, despite the paper's prediction that, "Victory will follow as surely as the shadow accompanies the substance,"[7] the fight to end the Corn Laws was both prolonged and bitter. Public demonstrations, frequent and large public meetings, and the agitation of papers like the *Economist* were all important in pushing for their removal, as was the determined work in Parliament of such opponents of the laws as Lord Clarendon. Perhaps just as important was the increasing scarcity, and thus increasing cost, of food in late 1845 and early 1846, as the first effects of the potato blight and a bad wheat harvest were felt throughout Europe.[8] As Lord Morley commented about the ruined fall grain harvest in 1845, "It was the rain that rained away the Corn Laws."[9] In response to a shortage of food, a number of European port cities had freed trade in grain late in 1845 and the Conservative prime minister Robert Peel was inclined to follow suit, especially as a remedy for what promised to be widespread famine in Ireland.[10] Nonetheless, there was much opposition to the ending of the Corn Laws in Parliament in both political parties. In late 1845, Peel's caucus split over the issue and he resigned. The Whigs under Lord John Russell could not form a government, and Peel soon returned, intent on ending the duties with Whig support. His government collapsed again shortly thereafter.

The *Economist* followed these developments closely. In early 1846 in an article provocatively entitled "The Great Crisis – A Warning to the Aristocracy" it threatened:

> We are now on the eve of the crisis on which so much depends ... This is one of those turning points in the history of nations which occur but seldom, and *which never recur* ... all the thin disguises which sophistry or ignorance have thrown around the question are now fairly torn away. It can no longer be represented as a labourer's question or a farmer's question. It is simply a landlord's question – that is, a question between cheap bread and dear bread – *between sufficient and insufficient food.*[11]

The paper kept up the pressure as Peel's proposals for a gradual elimination of the duties were debated in Parliament. Though the paper had immodestly suggested that those presenting arguments against the repeal of the Corn Laws "are sadly in want of the ECONOMIST, in order to infuse a little common sense" into the discussion,[12] at times its writers let their enthusiasm for ending the Corn Laws and their determination to apply the fairy dust of political economy to all questions get in the way of reason and common sense. Benjamin Disraeli warned in a debate in the house that ending protection would mean that English agricultural workers would be thrown out of work as imported wheat would replace domestically grown wheat. The *Economist* scoffed at this assertion, responding with a rather strange argument promising that high, capitalist agriculture would mean that any English disadvantage would soon be overcome:

> The less skillful the agriculture of any particular country, the more the inhabitants rely on the spontaneous and varying fertility of the soil and the seasons. … Now Hungary, and the part of Russia referred to by Mr. D'Israeli [sic], and the greater part of the United States and Prussia, in this respect, approximate Mexico. The people are rude agriculturalists, and trust mainly to the soil and the seasons. … Corn is nowhere really [the result] of spontaneous growth, but everywhere the produce of industry. The increase depends on labour becoming more skilful, and the price at all times the quantity of labour required to produce it. Unless agricultural labour, therefore, be more productive in other countries than in England, its produce cannot be sold for a less sum than that of the produce of our agriculture.[13]

While the *Economist* might have had a clearer vision of the theory of political economy than Disraeli, the young Conservative had a more realistic understanding of agricultural potential. The ending of the Corn Laws might have been unavoidable and their demise might have led to cheaper bread and lower costs for manufacturers, but it also stressed English agriculture and meant that England increasingly relied on imported wheat, while prices and agricultural profits fell.

"How Can Capital be Attracted to the Soil?"

The bill gradually eliminating duties on imported grain was given Royal Assent on 26 June 1846. Immediately afterwards, the *Economist* added a new section on agriculture to the paper each week. (Thankfully, it did not add "and Agricultural Monitor" to its already long title.) It used this new venue to clear the field for capital in agriculture. The first article in the new section declared that, with the elimination of duties, "Either land must be dealt with on commercial principles or it must go out of cultivation. … The problem therefore, now to be solved is, how can capital be attracted to the soil?"[14] A month later the paper congratulated farmers and "a very considerable portion of the landholders" that they were now talking about agricultural improvement. The paper cautioned, "They have much to learn, and much to forget, and more to do." Asserting that the *Economist* knew more about farmers "than any landlord," the paper found hope in the fact that though "perhaps slow," farmers were "eminently practical men of business."[15] Three years later, however, it was still commenting on how difficult this transition was, though it was confident that change would occur. The paper said, "It is slowly but certainly being forced upon the attention of landed proprietors and farmers, that land is to be regarded simply as an object of commercial enterprise, which must be dealt with solely with a view to profit."[16]

The *Economist* was a vocal proponent for what was known as high agriculture. This new version of scientific, improved agriculture focused on the widespread use of root crops, pasture, and manure to assist the production of wheat and permit a more limited use of fallow land. Most of the elements of high agriculture were little different from the improved agriculture championed by Arthur Young many decades previously: the need for large farms; improved pastures through the use of clover and fetches; the use of root crops for stall-feeding cattle; the importance of fertilizer, increasingly in the form of guano; and significant capital investment in draining land, fencing, farm buildings, and labour-saving equipment. Like Arthur Young, the *Economist* argued that competition and self-reliance required that farmers adapt to these changing circumstances and adopt appropriate business practices or be pushed from the land so their farms could be given to more efficient capitalists.

After 1846, the need for farmers to invest sufficient capital in the land replaced the Corn Laws as the paper's major preoccupation around agriculture. For the *Economist* the amount of capital a farmer had available to invest in the land should form the key determinant in their farming operations. It counselled, "Most failures and disappointments in farming arise from mistakes as to the amount of capital required to farm successfully."[17] If a farmer did not have sufficient capital, he should stay out of the market for land. And, when determining the size of the farm, "let him select a farm somewhat too small rather than the contrary."[18] The paper was so convinced of the importance of adequate capital that it often presented contradictory arguments about the benefits and disadvantages of large and small farms. On the one hand, it constantly argued for the advantages of large farms (and, as we will see below, opposed any suggestion that small farming could be productive, profitable, or socially appropriate). In 1847, for example, it argued that no one familiar with agriculture could compare districts "without being struck with the greater productiveness of large farms."[19] The next year, it reiterated – sounding very much like Arthur Young – "The farmer whose farm is large enough to employ three teams of horses and a proportionate number of labourers, will perform every act of husbandry better, and in better season, than he who can keep two teams or perhaps only one. And the farmer with five or seven teams, and labourers in proportion, will do still better."[20] On the other hand, it counselled landlords to reduce the amount of land each of his tenants had by at least a third, leaving them "a larger proportional capital" and thus able to "feel the benefits of higher cultivation."[21] One is struck reading the paper's discussion of the need for capital with the similarities to Arthur Young's arguments more than seventy years previously. It is telling that after seven decades of agricultural revolution, during which enclosure was meant to pave the way for the investment of capital in the land, there was, apparently, still such an obvious absence.

So Many Agricultural Rip Van Winkles

The *Economist* then began a campaign to identify hindrances to the application of capital to the soil. One of the obstacles to the investment of sufficient capital in agriculture, according to the *Economist*, was the nature of land tenure in England. Despite the paper's continual arguments against "traditional" land-lords who provided land for cheap rent to life-long tenants, the *Economist* also criticized landlords who charged high rents on short term leases. In the 1770s, Arthur Young and many of the other proponents of improved agriculture had championed the spread of thoroughly commercialized leases. Old practices of romantic England such as long leases for many lives were considered to be one of the major impediments to improved agriculture. The *Economist*, too, more than a half century later, felt the need to argue for such a thoroughly com-mercial view. Its attack on aristocratic privilege had included opposition to the landlords who let their land to same families for years, or lives, on end. It had likened the desire for long leases as a function of the "ancient attachment of the old English yeoman to his own little farm" but warned, "that system belongs to the past and is gone in this country for ever."[22]

Yet by the 1840s agriculture in England laboured under the worst possible land tenure system. The majority of land continued to be owned by a small number of aristocratic or wealthy proprietors: the 2,000 or so landholders identified by the 1873 *Return on the Owners of the Land* as controlling about one-half of the agricultural land in the country.[23] As the *Economist* freely ad-mitted, these landlords rarely had any real interest or knowledge of agriculture. As it said, "Nothing in this country is more distinct than the ownership of land, and the business of farming the land."[24] A situation in which "land is possessed by persons who do not know their business" or, more colloquially, in which "landowners, as such, are no more agriculturalists than shipowners, as such, are sailors," was one of the causes of the lack of capital invested in the land.[25] But the protection afforded by the Corn Laws and the shift to commercial-ized leases had, as predicted by Young, led to high rents despite the difficulties tenant-farmers demonstrated in making their farms pay.

This situation was only aggravated when the removal of the Corn Laws exposed British farmers to increasingly free trade in grain, despite the *Economist*'s assurances that imported corn could never be cheaper than English corn. The paper's remedy for this affliction was the rapid improvement entailed in adopting high agriculture through extensive capital investment.[26] But landlords, in pursuing their own self-interests as the *Economist* continually exhorted them to do, had responded to the demand for farms by increasing rents and letting farms on very short-term leases, often yearly. Without guarantees for recompense for improvements at the termination of the lease, farmers were naturally reluctant to engage in the improvements necessary to adopt high farming.[27] The paper denounced this as "the wretched system on which landed property is managed, preventing the outlay of capital, by reason of the insecurity and want of enterprise which it procures among tenant-farmers."[28] The *Economist* first argued that such improvements should be done by the proprietors who would benefit from better tenants and, consequently, higher rents. But it soon campaigned for a return to long leases as the best means to allow tenant farmers to engage in the desired improvements, arguing, with some exaggeration, "nine-tenths of the farmers of England are yearly tenants" and "so hampered by restrictions and reservations" that "a lengthened term of possession is indispensable to success in the business of farming."[29] The paper pushed for the adoption of a twenty-one-year lease as the standard, saying that proprietors would be more careful about the character of their renters, and the tenants would be more cautious in signing a lease and more willing to engage in improvements. It readily admitted, however, that landlords continued to benefit from high rents because of the competition for land and had little incentive by way of self-interest in changing their practices.[30] Over a decade after it began this campaign, the paper was still pointing out examples of tenants who had spent considerable sums on improvements to the land only to be thrown off their farms. The *Economist* warned, "We would hold up the case to farmers as a lesson that under no circumstances are they justified in embarking their capital in a farm ... without first securing a rational lease."[31]

In the opinion of the *Economist*, tenant farmers did not escape blame for the admittedly depressed condition of English agriculture. For years after the repeal of the Corn Laws, farmers complained about the price of wheat due to foreign competition. The *Economist* argued that these pressures only served to ensure the survival of the fittest farmers, those who adapted to permanent low prices with "changes in the mode of managing the land."[32] But the paper despaired that too much land was "in the occupation of tenants of little intelligence, who are very deficient in capital. They seem as compared with the active and enterprising modern farmers, like so many agricultural Rip Van Winkles, who have slept some 60 or 70 years."[33] Too many of them were "satisfied with existing practices and established routines in cultivation."[34]

The *Economist* was inclined to dismiss all claims to agricultural distress as a function of an attempt to reinstate protection. In 1851, for example, it noted, "If the assertions of party leaders in the one House of Parliament and Protectionist Peers in the other were to be accepted as evidence of agricultural distress, an unparalleled state of woe and impending ruin amongst English farmers might be taken to exist. … But, fortunately for farmers, … assertion is not proof." Instead, it argued, "a new era in husbandry is commenced" that would be marked by increased production through high agriculture.[35]

If 1851, two years after the final end of the corn duties, marked the beginning of a new era in farming, that era disappointed almost everyone. Through most of the first half of the 1850s, farmers complained bitterly that they could not make their farms pay at the prevailing prices and landlords increasingly worried that they could not find tenants for their farms. Though the paper's natural inclination was to dismiss all such complaints as romantic attachments to protection, by September of that year even the paper admitted that there was, in fact, some real distress, citing multiple instances brought to their attention of landlords who could not let farms that had come vacant. Even here, though, the *Economist* fell back on a familiar argument about the benefits of competition, suggesting "a little wholesome difficulty will in the end benefit both classes."[36] The paper returned to that theme the next week, saying that while the low prices created all sorts of problems, after this "period of transition" the farmer will be "in a far better position than formerly for carrying on his business with profit and security."[37]

The difficulties were not so easily overcome. Though the paper often asserted that the problems were associated with the continued prevalence of what it called "low" agriculture and would disappear with the widespread adoption of "high" agriculture, even the *Economist* seemed to lose some of its confidence in the magic of capital when applied to agriculture. High agriculture was associated, at least in the minds of the writers for the *Economist*, with the removal of permanent pasture, greater use of feed crops for livestock, and more land in tillage. Nevertheless, by the 1850s with low prices and problems with finding tenants, the paper was ready to admit that some land should be taken out of tillage and returned to permanent pasture.[38] Another important aspect of high farming was increasing reliance on imported fertilizers; most important among these was guano. The *Economist* thought guano to be almost miraculous in its ability to boost crops. As it said, "many curious things are narrated in history, but we remember none more curious than this almost miraculous conversion of the deposits of wild birds into a mine of wealth … in the increase it gives the vegetative powers of the soil."[39] The application of guano helped distinguish high farming from farming that took only "the natural produce of the soil." Its use meant that "the growth of corn may be enlarged to an extent that for all practical purposes we may call unlimited." By 1851, England was importing 116,295 tons of the stuff a year and, as the paper said, "the best and most progressive agricultural districts (have) become dependent upon the use of guano."[40] But supply was limited. Desperate searches were launched to find similar locales with the particular characteristics of the dried bird manure from the coast of Peru, but with little success; so important were these sources that Peru and the United States almost went to war over Los Lobos, islands encrusted with bird droppings, and England sought to insure Peruvian possession of the islands in return for a guaranteed price.[41] Only a few years later, guano was becoming increasingly difficult to obtain and was often "cut" with other substances; like any addict, farmers hooked on a new drug with no control over price and little over quality. By 1854, the paper was warning that supplies were predicted to end within ten years.

As troubles continued in agriculture, the paper adopted an even more strident tone about the natural selection that such difficulties entailed. It compared farmers thrown off the land because they could not compete to "the Indians … injured by the growth of a much more skilful and powerful people than themselves in a territory they exclusively occupied."[42] While prices briefly rose in the wake of the Crimean War, providing some relief to farmers, by the end of 1850s the *Economist* was once again remarking on the distress among farmers. A decade and a half after the end of the Corn Laws was celebrated as a means to bring the bracing wind of capitalism and competition to farming, the paper was dismayed by the continued lack of capital invested in agriculture and the position of the tenant farmers; it opined:

> The position, social and commercial, of tenant-farmers in England is more unsatisfactory and ill-defined than that of any other class. They are bepraised and petted, flouted and suspected by turns. They are denounced as narrow-minded and non-enterprising; or they are urged to expend their capital and their energies in the improvement of farms they hold on the most precarious tenures and under the most onerous conditions.[43]

This would sound like an impassioned defence of farmers were it not the *Economist* which had so often both praised and denounced them.

"Their Rude and Constant Labour"

There was, however, one other class more problematic for the writers of the *Economist*: rural workers. The "new era in agriculture" celebrated by the paper needs to be put in the context of the desperate plight of rural workers, who endured inadequate wages, unsteady employment, loss of access to common resources, deprivation of cottage gardens, and draconian restrictions of the New Poor Law. Their falling living standards and increased insecurity contributed to continued unrest, as fires lit up the landscape. As the *Times* commented, "Of a truth there is something rotten in our state of England."[44] While the major daily papers, especially the *Times* and the *Morning Chronicle,* reported often and sympathetically about the plight of rural workers and both provided articles trying to uncover the reasons for spreading arson (see chapter 4), the *Economist* most often sought to downplay the desperate situation facing rural workers. Its writing on rural workers and potential solutions to their continued poverty fit with its general approach. The only solution they proposed for workers' distress was higher wages resulting from the application of more capital in agriculture or migration to the cities – basically a constant reiterating of the arguments of Smith and Malthus, reinforced into the 1840s by the writing of Nassau Senior and John McCulloch. Workers needed constant lessons in self-reliance but were denied most opportunities of exercising that self-reliance; the *Economist* vehemently opposed common lands, allotments, or the provision of land to rural workers. Though the paper recognized the horrific lack of appropriate housing in rural England and repeated others' condemnation of the "war on cottages," it never discussed the need for cottage gardens and fought against the provision of potato land. Moreover, at a time when many writers – including the most prominent living political economist – were reconsidering the value of small-scale farming and arguing for the efficiency and social utility of peasant agriculture, the *Economist* mounted a full-scale attack on such thinking. It contradicted the writing of even some of its own correspondents, and presented often silly arguments to bolster its demand that nothing prevent rural England from continuing to be the "Elysium of the capitalist and the purgatory of the labourer," as Ravenstone had declared.[45]

The paper never disputed the low wages and destitution that afflicted much of rural England through these years. In its early editions, before the removal of the Corn Laws, it blamed rural poverty and fires on agricultural protection. In one of its early editions, for example, it quotes at length approvingly from a story in the *Liverpool Mercury,* another anti–Corn Law paper. The story captures many of the themes and much of the tone adopted by the *Economist.* The story blamed the "increasing number of incendiary fires" on:

> the manifold benefits which bad government has bestowed upon the country. The system of sliding scales, high rents, and large farms has ... ground down the wages of the agricultural labourers to some seven shillings a week ... and has reduced them to one common level of misery. ... the deformed wreck of a human being crushed by precocious labour, hunger, and exposure to the elements. ... What wonder that grinding, long-continuing, unbearable injustice has at length made the heart rise in madness.[46]

The *Economist* continued to cite reports from other papers, usually the *Morning Chronicle,* about "the dangerous state of feeling" among rural labourers.[47]

The *Economist* was equally disturbed by rural unrest but its proposed solutions to end the fires and ameliorate the condition of labourers were distinct from the sympathetic reports of other papers. As we saw in chapter 4, reporters in both the *Times* and the *Morning Chronicle* suggested the only viable solution was to provide rural workers with land. The *Economist* focused instead on the purported benefits of high agriculture. The paper adopted Nassau Senior's approach to the permanent condition of rural labourers; that is, as it argued in 1846, "at the best, the condition of the labouring peasantry must, ... be one of hardship; that is, their rude and constant labour will only supply them with the barest necessaries." Rural workers' wretchedness could only be ameliorated by increased wages; such an increase would be determined by the difference between "low farming and farming highly."[48]

This became the paper's mantra: only increased capital investment in agriculture in the form of high farming would relieve the plight of agricultural workers by increasing wages.[49] As the paper said in 1846, "The real object should be – first, to promote that increased application of capital to husbandry, which will raise the wages of agricultural labourers, by augmenting the demand for their services."[50] Or, as it argued the next year, "Labourers are starving within sight of acre on acre of land, on which they could easily raise ... the value of their wages three times fold. Why is this?" Arthur Young had asked the same question a half century earlier and his answer was to provide the labourers with that land. The *Economist* had an entirely different response; for the paper: "The short and general answer is, that the connecting link of capital is wanting."[51]

The paper asserted that the end of the Corn Laws, reducing the costs of food for labourers and bringing competition to farmers, would raise wages and put an end to the worst of the concerns of agricultural labourers. But along with their general disappointment with changes in agriculture, they needed to recognize there had not been a general increase in agricultural wages even well into the 1850s. When such raises were evident, the paper admitted that they occurred primarily because of increased emigration with the attraction of gold discoveries abroad, or migration to the northern industrial cities.

Migration to industrial cities was to be particularly celebrated. The *Liverpool Mercury* had described the "deluge of pauperism" flooding into the cities as the "safety-valve of the machine" preventing even more rural unrest.[52] In 1850, the *Economist* put a different spin on this migration and argued that labourers were "always glad ... to escape agriculture to commerce and manufactures."[53] By 1853, the *Economist* was celebrating the news from the census that the town population had now eclipsed that of the countryside and hoped more would follow.[54] A little over a year later, it crowed that such changes had "broken down the parochial and patriarchal barriers which made each spot of land a gaol, though a home, for a particular portion of the community, and the same progress will cause them to be entirely removed."[55]

But the writers for the paper were apparently a little confused about whether high agriculture would increase the demand for labour or not. On many occasions, the paper asserted that high agriculture used more labour, and in this way should increase wages.[56] Thus, agricultural labourers themselves should be the most in favour of the transition to high farming: "Low farming is to them synonymous with low wages and precarious employment; while high farming affords to the workingman good wages and constant work."[57] On the other hand, the paper also reiterated often that high agriculture meant producing much more with less labour. In 1846, in opposition to arguments that landlords should be required to employ more people, the paper was clear: "Putting aside the fact, that to improve cultivation is really to diminish the number of hands employed in agriculture, surely this demand is most unreasonable. Like other men, they pursue their own interest, and they hold the land to this end."[58] In 1850, it celebrated that, "There never was so large a crop grown and harvested at so little cost for labour." Three years later, it again remarked, "It is the essential quality of all agricultural improvements to produce more from the soil by less labour, and make fewer hands necessary to raise the quantity of food required. ... though a great deal more has been produced from a smaller surface, fewer hands have been required to produce it."[59]

Though occasionally the paper expressed some sympathy for agricultural labourers thus thrown out of work, more often it found fault with the workers themselves. In 1850, it argued that a large portion of the paupers found in rural areas were "men of dissolute and unsteady habits, whom nobody employs by choice or in regular work, and they very commonly consume with utter improvidence the large wages they earn during the summer months, and go into workhouses during the winter." Agricultural mechanization, reducing the demand for labour, "will form the most valuable protection to the farmer against his present dependence on occasional labourers."[60]

Valuable protection for the farmer perhaps, but little relief for labourers. Given the paper's belief that the best way to remedy distress in the countryside was to propel migration to the cities or out of the country, it staunchly opposed anything that might contribute to staying put. In explaining the disappointing effects of improved agriculture on raising wages, the *Economist* suggested that the fault lay in the way the effects of supply and demand were "modified" through the operations of the Poor Law. The Poor Law, of course, was attacked because it reduced the need for labourers to rely on their own initiative and steadiness: "Everything which detracts from self-reliance is sure to injure an individual or class acted upon." Though by the 1850s, the determination expressed by Poor Law guardians not to provide out of door relief under strict interpretations of the New Poor Law was praised,[61] the paper still found much to oppose in poor-relief operations. It argued that relief "has deteriorated the condition of the working class in rural districts ... It is nothing more than the application of a portion of the wage-fund to a purpose altogether unprofitable and unproductive."[62] Echoing Smith, the paper identified the Law of Settlement as a particular problem, as it interfered with the free circulation of labour. All of this meant that many districts continued to experience an apparent surplus of agricultural labourers, despite the promises of high agriculture.[63] Indeed, the paper argued in 1847 that they could find no evidence of improvement "either in the physical condition or the stubborn independence of the agricultural labourer" since the passage of the New Poor Law. This "stubborn independence" was partly to blame for the fact that, though the number of paupers on relief had declined since their height, there were still 2,000,000 paupers or one-eighth of the population. "How such an enormous evil is to be dealt with puzzles all ordinary political philosophy."[64]

The Labourer's Panacea

In its zeal to ensure that agricultural labourers benefited from a strict reliance on wage labour, the *Economist* opposed everything which might contribute to this "stubborn independence." It vehemently attacked any suggestion that the few remaining commons were of any use. Private ownership of land was the first step in "the emergence of a people from a barbarous condition." Without this first step there would be no appreciable investment of capital in land and, thus, no possibility of good cultivation. Those people who thought commons were beneficial to the poor were mistaken. "On the contrary," the paper reported, "the semblance of independent existence, scanty and most uncertain, is a temptation to indolent and irregular habits."[65]

Its campaign against allotments was particularly noteworthy. We have seen how various schemes to provide land to rural labourers had been proposed since the last decades of the eighteenth century. Since then, discussions of the need for allotments ebbed and flowed, often in relation to rural unrest. In the 1840s, partly in response to a renewed round of arson, new schemes were promoted by members of both the Commons and Lords, and by social reformers, many organized into the Labourers' Friend Society. We have seen (in chapter 4) how the sympathetic reporter for the *Times* had linked allotments to significantly improved living standards among rural labourers and argued that the presence of allotments led to a dramatic reduction in rural unrest.

As pressure mounted for the provision of allotments during the 1840s, the *Economist* went on the offensive. In 1844, for example, the paper admitted that a cure needed to be found for the problems in rural England "or property bids fair to be devoured between the poor-house on the one hand and the rick-burner on the other." But it warned that this could only be solved by increased wages through increased demand for labour. What it called the "the last and most popular *panacea* for all the labourers' ills – the allotment system" was, the paper said, "a more dangerous scheme and frought [*sic*] with more serious and frightful consequences than any which has been proposed." Allotments would not only "stagnate labour exactly on those spots where it is least needed," they would also divert labour from the employ of farmers where it could be combined with capital and thus become more productive. As the paper argued, "A pursuit ... for which the capitalist cannot pay wages should be instantly abandoned."[66]

Leading the attack in many ways was Lord Radnor. Radnor wrote a series of letters for the *Economist* opposing allotments and the provision of land to labourers. He couched his arguments ostensibly in opposition to the various regulations that usually accompanied such schemes, rather than opposition to relief for the workers themselves. In the same edition as the article cited above, Radnor raised all sorts of practical objections to allotments but suggested that even if they could all be met, "nothing but evil would ensue." He went on to compare the scheme to reinstituting slavery and to Irish poverty: "It was the slave who had provision grounds ...; the emancipated negro works *for wages* ... When this scheme is recommended by worthy people, it is always a matter of astonishment with me, that they do not look to Ireland ... Ireland is the land of allotments; is it not also the land of bad farming, poor farmers, low wages, and a distressed people?"[67]

The *Economist* and the *Examiner* newspaper entered into a dispute in 1844 prompted first by some statements by Radnor about his unwillingness to rent to small occupiers. In one particularly bizarre piece, the *Economist* had tried to argue that the allotments "offends the law of the Division of Labour" by asking the holder of the allotment and his family to do all the tasks involved in farming. The *Examiner's* joyful retort to this piece of foolishness was to claim:

> The real sin is not against the division of labour, but against the employer's claim to the man's whole strength for the day's work. The true dread is that the labourer will reserve some of his strength for cultivation of his allotment, and that his employer will not take all out of him for his fourteenpence a day, and have all the sweat of his brow. This is the task-master's avarice.[68]

The next year, Radnor again raised the spectre of Ireland, and added Malthus into the mix, in opposing a new plan to allow for allotments, citing "its unavoidable tendency to promote early and improvident marriages, and to give an unnatural stimulus to the increase of the population" and arguing that the plan would "lead to the indefinite increase of ... divisions of land, and thus, to many of the evils which now press so severely on the people of Ireland."[69] Silly arguments about the division of labour aside, the *Economist* and various correspondents to the paper identified some real issues with many of the proposed allotment schemes. One such scheme proposed by Robert Hyde Greg, a close ally in the anti–Corn Law fight and brother of the future writer for the paper, was particularly notorious, dictating what could be grown on the allotments, how much time could be spent on them, and prohibiting permaculture. One letter recommended by the paper, signed only by a "True Free Trade Labourer," both criticized Greg's plans and asserted that wage labour was somehow God's plan. In addition to the "negro" slavery and Irish poverty predicted by Radnor, this letter equated allotments to Chinese servitude. It said:

> What the capitalist always wants is, submissive neighbours in his labourers and plenty of them. The cottage garden scheme will certainly increase the number of his labourers ... it will add to their dependency and for a season will keep them quiet till they fall into a species of Chinese servitude ... To live on wages, and on wages only ... and finding its reward day by day in what it brings is in the order of nature and is the permanent condition of man and society. ... I shall embrace Mr. Greg's views when I am convinced that the regulation of selfish avarious [sic] politicians are superior to the wisdom of God.[70]

The paper occasionally endorsed cottage gardens for retired workers but continued to oppose allotments for the most of the next two decades. By the end of the 1850s, faced with continued rural poverty, and with Wilson distracted by India and Greg no longer at the paper, the *Economist* did soften its opposition slightly. In 1859 it still argued that farmers opposed allotments because they "induce labourers ... to withhold ... an unfair proportion of their physical power to bestow it on their own allotments." Nonetheless, it reported positively on an article by John C. Morton in the *Journal of Royal Agricultural Society* in which he had argued that an allotment "attaches a man to the locality in which he lives – it gives him employment for those hours both of his children and himself which would otherwise be wasted – it adds to the comfort of the home. ... All these things tend make him contented and respectable."[71] It is remarkable that more than a half century after Arthur Young and others had so enthusiastically and urgently appealed for cottage gardens and allotments for impoverished workers, after decades of similar comments by informed observers, the *Economist* could be surprised by a reiteration of their advantages, reciting almost exactly the benefits Young recounted for them.

"A Wasteful and Retrograde Misapplication of Human Labour"

Perhaps the *Economist*'s most vigorous denunciations, however, were reserved for anyone who suggested that small-scale or peasant farming could be advantageous. By the 1840s, in contrast to the paper's constant reverence for capital and its magic, there had been many decades of counterarguments attesting both to the benefits and productivity of small-scale and peasant farming. A long list of impassioned observers, some of them considered to be especially knowledgeable about agriculture and rural conditions, had detailed the re-markable productivity of cottage gardens, allotments, and market garden farm-ing – from Arthur Young, Sir Thomas Bernard, and William Cobbett to the commentator who wrote under the name Piercy Ravenstone.

In 1848, two important observers joined this list. In 1845, William Thomas Thornton, who would soon be a close associate of John Stuart Mill in the East India Company office, published an attack on Malthus's argument about over-population. In this, Thornton asserted that Malthus had the cause of population increase all wrong; only among the very poor were people likely to ignore the diminished prospects that too many children would bring. Misery, rather than preventing population increase, as Malthus proposed, was its "principal pro-moter." Thornton provided a survey of peasant livelihoods in a variety of regions of Europe and surmised that modest landholdings with limited needs in locales with relatively equitable distributions of wealth led to comfortable rural lives and insured against rapid population increase. In England, the early Poor Laws had contributed to the security of cottagers, commoners, and rural labourers and fos-tered identification with the parish. In contrast to Malthus's assertions, Thornton argued that the early Poor Laws had also worked to suppress population increase until a profusion of paupers tipped the scale, at which time, the Poor Laws al-lowed the already destitute to follow their own inclinations. Thornton laid the blame for this increase in pauperism, and thus the tendency for population to increase too rapidly, on the changes in agriculture; changes that had reduced the independence and viability of rural livelihoods by restricting access to land and forcing the rural poor to rely on wage labour. Thornton argued, "A vast extent of territory has been brought into cultivation, and great benefit it must be allowed has accrued …; but these advantages have been obtained at the expense of one unfortunate class, and that the one least able to afford it."[72]

In 1848, Thornton followed this up with the publication of *A Plea for Peasant Proprietors, with the Outlines of a Plan for their Establishment in Ireland.* Thorn-ton's 1848 book was both more powerful and more influential than his earlier contribution. In it, Thornton attacked both the prevailing idea that capital was the necessary key to the productiveness of land and that peasant farming led to an impoverished country. He asserted:

> Now since political economy was raised by Adam Smith to the dignity of science, its British professors have been almost unanimously of opinion that small farmers are incompatible with prosperity, either of agriculture or of agricultural labourers. Land, they assert, cannot be properly cultivated unless it be held in large quantities by men of capital.[73]

The constant reiteration of this argument had "prejudiced the minds of many against the admission of opposite evidence."[74] Thornton proceeded to test this evidence by examining the actual production of peasant proprietors in locales where they still had land: Belgium, Guernsey, the Channel Islands, Norway, and Germany.

In much of his work, Thornton argued against propositions put forward by John McCulloch, who along with Senior was the most vehemently anti-peasant of this generation of political economists. McCulloch had argued in his annotated edition of Smith's *Wealth of Nations* that any system of small-holding would lead to sub-division "until the whole land has been parcelled out into patches" and the entire population destitute. He reiterated in an article in *Encyclopedia Britannica* on cottage gardens the old saw that such pieces of land would lead to unwarranted independence for the cottager and "exempts him from the necessity of severe labour and unremitting application." For McCulloch this would lead to disaster. Thornton instead argued that his exploration of peasant farming had shown that the provision of land did not lead to rapid population increase: "those to whom fortune has been bountiful are, in general, proportionately careful not to forfeit her favours by matrimonial imprudence."[75]

In these places, peasants produced dramatically more from their land than larger farmers, with a much greater diversity of crops, and brought more to the market, thus supporting a larger population of small craftspeople and merchants. Thornton was particularly puzzled by arguments that peasants were not industrious: "But, of all the charges brought against small farmers the most amazing is that which represents them as slothful, so diametrically is it opposed to truth, which literally leaps into the eyes of all who are willing to look in the right direction. … their most distinguishing characteristic is ardent, constant, nay almost excessive, industry."[76]

Moreover, for Thornton, peasant proprietorship would lead to harmonious societies with a rural population that was neither servile nor rebellious; echoing Cobbett, he said, "A mere day labourer, half employed, and wretchedly paid, who is compelled to apply to the neighbouring landholders for a livelihood, and obtains from them only a miserable subsistence, not unnaturally regards his employers as oppressors, takes every opportunity of showing his spite against them by wonton aggressions, and is ready to listen to the harangues of seditious demagogues." Conversely, "Throughout western Europe, from the Polar to the Mediterranean seas, wherever there are peasant proprietors there likewise is an orderly and loyal rural population. … In the Channel Islands, Norway, Belgium, Switzerland, and Germany, there are no rick-burners, no breakers of thrashing machines, no riots among country people, and no secret disaffection."[77]

Though passionately and persuasively argued, Thornton's work, coming as it did from a relatively obscure civil servant working for the India Office, might have been relatively easily ignored by the *Economist*. But when Thornton's close associate in the India Office, John Stuart Mill, inspired by Thornton, added a vigorous defence of peasant farming in his 1848 *Principles of Political Economy*, it could not be ignored.

Mill cited many of the same people Thornton had and made many of the same arguments. He wrote, "The advantage ... of small properties in land, is one of the most disputed questions in the range of political economy." Mill went on to say that English writers ignore continental European assertions of the benefits of such small-scale farming primarily because they have little acquaintance with systems of peasant proprietorship and "have almost always the most erroneous ideas of their social condition and mode of life."[78] He cites Samuel Laing, a Scottish travel writer who had been resident in Norway for many years. In his 1842, *Notes of a Traveler*, Laing said:

> If we listen to the large farmer, the scientific agriculturalist, the political econ-
> omist, good farming must [depend on] ... large farms; the very idea that good
> farming can exist, unless on large farms cultivated with great capital, they hold to
> be absurd. Draining, manuring, economic arrangement, cleaning the land, regu-
> lar rotations, valuable stock and implements all belong exclusively to large farms,
> worked by large capital, and by hired labour. This reads well; but if we raise our
> eyes from their books to their fields, and coolly compare what we see in the best
> districts farmed in large farms, with what we see in the best districts farmed in
> small farms, we see, and there is no blinking the fact, better crops on the ground in
> Flanders, East Friesland, Holstein,. ... Minute labour on small portions of arable
> ground gives evidently, in equal soils and climates, a superior productiveness.[79]

Like Thornton, Mill also addressed the issue of population increase and after surveying the literature concluded, "I am not aware of a single authentic instance which supports the assertion that rapid multiplication is promoted by peasant properties."[80] Finally, Mill concluded:

> I conceive it to be established, that there is no necessary connexion between [peas-
> ant properties] ... and an imperfect state of the arts of production; that it is favour-
> able ... to the most effective use of the powers of the soil; that no existing state of
> agricultural economy has so beneficial an effect on the industry, the intelligence,
> the frugality, and prudence of the population ... and that no other, therefore, is on
> the whole so favourable ... both to their moral and physical welfare.[81]

Mill was by this time most certainly the best known and most highly re-
garded of this generation of political economists. His defence of small-scale farming and the inherent criticism of the claims for capital demanded a response. Despite its stated misgivings about the "wretched state" of English ag-
riculture, the *Economist* readily sprang to the defence of large farms and the necessity of capital.

Its earliest condemnations of small farms and peasant proprietorship were relatively mild. The paper observed, "Some have the idea that small farms are favourable to economy and increase of production. Experience teaches the reverse." Though it did not outline the experience referred to, the paper focused its criticism on arguments about the productiveness of labour, arguing that labour augmented by capital would always be more productive, and thus more beneficial to society and to the labourer himself, "than when left to its own clumsy and unassisted expedients."

As part of the evidence for this, the paper often remarked on the distinction between spade agriculture and ploughing. Some of those people supporting small-scale or peasant agriculture had argued that they produced more from small bits of land partly because spade agriculture was more efficient in such circumstances than ploughing. To dispute this, the *Economist* argued that if spade agriculture was so profitable to small farmers, it should be equally profitable to large farmers, who should thus set 500 labourers to work with spades on 1000 acres. But this was not done, because it was not profitable.[82] One writer to the *Morning Chronicle* recounted in a story a conversation he had with a French peasant who argued he produced more with a spade than he could with a plough. The writer than asked the peasant why large farmers did not do so. The peasant said it would cost the farmer too much in labour. "Here in lies the fallacy," the writer said. All labour is either productive or not; the peasant simply did not understand that his labour was not productive. The *Economist* agreed with this assessment wholeheartedly. "So far from being advantageous to promote spade-cultivation," it reasoned:

> [W]e deem it to be a wasteful and retrograde misapplication of human labour. It has been said that the owner of a small holding is ever industrious, ... but it may be asked what benefit is that to himself or to the community, if ... his isolated labour is far less productive than his labour when employed in connection with capital and in combination with other labourers under the superintendence of a capitalist with skill and enterprise?[83]

After the initial publication of Thornton's *A Plea for Peasant Proprietorship* the paper engaged in a review of this work. The *Economist* (in an article that would appear to have been penned by Hodgskin) suggested that Thornton had produced a careful study that should be read alongside McCulloch's works cited above. However, it went on to argue that Thornton's work had no real relevance to England. It reiterated that the productiveness of labour was the source of all wealth. The question of large or small was of as little importance in farming as it was in other forms of manufacture. But, it said, progress implied the expansion of fortunes and thus the increasing size of all endeavours. The division of land into small farms was a symptom – but not the cause, necessarily – of a lack of progress, of a society and people "hemmed in." "We apprehend, therefore, that the division of land into small portions … is more to be regarded with disfavour, as a sign of society coming to a stand-still, with all the evils of a stationary or declining condition." The paper went on to admit that in England such progress had benefited the rich and "circumstances … gave the owners of capital great and increasing advantage and superiority in relation to the labouring classes." But, it declined to identify specifically those "circumstances."[84]

After Mill published his *Principles* later that same year, the paper became more strident in its denunciation of peasant farming. In November 1848, it admitted that a "certain number of farms from 50 to 100 acres" in each district would be advantageous "as stepping stones to the thrifty agricultural labourer in working his way into the condition of a farmer." But, they asserted, "all the quotations made by Mr. Mill … prove the painful frugality and unremitting and ill-rewarded toil" of the peasant proprietors of France, Italy, Germany, and Switzerland. The paper concluded, in an argument hauntingly similar to Young's early (and subsequently abandoned) discussion of the difference between French and English rural populations, "We have no doubt that the division of the classes dependent upon the land, into proprietors, tenants and farm-labourers, … will be found to be an important onward step in the progress of civilisation. … It will be found that constant and regularly paid agricultural wages will conduce more to the comfort and advancement of our labourers than the precarious independence of peasant farming."[85] In 1850, in a further attack on Mill, the paper disparaged "political economists of some note – great friends of the people – who lend their influence to the scheme of sending people back on the land." It went further in condemning any scheme to provide agricultural workers with land:

> A petty agriculture and garden cultivation may be very pleasant occupations for persons with small independent incomes; here and there they may eke out a peasant's means of subsistence. … it might drive the people back to serfdom; it would never advance their independence. It might make England like Ireland … and counsel the people amiss … divert them from the course of improvement they have entered on to become something like pauper occupants of small allotment of land, or inhabitants of self-sustaining villages.[86]

The next year, it continued its attack on both peasant farming and Mill. The *Economist* warned:

> The belief that land occupied in small farms, where cultivated with great industry, is more productive than when occupied in farms sufficiently large to insure the combination of labour, good implements, and stock – in short, capitalist enterprise – may be said to be something more than a popular fallacy when we find

so philosophical a writer as Mr. J.S. Mill according to it. This fallacious notion is everywhere contradicted by facts and experience. Usually petit-farming is a miserable affair.[87]

The paper warned that not only was such farming miserable for the peasants, it would also lead to a collapse of manufacturing because peasants would produce goods for themselves. And, of course, it refused to countenance arguments that peasant farming would not lead to a disastrous increase in the agricultural population.[88]

The paper did not cite examples of the "facts and experience" to which it referred. But it soon felt the need to ignore evidence provided by one of its own writers. Given the *Economist*'s determination to prove small farming harmful to the rural poor, it must have been particularly distressing for Wilson when the paper let three articles on French farming from an unnamed correspondent slip through in 1855. In April, a story for the paper surveying French husbandry said, "In most places the size of the various patches proves that the extent of the land occupied by one person must be small. … Nothing, however, can exceed the clean and careful cultivation which is universal." And, the story suggested that England might have much to learn from France.[89] In September of the same year, presumably the same correspondent remarked, "The more we wander through the rural districts of France, the more we are impressed with the intelligence and industry of the French peasantry."[90] A little more than a month later, the correspondent provided a description of the Valley of Isere that resembled the description of well-managed cottage gardens provided by Trevor Burnard more than half a century previously:

> This tract of the country is one which exhibits most completely the system of small properties and peasant proprietors. … There are no agricultural labourers for hire, each family depending on the labour of its own members. … Surrounding each field are walnut trees of large size, and across from them are alternate rows of mulberry trees and vines. … Melons and pumpkins grow here in great profusion. … The cultivator of this district … has, besides his cereals, roots, and green crops, three sources of profit from his land – first, the mulberry leaves for his silk worms; next, his walnuts, which are made into oil; and thirdly, his vines. … A fair was being held, where we saw an immense concourse of the peasantry in their best attire. … The men … looked as intelligent and respectable as the great body of farmers assembled at one of our own country fairs … and they appeared to be enjoying themselves in that easy, quiet, polite way which is characteristic of the whole population of France.[91]

One can't help but wonder what debates the publication of such stories commenting so favourably on French peasant agriculture in the midst of the distress prevailing in the English countryside prompted among the inner circle in the *Economist*. One searches in vain, though, for similar stories in subsequent editions of the paper. When in 1861 William Trotter had the temerity at a Farmers Club meeting to suggest, "I have not been able to discover that large farms have much advantage over small ones. I admit the tendency is to the increasing of size. I see some evil in this, but it partakes of the general tendency of the age, which is that of collecting wealth into heaps and population into dense masses," the *Economist* responded that large farms and heaps of wealth, were, indeed, a sign of progress: the "natural tendency of increasing wealth and prosperity."[92]

There appeared to be little evidence of such a tendency to prosperity in rural England. Through the 1850s, the situation for agricultural labourers was almost uniformly bleak. Though the *Economist* had on occasion joined in the chorus denouncing the war on cottages and recommending more be built, it opposed cottage gardens and soon expressed ambivalence about calls for cottages. When the *Morning Chronicle* published a series on the problems rural labourers had in obtaining habitation, the *Economist* found reason to oppose most of their plans, arguing that "we must not be led away by a desire for the elevation of the working class."[93] Meanwhile, more than a decade later, the first national survey of agricultural labourers' accommodation reported that of the 5,375 cottages surveyed, there were 8,805 bedrooms for 25,000 people. At a time when the Poor Law mandated a minimum airspace of 500 cubic feet per inhabitant of workhouses, cottagers enjoyed less than a third of that.[94] That same year, Dr. E. Smith presented a report to Parliament on the diet of the working class. He reported that in agricultural districts close to half of the people were chronically malnourished because of an absolute lack of food. The *Economist* was shocked but counselled, "The only real remedy is an increase of wages to be repaid by higher cultivation, the use of machinery, and *the increase of power to be obtained from the human machine when you give him enough oil*."[95]

Chapter Nine

Ireland: "They Lie Beyond the Pale"

The *Economist* was most concerned with ensuring the triumph of capital in England. But the paper also focused significant attention on other places further afield. The *Economist* wrote often and at length about Ireland, incorporated into the United Kingdom of Great Britain and Ireland through the Act of Union in 1801. Issues around the application of capital to the improvement of agriculture – and the accompanying dilemma of what to do with the multitude of under-tenants farming tiny plots of land (cottiers) – drew significant attention from the paper even before the failure of the potato crop beginning in 1845 devastated Ireland. As we have seen, for more than four decades before that point, the purported lessons of Ireland – the poverty and overpopulation that threatened England if it allowed a proliferation of peasant farming – were a constant threat trotted out whenever the shift to large-scale capitalist agricultural improvement was questioned. Being "beyond the pale" (the circle of control and influence of Normal lords surrounding Dublin in the thirteenth to sixteenth centuries) was an often-used evocation of Irish backwardness.

During the famine years, between 1845 and 1850, the *Economist*, mirroring much of the British populace, struggled to find an appropriate response to the distress. The *Economist*'s articles were sometimes sympathetic and concerned, but the paper more often fell back on harsh remedies derived from its rigid application of "nothing but pure principles" that counselled eliminating aid and dispossessing cottiers. Wilson and the *Economist* were especially influential in promoting policy to do with Ireland. From 1847 until 1852, Lord Clarendon (George Villiers) was the Lord-Lieutenant of Ireland. Clarendon was an old associate of Wilson from the anti–Corn Law struggles, and a personal friend. During Clarendon's rule, the paper unstintingly complimented the Lord Lieutenant in its stories. Letters between Wilson and Clarendon also made it clear that the Lord Lieutenant sought advice and inspiration from the paper.[1]

More than one million people died of famine or related diseases in Ireland between 1845 and 1851. Another million and a half people emigrated; Ireland lost about a quarter of its population. Emigration in large numbers continued for decades following the famine; by the end of the century, Ireland's population was half of what it had been before the famine. For more than fifty years, historians and others have debated the responsibility the English government should bear in these deaths. From Cecil Woodham-Smith's classic *The Great Hunger* in 1962 to Tim Patt Coogan's account more than half a century later, authors have argued that a blind faith in neo-liberal policies contributed decisively to the more than a million deaths and avalanche of poor emigrants.[2] Many of these accounts have asserted that the British government engaged in a process that was at best short-sighted and ignorant and at worst deliberately genocidal. Yet no historian has analysed the important role the *Economist* played in coaching, cajoling, and inspiring the Russell government to apply strict and harsh lessons from political economy to Ireland. If the British government deserves to be labelled genocidal because of its actions in Ireland, then the *Economist* was constantly at its shoulder urging harsher treatment. Through the years of the famine, the paper kept up a continuous, if sometimes erratic, demand that the principles of political economy be applied to Ireland and that Ireland be "cleared" to make way for capital. In this instance the fairy dust of political economy turned particularly toxic.

"Almost Idiotic Wretchedness"

Ireland held a special place in the English economy and politics. Land ownership was even more concentrated in Ireland than in England itself; 90 per cent of the land was owned by 5,000 landlords, many of them absentee English owners who could trace their ownership from the allocation of land following Cromwell's subjugation of Irish revolt in the seventeenth century. Many of England's most powerful aristocrats also owned estates in Ireland. Most of the land was handled by agents and leased out to tenants, many of whom then divided the land among under-tenants, who often let out their land in even smaller parcels. The result was a large population of families on small plots of land – cottiers – who provided work for larger tenant farmers but who depended on their plots of land for much of their subsistence. Increasingly cottiers concentrated on potatoes, augmented by dairy and, more often, pigs. By 1841, there were about 2.3 million landless labourers out of a population of a little more than 8,000,000 people; there were 135,000 holdings of less than one acre and almost half of the rest of the 440,000 farms in the country were no larger than 10 acres. About half of that population depended on the potato for the bulk of their food.[3]

Most accounts of rural Ireland in the late eighteenth and early nineteenth centuries stressed the poverty of cottiers. They lived in "wretched hovels" worse than anywhere in Europe, according to J.G. Kohl. "Misery, naked and famishing

... covers the entire country," or so thought Gustave de Beaumont in the 1830s.[4] The 1841 census reported that of the 1.8 million homes in the country, close to a million were "mud huts," with almost 500,000 of them consisting of one room.[5] One article in a Belfast newspaper in 1845 recounted the correspondent's horror on encountering dwellings that, "looked to me like the abodes of extinguishing hope – forgotten instincts – grovelling, despairing, almost idiotic wretchedness. I did not know there were such sights in the world. I did not know that men and women, upright and in God's image, could live in styes like swine, *with* swine – sitting, lying down, cooking, eating in such filth."[6]

This poverty was often considered to be largely the result of population growth. Estimates of Irish population levels prior to the first census, which was carried out in 1821, were based on hearth taxes and other indirect means, many carried out by Kenneth Connell in the 1950s.[7] Re-examining these and census figures, Cormac O'Grada has calculated that the population of Ireland was slightly over 3 million in the middle of the eighteenth century, rising to 6.8 million by the time of the 1821 census, and reaching just over 8 million twenty years later.[8] Malthus, for one, argued in a letter to David Ricardo in 1817 that the "predominant evil" in Ireland was "a population greatly in excess of the demand for labour." He continued, "The *Land* in Ireland is infinitely more peopled than in England, and to give full effect to the natural resources of the country a great part of the population should be swept from the soil into large manufacturing and commercial towns."[9]

Closely associated with the evils of an excessive population was the effect of extensive potato cultivation. So often repeated that it became a truism, it was argued that potatoes made living too easy for the Irish cottier and thus prevented them from being compelled to further industry. Remember the discussion between Malthus and Ricardo outlined in chapter 5. Despite Ricardo's cautions expressed in that exchange, the need to break the links between dependence on the potato and the independence (and supposed indolence) of the cottier was constantly reasserted. J. Curwen, in a pamphlet in 1818, outlined the supposed curse of the potato:

> The potato, which in some points of view may justly be regarded as one of the greatest blessing to our species, is capable of operating the greatest calamities, ... for as the cultivation of a single statute acre may successfully and easily be attended by one individual and as its produce on an average would give food for at least ten persons the year round ... what chance is there for manual exertion in such a society among whom a patrimonial aversion to labour and an habitual attachment to idleness are paramount to every consideration.[10]

J. Stanley, in an 1836 booklet warning about the extension of the Poor Laws to Ireland, argued, "If there was no potato, there would be no cottier – that foe to the agriculturalist – and land would be legitimately cultivated by capital."[11] An official government report in 1845 asserted that the "population is pushed much beyond the industry and present resources of the country" and blamed the potato and "the cheapness of the nourishing root" for this population growth.[12]

There were some counterarguments. In his 1780 *Tour of Ireland*, Arthur Young argued that the Irish peasant could be most industrious; if waste lands were given over to them on good leases, they would turn the country into the most productive garden. Young, like many commentators, was struck by the health and physical well-being of the cottier and he attributed this, as did Adam Smith, to the abundance of the potato. Young said, "When I see the people of a country in spite of political oppression with well formed bodies, and their cottages swarming with children; when I see their men athletic, and their women beautiful, I know not how to believe them subsisting on an unwholesome food." He went on to suggest, "If anyone doubts the comparative plenty which attends the board of a poor native of England and Ireland, let him attend to their meals."[13] Indeed, it is now well established that substantial Irish population growth through the late eighteenth and early nineteenth centuries was the result of significantly lower levels of mortality and longer life spans than prevalent throughout Europe and not a particularly high birth rate.

Despite the apparent backwardness of Irish agriculture, and despite the vaunted opinion held by agricultural improvers of their activities in England, Ireland became an important source of food for England. During the latter half of the eighteenth century, Ireland provided England with half of its agricultural imports. In 1801, Ireland was added to the Union, freeing trade between the two even further. By 1824, trade between Ireland and England was completely free of restraints and Ireland was providing more than 70 per cent of England's basic food imports. In addition, abetted by more efficient steam ships, by the 1830s Ireland was regularly shipping more than 600,000 head of cattle, sheep, and pigs to Britain.[14] As James Belich has argued, "It was Ireland that made up the difference between British food output and food consumption during the first decades of the Industrial Revolution."[15]

"Wanderers on the World's Bleak Common"

Decades of subdivision of tenancies to cottiers had created a nest of problems. Landowners, absentee or not, relied on agents or tenants to rent out their land but exhibited an "excessive compulsion with the size of their rents," in the words of Kenneth Connell.[16] Most often this meant increasing subdivision of the land in the con-acre system, whereby a cottier would get a plot of land, often an acre or two, on a yearly contract in return for an elevated rent, often paid for through work calculated at very low wages.[17] Population increase, the attractions of potato land, and – perhaps – the lack of alternative employment meant there were ready applicants for such land. As Young observed, many a landlord found that "the little occupiers were the *best* pay they had on their estates." Young considered the principal tenants, occupied in letting out land to cottiers, to be the "most oppressive species of tyrants. … Not satisfied with screwing up the rent to the uttermost farthing, they are rapacious and relentless in the collection of it."[18] As estate owners sought to improve their estates and respond to new opportunities in the export markets, they often did not renew leases with the principal tenants or intermediaries and demanded that the land be turned over to them absent of cottiers. The under-tenantry had little protection in such cases and were usually thrown from the land.

By the 1830s, there were increased calls for the government to do more to protect and encourage the investment of capital in Ireland. "Improving" landlords were frequently met by protests from tenants and "agrarian outrages" not dissimilar to those afflicting England itself. Linked to concerns about rural unrest was a growing demand for a Poor Law in Ireland, modelled in some ways on the new 1834 English Poor Law. Debates around the introduction of the Irish Poor Law were heated. Nassau Senior, who eventually became one of the commissioners of the long-running Royal Commission for inquiring into the poorer classes in Ireland, disagreed with the introduction of any relief. When Lord John Russell in a speech in Parliament remarked that the Irish poor, "through no fault of their own," were constantly in want, Senior was quick to disagree. He said, "If the Irish labourers allow their numbers to increase without any reference to the means of subsistence, a portion of them, must every year … perish from want … I cannot admit that it would occur *without any fault of their own*." Senior went on to argue that the only remedy for Ireland was to reduce the population and increase the amount of capital invested in the country through the elimination of small holdings. As he said, "The only remedy is treating the land not as a source of subsistence, but as a machine for the investment of capital."[19] Elsewhere, Senior had reiterated that the problem lay in land held by cottiers. In a letter to Lord Howick, he said, "The land is occupied in such minute portions, and generally infested by so numerous a population, that the agricultural capitalist cannot find a field for his exertions."[20]

Sir George Nichol, who was most responsible for writing the final report of the commission before the law was passed in 1838, made it clear that the intent of the Irish Poor Law was to make Ireland more attractive to capital by taming cottier unrest and making it easier to remove them from the land. He argued that while there had been much progress in Ireland since the Act of Union in 1801, this prosperity was not evident in rural areas primarily because the influx of capital had been overwhelmed by the increase of population. Moreover, the cottier had come to see their plot of land "as conferring an almost interminable right of possession." The struggle for land meant, according to Nichol, that "the peasantry have combined and burst through the restraints of law and humanity."[21] Despite the opposition of Senior, the Act for the More Effectual Relief of the Poor in Ireland was passed in 1838. Like its 1834 English cousin, the 1838 Irish Poor Law relied heavily on the horrors and "moral disagreeableness" of the workhouse as a way both to reduce the costs of poor relief and to guard against indolence.[22] Unlike in England, the Irish Poor Law did not stipulate a "right" to relief and it relied even more heavily on the workhouse.

In 1843, as conflict over land continued and threatened to prevent further agricultural improvement, the Peel government created a Commission, commonly called the Devon Commission after its chair, the Earl of Devon, an Irish Conservative landowner, to examine the issue. The focus of the commission was on the relationship between landlords and substantial tenants. The commission reinforced the right of landlords to evict tenants, but also asserted the need for landlords to compensate tenants for improvements to the land. The commission, which reported in 1845 on the cusp of the famine, was important in helping shape the nature of some subsequent land legislation in Ireland but it did little to address the most pressing issue: What was to become of cottiers who were not tenants to the landlord in these cases? The commission heard testimony of clearances carried out "for the purpose of consolidating small tenements into larger holdings," described as "generally accompanied with much misery and suffering to those who were removed." The commission went on to say that too often such movements occurred "without sufficient reference to the future fate of the people removed," and observed that "their ejectment … brought absolute destitution."[23] But it did little to address the real problem. In 1844, the *Economist* remarked that even while the commission was meeting throughout Ireland, "the system of eviction" continued. The paper reprinted part of a story from the *Waterford Chronicle* about the police and bailiff taking possession of lands on which the four principal tenants had fallen in arrears on the rent. While only these four had fallen behind, their under-tenants, twenty-three families who had all paid their rent to the principal tenants, "were cast homeless and friendless from their dwellings, wanderers on the world's bleak common … It was truly a heartrending sight to behold them, with their families assembled in groups, lighting fires by the ditch side to boil a few potatos [*sic*]."[24]

"Frightful Spectacles as no words can describe"

If Ireland presented the threat of a teeming, impoverished, rebellious rural population in the early 1840s, the spectacle became much more alarming after a fungal infection hit the potato crop throughout Europe in 1845. The blight continued in Ireland for the next four harvests, devastating the major food crop for the bulk of the population and spreading horrible famine in its wake. If a population that was too large, too independent because of the ease of subsistence, and too dependent on the potato was the "predominant evil" in Ireland before 1845, then the famine and its aftermath provided the most effective remedy. As Charles Trevelyan, the Assistant Secretary to the Treasury in the Russell administration and the man most responsible for policies in Ireland – knighted for his service to the crown during the famine – remarked:

> The famine is a direct stroke of an all-wise and all merciful Providence, which laid bare the deep and inveterate root of social evil [unchecked population growth]. The famine was the sharp but effectual remedy by which the cure is likely to be affected. ... God grant that the generation to which this opportunity has been offered may rightly perform its part.

Or, as one landlord declared, "Nothing but the successive failure of the potato ... could have produced the emigration which will, I trust, give us room to be civilised."[25]

The Peel administration felt compelled to provide some relief, but given the heated political debate surrounding both Ireland and poor relief, Peel stepped cautiously. Privately, almost secretively, he arranged for banker friends to provide funds for the purchase of "Indian," that is, North American, corn meal to be distributed. While this measure almost certainly saved some lives during the first few months of the famine, it was both too meagre – just over £100,000 worth – and not particularly successful: even poor Irish did not take to the meal and there is evidence that it was substantially lacking in nutritional quality.

The administration of Lord John Russell that succeeded Peel's in 1846 was more tied to ideas of laissez-faire political economy in its approach to relief. It sought to clarify land tenure in Ireland through an Encumbered Estates Act that would allow the sale of mortgaged estates and permit new owners to clear their lands of tenants and cottiers more easily, while hopefully attracting capital and agricultural improvers to Ireland. Part of the government's effort was focused on revising poor rates and taxes upwards to ensure that Irish landlords paid for Irish relief. The destitute were to confine themselves to poor houses – in effect giving up their rights to their tiny plots of land – to receive relief. As disease and hunger took its toll, the death rate in workhouses reached astonishing levels, in excess of twenty-five per thousand each week in 1847. Perhaps in a more readily grasped statistic: the Cork Union Workhouse experienced a death an hour through the worst years of the famine. One report from Carrick-on-Shannon in early 1847 said that in a poor house of 1,050 inmates, there were twelve deaths a week. Still, there were three people applying for each space available. The correspondent reported, "Famine and wretchedness presented themselves in the most striking manner; ... the children, in particular, were reduced almost to skeletons, their hands like claws of birds, their arms and legs wasted until there was little but bone. … It is with a perfect knowledge of the state of things within, that the poor Irish, entreat for admission into this pestilential workhouse."[26] As James Donnelly said, "Resigned to death many entered the workhouses only to assure themselves a coffin at public expense."[27]

The Russell government also relied on work gangs, in which the hungry poor were put to work on public works, in agricultural improvement projects, or in building railroads. Trevelyan was constantly worried, however, that such duties would keep people from relying on their own initiative. In a self-congratulatory piece about his role in Ireland published in the *Edinburgh Review* in 1848, he reported that to ensure that those who could make a living elsewhere relied on their own initiative, he arbitrarily struck 20 per cent of the people receiving work relief off the list in March 1847 and engaged in successive reductions following; "and the crisis passed without any disturbance of the public peace or any perceptible aggravation …" As Trevelyan saw the issue: "The great evil with which we have to contend is not the physical evil of the famine, but the moral evil of the selfish, perverse and turbulent character of the people."[28]

"Martyrs to the cause of human improvement"

It was in this context – this horror with its buried promise of redemption – that the *Economist* sought to refine the science of political economy and apply it to a distressed Ireland. To read the paper through these early years with the benefit of hindsight, anticipating the famine and the deaths, prompts a shudder at what was to come and amazement at the deliberate blindness of those who commented on Ireland.

Before the famine, the paper occasionally recognized the prevailing poverty in Ireland, but argued that it saw reasons to be confident about future prospects if Ireland continued on the road to agricultural improvement. In January 1845, *The Economist* commented on the "great and general improvement" over the last two years, the "miraculous conversion to temperance of the most intemperate people on earth," and attributed this to the demand for Irish agricultural products in the industrial cities of England.[29] As with every other issue, the paper vehemently argued that free trade and, specifically, the end of the Corn Laws would provide the most benefit to Ireland. The paper did not ignore the concerns raised about land problems in Ireland. In 1844, it commented that it understood "That those who own the soil may not exercise their rights in the wisest and justest [*sic*] way." Still, it argued there was no excuse for an "interference with the right of private property" and asserted that, "the real grievance of Ireland is – that there are more people in it than are profitably employed …"[30] One response to this article came from Joseph Crook, who said in a letter to the editor, "The MONSTER GRIEVANCE OF IRELAND IS THAT ENGLISHMEN ARE EATING AT THE IRISHMAN'S TABLE, CLEARING EVERYTHING

OFF, LEAVING NOTHING FOR HIM BUT TO REJOICE ON POTATOES ...
The life's blood of the Irish people is wrenched out of their hands!"[31] The paper
used this letter as an opportunity to provide yet another lecture on the benefits
of free trade and the ending of the Corn Laws. The paper argued somewhat
contradictorily that the best way to feed the Irish was for Ireland to export more
food to an industrializing Britain.[32]

The *Economist* never fully addressed concerns, even in those pre-famine
days, about cottiers starving while their country exported the best of its food,
stated so forcefully by Joseph Crook. When Daniel O'Connell (one of the leaders of the campaign to repeal the Union and the most popular politician in Ireland) gave a speech in London describing the "wretched" condition of Ireland,
complaining that while millions of people were hungry Parliament concerned
itself with funding a College in Ireland, and proclaiming, "feed the starving
population of Ireland before you think of educating them," the *Economist* provided a taste of what political economy had in store for an Ireland soon faced
with hunger on a very different scale. It responded to O'Connell, "We do not
like the eternal cry of 'give' 'give' pressed on governments from Ireland ... It is
not good for a people to be taught at every turn that *governments* can do them
much good. ... A lesson of SELF-RELIANCE taught them by a man of such
infinite resources ... would be the best thing that ever has been done for Irishmen or Ireland."[33] Clearly the paper's definition of self-reliance was somewhat
limited; it precluded any movement meant to direct Irish agriculture for its own
population or even any suggestion that might provide incentives for Irish industry. And it surely did not include any idea that cottier or peasant agriculture
was dramatically more "self-reliant" than wage labour.

Along with concerns about Ireland's proclivity to request assistance, the paper was most troubled by rural unrest. Through the summer of 1845, before
the famine was felt, the paper commented in alarmist language about the violent tendencies of Irish rural society. It labelled one relatively minor incident "a
dreadful conflict between the police and the peasantry." In the same edition the
paper suggested that these rural outrages "opens up to view a state of society ...
to which there is no parallel in Europe." Slightly later in that summer, the paper
reported on "a state of terrorism" leading many of the "leading gentry" to seek
refuge in Dublin.[34]

In Ireland, though, just about everything depended on the potato. There
had been periodic failures of the potato harvest in parts of Ireland in previous
years, most notably in 1822 and through a few years in the middle of the 1830s.
They were mostly localized and, while brutal for the cottiers whose crops were
affected, they did not lead to widespread trouble. The 1844 harvest looked especially good. The *Limerick Chronicle* said the crop was the "best on record"
and commented on how "the poor man's harvest ... exhibits in the smallest
gardens an amazing quantity of this inestimable root."[35] By the end of the next

summer, the signs turned ominous. As the *Economist* said, "The most serious apprehensions are beginning to be entertained" as the cold and wet weather of July continued into August.[36] A month later, the blight was becoming more apparent and its breadth, not only through Ireland but in Britain and across Europe, more obvious. There ensued a desperate search for the cause and a remedy. By October, the *Economist* reported, "Accounts from Ireland are appalling and distressing. Habitually subsisting on the lowest food, there is no gradation between their usual existence and starvation."[37]

In the midst of the deepening famine, there were multiple calls to restrict the export of food. The *Freeman's Journal* reported in November 1845 that in the last week the port of Galway alone sent 3,448 tons of oats, 800 quarters of wheat, and 8,546 quarters of barley and asked, "Will the executive still persist in alleging that it is 'premature' to take active measures for the alleviation of the miseries with which we are threatened, when in some districts famine is already imminent, while the rapid increase in the export of 'bread stuffs' threatens, in no long period of time, to leave us utterly unprovided with a substitute for the decomposed potatoes?"[38] Others took more direct action; that same month the *Limerick Chronicle* reported that they expected there would soon be riots to prevent potatoes from being exported. Two additional companies of soldiers were "held in readiness to march" to Galway should they be needed.[39] By the next month, the situation was becoming increasingly dire. One letter to the paper warned that no one yet knew what to make of the blight or how to eradicate it. "The evil is without precedent, and I fear without hope. … There will not be food for three-fourths of the people of Ireland before May next. The children's wailings, the mother's woes, the father's sorrow, the plague that follow famine, are all near at hand."[40]

The *Economist*'s response to this increasing alarm was a combination of opportunism and blindness. Its primary consideration was to use the famine as another, and most powerful, argument for the elimination of the Corn Laws. Admitting that it was difficult to see that every steamship on its way to the continent was loaded with potatoes, it cautioned, "We would place no restriction on exports; but we would remove all restrictions from imports; and then we might rest satisfied that no exchange would take place that was not beneficial to the country."[41] It kept up an incessant clamour that the elimination of the Corn Laws was the most effectual remedy for the famine. As it did for England itself, the paper advised putting aside all other attempts at legislation until the Corn Laws were ended. When it finally appeared that they would get their most ardent desire and that the Peel government on its last legs would pass such legislation, the paper presented a rosy and completely unrealistic picture of the future, suggesting reports were favourable about the disease and that with the passage of the law "the pestilence, which at present hangs over the unhappy country, may be in some measure averted."[42]

After the ending of the Corn Laws, with little relief for Irish hunger in sight, there was continued popular opposition to food exports, expressed most directly through attacks on those transporting foodstuffs, ranging from harassment of dairy maids taking milk out of a local region, to blocking roads to prevent the internal movement of grain, to much larger battles to prevent shipments of wheat out of Ireland, to riots looting bakeries and granaries similar to those occurring only a few years earlier in England itself. In October 1846, the *Cork Examiner* reported that "an immense number of people ... came here this morning with clubs, determined to sack and pillage the town." Military gunboats were deployed on the Blackwater River to protect grain cargoes. Around the same time, in Dungarven, 12,000 people attacked the bakeries and were only stopped when the Dragoons fired on the crowd.[43]

The *Economist* kept up its opposition to any notion of restricting exports. In Parliament, Lord Bentinck, argued that Ireland grew enough food to feed itself, part of the legacy of the protection of the Corn Laws. The *Economist*, though, asked if that grain were kept in Ireland, "where are the three millions of quarters to come from for the people of Great Britain? ... Lord Bentinck's boast is, that the food which was raised for the people of England ... will now be available for the Irish. ... He would starve the English to relieve the Irish."[44] The paper provided a history lesson drawn from its own peculiar reading of the Bombay famine in 1812. According to the paper, in response to calls to prevent the port from exporting rice, the Bombay government instead adopted "the *manly* step of declaring the port of Bombay shall not be shut under any circumstances [emphasis added]." Bombay merchants exported rice in great quantities and, the *Economist* said, the consequences were most satisfactory as market forces prevailed. The paper drew its history lesson from a travel volume written by an English sea captain. The *Gazetteer* of the Bombay presidency, in contrast, described widespread death and how, "Dogs, by feeding on human flesh, grew strangely fierce. I have seen a pack of them carry off a living child from its sick mother's arms. I have seen them day after day waiting round the dying, ready to feast on their bodies."[45]

The calls to block exports continued: in 1847, an editorial in the *Nation*, a Dublin newspaper supporting the end of Union, reported that though the potato crop had failed again, the grain crops were good. "And now the thing for Irishmen to consider is this," the editorial suggested, "– no people on the globe was ever put to such a problem before – how to get leave to eat the bread that God has sent them." It went on to say that shipping Irish grain to England is termed "'civilisation' and 'the enlightened spirit of commerce' ... so that whoever dies of it may congratulate himself that he is a martyr to the cause of human improvement and the progress of the species."[46] In 1846, Ireland exported over 1,200,000 quarters of grain to England and over 900,000 head of livestock; by 1848, grain exports increased to over 1,300,000 quarters.[47] The *Economist* called all proposals to restrict the export of food "wild schemes." "Trade," the paper argued, "without any other stimulus than the present great profit to be gained by bringing food from all parts of the world, has ransacked every market, and will bring hither every atom of food which can be honestly procured and fairly paid for."[48]

The paper also opposed any measures designed to sell grain cheaply. Hoarding grain for profit was part of the "naturally appropriate social duties" of those with surplus product.[49] This was one of the reasons it cited for opposing food aid. Such aid reduced the price of grain below what it could have obtained in the market if aid had not been given, harming those who hoarded grain with the intent of making a future profit. As the paper said in 1846, "even in ill-fated, half-starved Ireland, there are little stores kept back for scarcity … the persons who had kept them back were cruelly and unjustly, forced by the government interference, to carry their stocks prematurely to the market … the interference of the government severed the order of nature, deprived human providence of its well-merited reward, and destroyed the motives for frugality and care."[50] It continued this refrain throughout the famine; in 1847, it defended those merchants who had bought up the "Indian" corn meal brought into the country through the efforts of Peel in 1846 with the intent of driving up the prices. "Instead of reproach," the paper argued, "those gentlemen who had confidence in the principles of trade, and courage to act on them … deserve great praise." It went on to warn, "But the want of faith in principle is a vice of the age … Smith has made, as Newton made, a great branch of science, peculiarly British; and should we want faith in his principles, it will lead to more disastrous results than the loss of scientific reputation. We shall falsify the principles on which, at this moment, the human race are [*sic*] fixing their hopes."[51]

"Laws to force back society to the dark ages"

In the face of increasing calls for policies to alleviate the horrible distress in Ireland, faith in principles became a kind of mantra for the paper – a talisman they applied to each question they examined: "We totally deny that what is wrong in *principle* can be right in practice."[52] In the eyes of the writers for the *Economist*, what was wrong in principle was any form of food aid, or relief work, or, as they repeated time and again, any policy that tried to feed the Irish. While its criticism of government policy in Ireland became more muted after the Whig administration of Lord John Russell, of which Wilson was a member, took power, and the paper became especially supportive on specific issues after Lord Clarendon became Lord Lieutenant, it continued to argue against aid until well after the famine ended. As early as November 1845 the paper was warning, "Charity is the national error of Englishmen. Alms-giving is considered by us as the certain panacea for most social evils. … There is … a sort of undefined resolution that *something must be done* to prevent our poor from dying of starvation ... To put food into the mouth of a poor man who cannot purchase it, is to take it out of the mouth of another man, only a degree less poor, who could and would have purchased it."[53]

As the Peel and Russell governments tentatively and gingerly began to provide minor sorts of relief for the dying in Ireland, the paper continued to rant against any such practice. In March 1846, the paper opined in an article entitled "Feeding the Irish," "We thought this had been so clearly demonstrated by Mr. Malthus to be an impossibility, that we feel only astonishment at its being proposed. To us it appears like calling on us to unlearn the first rules of arithmetic, and do our sums by the assertation that two and two make five." It went on to argue, "It is no part of the duty of a government to feed the people, or any portion of the people."[54]

As the extent of the famine became clearer and the number of deaths began to rise, there were heightened calls for more effective government policy. The *Morning Chronicle* warned in April 1846, "Famine is clutching its gaunt finger closer and closer upon the wretched peasantry." A few months later the *Clare Journal* besieged the government, "We feel it absolutely necessary ... to take immediate steps to satisfy the clamours of a starving people."[55] But, the *Economist* continued its campaign against aid. In May 1846, it warned about the "frenzied howl" coming from Ireland:

> There is a great outcry for the Government to feed and ... employ the unemployed and hungry people ... In Ireland it is notorious that people do not help themselves, and it is equally notorious that Ireland has been the pet of our legislature. ... If we had to seek an example ... of benevolently meant interference producing nothing but evil, we should refer to Ireland. ... The outcry in Ireland and in some part of England for the Government to employ and feed the Irish, is the wail of unthinking suffering and ignorance, and were it acted on, would only prolong the imbecile pupilage which is now the condition of the Irish? [*sic*]"[56]

For the paper, government assistance, whether direct aid or relief work, had only prolonged the suffering. Though exporting food, Ireland was not "exporting" enough people. The "light work and good pay" provided by the government had kept the people at home. Such a system suited the Irish temperament as, "They cleave to their country and to dole out a scanty subsistence, as the reward for inefficient, unskilful, unprofitable toil ... is the very way to keep them at home ... It seems scarcely possible to aggravate the social evils of Ireland; yet that has been done by benevolently supplying the people with food and employment."[57]

The *Economist* continued to warn about the effects of aid provided to the Irish. Even as the Russell administration made harsher laws for the provision of relief in the midst of the famine – insisting more rigorously on work in return for assistance and placing more of the burden of paying the costs of relief onto Irish landlords – the paper complained about the misguided principles. "The truth is," it said, "it is no man's business to provide for another. Still less is it the business of the Government." It also felt compelled to complain about "liberal contemporaries, who forgetting all the truth which the masters of economic science meant to impress on the world seventy or eighty years ago have gone back to mischievous errors that prevailed before Smith wrote or Malthus lived."[58]

Eventually inured to the fact that the Russell administration would continue to offer some, if paltry, levels of work relief – and as Trevelyan worked assiduously to reduce the numbers who could rely on such relief – the *Economist* insisted that such dependence must be the absolute last and starkly unwelcome prospect for all. In response to a deputation from the County of Cork, which had asked that relief wages be raised to a level that would allow a family to exist, the paper warned:

> To pay them, not what their labour is worth, not what their labour can be purchased for, but what is sufficient for a comfortable subsistence for themselves and family. ... Do they not see that to do this would be to stimulate every man to marry and to populate as fast as he could, like a rabbit in a warren – in other words, that to apply this to Ireland would be to give brandy to a man who was lying dead drunk in a ditch.[59]

The paper also repeatedly asserted, without providing any evidence, that the Irish were genetically prone to rely on charity. It warned in early 1847 that employers could find few workers and cottiers were even abandoning their fields because government relief work proved to be too attractive. Government measures had converted "a period of distress arising from natural causes, into one of unusual comfort and ease [while] ... the country has been reduced to one great and abandoned waste."[60] In perhaps its most intemperate article, in response to a question posed in the *Times* – "How are the people of Ireland to be fed and employed?" – the *Economist* engaged in a remarkable rant, in which dying from hunger became part of "the order of nature": "It is clearly the duty of individuals each to provide for himself. If they do not they naturally perish and die, and it is attempting to thwart the order of nature, for the Government to prevent their doing that duty." It continued its attack on any aid even after the Russell government came to power, warning in 1847, "Laws to employ, and laws to feed the people, ... are laws to force back society to the dark ages ..."[61]

The continual refrain from the paper through the five next brutal years of starvation and death was that, as it said on Christmas Day 1847, when one might have expected an expression of charity at perhaps the very worst period of the famine: "Till you make the people of Ireland rely upon themselves and their own resources you do nothing."[62]

"The failings of the race prevail"

Along with asserting that the government had no business trying to feed the people, the *Economist* was most intent on trying to push the government to enact policies that would remove the cottier from the land and free Ireland for the investment of capital in agriculture. The paper was adamant that there was no room in the civilized world for an Irish peasantry. In the opinion of the paper, increasingly, clearing land for the investment of capital required coercion and repression.

We have seen in the last chapter how the *Economist* held a complex, often ambiguous, relationship with landlords. The paper often saw landlords as the enemy in their struggle to end the Corn Laws, and portrayed traditional, large landowners as one of the major impediments to the most advantageous alignment of agrarian capital. Conversely, improving estate owners, such as Radnor, were essential to the success of the transformation the paper most ardently urged for the English countryside. And, of course, absolute respect for the rights of property was perhaps the single most important element of both Adam Smith's and Robert Malthus's arguments about the basis of political economy.

The *Economist*'s approach to land questions in Ireland, especially in the early years of famine, reflected these conflicting tendencies. In April 1846, a landowner named Gerrard, determined to turn her estate into pasture, evicted sixty-one families. (The *Economist* identified the owner first as a Mrs. Gerrard, but in subsequent stories referred to Mr. Gerrard.) The paper's first story about the affair said that various testimonies made it clear that the land had been improved by the "peasantry" while mostly ignored by the owner. The *Economist* wrote, "We say the law is unjust – that the soil has originally little or no fertility – that nearly all of its fertility is imparted to it by labour – and the law which confers on the owner of the soil nearly all the fruits of the peasant's toil, … is the parent of crime." The paper went on:

> We are well aware of the sacredness of the right of property; but when we find that our respect for that of the Irish landlords leads to the impoverishment and degradation of the people, making them at once paupers and criminals – when we find that this so-called right and its consequences fill Ireland with beggars and assassins – we are driven, by the numerous practical evils into which the maintenance of the right has involved us, to call in question the right itself.[63]

The paper continued to discuss this case and its broader implications in its leaders for the next few weeks. The paper expressed doubts about landlords' promises that given security they would improve their land and provide employment. "What have they done for the people of England and Scotland," the paper asked, "where their lives have been as safe and their property as cherished as an infant in the arms of its mother?" Nonetheless, the paper arrived at the conclusion that clearing the land "is a necessary consequence of the landlords' legal rights, and that to secure them is to hasten the clearing." Progress everywhere is marked most determinedly by agricultural improvement, "to produce more food by less labour":

> To give security therefore, to the lives and property of the landlords – supposing them, being so secured to use their property in the best manner, making the land the most productive possible – is to hasten the eviction of the tenantry, and prepare for the Irish people still greater calamities and still more intolerable woes. This is the great problem for consideration: – By giving security to the property of the Irish landlords, and so promoting agricultural improvements, by which the whole community can be most advantageously fed, we shall infallibly doom the bulk of the Irish peasantry, like the Indians, to extermination ... The peasantry stand in the way of improvements required by the interest of landlords and of society ... They lie beyond the pale.[64]

Nevertheless, the paper warned the next month that any "possible cure" for Ireland needed to recognize some essential facts: the multitude of the Irish could "not be controlled by police staff, by bayonet, or by gun ... there they are, suffering from hunger and destitution, rendering life and property insecure, and spreading their own contagious evils abroad ... This people cannot be exterminated – these sentiments cannot be *evicted*." Thus, "Till the people be either employed or fed, or swept away, there can be no security, and little or no improvement." Initially the paper appeared to opt for "employed and fed" by pronouncing in favour of the campaign led by some prominent public figures, including Thornton and J.S. Mill, to prompt the government to provide small farmers access to waste lands. The paper would prefer if the landlords set themselves to improving waste lands, but if they would not the state should take over the land for a nominal fee and turn it over to peasants to improve. The paper admitted this might lead to "a still greater multitude than at present of turbulent, craving, and unskilled peasantry, quarrelling over scraps of the soil, and making civilisation impossible." The *Economist*, however, was convinced that free trade would lead to manufacturing employment that would pull enough people from the land to prevent this in the long run.[65] This series of articles was the most favourable treatment the paper would bestow on small farmers or cottiers. The next month the Peel government fell, to be replaced by the Whig administration of Lord John Russell. William Rathbone Greg was brought in to write for the paper, initially focusing his articles on Ireland, and the *Economist* apparently lost all of its sympathy for cottiers, increasingly opting for "swept away" as the best possible solution for Ireland's woes. Borrowing a title from a pamphlet published two decades previously, the paper printed another series of articles entitled "Ireland – Its Permanent Evils and their Remedy." The underlying argument of the articles was that temporary solutions to the current "distress" that did not address Ireland's underlying troubles would aggravate the problem. Paramount among these deep-seated problems was the existence of a population of cottiers and the lack of a vibrant class of agricultural capitalists who would improve the land and employ labour. Moreover, echoing some of the evidence presented to the Devon Commission, the paper argued that this "multitude of wretched families" now "regard the land they have once held as belonging to them, *whether they pay rent or not*, and … retain forcible possession of it accordingly." The resulting violence perpetrated by cottiers prevented any investment in agricultural improvement. The paper that had only a year previously expressed a measured opposition to mass ejections of cottiers and a sympathy for the families so treated dramatically changed its tune. Such evictions occurred, the articles now said, because at the termination of the long lease once given out to principal tenants, the owner:

> regains possession of his estate, he finds it swarming with a wretched population living in pig-styes; the land exhausted and ill-used … and the whole property … an almost worthless possession. If he has the natural and laudable feeling of anxiety to make his newly-recovered property both profitable and creditable to him, … [t]he landlord is looked upon as a cruel oppressor. *Yet, in our own country, as leases fall out small farms are constantly thrown together to form larger ones, and no one dreams of finding fault with the proprietor, but, on the contrary he is generally looked upon as an active and improving landlord who knows what he is about.*

Ignoring the seven decades of unrest and destitution that accompanied this process in England, (and the decades of English restrictions on Irish industry), the article identified the difference between Ireland and England as the absence of manufacturing employment. The fault for this lack of investment of capital in manufacturing lay in "The reckless character and foolish violent conduct of the Irish [which] have not only prevented the establishment of those manufactures which would speedily have rescued them from misery, but have driven away those they once possessed."[66]

This article marked the beginning of a dramatic change in the way the *Economist* wrote about Ireland. Articles in the paper, most written by Greg, who had never been to Ireland, now focused on the need for security and stability, supported evictions and the "extinction" of the cottier, and increasingly blamed both poverty and unrest on the racial deficiencies of the Irish. The next week, in the second instalment of the series, the paper started its lead article with:

Ireland presents the singular anomaly of a people who murder each other in order to obtain a patch of land, which when obtained, they only half cultivate – who are constantly clamouring for employment, and yet outrage and ruin those who proffer it to them. … Their agriculture, as might be expected from poor and ignorant cottiers, is of the rudest and most inefficient kind, yet they resent as an injury deserving death, any attempt to improve it.

The next week, the third instalment argued that the absence of capital could be traced to peasant-led unrest that needed to be curtailed at any cost, citing "a reckless and lawless insubordination … an entire repression of liberty in the application of capital … by a popular tyranny." The paper warned, "Whatever steps, therefore, are taken for the permanent improvement of Ireland, will be entirely futile, unless accompanied by measures, that, at any costs, will give that necessary security and safety." So important was the necessary security for capital, the paper went on, "We should be prepared to arm the government with powers, even though apparently despotic, if it were found necessary for the effectual repression of existing outrage, and for securing the administration of *justice*, in reality, if not form." This repression would be necessary, it expected, because the "first right" the paper proposed to enshrine in its vision of Ireland was the right of landlords to eject all tenants not under lease. Indeed, it said, "we would regard those landowners who refuse to allow men to live like pigs on their property, and who reduce the population upon it to the number required for the fullest and highest cultivation of the soil, as benefactors and … wise and benevolent men."[67]

By October of that year, the *Economist* had also apparently abandoned its support for providing waste lands to peasants; again, opposition to this was voiced in reference to the defects of the race. The paper asked:

[W]hat earthly reason have we for anticipating that a set of peasants who, when *tenants* of the soil … were indolent, unenterprising, living from hand to mouth, … multiplying like rabbits, satisfied with potatoes for food, rags for clothing, pig-styes for shelter would … become prudent, provident and improving … would eschew potatoes, marry late, cultivate agricultural improvements? We must never forget the character of the Irishman is singular.[68]

From this point, the paper was consistent in its stance that providing land to the Irish poor would exacerbate the problem rather than amend it. This idea was repeated by the Lord Lieutenant and shared with Wilson regularly. In December 1847, for example, Clarendon told Wilson that they would never be able to give capital a decent chance in Ireland without a depletion of the population.[69] In 1851, the paper reported, "We remain unshaken in our conviction, long ago expressed, that Ireland's way out of her difficulties does not lie through the transformation of her people into a race of peasant proprietors." Forgetting its steadfast opposition to peasant proprietorship in England, the *Economist's* justification for such an argument was a racial one:

> Some [races] are impelled to ceaseless toil and untiring acquisition by an *onwardness* of nature (if we may coin a word) ... the Anglo-Saxons are of this order of humanity. Others ... are impetuous and impulsive, but not indefatigable nor enduring – preferring the enjoyment of life to its improvement ... and of such men is the Irish nation made. ... Such being their character, it is not difficult to foretell the consequences of erecting them into a nation of small proprietors ... They would pinch, they would scrape, they would toil with unheard of assiduity, till they had contrived to save the sum needed for the purchase of the five or ten-acre freehold. They would then have attained their paradise – an estate and a cabin of their own. They would draw the curtains and rest. They would marry; they would beget children after the prompt fashion of their tribe ... As their sons grow up, they would add a room or a shed to their cabin ... "Ireland for the Irish" ... means the cabin for the pigs, rags for the peasant, potatoes for the population.[70]

Given this view of the Irish character, the paper increasingly focused on the need for repression as its response to the famine. It was particularly opposed to the popular pressure for tenant-right, variously perceived as being either a right to payment for improvements, or against the termination of a lease if rent continued to be paid, or against the eviction of cottiers at all. In 1847, the paper lamented that, "Contrary ... to the expectations of some politicians, the Irish have not been taught quietness by being exposed to starvation," and warned that any confirmation of tenant right would be "a fatal check to social progress."[71] It even tried to argue that relief money was being used by cottiers to buy arms "with which they carry out that war against the payment of rent."[72] How influential the paper's continual appeals for repression were can be judged to some extent by the letters from the Lord Lieutenant. In 1848, he wrote to Wilson saying, "I am curious to hear how your Articles have been received by the middle classes and large constituencies in England and whether they are prepared to go to your lengths."[73] Two years later, Clarendon commented, "I still feel like the Governor of an ill-guarded jail, obliged to keep constant watch over the inmates."[74]

Repression continued to be justified through reference to the unique character of the Irish race. In December 1847, the paper first trotted out a horse it would ride for some time: the Irish could be reformed when surrounded by their betters, but they were irredeemable at home, "reckless of consequences and apparently without the slightest interest in social order." At first it suggested, echoing Nichol, this was because the cottier could not find employment and "cling to the land."[75] But soon the paper was making a more direct reference to race in their explanations for Irish troubles. A remarkable article in 1848 began with: "Thank God! We are Saxon!" and then went on to compare the "solid, slow, reflective, phlegmatic temperament" of the Englishman to the "savage Celt" and "flighty Gaul." For the paper, "The Frenchman is a civilized Celt. The Irishman is a barbaric Gaul ... both are set on fire by watchwords. ... What is communism in France, becomes highway robbery and burglary in Ireland."[76] Eighteen months later the paper continued to argue that "Irish turbulence, Irish menace, Irish recklessness of life, Irish disregard for the rights of property" were preventing the investment of English capital in Ireland and, consequently, landowners found it impossible to "deal with it [land] in the way modern science has pointed out as the most profitable."[77] Even in 1850 as the famine neared its end, the *Economist* continued to use arguments about race to rationalize the failure of its prescriptions for Ireland:

> Whenever the Irish peasantry are so situated, either by subordination of their position or by minority in numbers as to take the tone from those above them and those around them, they succeed and advance. Whenever they are so dominant, either in numbers or influence, as to overpower such foreign elements of amendment as may have settled among them – or where they are without a strong, large and prominent admixture of such foreign superiorities – the failings of the race prevail, they sink rapidly in social condition. ... At home the Irishman is alone, dominant, and uncorrected; he is among Irishmen with the same constitutional failings as himself, from whom he can derive only encouragement for all those qualities which need enlightenment, shaming, and correction.

Perhaps worst of all, according to the paper, "They still sigh for the potato."[78]

By 1850, the worst of the famine was over. The potato crop that year was adequate and the terrible scenes of hunger and accompanying disease occurred less often. Though death rates in poor houses remained high, they were a fraction of what they had been in 1847 and 1848. Other elements of the famine years remained, though: rural "outrages" continued as the push for tenant-rights intensified, and the hungry continued to crowd onto ships for America and elsewhere. The *Economist* was both heartened and a bit frightened by the success of this "sharp but effectual remedy." In 1849, it had argued that "The failure of the potato crop ... has produced a greater social revolution in Ireland than perhaps ever occurred in any country within so short a period." Land was no longer encumbered or burdened with a multitude of cottiers. The paper celebrated the fact that in its estimations no less than one-third of the land was in the market. "Farms can be had on long leases, on such terms as would in any other part of the United Kingdom secure an ample fortune to the cultivator in a few years."[79] Clarendon reported in a letter to Wilson that with the passage of new legislation and cleared estates, "men having the command of capital may select some of the finest land in the world."[80]

The paper was almost euphoric about the way this remedy had transformed Ireland. In 1852, in a statement that must have been seen as cruel and perverse to those still lining up to take crowded ships to untested destinations and still burying the dead, the paper argued that though the loss of population in Ireland during the famine was only matched by the loss of life in Peru and Mexico with Spanish conquest:

> Yet, already this remarkable event seems vanishing from our memories, and mighty heaps of dead and mouldering villages are hidden by a few smiling farmhouses and the increased prosperity for those who are left. … The healing hand of nature is fast closing the wounds she made, and with her wanted benevolence she seems not to have removed a terribly diseased limb till it was necessary to save the body, and she is now restoring it to health and vigour unknown for ages … The famine was only an active paroxysm of a long-standing chronic disorder.[81]

Though the paper had strongly pressed the Russell government to follow policies designed to ensure that the multitude of cottiers should "be swept from the land," and had privately encouraged Lord Clarendon in that opinion, by the time of the 1851 census, even its writers were shocked by how well they had succeeded. The census indicated that the population had declined by at least 1,600,000 people since 1841. And yet the population continued to fall. The paper commented on how emigration was proceeding "at a rate to terrify those who once so strenuously endorsed it."[82] A half decade later, the paper observed that emigration continued apace; the population now 2,000,000 less than it had been in 1841. Ironically, the paper now argued, "The ultimate test of progress is the continued increase of the people, and as long as they continue to decline in number no other criterion of national welfare is worth much consideration."[83]

But perhaps the population continued to decline because those in power were still intent on amputating the "terribly diseased limb" represented by cottiers. When new movements were launched to benefit peasant proprietors, the *Economist* warned that this was "a step of the most singular and perilous regression – it is administering a poison under the pretext of a remedy." Again, its opposition to such a plan was both a "principled" stand against peasant proprietors and a racist argument about the nature of the Celtic peasant; the paper advocated for "redeeming Ireland … by inoculating it with a large admixture of Scottish and English blood."[84] Irish cottiers and peasants continued to obstinately dissuade capital through agrarian outrages, prompted, the paper opined, by "The old feeling of the peasantry that the possession of land alone stood between them and starvation … the obscure but inveterate notion of a *right to land*." And, again, they counselled repression, suggesting, "Civilised institutions are for civilised nations."[85]

A decade later, despite the unprecedented collapse of the Irish population, the same problems perversely remained. By 1863, the paper could report that through death and emigration the population was four million less than it would have been. This collapse "must rank as among the most startling events of history. ... The surplus population has to a great extent disappeared." The paper foresaw the "promise of a brightening future." And yet the amount of land cultivated in potatoes continued to increase, and that under cereals decline, and the paper was once again talking about "agrarian crime of the worst order."[86] Perhaps the appropriate question is: Exactly what was the true crime of Ireland and who were its culprits?

Chapter Ten

Cooked Land, Cotton, and Slavery

A milestone of sorts was passed in England shortly before the *Economist* arrived on the scene. In 1841, out of a total English population of 14,995,000, over 8,000,000 people lived in the fourteen counties classified as "manufacturing" counties.[1] A decade later, 54 per cent of the English population lived in towns or cities.[2] That this shift from a predominantly agricultural and rural population to one that was increasingly urban and employed in manufacturing took so long despite close to a century of falling rural wages between 1750 and 1850 says something about the hold the parish continued to have on those who dwelled there. It also says something about conditions in the manufacturing cities. People were not drawn to the cities; they were expelled from their parishes by poverty and abysmal housing.[3]

The county with the biggest increase from 1801 to 1841 was Lancashire, which almost tripled in size during those years.[4] Lancashire in general, and its urban seat, Manchester, were the focus of England's rapidly burgeoning cotton manufactures. Wilson, Greg, and the *Economist* in general were closely connected to Manchester and to cotton interests. Greg, of course, came from an important cotton milling family. Wilson had deep connections to cotton interests as well. The epicentre of the anti–Corn Law struggle was in Manchester and its foremost politicians, John Bright and Richard Cobden, led the fight. Wilson developed close relations with them early in the struggle. As the paper grew in influence, Wilson became deeply associated with manufacturing interests in Manchester, writing almost weekly for the *Manchester Guardian*.[5]

Manchester relied on cotton, huge cargos delivered to the wharfs at Liverpool to feed the multiplying cotton mills of the city and employ the millions who depended on their continued production. The need to guarantee that cargo meant the *Economist* and Wilson also became deeply enmeshed in questions of slavery, especially in the United States, and debates about policy in India. It was perhaps around the question of slavery in the United States that "pure principles" failed the paper most egregiously and about which the paper was most decidedly on the wrong side of history.

India, too, proved problematic. India was important to Britain, of course, for all sorts of reasons. One of them was as the potential saviour for Manchester cotton interests dependent on an increasingly threatened supply from the American South. Making India play that role required investment, which required security and control. Increasingly, even Wilson and the *Economist* had doubts about the ability of private interests to lead the charge in India. Both Wilson's and the paper's counsel on India was affected by Wilson's interests as one of the founders, in 1853, of the Chartered Bank of India, Australia, and China.[6] Thus Wilson, despite the paper's constantly repeated warnings about the dangers of government involvement in the economy, became closely associated with a scheme for what was essentially a public guarantee for investment in railways designed primarily to energize Indian cotton production. And equally paradoxically, he died in India campaigning for an income tax. Charles Trevelyan, who so successively terrorized the poor in Ireland, emerged in India as Wilson's bête noire.

As was the case with its writings on Ireland, serious doubts about the ability of other, "darker," races to respond effectively to the principles of political economy crept into the paper's generally celebratory articles. As the *Economist* became more disillusioned with the results of the application of the fairy dust of political economy in the 1860s, and as the paper took stock following the death of Wilson, it increasingly hinted at even darker interpretations of the relationship between Britain and these "others," interpretations that contained within them the seeds for the brutality of late nineteenth-century imperial pursuits.

"In the Service of Tireless Machines"

By the late eighteenth century, British cotton textile producers had, through a series of mechanical and technical innovations applied to weaving and spinning, managed to dislodge Indian weavers from their long-held place of dominance in the production of cotton cloth. With increasing capital and labour invested in cotton production and centred in Lancashire, cotton textiles became the most important manufacturing sector of the British economy. Though agricultural labour was still the most common occupation in England at the middle of the nineteenth century, and domestic servitude second, cotton manufacturing was third, employing more than a half a million workers directly.[7] Its importance ran even deeper: cotton cloth made up more than 40 per cent of British exports by value by the end of the 1840s; the *Economist* estimated that cotton manufacturing and trade employed close to four million people in Britain.[8] It was through cotton that Britain industrialized; as Eric Hobsbawm wrote, "whoever says Industrial Revolution says cotton."[9]

Initially cotton mills such as Samuel Greg's Quarry Bank Mill were located along waterways in Lancashire so that they could run on water power. For the majority of their workforce they often used children farmed out from local poor houses or women deprived of steady agricultural labour and bereft of cottage or common land. Increasingly through the first couple of decades of the nineteenth century, these mills were replaced by new ones running on steam power. By 1835, there were more than a thousand cotton mills in Britain and two-thirds of them ran on steam power. Steam mills no longer needed to be located in outlying areas on watercourses; they soon clustered mostly in Manchester. Though the mills continued to use large numbers of women and children, as mill equipment became more complex and as the industry centralized, men soon made up the majority of the workers.[10]

Manchester then became the epitome of early industrial Britain, and it was in Manchester that industrialization's debilitating effects were most evident. The *Economist* might applaud the industrial cities as safety valves to vent off the pressure of displaced rural workers, and talk about how such workers embraced manufacturing employment. Nassau Senior might describe cotton mills as pleasant locales of fresh air and light, fit to raise children whose work was little more than play. We have other descriptions, though. James Kay-Shuttleworth, a doctor intent on investigating the causes of a typhus outbreak in Manchester in the 1830s, described "Prolonged and exhausting labour, continued from day to day, and from year to year. ... The dull routine of a ceaseless drudgery, in which the same mechanical process is incessantly repeated. ... To condemn man to such severity of toil is, in some measure, to cultivate in him the habits of an animal." He described workers living "in squalid wretchedness, on meager food." The workers and their families were "crowded into one dense mass, in cottages separated by narrow, unpaved, and almost pestilential streets, in an atmosphere loaded with ... smoke and exhalations."[11] Shuttleworth was not alone in his assessment; Frederich Engels's classic *The Condition of the Working Class in England*, first published in German in 1845, was largely drawn from his close association with Manchester. He argued that it was in these towns that "the social war ... is openly declared ... the powerful few, the capitalists, seize everything for themselves, while to the weak many, the poor, scarcely a bare existence remains." Labour, "buried alive in the factory, in the service of tireless machines, is experienced by the workers as torture of the severest kind."[12] But, or rather because of this poverty, as one well-to-do inhabitant calmly responded to Engels's tirade about the horrible living and working conditions, "And yet there is a great deal of money made here." Or, as Alexis de Tocqueville remarked after a visit in the 1830s, "From this filthy sewer pure gold flows."[13]

One ingredient was needed more than any other to make this gold continue to flow: cotton. British industrialization – indeed the key ingredient of European industrialization through the nineteenth century – was, bizarrely, completely dependent on a raw material Europe could not and did not produce. As cotton manufacturing expanded, the amount of raw cotton demanded by the industry reached dizzying heights. Through the eighteenth century, Britain depended on a diverse mix of cotton producers: West Indies, Brazil, Egypt, and other parts of the Ottoman Empire. By the beginning of the nineteenth century, all of these sources were dwarfed by India and, most especially, the southern United States. Britain was importing just under a million bales of cotton a year in the first half of the 1830s; a decade later this had increased to over 1.5 million bales. By then India was providing just over 200,000 bales a year, and the southern United States close to 1,200,000 bales.[14] By the end of the 1840s, imports increased to two million bales; as the *Economist* pointed out, the "daily food of *hundreds of thousands* of our fellow countrymen" depended on the continuous flow of almost 40,000 bales of cotton a week.[15]

India's eclipse as a source of raw cotton for England was mostly the result of a cotton and slave revolution in the American south, as first Old South and then new lands in the American southwest were opened up to cotton cultivation. The key to this expansion, beyond new fertile lands, was an explosion in the numbers of slaves in the United States, what the *American Cotton Planter* in the early nineteenth century called, "the cheapest and most available labor in the world." It was not just available and cheap. As Edward Baptist has made painfully clear, a brutally efficient work regime – "millions of measured lashes" – insured that cotton production on the rich lands of the new south continued apace, and Manchester got its cotton at constantly, if unsteadily, falling prices despite the explosion in demand.[16] And the machines continued, tirelessly.

"A Curious Fact in the Natural History of Man"

In a story on slavery in the United States and the cotton trade in 1850, the *Economist* offered the opinion that, "We are never more likely to be wrong than when we are extremely proud of being right."[17] This might serve as a fitting description of the paper's arguments about slavery, the slave trade, and the cotton supply. The *Economist* continually asserted that it abhorred slavery and yet it constantly opposed measures designed to quicken an end to slavery.

Throughout the 1840s and into the 1850s, there was regular discussion in the paper about the slave trade as Britain attempted to enforce its prohibition against slaving on the African coast north of the equator. Debates also centred on the question of preferential tariffs for British West Indian sugar producers, or, alternatively, prohibitions against sugar from those countries, mostly Brazil and Spanish Cuba, using slaves. Not surprisingly, given the extent of British trade and capital investment in Brazil, the *Economist* was staunchly opposed to increased tariffs on Brazilian sugar. In a leader in 1843 the paper said, "We trust we shall be among the last who will ever be found advocating the continuance of slavery, or opposing any *legitimate* means for its extinction." But it argued that increased tariffs on slave sugar were not one of those legitimate means.

Its opposition to these was twofold: on the one hand, the paper asserted that to be consistent such measures should apply to all slave-produced goods from all countries, including cotton from America. On the other, it tried to make an unconvincing argument that protecting West Indian sugar production by tariffs would drive up the price of labour in the West Indies; other countries producing sugar would never be able to abandon slavery because they would need to match the price of labour in the West Indies for their newly freed slaves, as if there were, miraculously, free movement of labour across the former slave and plantation colonies of the Americas.[18]

The paper offered contradictory opinions about whether the anti-slavery squadron off the coast of Africa was a *legitimate* means or not. In 1858, the *Economist* felt compelled to condemn an argument made by William Hutt in Parliament. Hutt had said that as long as there was demand for slave-produced products, it would be impossible to stop the slave trade. The law of supply and demand would find some way to insure the demand was met. He advocated proscriptions or tariffs against slave-produced goods. The paper felt the need to rescue the principles of political economy from those who would use it incorrectly. "Now we must enter our earnest protest," it said, "against language of this sort, as calculated wholly to obscure the true principles of political economy, and ... to diminish seriously the willingness of the public to recognise the validity which they have." The paper went on to argue that the law of supply and demand was "simply a ... tendency" that could be discouraged. "The whole meaning of dignity of economic science is clouded by treating the law of demand and supply as a physical law which *cannot* be thwarted." The paper went on to suggest that the interdictions of the slave supply was one of those effective means of thwarting the law and "have counteracted the tendency of demand to produce supply in that particular instance."[19]

This would have been an impressive example of the *Economist* sensibly suggesting limits to economical laws if it had not argued the exact opposite, and in much more inflammatory language, for much of the preceding decade. In 1843, the paper commented on the case of a ship that had been seized on suspicion of being involved in the slave trade. In agreeing with the acquittal won by the ship's owners, the *Economist* warned, "the slave trade will not be put down by prosecutions. So long as there is a *profit*, so long will there be individuals ready to engage in smuggling, either dead goods or living beings." Two years later, when Hutt first put forward a motion to fund a further joint French and English patrol, the paper again questioned attempts to end the slave trade, while reiterating many of the arguments apologists for the trade had made for centuries:

> It never for one moment entered the minds of those who sought to redress the great existing evil, that Africa had a vast, uncivilized, and unfed population; while America and the adjacent islands possessed ... an ample opportunity of affording

civilisation, employment and support to that race. … The evil … was not in the removal of the African labourer to the West. On the contrary that was in itself a positive good. The evil was wholly in the condition to which he was consigned. … Abandon attempts to end the slave trade, but bring in efforts to bring "free" black labourers to the Americas and slavery will end.[20]

The paper continued to make similar arguments about West Africa and African labourers for the next decade. In 1848, it asserted once again in opposition to a bill to fund the squadron that if it managed to "hermetically" seal Africa from the slave ships this will have "confined the most hopeless barbarism within itself. We have shut out the only means … the only practical mode which has yet been discovered, by which communication can be opened and maintained between Africa and the civilised world." The paper went on to repeat word for word what it had printed two years previously, except ending its diatribe with, "It was against the interests of all to maintain slavery and abolish the slave trade." Later that year, it added another plea against prohibiting the slave trade:

> To prohibit the transport of Africans as labourers to Brazil will only make what might be a decent, well-regulated emigration, a smuggling trade, pregnant with horrors. … our terrible and lamentable failure on the coast of Africa, adds one to the many proofs before in existence that progress is not to be hastened by prohibitions and restrictions, however benevolently intended; and all attempts to forcibly promote what some persons regard as improvements, only retard the moral and physical development of the species.[21]

Later that year the paper offered a broad sweep of history in justifying both slavery and the slave trade. In a strange history of West Africa, it argued that since the European encounter with Africa, West Africans have been "transported into other countries" as slaves. "We do not apologise for this any more than we apologise for earthquakes; we notice it as a curious fact in the natural history of man."[22]

"The Beneficent Whip of Hunger and Cold"

The *Economist* demonstrated an equally contradictory view about labour in the West Indies. The paper opposed planter attempts to maintain preferential tariffs for West Indian sugar and often suggested West Indian planters were seldom good managers of their properties, "terrified by a temperature of 130 degrees in the sun." "The curse of Jamaica," the paper said, "is that the planters continue to cherish the habits of slaveowners after they have got a population of free labourers."[23] While the paper favoured the emigration of West African labourers to the West Indies, it opposed plans to bring in "coolies" from India and China, arguing that such transport would make their labour more expensive than it was in India itself and, besides, Chinese "coolies" bring with them "depraved heathen habits."[24]

Initially, the paper seemed to suggest that emancipated former slaves would soon adopt a vigorous work ethic when planters stopped trying to treat them as slaves. In 1849, Thomas Carlyle, the Scottish writer and lecturer, had argued in a paper entitled "Occasional Discourse on the Negro Question" that a new form of slavery needed to be imposed on the West Indies to prevent former slaves from living off the fruits of the land; "Sitting yonder with their beautiful muzzles up to their ears in pumpkins … while the sugar rots round them because labour cannot be hired."[25] At first the *Economist* dismissed Carlyle's comments, saying he evidently borrowed his opinions "from the complaints of planters who live at home." The paper cited a story from the *West Indian*, a paper in Barbados, talking about how the sugar boiling house works from 5:00 am to midnight. The *Economist* suggested, "There must be a Ten Hours Act to put a stop to the lazy Negroes working nineteen hours in the day," arguing that there appeared to be a better spirit of industry at work in the West Indies.[26] The paper also seemed to agree with the opinion of Edward McGeachy, the Crown Surveyor for Jamaica, who said that cotton planters would find plenty of labourers for wages, as the people want money and "besides, the labour of a cotton plantation is one of the lightest possible work: old and infirm persons, women, and children may perform it." McGeachy also suggested, after having visited the United States, that slave labour there "seems very expensive, the amount of feeding and clothing, care and attention which they receive, astonished me. They are really as happy a set of looking people as I ever met with and their masters kind and indulgent in the extreme."[27] Surely, both he and the paper thought, Jamaica's poor ex-slave population could easily compete with such pampered slave labour.[28]

But those who would drive ex-slaves to labour on sugar or cotton plantations found themselves faced with the problem farmers believed they confronted in England itself: self-provisioning made labour more independent. Testimony in the House of Commons warned that slaves in Jamaica, as in other locales, had come to see provision land provided for them on the plantation as their own. On this land they could provide for their own needs through one day of labour a week. With the threat of independent labour looming, "emancipation" in 1834 had been followed by a six-year apprenticeship in which ex-slaves were meant to be forced to labour for forty hours a week without wages, and by the passage of various provisions making it difficult for ex-slaves to claim land. Nonetheless, a large percentage of ex-slaves had established themselves on their own land for self-provisioning, producing food for markets, and coffee for export. A long line of planters and British administrators on the island denounced their continued reluctance to labour for wages and their preference for working their own provision grounds.[29] As one magistrate in the 1850s claimed, "Their march back to barbarism has been rapid and successful."[30]

In 1846, the *Economist* had printed some long correspondence from William Smith, a resident of Jamaica. Smith argued that the sugar plantations refused to pay high enough wages. Wages in Jamaica did not just need to reflect the cost of the "necessities of the negro," which were very low; rather, they needed to meet the competition for that labour provided by the provision grounds. "The planter, must therefore, pay more than the negro can earn by working for himself."[31] The *Economist* seemed to agree with this argument, and provided a strange interpretation of English history as an example to the Jamaican planters. The paper said, "Labourers in England could not draw from the cultivation of small allotments of land, unaided by implements, manure, and draining and other improvement, an income equal to the wages they receive by combining their labour with farmers' capital." Thus, they suggested, labourers had willingly embraced giving up such land for a reliance on wage labour.[32] This was simply a fantasy masquerading as economic history, of course, considering the long history of falling wages and constant demand for land of their own on the part of English rural labourers, and at the very moment of widespread arson in the English countryside.

Soon, though, the paper joined those expressing disappointment in the apparent unwillingness of Jamaican ex-slaves and their descendants to abandon their own small farms to labour on plantations producing cotton or sugar. By 1859, less than a decade after it had dismissed Carlyle's argument, the paper warned:

> We think the philanthropic party, in their tenderness for the emancipated Africans, are sometimes not a little blind to the advantages of stern industrial necessities. We are no believers in Mr. Carlyle's gospel of the "beneficent whip" as the bearer of salvation to tropical indolence. But we cannot for a moment doubt that the first result of emancipation was ... to substitute [for] the worst kind of moral and political evil, one of a less fatal but still very pernicious kind ... They were suddenly liberated ...; they became free beings but without the discipline to use freedom well...They found themselves ... in a position in many respects analogous to that of people possessed of a moderate property in England, who can supply their principal wants without any positive labour. ... [T]he Negroes in most of the West Indian islands ... wanted nothing but the plantains they could grow almost without labour, and the huts which they could build on any waste mountain land without paying rent for it. ... when the spur of physical tyranny was removed, there was no sufficient substitute for it ... in the wholesome hardships of natural exigencies. The really "beneficent whip" of hunger and cold was not substituted for the human cruelty from which they had escaped.[33]

Again, this is pure fantasy given the copious testimony we have describing the hard work employed on and abundant harvests received from Jamaican peasant holdings on land they had been able to pry out of the hands of plantation owners or carve out of interior forests. As one correspondent told the paper two years later, "Every family has its pigs, fowls and gardens to take care of, and will not leave them ..."[34] Measures meant to force ex-slaves to abandon their pigs in favour of labour for capital were at the core of the Morant Bay "peasant war" in 1865, which left more than four hundred people dead.[35]

"Can Slavery Be Abolished?"

Though the determination to invigorate cotton cultivation in Jamaica contributed to the repression that fertilized the Morant Bay rebellion, Jamaican cotton was never seriously considered as an alternative to American cotton for Manchester. The *Economist* was almost obsessively concerned with the supply of cotton. The paper continually tracked importation, consumption, and reserves. In the first edition of every month, it gave a summary of the world supply and expected crops. Even in the 1840s, with plentiful supplies and reasonably favourable prices, it demonstrated significant anxiety about this most precarious engine of British industry. Discussions of American cotton production involved the *Economist* by necessity in debates about slavery in the United States. The paper had no illusions about the links between American cotton and slavery. It developed a unique formula for accounting for the continual increase of cotton production. In 1849, it argued that the slave population of the United States increased at an annual rate of 3 per cent, and the cotton crop could be expected to do so as well. A decade later, it simplified this equation, asserting that each new slave produced one extra bale for export.[36]

The paper asked its readers and itself on a number of occasions: "Can Slavery be Abolished?" The paper affirmed, "Our reason and our hearts call on us to abhor it and strive against it." But it always managed to find justification for not doing so, for answering that question in the negative. Much as it had in the argument against an embargo on slave-produced sugar, it tried to find justification for not actively opposing slavery by broadening the discussion; "Where is this moral crusade to stop? ... The condition of the large masses of the population in India under our dominion is no better than slavery." Moreover, the paper argued, abolishing the use of American grown cotton "would make a fearful hole in society." And immediate emancipation was, at any rate, impossible: "Are the planters to vacate the lands for [their 3,000,000 slaves]? Are they to become the servants of the negroes?" Thus, the paper counselled, "We must have patience with its existence."[37]

Patience required waiting for the lessons of efficiency. The paper professed to believe that the greater efficiency of free labour would end slavery: "Wherever there is a slave there must be a keeper: there are no prisoners without gaolers."[38] But the paper rejected any movement to hasten that inevitable prospect. From the 1840s on, it continually argued that it was neither appropriate nor effective to offer any advice to the Americans about the ending of slavery and warned that, "[Z]ealous haste to promote emancipation by force is sure to retard it" and reminded its readers that "sixteen hundred millions (dollars) of property in slaves" was at stake and worth considering "in the balance against the gratification of ignorant zeal."[39]

As the struggle over slavery grew more heated in the United States and as the *Economist* began to perceive a growing threat to Manchester's supply, the paper developed a particularly useful discourse – that is, useful to the argument that it abhorred slavery while it tried to protect the supply of American cotton. The paper argued first that the best means for ending slavery was to limit slavery's access to new territory. Secondly, it suggested that the dissolution of the United States would not be catastrophic if done peacefully, and should be readily agreed to by the North. Thirdly, if war was inevitable, the paper counselled that the best way to end slavery was to hope for a quick southern victory sufficient to allow the South to press for an end to the war and secession. These assertions required some intricate manoeuvring.

The paper's argument that slavery required new territory was based on its perceptions about the necessity of capital investment in agriculture. Slavery, it suggested, could only be competitive in fertile land that required no significant investment to maintain productivity. This required an agricultural frontier. Without it, the inevitably diminishing yields would insure that slavery could not compete with wage labour. It was slave lands' "power of indefinite expansion alone (that) gives its increasing value to slave-labour. ... The more you draw on human powers to supplement the failing powers of nature, the more ineffective slave-labour becomes. ... We believe, therefore, that the political *non-extension* of slavery is the most essential condition for the paralysis and annihilation of the slave-system."[40] While there is little doubt the dramatic expansion of cotton production in the new South benefited from the stored fertility in soil that had not been farmed for a very long time, the paper never clearly explained why it would not be as profitable to fertilize with slave labour as with wage labour. And certainly it recognized that the American South, cotton lands included, was already a strong competitor in the scramble for sources of guano. The paper also argued that it was somehow the ambitions of the North that sought to envelope Mexico and the Caribbean into the union and thus extend the boundaries of slavery. Thus, for the paper and, it presumed, to all Englishmen, "the actual separation between the North and South, which seems an essential preliminary to any adequate seclusion and, so to say, *suffocation* of the peculiar institution, in a limited area of its own, will be a welcome event."[41]

As conflict between the North and the South grew closer, the paper more often fell back on an argument about the benefits to be derived from the break-up of the union. In 1856, in the wake of conflict in Kansas, it said:

> We know well with what sort of panic terror the idea of dissolution of the Union is received by nearly all Americans ... We confess ... that we have never been able to discover what the Free states should lose by a severance from the Slave States ... and we have a very decided opinion ... that an amicable dissolution of the Union ... would be the greatest blessing to America, the greatest security to Europe, and an event of the brightest augury to the future civilization and progress of the race.[42]

As war drew closer at the beginning of the new decade, the paper portrayed the coming conflict in stark terms: "In no other quarter of the world are good and evil so distinctly in conflict as is just now the case in America."[43] While this statement was meant to burnish the *Economist*'s anti-slavery credentials, the paper was less than clear about where the good and evil lay. After South Carolina declared its intent to secede, the paper immediately called on Britain to recognize the new state. It also suggested that the secession of South Carolina and those states that might join it should not be "in any way injurious to Great Britain." Indeed, the paper thought that secession might be beneficial, as it would curtail the growing and unreasonable aggressiveness of the United States. As the paper suggested, a weakened America would be "somewhat less aggressive, less insolent, and less irritable."[44] Or, as it later argued, "The dissolution of the Union will prove a good to the world." The United States had risen so fast and so powerfully that "no other nation could stand up against them. ... They were so rough, so encroaching, and so overbearing, that all other Governments felt, as if some new associate, untrained to the amenities of civilised life, and insensible alike to the demands of justice and of courtesy, had forced its way into the aeropagus of nations."[45]

After South Carolina forced the evacuation of federal forces at Fort Sumter in April 1861, the *Economist* published a long article calling for the end of hostilities and the recognition of secession. Their reasoning for such an argument was interesting. The secession of the South would leave the North morally free from the taint of slavery. The Slave States would be "left with a noble empire and an almost boundless field." But the paper, nonetheless, hoped this new slave republic in which "slavery is a recognised and *undisputed* system" would somehow work to ameliorate the condition of slaves. The paper ended by arguing that a war to end slavery might be a "righteous war," but that was not what the war was about.[46]

In subsequent articles, though, it made it clear it wanted no truck with a war to end slavery. When some in the North began to talk about promoting slave opposition to their masters in the South, the paper, despite once again reiterating its opposition to slavery – "too well known to need repeating" – labelled such a tactic "an enormous crime." And when General Freemont in Missouri declared that he would free the slaves of anyone who fought against the union, the paper went into full battle mode. Warning that this would "set free 100,000 semi-savages, without preparation, without security against their possible conduct on receipt of their unwonted liberty," the paper called on "all the soberer, and wiser, and gentler spirits of the Union … – will not all who shrink from suffering, loathe rapine, and abhor blood – cry out against the in-auguration of a policy which, if it means anything, means Negro insurrection, servile war, outrages and horrors without number and name."[47]

When Lincoln issued the preliminary Emancipation Proclamation in September 1862, declaring all slaves held by rebels to be free, the paper registered its disbelief, both in the reasons for and the significance of the proclamation. The paper argued that Lincoln would never have issued the proclamation if he believed the North would defeat the South, as "it is not intelligible that he should intend to recover it with four millions of liberated, masterless, disorganised Negroes. … Is it not as certain as any future event can be … that if, in the middle of next year, the Federals find themselves conquerors and masters of a submitted South, they will treat the proclamation as a mere waste of paper, and behave to the Negroes precisely as their own masters have always done?"[48]

The paper's incredulousness about both the sincerity and benefits of the Emancipation Proclamation stemmed mostly from its perception about the possible alternative measures for the organization of society. As it said when questioning the Proclamation itself, "Can there be anything except a mere change of owners? The Blacks will be there still, four millions in number. The soil will be there still, countless acres in extent. Is it conceivable that the Northerners will regard the Blacks as having any function except to cultivate the land, or any right except to earn a subsistence?"[49] This argument foretold a deepening and chilling prescription for dealing with other races that would find even more virulent expression in the *Economist* in years to come.

Despite heightened concerns about the impact of war on the supply of cotton, the *Economist* most often expressed cautious optimism. While worried about the heavy reliance on one source for so much of its cotton, the paper suggested there was little reason for immediate concern through the 1850s, doubtful as it was that hostilities would, in fact, break out or that American planters would allow anything to interfere with their desire to grow and sell cotton. Even after 1861, when the North blockaded southern ports capable of shipping cotton, the *Economist* was certain that a significant amount of cotton would "leak" through the blockade, primarily through Mexican ports. Furthermore, "we share to a considerable extent the instinctive conviction of the Lancashire merchants and manufacturers, that an article grown by an eager seller and consumed by an eager buyer *will* find its way from one to the other."[50] So much for the law of supply and demand being only a "tendency" capable of being discouraged by inconvenience.

As the war deepened, the supply of cotton was soon more circumscribed than the *Economist* had predicted. Even with prices for raw cotton more than quadruple what they had been before the outbreak of the war, and other areas dramatically increasing their exports to Manchester, mills curtailed hours, many shut down, and others complained they were losing money given the limitations and prices of the supply.[51] The paper encouraged more extensive cultivation in other areas, but remained convinced that no matter the outcome of the war, cotton from the US South would flow to Manchester much as it had before the war. In 1862, it stated with some confidence:

> We do not believe the war will be on much longer. ...We do not believe the North will subjugate the South. We scarcely expect Mr. Lincoln will venture on an abolition proclamation, or that it will produce much practical effect even it does. We expect that, ere long, agricultural industry will be restored to its old channels, and capital and labour something like its old relations; and therefore, that the cotton crop of the States will once more be available to the British consumer.[52]

Almost two years later, well after the Emancipation Proclamation and when the tides of war had turned decisively against the South, the paper opined:

> We do not believe that fertile land in the hands of so energetic a people as the Americans will ever be suffered to remain untilled. We do not believe that in a Country inhabited and governed by so peremptory and impatient a people as the Americans, four millions of men, even though by nature they be black and lazy, will ever be suffered to squat in idleness, and become a standing nuisance and burden to all around them. We believe that if they remain slaves they will have to cultivate the land under compulsion and for a maintenance; and if they become either absolutely or conditionally free they will have to cultivate the same land under the inducement of wages or some other inducement equally cogent. ... [A]s soon as belligerent obstacles are withdrawn, American cotton will find its way into Liverpool as before, and in ample quantities.[53]

"An Admirably Rounded Empire"

India was the natural alternative to precarious supplies of cotton from the US South. British interest in India had often been closely tied to the allure of profits to be garnered from cotton cloth. Until the middle of the eighteenth century, the English East India Company (EIC) was just one of a number of European corporate trading companies operating in ports in Asia and the

Indian subcontinent, and not usually the most successful of them. While trade involved a range of goods, the most valued cargo in the wide circle of the Indian Ocean and the South China Sea trade was cotton cloth.[54] Following the Battle of Plassey in 1757, the East India Company slowly emerged as the dominant military force in the Bengal region. For the first couple of decades, the EIC and its factors worked at tying Indian weavers to Company contracts.[55] Over time, though, the EIC became less a trading company and more a fully governing body, relying increasingly on land taxes. Using such taxes to fund its army, the EIC expanded both British and EIC control over the subcontinent through conquest; long military campaigns in the early nineteenth century brought much of south-central India under EIC control and further campaigns in the 1840s did the same to the Punjab. British officials, particularly Lord Dalhousie, who was governor-general of India from 1848 to 1856, also used a questionable expression of political dominance, the Doctrine of Lapse, whereby independent princely states were taken over when the ruling prince had no legitimate male heir. Dalhousie, particularly, employed this strategy to expand British and EIC control over potential cotton-growing regions.[56]

From its inception, the *Economist* felt compelled to tread a middle ground: opposed to empire and conquest, but conscious of the commercial opportunities opened up by EIC territorial expansion; detesting monopoly but often defending the EIC from criticism. These tensions were apparent in the careers of its two most revered inspirations: Smith denounced the East India Company in particular and mercantile trading empires in general; Malthus had been a faithful servant of the company most of his adult life. In addition, Manchester cotton interests were often especially critical of the East India Company, arguing repeatedly through the first half of the nineteenth century that the company was responsible for limiting cotton exports from India. Wilson, while close to Manchester cotton interests, was also deeply involved with the East India Company through his position, assumed shortly after first being elected, on the Board of Control, meant to provide supervision over the Court of Directors of the company.

British society in general reflected this ambivalent attitude to the EIC. The company was tremendously powerful and influential. Tariffs on EIC imports provided one-quarter of British government revenue in the late eighteenth century. EIC tentacles reached deep into parliament through its control over rotten boroughs and the votes of more than one hundred MPs who had invested in the company. In addition, many British government administrators, like Charles Trevelyan, moved back and forth between administrative posts in the company and the British government.[57] Nonetheless, there was also significant opposition to the company in Britain. The first governor-general of Bengal, Warren Hastings, was subject to a very public prosecution in London, continuing over seven years. He was accused of misconduct and corruption, but in many ways his trial was the result of growing British public discomfort with the rapid expansion of EIC-controlled territory and opposition to the extravagant wealth of company administrators and factors returning from India.[58] The occasion for the renewal of the company's charter every few decades occasioned intense debate about the company's role and privileges. Late in the eighteenth century, a government-appointed Board of Control was imposed and East India Company trading monopolies were steadily eroded in the early nineteenth century. The extension of the charter in 1833 effectively ended the EIC's role as a trading company within India and meant the EIC was almost solely after this an administrative and governing entity.

Torn in its allegiance to cotton interests on one hand and the EIC on the other, and between liberalism and empire, the *Economist* found itself making complex arguments about the idea of empire. In 1843, for example, when the EIC armies conquered Sindh, the paper argued that "atrocious monopolies" needed to be broken up and replaced by "responsible government." "India," it argued, "should no longer be considered a retreat for the needy nobleman and adventurers – a nest where every packed goose and vulture may feather themselves at the expense of the happiness of millions." It criticized past aggressions by the EIC but nonetheless argued "we are now so situated that we cannot sit quietly still and witness anarchy, confusion, and murder, upon the borders of our territories."[59]

The paper returned repeatedly to the same arguments. It disagreed with empire, detested monopoly, and rejected conquest, yet found that circumstances continually required that Britain and the EIC expand empire through conquest. After the second Anglo-Sikh War, which resulted in the annexation of the Punjab, the paper concluded, "It is difficult ... without a feeling of melancholy alarm to reflect on the successive annexation of territory in India and behold ourselves constrained by a terrible necessity to pursue a course of conquest and aggrandizement." The paper rued the fact that Britain was "forced into the alarming position of great conquerors." It suggested that this had occurred partly because EIC officials were too greatly influenced by their close intimacy with the people of Asia, "amongst whom they live, amongst whom a love of conquest is yet a passion, and whose creed is war." At the same time, it celebrated the fact that the Indian empire was now "admirably rounded" and its expansion "puts us in possession of the key to the whole commerce of Central Asia." The paper argued that liberal imperialism needed to distinguish itself from ordinary empires by "making the people by ... prosperity forget that they have a foreign master."[60]

"Cooked Land"

The *Economist*'s prescriptions for making the people forget they had a foreign master revolved around the need to make Indian agriculture more productive.

Fortunately for Britain, this also meant that India would better provide it with many of the tropical products it desired. Such productivity would also by necessity provide an avenue for British capital. The "incessant and inextricable insertion of capital into the land" was the fertilizer necessary to turn unimproved land it into "cooked land" capable of producing both more goods and more profit. It was also, the paper argued, the only means possible to end India's peculiar "arrested civilisation."[61]

The paper often expressed wonder at the immense potential represented by British control over India. In 1844, it suggested that an India under British control, infused with English energy and capital and linked to world trade, would change the world. It would, for example, abolish the use of slavery in sugar production by flooding world markets with cheap sugar:

> With labour more abundant, and cheaper than any other place in the world – with the richest soil and the best climate – with improved tenure of land – with English enterprise and capital – and with the spur and stimulus of competition and coming of free trade, it is not difficult to foresee that the cheap free produce of India will abolish slavery throughout the world; and that we shall be shippers of sugars to continental Europe, as we are now of indigo and other Indian produce.[62]

A few years later, the paper reiterated India's grand promise: "There is scarcely one important article of tropical produce which is consumed in this country, either as the raw material of our manufactures, or as an article of daily use, for the production of which India is not as well, or better, adapted than any other country."[63]

Manchester commercial interests viewed India as a potential major supplier of raw cotton and pressed various measures on governments to help foster such exports. They most often blamed the East India Company for not assisting in those efforts either by not providing sufficient infrastructure for cotton exports, or by imposing a land tax that inhibited the spread of cotton cultivation.[64] In reality, the export of Indian raw cotton to England was constrained by a number of different circumstances, many of which were not related to East India Company rule. There continued to be substantial demand for raw Indian cotton both internally, for Indian weavers, and in China, which took about one-third of the Indian crop each year. These combined to raise the price of Indian cotton, in most years, above that of cotton from the southern United States. In addition, the predominant cotton variety in India, Surat cotton, was a short staple cotton not well suited to Manchester manufacturing interests, who most often used mid-staple cotton for both the warp and weft of cotton cloth. Attempts to introduce Bourbon or Upland mid-staple cotton to India were generally unsuccessful, primarily because their root systems were less robust and they needed more water than indigenous cotton varieties.[65] Nonetheless, there were numerous studies and reports reiterating the promise of Indian cotton, with most asking why this promise was not met. One that garnered some particular attention was a talk given to the Royal Asiatic Society in 1839 by John Briggs and later published as a pamphlet. Briggs sought, in his words, "to show to this meeting, that India, with her free population, may supply cotton in any requisite quantity as good, and cheaper, than America or any other country can with slave labour."[66] Briggs pointed to significant artificial obstacles to such exports, most notably the debilitating effect of the land tax imposed by the EIC, and the lack of transportation.[67]

Through most of the 1840s and into the 1850s the *Economist* seemed to agree with Briggs and others. In 1846, for example, it argued that "with proper management, India is capable of furnishing a supply of cotton equal to the consumption of the whole world." And in 1847 it published a five-part series dedicated to the question "Why does not India Supply us with Cotton?" The paper started the series saying, "Scarcely a week, nay, scarcely a day passes, that this question is not asked." In the second article, it reiterated the argument that, "In a word: there is in India land capable of growing five hundred times as much cotton as annually brought to England; and it may be truly said to be the natural region for supply of cotton to the universe."[68] Like Briggs and others, the paper placed the blame for the lack of cotton exports from India on the system of land tenure and land tax leading to a paucity of capital investment in land, and the lack of infrastructure. Both the paper and Wilson became intimately connected with schemes for changing both of these.

Like the Manchester interests, the paper blamed the land tax system for the lack of capital investment in Indian agriculture. Since near the end of the eighteenth century, the EIC had relied for the majority of its income on a land tax. The nature of that tax differed in various regions of British-controlled India. Initially based on the grant of the *Diwani* to the EIC by the overpowered ruler of the Bengal, land taxes in the Bengal were regularized by Lord Cornwall in 1793 in a system often called the Permanent Settlement. *Zamindars*, who had previously held different relationships to the land in different locales but who were generally a form of tax agent extracting rents from farmers, were given a more permanent claim over the land; in return they were to provide the EIC a fixed, long-term rent.[69] EIC officials in other regions of India believed they saw many inequalities and disadvantages with this system and implemented other varieties of land tax. In the Madras region, the *ryotwari* system collected a tax more directly from Indian peasants and small farmers, while in parts of Northern India the EIC collected the land tax from village headmen. There was much debate in the EIC at the time, and among historians since, about the varying effects of these systems.[70] The impact on peasant livelihoods throughout India was uneven, but in much of the subcontinent, no matter the land tax system, increased tax/rents that were not dependent on the bounty of the harvest, the vicissitudes of fluctuating markets, and the reliance on local money lenders to pay rent in times of stress led to declining peasant livelihoods through much of India during this period.[71]

The *Economist* argued that each of the systems prevented investment of capital and cooking the land, either because investors had no access to land, or land tenure was made insecure by the terms of the tax, or those seeking cotton were left to "extract it from unhappy cultivators."[72] It often argued that the tax needed to be lowered if cotton was to be grown.[73]

As Wilson developed closer connections to the EIC, the paper changed its tune. While still concerned about the limited amounts of cotton coming from India, it took a more positive approach to the land tax. It argued that the permanent or perpetual settlement of land taxes had provided security to Indian agriculturalists and would lead to progress. In the context of the debate about the extension of the company's charter in 1853, the paper engaged in a full-scale defence of the EIC's activities in India. It said, "It is a notorious fact, known to everyone, who has the slightest acquaintance with India, that the terms upon which land was formerly held by ryots have undergone great modification and improvement ... By this means the cultivator is secured in all the advantages which can be obtained by increased and improved cultivation." The paper went on to argue that the improved conditions of Indian peasants could be demonstrated by the growth in exports from India: cotton exports had tripled between 1833 and 1850; hemp had increased tenfold; silk by a third. In response to criticisms that these exports were instead "evidence of the increasing exactions of the Government," the paper pointed to the rise in imports from England, which had more than tripled, as more than sufficient refutation of such an argument.[74] (It might be noted here that this assertion was made at the same time the *Economist* was arguing, elsewhere, that Indian ryots were living in conditions no better than American slaves.) Both Wilson and the *Economist* eventually professed to believe not that the Indian ryots were too heavily taxed, but that the land tax should remain and an income tax added to the "exactions" to help pay the costs of empire. And of course, Wilson's role in the Bank of India, Australia, and China, and the desire to overcome EIC opposition to the bank's charter, certainly played a role in shaping Wilson's opinions.[75]

The paper continued its defence of the EIC the next year, but its arguments were increasingly tinged with pessimism about change. In January, the paper argued that some areas of India had been under EIC rule for twenty-five years. The Company had been able to "maintain an immense territory, filled with jarring interests and conflicting superstitions in an undisturbed tranquility never known before." India, "under the rule of the Company, has made considerable progress." But, it warned, "almost every foot of land is owned and occupied – and the great problem is, how the habits of nations, reputed for ages to be almost unchangeable and unchanged, can be altered and improved."[76] An increasing antipathy to the "Hindoos" would soon become a much more pronounced element in the *Economist*'s stories about India.

"One of the Most Important Propositions of Modern Times"

One of the reasons for the paper's staunch defence of the EIC no doubt had much to do with Wilson's increasing connections to the company. Along with concerns about the land taxes, most complaints about EIC policy asserted that it had not done enough to create infrastructure to facilitate trade, especially to assist in cotton exports. This started to change in the 1840s when, under Lord Dalhousie, the government of India began to invest substantially in the maintenance of roads and the dredging and improvement of canals. The most ambitious of these plans, however, revolved around railways. The *Economist* had always been a strong supporter of railways, despite Spencer's somewhat jaundiced experiences in the industry. It had occasionally expressed concern about over-investment in railway schemes in Britain and had cautioned that attempts to attract too much capital had crowded out "honest plod and fair industry." But despite concerns about fraudulent schemes, the paper had opposed government regulation of railway investment as "interfering and meddling."[77]

It is somewhat surprising then that Wilson should have become so intimately connected with plans for what became essentially a government-secured and fully regulated scheme for the construction of railways in India. In 1846 the EIC sponsored a plan through which the company would guarantee returns to British investors providing capital for railway construction in India. The *Economist* supported this idea strongly; as the paper said, "We have always regarded the establishment of railways in India as one of the most important propositions of modern times." Not only would railways assist in increased cotton exports and more generally help "cook" the land, but they would also increase the reach of the EIC armies and dissuade rebellious princes.[78]

Wilson was personally invested in many of these proposals. In 1859, in a note to the first viceroy of India, Wilson claimed that he (i.e., Wilson) "was almost alone instrumental in beginning the Railway system."[79] This was an exaggeration; the company first proposed the idea in 1846 before Wilson was elected to parliament. But after he was elected in 1847 and appointed to the Board of Control, he and the paper did become the scheme's staunchest supporters. His daughter remembers Wilson, while Secretary of the Board of Control, devising plans and maps for the railways at their dining room table.[80] Two lines using this plan were approved by Parliament in 1849.[81]

Under the plan the EIC guaranteed a 5 per cent return on all capital invested for ninety-nine years.[82] The EIC was the effective government of most of the subcontinent and, as we have seen, it received most of its income from land tax charged, ultimately, to ryots. Most of the railways, designed primarily to meet either administrative/military demands or tap potential cotton growing regions, did not return a 5 per cent profit until well into the twentieth century. This is not surprising, given there was little incentive with the guarantee to do so. As one shareholder said in 1851, "I care nothing about the line or what is done with the money, so only that it is spent to secure the 5 per cent."[83] Thus, the long-term effect of the railway scheme was a massive transfer of wealth from Indian peasants and farmers to British stockholders. In addition, as the paper rejoiced when the plan was passed by the House: "The enormous importance of improved means of communication in India as the only requisite for developing the extraordinary resources of that country, as the largest and richest field of production for some of the chief raw materials of our manufactures, such as cotton, silk, hemp, and indigo ... is now well understood and fully acknowledged."[84] Even in the years immediately following the rebellion, the paper argued for greater urgency in the construction of railways, "as the only means by which we can hope permanently ... to bring in the abundant labour of the millions of fellow-subjects in India ... and thus to give the best practical check to the growing attractions of Slavery and the Slave-Trade."[85] By 1861, reportedly, the Government of India, had raised £33,000,000 and paid £5,000,000 in interest through the railway scheme.[86]

"Every Act of Treachery and Ferocity"

Meanwhile, storm clouds gathered. In 1855, a substantial revolt occurred in eastern India among Santals protesting the land tax. While the paper first dismissed the revolt as isolated and not particularly important, when it proved difficult to curtail the *Economist* professed to see dark portent in it. "A speck on the eastern horizon," the paper warned, "has so often grown into a cloud. ... [P]eace in India is treacherous; to be cherished, indeed, but still jealously and vigilantly watched. ... a country which is still, and must be for some years to come, held by the sword."[87] The portents continued to arrive: in April 1857, in a review of a pamphlet written by Major Andrew Crawford entitled "Remarks on the Indian Army," the paper pointed out that, "we still hold it, as we obtained it, by the sword ... and the people are not yet enlightened enough to have become enamoured of our milder and juster [*sic*] sway. We are a handful of Europeans among scores of millions of Asiatics ..."[88]

A few months later, news of the Great Rebellion began to arrive in Britain. The *Economist* first dismissed the rebellion as "this sudden outbreak of panic and fanaticism in the Bengal Army" and attacked any suggestion that the rebellion was more than simply a limited mutiny in the army.[89] While it continued to hold this stance, the paper soon suggested the causes of the revolt were linked to a broader discontent with progress, arguing that the Sepoy army was threatened by "being rapidly undermined by intellectual forces which they are perfectly helpless to arrest." The paper advised the continuation of current policies and, especially, the rapid expansion of railways through which "the resources of districts and populations hitherto so neglected can be developed and large *aggregate* returns ultimately realised."[90] The paper contradictorily clung to the idea that the rebellion was a simple, and limited, mutiny among sectors in the army, castigating those who suggested otherwise, while also arguing that it demonstrated the natural tendency of the population to barbarity. Almost a year after the revolt, the paper was still protesting against those who portrayed the rebellion as a symptom of general discontent with British rule and it briefly opposed the India Bill removing the EIC from control over the Government of India. Soon, however, the paper both admitted the serious nature of revolt and used the revolt as justification for a more coercive approach to both governance and the economy.

Near the end of 1857 and into the new year, the *Economist* produced two articles suggesting the benefits that Britain might derive from the rebellion. In the first, the paper argued:

> The mutineers have revealed in unmistakeable colours – not to ourselves only, but to the whole civilised world – what would be the result of leaving India to her own control. ... We now see written legibly in the records of every act of treachery and ferocity ... what India could become, if abandoned by the British power. ... It would not be mere barbarism, but something far worse than barbarism, which would sweep over Hindostan if once our hand were withdrawn.[91]

The next month the paper was even more explicit about the lessons that should be drawn from the rebellion. The paper said if one ignored the English suffering:

> we might ... look upon these horrors as almost pure gain to the power and influence of our Government. They have revealed the marvelous constitution of the native mind in characters so broad and strong. ... Everywhere it is felt that England, and England alone, can save India from herself. ... No events less horrible could have strengthened our hands so powerfully. ... the details of the revolt have vindicated us from the charge of enforcing an unjust and arbitrary yoke as nothing we could have done or said could possibly have vindicated us.[92]

The treatment of Indian ryots and others thus vindicated, the *Economist* articulated a complex, and occasionally contradictory, argument about what England needed to do in India. Though stating time and again that England continued to hold India by the sword, it counselled that it could not rule India through fear, rather "our chief object, to which all other must yield in prominence, is to govern India for the highest well-being of her people." But how to do this was often disputed. The paper argued that land settlement and the land tax needed to be altered to encourage the consolidation of a landed aristocracy, partly because they provided support to the government, and partly because the peasantry had not yet been influenced sufficiently by the "gentler" treatment of the EIC to come to the aid of the government. Moreover, even the abuse of power by a landed aristocracy was beneficial if it "breaks the dead level of native society."[93]

The paper also articulated two complementary arguments. Firstly, heightened cotton production in India would require European control over land and production, and, even so, India would not provide the long-term answer for England's cotton woes. For that, Britain would need to look to new fields in Africa. Both in its own stories and in those they printed from other sources, the paper more forcefully made the argument that for cotton production to increase in India, it needed to be in the hands of Europeans, either as owners of the land or as agents sponsored by the government to contract for cotton. The paper had hinted at this argument in the 1850s, but after the rebellion, with the paper under the direction of Walter Bagehot, it became a central part of the *Economist*'s concerns. In 1862, it published a five-part letter from a J.W.B. Money, who had long been resident in India. Money argued at length that "the direction of Indian cotton must pass from the native to the European," suggesting that 2,000 European cotton planters be provided with 20,000 acres each, employing 10,000 families. Under such a system, within four years they would export 4,000,000 bales.[94] In the absence of direct control of the land, the government needed to do more to prompt cotton cultivation and marketing by establishing a system of government agents charged with collecting specific amounts of cotton. Though this was not initially perceived as the system of obligatory cultivation of cotton that would be used so notoriously in Africa, it came very close. In the face of the expected criticism that this was a significant contradiction of the ideas inherent in a free market and limited government involvement, the paper provided an awkward defence: "Where there is no intelligent population to lead the way, a Government must do what in more civilised countries can safely be left to private enterprise. ... To interfere now for the promotion of an improved and extended growth of cotton is not to interfere with the laws of supply and demand, but ... to enable those laws to operate."[95]

The paper's second argument was that Britain should look farther afield for its cotton in the future. Though such semi-coerced cultivation in India might temporarily help solve the problem of a reliance on US cotton, the paper doubted Indian cotton could ever compete in price. In the long run the paper suggested West Africa would provide a more enduring remedy and urged speedy "settlement and civilisation" of the continent.[96]

These arguments were frightening portents of the future. By the 1860s, as the *Economist* faced evidence that the elixir of capital, free trade, and laissez-faire was being met on all sides by opposition it could only ascribe to barbarism and superstition, it increasingly counselled coercion and repression. In 1861, in commenting on the need to organize labour into new "sources of prosperity" the *Economist* engaged in an only slightly disguised call for a new form of slavery:

> The one necessary essential to the development of these new sources of prosperity is the arrangement of some industrial system under which very large bodies of dark labourers will work willingly under a very few European supervisors. It is not only individual labour which is required, but organised labour, labour so scientifically arranged that the maximum result shall be obtained at a minimum of cost … All of these ends were secured, it must freely be acknowledged, by slavery. For the mere execution of great works cheaply no organisation could be equal to that which placed the skilled European at the top, and made him despotic master of the half-skilled black or copper-coloured labourer below. … [C]ivilisation, after a protracted struggle with its own interests and prejudices, has resolved to discard slavery from its working system. A new organisation therefore must be commenced … If, however, complete freedom is to be the principle adopted, it is clear that the dark races must in some way or other be induced to obey white men willingly. … in *the tropics Nature has given man the benefit, or the curse, of a perpetual poor law, a prodigality of food which of itself establishes a minimum of wages.*[97]

A few years later the paper, in an article ostensibly about the economic rewards of employing justice in dealings with "dark races," provided a chilling prediction of its view of English destiny – "it is probably the destiny, it is even now the function, it is certainly the interest of the European, and more particularly of the English family of mankind, to guide and urge and control the industrial enterprises of all Asia, of all Africa, and of those portions of America settled by African, Asiatic or hybrid races."[98]

"Take Care of My Income Tax"

Shortly after the Government issued the India Bill, imposing direct British government control, the new Secretary of State for India, Sir Charles Wood, asked Wilson to agree to take the position of Finance Minister in the Council of India established to work alongside the Viceroy, Lord Canning. Wilson was reluctant to take the position but seems to have been compelled by a sense of duty to accept. In 1859, Wilson, his wife, and three of his daughters set sail for India.

Wilson was convinced that Indians needed to be taxed more heavily to pay a greater share of the cost of empire (and the increasing railway interest). The paper became his public voice, suggesting that the land tax should be considered rent, rather than a tax, and be paid readily and cheerfully. Viewed in this way,

Indian subjects were, the paper argued, the least taxed subjects of the British Crown anywhere in the world. Moreover, both Wilson and the paper argued vehemently against the idea that Britain should take on any of the debt of the Government of India.

Even before setting sail for India Wilson was convinced that India needed an income tax.[99] In his first letter from India to his son-in-law and soon to be new editor of the paper, Walter Bagehot, Wilson enthused, "What a wonderful country to tax."[100] He quickly got to work devising a plan for an income tax he hoped would provide £3 to 4 million for the government.[101] Wilson viewed his control of the Indian exchequer as the major cog in "an unruly empire" that "needed to be governed on the principle of forcing civilisation at every point."[102] He was encouraged in his efforts by letters of support, including one from the Prince Consort, Albert, who counselled him to hold true to "unalterable truths of the laws of political economy taught by abstract science." He remarked, "India is a wide field for their application" that should not be impeded by "local peculiarities."[103]

Though there was some disagreement with Canning about the level of income at which the tax should begin – Canning intent that the tax should not apply to soldiers in the Indian army – Wilson initially met little resistance among British administrative officials to the tax. Charles Trevelyan, now back in India as the governor of the Madras district, was opposed to the tax, however. He argued that such a tax was both unnecessary and would lead to widespread rebellion.[104] When Wilson ignored his opposition, Trevelyan convinced the Madras Council to place in its minutes heated opposition to the tax, also warning of the probability that it would lead to spreading rebellion. He, then, took the unprecedented step of having the minutes made public.[105] Pandemonium ensued as the Indian press publicized the dispute and Trevelyan's prediction of unrest. Wilson struggled to save his tax. Suffering from dysentery, he refused to leave his work and the heat of Calcutta until too late. He died on 11 August 1860. His last words were reportedly, "Take care of my Income tax."[106] The *Economist* marked his passing with a reprinted short notice from its old antagonist, the *Times*, adding: "The conductors of the journal do not feel they can at present do more than record this mournful event in the words of others. It has come too suddenly on them."[107]

Chapter Eleven

Conclusion: "The Home-made Civilization of the Rural English"

In one of his delightful books about his life in Farnham, Surrey, George Sturt provides us with a vision of a "civilization" he imagines is in its last days. Writing at the beginning of the twentieth century, Sturt tells us that he recognizes in the inhabitants the remaining vestiges of a "peasant tradition." This "home-made civilization of the rural English" according to Sturt, "permitted a man to hope for well-being without seeking to escape from his own class." Sturt draws a picture of a still-lingering society in which, "people could find … not only a method of getting a living, but also an encouragement and a help to live well." The region of Surrey Sturt describes was not well-favoured land. Sturt says, "The cottagers had to rough it, to dispense with softness, to put up with ugliness; but by their own skill and knowledge they forced the main part of their living out of the soil and materials of their own neighbourhood."[1] Sturt argued that the most obvious lingering effect of that tradition was "self-reliance." He says, "Anyone personally acquainted with the villagers knows how their life is one continuous act of unconscious self-reliance."[2]

Sturt's description of unrelenting self-reliance is strikingly at odds with the way the term was used by the apostles of inequality discussed in this book. From Arthur Young through Malthus and Senior to the writers for the *Economist*, they obsessed over the need to force self-reliance on the rural poor. But their vision of self-reliance was blinkered, a kind of code for not going "on the parish" but instead relying on money wages, no matter how miserly and sporadic. As we have seen, Arthur Young eventually recognized the fallacy of such a strategy; he came to realize that forcing the rural poor to rely exclusively on wages meant inevitably increased poor relief and more misery. Young's solution was to contribute to the diversity of household income by increasing the opportunity for self-provisioning through cottage gardens or allotments. Young and the gallery of large landowners in the Board of Agriculture and Internal Improvement who championed the provision of such land tapped into the most ardent desires of the rural poor, if we can judge from the writings of contemporaries and those, like Sturt, who sought to reconstruct a vision of a "peasant civilisation" decades later.

Sturt's description of the "home-made civilization of the rural English" would be familiar to anyone who has either worked in or studied peasant or poor rural communities. Livelihoods seem always to be pieced together from a mix of hard work, ingenuity, and anxiety. Getting the most from small pieces of land was a hard-won craft built from experience; making a living and raising a family in such circumstances was an art, employing if not always embracing a diverse range of opportunities. In some studies of the poor in England in the late eighteenth and early nineteenth centuries, this imaginative frugality has been called "an economy of makeshifts" (borrowing the phrase from French historical studies on the poor).[3]

What went into an economy of makeshifts? Wage employment was always an important part of most rural families' income; poor relief, especially before 1834, was important, as was household handicraft production.[4] But these sources of income were almost always coupled with a diverse range of other activities: dependence on common resources, either through recognized common right or more informal types of arrangements; and, of course, cottage gardens or allotment plots. Determining the relative mix and value of these various activities has proven to be difficult and not without dispute.

We discussed earlier competing interpretations of the value of common resources before enclosures. Various studies have estimated the percentage of families in different parts of England in the late eighteenth century who might have had official common right as between 4 per cent who owned common right dwellings in Campton and Shefford,[5] to 15 per cent renting common right cottages in the south and east of England.[6] Some scholars have suggested that the predominance of wage labour meant that the bulk of rural inhabitants formed a "proletariat" in the early nineteenth century. Leigh Shaw-Taylor, for example, has argued that only a small percentage of the rural labourers in the south and east of England had sufficient common right to keep a cow. He asserts, "Only the keeping of cows was sufficiently valuable to confer any real degree of independence of wage labour."[7] We must thus, according to him, consider the majority of rural labourers to be thoroughly proletarianized. The proposition that the rural poor in England and Wales were essentially only wage-earners also fits into the argument of those, like Robert Brenner, who focus on a more or less seamless transition to industrial wage labour as being a key component of English economic success in the nineteenth century.[8]

Other authors have argued that the commons was much more important than these views suggest. Jane Humphries, R.W. Malcolmson, and Jeannette Neeson among others have convincingly argued that the range of activities carried out on the commons, or on the fringes of the commons, especially by women and children, was much more diverse and much more important in family livelihood than the restricted focus on the rental of common right cottages or holding sufficient common right to keep a cow. Access to common resources was not always restricted to those with common rights nor always related to having a right to open fields or the stint of a cow. Even "landless" commoners gathered part of their livelihood from the commons: gleaning might make up 5–13 per cent of the grain needs of a family; gathering fuel and other material from common wastes and forests often added significantly to family income; keeping geese, even plaiting straw, all of which were often functions of informal access to common resources, added together made up more than a considerable portion of such makeshift family incomes.[9]

Focusing solely on wages for the rural poor in contemplating rural lives, as the early Young, political economists, the various poor law commissions, and the *Economist* all wished to do, is particularly problematic into the late eighteenth and early decades of the nineteenth century as "full" employment for rural labourers became increasingly scarce, especially in the southeast. Such a focus seems especially inattentive to the lives of the rural poor if we add self-provisioning and market-gardening from cottage gardens and allotment lands to the diversity outlined above. While the right to keep a cow as recognized common right may have, in fact, been most cherished, it was certainly not the only thing which helped in self-provisioning, provided some independence from a strict reliance on increasingly sporadic wage labour, and prevented going on the parish or into the dreaded workhouse. Viewed from a different perspective, the thirty families "round the skirts" of the commons at Horton Heath that William Cobbett described would need to be disregarded in such a consideration. Let us remember, instead, what Cobbett found on these tiny pieces of land: there were a few cows, but there were also more than a hundred beehives, sixty pigs, and five hundred head of geese and chickens. As Cobbett said, "The cottages consisted of fathers, mothers, and children, grandfathers, grandmothers, and grandchildren, or more than two hundred persons! [I learned to hate] a system that could lead English gentlemen to disregard matters like these."[10] As historians, perhaps we should be equally leery of such disregard.

It has proven to be remarkably difficult to calculate the contribution of small cottage gardens and allotments to rural livelihoods, whether carved out of commons wastes (as in the families at Horton Heath) or rented from lords or farmers (as in Brinton Abbot). Some studies have found that self-provisioning contributed only a very small proportion of the income of rural households, perhaps as little as 2 per cent in some regions.[11] This seems remarkably low and not consistent with other evidence. Barry Reay has argued that in the middle of the nineteenth century some 16 per cent of the average income of a household came from the garden allotment.[12] Contemporary evidence makes it clear that such produce was immensely important to rural livelihoods. Small cottage gardens were often associated with keeping bees, raising a pig or two and geese and other fowl; numerous commentators suggested hives alone might cover the cost of rent for a rood or two of land.[13] While a cow was considered to be a uniquely important contributor to household incomes, some estimates suggest that a pig could contribute close to 20 per cent of a full wage income for a year, or about one-half the value of a cow.[14] We might be advised to remember the care with which the collier's wife discussed in chapter 3 nurtured her pig as part of her diversified small holding.[15] William Cobbett's Cottage Economy was based around the trinity of Bread, Beer, and Bacon; as he said, "A couple of flitches of bacon are worth fifty thousand Methodist sermons."[16] It is perhaps hard to put a value on Methodist sermons, but certainly others echoed Cobbett's assessment of the value of the pig to the family economy. Between one-quarter and one-half of the rural households kept a pig at the middle of the nineteenth century and, as Walter Rose remarked in recollections of English village life from the 1870s to the 1880s, "Life without a pig was almost unthinkable."[17]

The multitude of reports of the remarkable productivity of cottage gardens – the extraordinary care and importance cottagers placed on them – that were recounted in the pages of *Annals of Agriculture* or in the journal of the Society for Bettering the Condition of the Poor may have depicted exceptional cases. But if so, there were many of them. Though Brinton Abbot worked for wages for Squire Fairfax, from whom he rented land, Abbot would surely not have rated those wages more highly in his family economy than his rood of land. Even some of the reports to the Poor Law Commission that expressed opposition to rural labourers' small gardens admitted that a family could live in moderate comfort from the income of a few acres of garden land. Numerous other accounts we have examined suggest that the cottage garden or allotment made the essential difference between an impoverished existence dependent totally on wage labour and the ability to carve out a more secure livelihood by following the art of making a living out of little bits. As Arthur Young reported, "Nothing could be clearer than the vast importance which all these poor people scattered as they are through many counties, and affected by circumstances so extremely various, attach to the object of possessing land, though no more than to set a cottage on."[18]

By the middle of the nineteenth century, as "high" agriculture became the new clarion call and as the New Poor Law made going on the parish more difficult or less attractive, the *Economist* newspaper celebrated the diminished hold of the parish for England's rural inhabitants, congratulating itself that the changes then under way had "broken down the parochial and patriarchal barriers which made each spot a gaol, though a home," and predicting that "the same progress will cause them to be entirely removed."[19] It is true that England experienced fairly dramatic population shifts through the first few decades of the nineteenth century. By 1851, for the first time, the majority of the population lived in towns or cities. Not only did the proportion of agricultural labourers fall, but their absolute numbers also declined after 1851. Still, we should not make too much of this shift, nor conclude that it was either inevitable or welcomed. The real standard of living for agricultural labourers had declined for close to a century by that time. Nonetheless, it would appear the embrace of the parish for much of the rural population remained both strong and welcome. While some, clearly, were held in place by the Law of Settlement and other restrictions that inhibited some types of mobility, for most the parish was always more "home" than "gaol." As Keith Snell has detailed in his careful study of parish relief records, "A strong case can be made for 'invigorated localism' in the mid-nineteenth century, lasting through to the 1870s or beyond."[20] Certainly, again, this accords with the evidence from contemporaries. Testimony after testimony through the first half of the nineteenth century reiterated the hold of the parish, the benefit of community, the attraction of long-known neighbours, and the comfort of familiar land. Though Cobbett often romanticized an ideal country life, he spent much of his adult life trying to get back to a farm, a parish, and a community he remembered from his childhood near Farnham, Surrey. He eventually found it at his farm in Botley, "the most delightful village in the world … with neither workhouse, nor barber, nor attorney, nor justice of the peace," according to Cobbett.[21] George Eliot suggested in *Daniel Deronda* published in 1876:

> A human life, I think, should be well rooted in some spot of a native land, where it may get the love of tender kinship for the peace of the earth, for the labours men go forth to, for the sounds and accents that haunt it, … a spot where the definiteness of early memories may be inwrought with affection, and kindly acquaintance with all neighbours, even to the dogs and donkeys, may spread not by sentimental effort and reflection, but as a sweet habit of the blood.[22]

George Sturt was, perhaps, somewhat less romantic, but he, too, writing at the turn of the century, remarked continually about the hold of place, the value of a shared culture of labouring on the land, and, of course, the self-reliance of country folk.

Perhaps the manufacturing centres of northern England, such as Manchester, or the siren song of gold strikes, or even the promise of land of one's own in some distance place, acted as a "safety valve" venting the resentment and frustration bubbling over in destitute rural parishes, as the *Liverpool Mercury* could argue in 1844.[23] But one feels driven to ask why there was the need for such a release. If the hold of the parish was so powerful, if a rural household under the thrall of the "enchantment of property," as Young would eventually come to admit, would lend itself to such industry and productivity that a small piece of land could make the difference between poverty and modest comfort, if cottage gardens produced many times the amount of food of the normal husbandry in a country that was chronically short of food, if the self-reliance of poor country folk led naturally to creative independence, why the continually repeated demand that they rely on only wage labour through this century of calamity for the rural poor?

The answer would appear to lie in faith in the magic of capital, the constant warnings about the dangers of population increase, and a continual demand for labourers dependent on meagre wages. Arthur Young, the most celebrated commentator on English agriculture in the last few decades of the eighteenth century, asserted constantly the need for capital to improve agriculture and to make it more productive. Perhaps haunted by his own failures at farming, caused, he said, by his inability to command enough capital, he continually argued that only enclosure, improved agriculture on large capital-intensive farms, and wage labour could lead to progress. Eventually he concluded that not capital but the industry of cottagers on their own land was the answer both to the short-term food crisis of the 1790s and to enduring poverty. His eloquent calls for land for the rural poor, along with the articulate and often moving accounts of some fellow members of the Board of Agriculture and Internal Improvement, had little effect, drowned out in the chorus of those singing the praises of capital and chanting warnings about population increase. The result was deepening poverty and heightened rural unrest.

Farmers and landowners terrified by the prospect of "saucy" labourers not dependent on wages were joined by a series of writers, Malthus in the lead, who warned that the provision of land for the rural poor, especially if they came to depend on the land more than on wages, would lead to disastrous population increase. The early Young, Malthus, Senior, and the *Economist* all, time after time, argued that the road to prosperity lay in the trinity of large landowners renting land to capital wielding farmers and rural wage labour. They rhapsodized about the benefits of capital, the "universal opulence" that would ensue from the division of labour, and painted apocalyptic images of the damage that any interference with the "natural law" of supply and demand would cause. Not everyone was enthralled. As the critic writing as Piercy Ravenstone argued, if capital was the key to prosperity, why were workers starving while England was "oppressed with capital even to plethory."[24] Despite such criticism, what accolades called the "science of political economy" increasingly dominated discussion of the economy and policy and, for a time, crowded out alternative arguments about ways of organizing society and the economy.

The *Economist* newspaper was an important weapon in the war waged to favour capital. The paper redoubled arguments about the need for capital and the dangers of allowing rural labourers access to land. It was especially vehement in its denunciations of any suggestion that small, peasant farming could be productive, arguing constantly that labour "left to its clumsy and unassisted expedients" could never foster increased production nor well-being. As it warned,

"A pursuit ... for which the capitalist cannot pay wages should be instantly abandoned."[25] The *Economist* also sought to reinforce the lessons of political economy in discussions of Ireland, especially during the famine years, to the issue of slavery and the US Civil War, and to British rule in India. Through it often made complex and occasionally silly arguments, the paper continually tried to apply what James Wilson, the founding editor, proclaimed to be "nothing but pure principles"[26] to all the momentous issues confronting the country. In the desire to clear the way for capital and to insure the victory of what Adam Smith had declared to be the path to "natural liberty," the *Economist* increasingly advocated repression, found excuses for the continuation of slavery, and cautioned that new "sources of prosperity" required some system "under which very large bodies of dark labourers will work willingly under a very few European supervisors."[27]

By the second half of the nineteenth century, some of the sting was out of political economy, though it was never abandoned in England to be tried in Siberia as the *Times* advised. Laissez faire was no longer held in such high esteem. William Thomas Thornton and John Stuart Mill made cogent and powerful arguments about the benefits and economic prospects of peasant agriculture. Capital intensive (high) English agriculture was not able to compete with foreign grain and England experienced a modest reversion to smaller farms. And a couple of decades later, the most enduring critique of political economy, volume 1 of *Capital*, was published, though not in English until near the end of the century. Through everything – a century of declining wages and falling living standards; a half century of rural unrest, arson and riot, and protest; a century when the simple expedient of providing the industrious rural poor with land was rejected; a century of the triumph of capital; a century of a grand experiment with the fairy dust of political economy – the rural poor were at the centre of it all, "one foot already in the swamp of pauperism."[28]

Notes

1 Introduction: "The Multiplication of Wretchedness"

1 Arthur Young, *The Farmer's Letters to the People of England containing the Sentiments of a Practical Husbandman*, Vol. 1, 3–4, 9–10. (Note: Young converted the single volume original into two volumes for the 1771 edition. The second volume is entitled *The Farmer's Letters to the Landlords of Great-Britain*. It is not clear why the title changed; the second volume resembles his later Tours in substance and is no more or less directed at landlords than volume 1, which kept the original title.)

2 Young, *The Farmer's Letters to the People of England*, Vol. 1, 201, 292, 295.

3 *Economist*, "Agriculture: Land; its Uses and Abuses," 4:150 (11 July 1846): 893–4.

4 *Economist*, "Scarcity of Labour," 13:628 (8 Sept. 1855): 979–80.

5 *Economist*, "The Poor Law and the Commissioners," 5:195 (22 May 1847): 577–8.

6 The first national survey of agricultural labourers' accommodation cited in Alan Armstrong and J.P. Huzel, "Labour II: Food, Shelter, and Self-help, the Poor Law and the Position of the Labourer in Rural Society," 729–835; G.E. Mingay (ed.), *The Agrarian History of England and Wales (AHEW)*, Vol. VI., esp. p. 748.

7 Report of Dr. E. Smith cited in *Economist*, "The Food of the English Labourer," 22:1102 (8 Oct. 1864): 1252–3.

8 Arthur Young, *Travels in France during the years, 1787, 1788, and 1789*, 254.

9 Piercy Ravenstone, *A Few Doubts as to the Correctness of Some Opinions Generally entertained on the Subjects of Population and Political Economy*, 5.

10 Ibid., 207. (See chapter 6 for a fuller discussion of Ravenstone's identity.)

11 Letter from Wilson to his wife, reprinted in Emilie Barrington, *Servant of All: Pages from the Family, Social, and Political Life of my Father James Wilson*, Vol. I, 77.

12 *Poor Law Commissioners' Report of 1834*, 1:3.

13 Important among these works are the studies by Keith Snell, especially *Annals of the Labouring Poor*; Alan Armstrong, *Farmworkers: A Social and Economic History 1770–1980*; Barry Reay, *Rural Englands: Labouring Lives in the Nineteenth*

Century; and, of course, E.P. Thompson, *The Making of the English Working Class*, esp. ch. 7. The important ways their work has informed my own will be apparent in the various chapters.

14 A fuller historiography of writing on enclosure follows below. Here I would mention the early twentieth-century works that helped trailblaze studies of enclosure: George Sturt, *Change in the Village* originally published in 1912 and J.L. and Barbara Hammond, *The Village Labourer,1760–1832: A Study in the Government of England before the Reform Bill*. More recent works of note on the effects of enclosure are Jeannette Neeson, *Commoners: Common Right, Enclosure and Social Change in England, 1700–1820* and Jane Humphries, "Enclosures, Common Rights, and Women: The Proletarianization of Families in the Late Eighteenth and Early Nineteenth Centuries."

15 A noteworthy exception is Jeremy Burchardt, *The Allotment Movement in England, 1793–1873*.

16 Most noteworthy are Ruth Dudley Edwards, *The Pursuit of Reason: The Economist 1843–1993* and Angel Arrese Reca, *La identidad de The Economist*. There is also one PhD dissertation on Wilson: James Moncure, "James Wilson and The Economist, 1805–1860." My book was submitted to the publisher before Alexander Zevin's wonderful *Liberalism at Large: The World According to the Economist* was published. I have, though, used it when I could as I have made revisions.

17 Ravenstone, *A Few Doubts*, 294.

18 *Economist*, "Conflict of Peasantry and Landlords," 4:137 (11 April 1846): 467–8.

19 The quote comes from *Economist*, "The Deficiency of Labour in the West Indies," 17:829 (16 July 1859): 784–6.

20 *Economist*, "English Feelings Toward America," 19:944 (28 Sept. 1861): 1065–7.

2 "The Yoke of Improvement"

1 Young, *Farmer's Letters to the People of England*, 201.

2 J.D. Chambers and G.E. Mingay, *The Agricultural Revolution*; Mingay, "Introduction," 1–7, in *The Agrarian History of England and Wales, Vol. VI, 1750–1850*; Jones, *Agricultural Enlightenment*.

3 Overton, *Agricultural Revolution in England*; E.A. Wrigley, "Country and Town," 217–42, esp. p. 233. This argument is what Robert Allen, in 1992, called the "agrarian fundamentalism" that marked English historiography about the industrial revolution. He suggests it consists of three elements: modernization of rural institutions in the late eighteenth and early nineteenth centuries led to a technical revolution in agriculture that increased productivity; this increased productivity boosted early industrialization by providing both capital and labour for industry; the growth in inequality in this period was necessary for such industrialization. He suggests this fundamentalism is common to both "Tory" and Marxist approaches and disagrees with all three contentions. Robert Allen, *Enclosure and the Yeoman*, esp. 3–10.

4 Gazley, *The Life of Arthur Young*, 1.

5 G.E. Fussell, "My Impressions of Arthur Young," 135–44, esp. 144.

6 *Return of Owners of the Land, 1873 … presented to Both Houses of Parliament.*
   Also see John Bateman, *The Great Landowners of Great Britain and Ireland*; and
   F.M.L. Thompson, "The Social Distribution of Landed Property in England since
   the 16th Century," 505–17.

7 Christopher Clays, "Landlords and Estate Management in England," 119–251, esp.
   163.

8 For the importance of the example of garden agriculture see Peter Bowden, "Agricultural Prices, Wages, and Farm Profits," 1–118, esp. 95; Malcolm Thick, "Market
   Gardening in England and Wales," 503–32, esp. 530. On the other hand, Robert
   Allen argues that much of this agricultural improvement was the product of yeoman farmers. Robert Allen, *Enclosure and the Yeoman*, esp. 18–19.

9 Peter Bowden, "Agricultural Prices," 74; Keith Wrightson, *Earthly Necessities:
   Economic Lives in Early Modern Britain*, 276; G.E. Mingay, "The East Midlands,"
   89–128, esp. 119.

10 Cited in Wrightson, *Earthly Necessities*, 282–3; see also Christopher Clays, "Landlords and Estate Management in England," 119–251, 172–5; Allen, *Yeoman*, 97.

11 Thirsk identifies Suffolk, Essex, Herefordshire, Kent, Devon, Somerset, Cornwall,
   Shropshire, and Worcestershire among these. Joan Thirsk, "Enclosing and Engrossing, 1500–1540," 54–109, esp. 57.

12 Wrightson, *Earthly Necessities*, 274.

13 See Eric Evans, Paul Brassey, David Hey, G.E. Mingay, Joan Thirsk, and B.A. Holderness in Thirsk, *AHEW I*.

14 Thirsk, "Agricultural Policy: Public Debate and Legislation," 298–388, esp. 380–1.

15 Bowden, "Agricultural Prices," 73.

16 Robert Brenner, "Agrarian Class Structure and Economic Development in
   Pre-Industrial Europe," 30–75, esp. 63–8.

17 See, for example, Ellen Melksins Wood, *The Origin of Capitalism: A Longer View*;
   Larry Patriquin, "Agrarian Capitalism and Poor Relief in England, c. 1500–1790"
   3–50, in *The Capitalist State and Its Economy*; Neal Wood, *John Locke and Agrarian Socialism*, esp. 110–11; David McNally, *Against the Market: Political Economy,
   Market Socialism and the Marxist Critique*, esp. 8.

18 Thirsk, "Introduction," esp. xxxi.

19 Robert Allen, *Enclosure and the Yeomen*, 79.

20 J.M. Neeson, *Commoners: Common Right, Enclosure and Social Change in
   England, 1700–1820*, 313.

21 Nicola Verdon, *Rural Women Workers in Nineteenth Century England: Gender,
   Work, and Wages*; K.D.M. Snell, "Agricultural Seasonal Employment: The Standard of Living and Women's Work in the South and East, 1690–1860," 421–3.

22 Lynn Hollen Lees, *The Solidarity of Strangers: The English Poor Laws and the People, 1700–1948*, esp. 11; Keith Wrightson, *Earthly Necessities: Economic Lives in
   Early Modern Britain*, esp. 213–21; Paul Fideler, *Social Welfare in Pre-Industrial*

England; Steve Hindle, *On the Parish? The Micro-Politics of Poor Relief in Rural England*; Samantha Williams, *Poverty, Gender and Life Cycle under the English Poor Law, 1760–1834*; K.D. Snell, "Pauper Settlement and the Right to Poor Relief in England and Wales," 375–415; K.D.M. Snell, *Parish and Belonging: Community, Identity and Welfare in England and Wales, 1700–1950*.

23 Robert Woods, *The Demography of Victorian England and Wales*, 364–71; John Komlos, "The Secular Trend in the Biological Standard of Living in the United Kingdom, 1730–1860," 115–44; Stephen Nicholas and Richard Steckel, "Heights and Living Standards of English Workers during the Early Years of Industrialization, 1770–1815," 937–57.

24 E.A. Wrigley, *Continuity, Chance, Change: The Character of the Industrial Revolution in England*; see also Robert Allen, "The Nitrogen Hypothesis and the English Agricultural Revolution: A Biological Analysis," 182–210. Wrigley's work, though useful and informative, is marked by the disregard for differences in the ability to improve soil fertility between large-scale and small-scale agricultural production. See Joan Thirsk, *Alternative Agriculture* for a discussion of earlier models of advanced organic agriculture in smaller scale production in England.

25 V.M. Lavrovksy, "Parliamentary Enclosures in the County of Suffolk (1797–1814)," 186–208; J.D. Chambers, "Enclosure and Labour Supply in the Industrial Revolution," 319–43, esp. 334; Neeson, *Commoners*, 244–6.

26 Overton, "Re-establishing the English Agricultural Revolution," 1–20; esp. 20; see also his *Agricultural Revolution in England: The Transformation of the Agrarian Economy, 1500–1850*, esp. 116–17; E.A. Wrigley, *Energy and the English Industrial Revolution*, esp. 29; M.E. Turner, J.V. Beckett, and B. Afton, *Farm Production in England 1700–1914*, esp. 230; Peter Jones, *Agricultural Enlightenment: Knowledge, Technology, and Nature*.

27 Manley, "Usury at sixpence," cited in Joyce Oldham Appleby, *Economic Thought and Ideology in Seventeenth-Century England*, 146.

28 Michael Turner, *English Parliamentary Enclosure: Its Historical Geography and Economic History*, 176–8; Paul Brassley, "Northumberland and Durham," 47; Joan Thirsk, "The Southern Midlands," 173; David Hey, "Yorkshire and Lancashirem," esp. 62; B.A. Holderness, "East Anglia and the Fens," 197–328.

29 J.D. Chambers, "Enclosure and the Labour Supply in the Industrial Revolution," esp. 336.

30 Leigh Shaw-Taylor, "Labourers, Cows, Common-Rights and Parliamentary Enclosure: The Evidence of Contemporary Comment c. 1760–1810," 95–126, and his "Parliamentary Enclosure and the Emergence of an English Agricultural Proletariat," 640–62. His work responds to the most widely cited recent work on the importance of the commons, J.M. Neeson, *Commoners*. Also see Jane Humphries, "Enclosures, Common Rights and Women: The Proletarianization of Families in the Late Eighteenth and Early Nineteenth Centuries," 17–42. For a description of the operations of a Midland commons see W.E. Tate, *The English Village Community and the Enclosure Movements*.

31 John Howlett, *Enclosures, A Cause of Improved Agriculture...*, esp. 71–2, 79–80.

32 Cited in J.L. and Barbara Hammond, *The Village Labourer*, 58.

33 John Billingsley, "Uselessness of Commons to the Poor," *Annals* 31 (1798): 27–32, esp. 31.

34 Chambers and Mingay, *The Agricultural Revolution*, 84.

35 Townsend, *A Dissertation on the Poor Laws*, 27, 35–6.

36 Arthur Young, *A Farmer's Tour through the East of England*, 361.

37 "Report from the Select Committee on the Poor Laws," *House of Commons Papers* 462, 1817, p. 4. Note: the committee had clearly been influenced by Malthus in the wording of this assessment.

38 John G. Gazley, *The Life of Arthur Young*, 306.

39 Arthur Young, *Autobiography of Arthur Young*, 28. This version of Young's life is interesting. It was edited by Matilda Betham-Edwards. Betham-Edwards was a late Victorian travel writer and novelist, writing mostly in French. She also edited a version of Young's *Travels in France* in 1892, and is considered to be particularly sympathetic to peasant proprietors in her French writing; Joan Rees, *Matilda Betham-Edwards: Novelist, Travel-Writer and Francophile*. See also Barbara Laning Fitzpatrick, "Arthur Young and 'Ten or a Dozen Booksellers': The Publication of the *Universal Museum* in 1762," 35–43.

40 Young, "Memoirs of the Last Thirty Years of a Farming Life," *Annals* 15 (1791): 152–82, esp. 154.

41 Young, *Autobiography*, 29; Young, "Memoirs," 154.

42 C.E. Mingay (ed.), *Arthur Young and his Times*, 4.

43 Cited in Henry Higgs, "Arthur Young (1741–1820)," 1885–1900.

44 Constancia Maxwell (ed.), *Travels in France during the Years, 1787, 1788, and 1789*, xiii.

45 Young, *Autobiography*, 46–7, 52–3.

46 Ibid., 76–7; also footnote 1, page 100, from Matilda Betham-Edwards.

47 Young, *Autobiography*, 210–23.

48 See J.D. Chambers and C.E. Mingay, *The Agricultural Revolution*, 73–5; Robert Allen and Carmac O Grada, "On the Road Again with Arthur Young: English, Irish and French Agriculture during the Industrial Revolution," 93–116; Liam Brunt, "Rehabilitating Arthur Young," 265–99; Peter Jones, "Arthur Young (1741–1820), For and Against," 1100–20.

49 See Young, *Annals* 15 (1791): 170–1, for one such complaint. See Nicolas Goddard, "The Development and Influence of Agricultural Periodicals and Newspapers, 1780–1870," 116–21 for the latter figure.

50 See Rosalind Mitchison, *Agricultural Sir John: The Life of Sir John Sinclair of Ulbster, 1754–1835*, esp. 111, 141, 225.

51 Young, *Autobiography*, 223.

52 Young, "Board of Agriculture," *Annals* 31 (1798): 343–59.

53 Young, *Political Arithmetic* Part 1, 199.

54   In Young, *Annals* 16 (1791): 480–607, esp. 502.
55   Young, *General View of the Agriculture of Oxfordshire, drawn up for the consideration of the Board of Agriculture and Internal Improvement*, 35–6.
56   Constantia Maxwell (ed.), *Travels in France*, xxxii.
57   See for example Young, "Tour to the West" *Annals* 6 (1786): 17–151, esp. 130.
58   Young, *A Six Months' Tour Through the North of England*, 495–6.
59   Young, *A Farmer's Tour Through the East of England*, 218–19.
60   John Sinclair, "Essay VII: Substance of a Speech in a committee of the whole house," 188, 206. Sinclair's address to the first meeting of the Board is in *Annals* 23 (1794): 200–17.
61   Sinclair in Appendix B, *Report of the Select Committee on Waste Lands* (1795), 204.
62   Young, *Travels in France*, 313; Sinclair, "General Enclosure Bill," *Annals* 26 (1796): 85; "General Enclosures Act," *Annals* 35 (1800): 140–2. J.L. and Barbara Hammond argue that these were unsuccessful primarily because various elements in Parliament made significant amounts of money during the approval of each Enclosure Bill. *The Village Labourer*, 76.
63   Young, *Political Arithmetic*, 288–9.
64   Young, *Travels*, 278, 254, 469, 279.
65   Lees, *Solidarity*, 84.
66   Young, *Farmer's Letters*, 295.
67   Young, *Tour Through the East*, 86.
68   Mills, "Account of a Hundred Houses of Industry," *Annals* 6 (1786): 331–50.
69   John Crutchely, "On Management of the Poor in Rutlandshire," *Annals* 22 (1793): 416–26.
70   Young, "A Week in Essex," *Annals* 18 (1792): 391–444.
71   Thomas Ruggles, *A History of the Poor: Their Rights, duties and laws respecting them*, 35.
72   Jeremy Bentham, "Situation and Relief of the Poor," *Annals* 29 (1797): 393–427, esp. 418–19.
73   Young, *Travels in France*, 347.
74   Young, *The Example of France, a Warning to Britain*, 20, 58.
75   See Young, "French Events Applicable to British Agriculture," *Annals* 18 (1791): 486–95; Young, "A Farmer's Letter to the Yeomanry of England," *Annals* 27 (1796): 49–54; the same title, *Annals* 28 (1797): 177–87; Young, "Yeomanry Corps," *Annals* 38 (1802): 148–51.

3   "The Enchantment of Property"

1   M. Bethan-Edwards (ed.), *The Autobiography of Arthur Young with Selections from his Correspondence*, 433.
2   Ibid., 354.
3   H. Phelps Brown and S.V. Hopkins, "Seven Centuries of Building Wages," 296–314; Alan Armstrong, "Rural Population Growth, Systems of Employment and

Incomes," 641–728; Keith Snell, *Annals of the Labouring Poor: Social Change and Agrarian England, 1600–1900*, 37.

4 Keith Snell, *Annals of the Labouring Poor*, 47, 130; Samantha Williams *Poverty, Gender and Life Cycle under the English Poor Law, 1760–1834*, 131–7.

5 Roger Wells, *Wretched Faces: Famine in Wartime England, 1793–1801*, 61–9.

6 *Economist*, "The Food of the English Labourer," 22:1102 (8 Oct. 1864): 1252–3.

7 William Cobbett, *Rural Rides in the Counties of Surrey, Kent, Hampshire, etc.*, 30, 28.

8 J.M. Neeson, *Commoners: Common Right, Enclosure and Social Change in England, 1700–1820*, 189–235; Jane Humphries, "Enclosures, Common Rights, and Women: The Proletarianization of Families in the Late Eighteenth and Early Nineteenth Centuries," 17–42.

9 Reprinted in the *Times* 10 August 1787, 2–3.

10 David Davies, *The Case of Labourers in Husbandry Stated and Considered*, esp. 52, 33–4, 73–4, 135–6.

11 Cobbett, *Rural Rides*, 134, 206–8. (In all instances throughout, the emphasis in quotes is from the original unless otherwise stated.)

12 Michael Turner, *Enclosures in Britain 1750–1830*, 53–64, has an extended discussion of the various debates around the financial costs of enclosure.

13 Jane Humphries, "Enclosures, Common Rights and Women: The Proletarianization of Families in the Late Eighteenth and Early Nineteenth Centuries," 17–42; J.M. Neeson, "English Enclosures and British Peasants: Current Debates about Rural Social Structure in Britain, c. 1750–1870," 17–31; See the debate between Lofft and Ruggles in various editions of the *Annals*, esp. 9 (1788): 165–7; 10 (1788). Both Lofft and Ruggles wrote regularly to the journal. See also Peter King, "Gleaners, Farmers and Failure of Legal Sanctions, 1750–1850," 116–50.

14 George Sturt, *Change in the Village*, 132–5 (originally published under his pseudonym, George Bourne).

15 J.L. and Barbara Hammond, *The Village Labourer*, 97.

16 Arthur Young, *Political Arithmetic*, 95.

17 Ibid., 93.

18 Adam Smith, *An Inquiry into the Wealth of Nations*, 78–9.

19 Michael Rose, "Settlement, Removal and the New Poor Law," esp. 27; Williams, *Gender*, 82–3; Keith Snell, "Pauper Settlement and the Right to Poor Relief in England and Wales," 375–415; and his *Parish and Belonging*, 98–102.

20 Young, *Political Arithmetic*, 95.

21 Cobbett, *Rural Rides*, 39.

22 *Economist*, "Rural Labour as Affected by the Law," 5:187 (27 March 1847): 354–5.

23 G.E. Mingay, "The Course of Rents in the Age of Malthus," 85–95.

24 Alan Armstrong and J.P. Huzel, "Labour II: Food, Shelter and Self-Help," in, esp. 747–8.

25 The yearly expenditure on poor relief multiplied 5X between 1750 and 1803. Lynn Hollen Lees, *Solidarity*, 84.

26 Hammond, *The Village Labourer*, 165. For a fuller discussion of the Poor Law see Steve Hindle, *On the Parish?: The Micro-Politics of Poor Relief in Rural England*; Lees, *Solidarity*; Paul Fideler, *Social Welfare in Pre-Industrial England*. An essential source is *Poor Law Commissioners Report of 1834*.

27 Young, *Annals* 15 (1971): 152–82, esp. 177.

28 Young, *Autobiography*, 285–8; Wilberforce's work, published in April 1797, was a long treatise on the need for people to express gratitude for Christ's suffering in active and heartfelt caring for those around them: "True love is an ardent, and an active principle." Wilberforce, *Practical View*, 69.

29 Henry Higgs, "Arthur Young (1741–1820)."

30 Patricia James, *Population Malthus: His Life and Times*, 137.

31 Redcliffe Salaman, *The History and Social Influence of the Potato*, 511.

32 Young, *Observations on the Present State ...*, 42–4.

33 Young, *A Tour of Ireland*, 30–3.

34 Young, *Travels in France*, 54.

35 Ibid., 50, 88.

36 See Sir John Sinclair, "General Enclosure Bill," *Annals* 26 (1796): 85.

37 Young, "On the Advantages of Cottagers Renting Land," *Annals* 26 (1796): 227–45.

38 This is from *Annals* 1 (1784): 124–8.

39 CIVIS, "Management of the Poor in Leeds," *Annals* 27 (1796): 408–29.

40 See *The First Report of the Society for Bettering the Condition and Increasing the Comforts of the Poor*.

41 Thomas Bernard, "An Account of a Cottage and Garden," *Annals* 30 (1798): 1–9.

42 Joseph Scott, "Crops, Markets, Poor, etc.," *Annals* 36 (1800): 376–8.

43 Included in Sir John Sinclair, "Observations on the Means of Enabling a Cottager to Keep a Cow by the Produce of a Small Portion of Arable Land," *Annals* 36 (1800): 231–48.

44 John Parkinson, "Cottagers' Land," *Annals* 36 (1800): 360–3.

45 Sir William Pulteney, "Accounts of Cottagers," *Annals* 44 (1806): 97–111.

46 Ibid.

47 Sinclair, "Observations on the Means," esp. 234, 241, 245–6.

48 Arthur Young, *Annals* 33 (1799): 621–9.

49 Arthur Young, "Conduct of Workhouses," *Annals* 31 (1798): 382–8, esp. 388.

50 Arthur Young, "On the Price," *Annals* 33 (1799): 625.

51 Arthur Young, "On the State of Poor," *Annals* 34 (1800): 186–91.

52 Cited in Arthur Young, *General Report on Enclosures*, 17.

53 Arthur Young, "Effects of Enclosures," *Annals* 36 (1800): 114–19.

54 Arthur Young, *An Inquiry ...*, esp. 7, 12, 42–3; this was also printed in *Annals* 36 (1800): 497–547.

55 Arthur Young, *General View of the Agriculture of Oxfordshire*, 35–6.

56 Arthur Young, "Minutes Concerning Parliamentary Inclosures in the County Bedford, Taken on the Spot by the Editor," *Annals* 42 (1804): 22–58 and 479–501, esp. 27, 497.

57   Board of Agriculture, *General Report on Enclosures*, 32–3, Appendix I.

58   Young, *Autobiography*, 360–1.

4 "A Rooted Hatred Between the Rich and the Poor"

1   *Times*, 25 November 1830, p. 2.

2   *Times*, 23 March 1844, p. 6.

3   Young made this call often and for many years. The quote comes from Arthur Young, "Means of National Tranquility," *Annals* 18 (1792): 144–50. See also "French Events Applicable to British Agriculture," *Annals* 18 (1792): 486–95; "A Farmer's Letter to the Yeomanry of England," *Annals* 27 (1796): 49–54; and similar title *Annals* 28 (1797): 177–87. Young also expressed these warnings in his *Travels in France during the Years 1787, 1788, and 1789*.

4   Young, *An Inquiry into the Propriety of Applying Wastes ...*, 13.

5   J. Boys, "Crops and Poor," *Annals* 36 (1800): 368–70.

6   Ruggles, "Land for the Poor," *Annals* 36 (1800): 354–5.

7   "Speech of the Right Honourable Lord Carrington, Board of Agriculture, March 15, 1803," *Annals* 37 (1801): 231–48; Young, *Autobiography*, 363.

8   Young, *Autobiography*, 358.

9   Cobbett, *Rural Rides*, 903; Young, *Autobiography*, 315; Hugh Wyndham, *A Family History, 1688–1837*.

10   Young, *Inquiry ...*, 159.

11   Sinclair, "Observations on the Means of Enabling a Cottager to Keep a cow by the Produce of a Small Portion of Arable Land," *Annals* 36 (1801): 231–48, esp. 241.

12   Billingsley, "Uselessness of Commons to the Poor," *Annals* 31 (1798): 27–32.

13   "Extract from An Account of the Advantages of Cottagers Renting Land," *Reports of the Society for Bettering the Condition and Increasing the Comforts of the Poor* vol. 1 (1798), 93–101, esp. 101.

14   Cobbett, *Cottage Economy*, 144; see also William Reitzell, ed., *The Autobiography of William Cobbett*, 107–8.

15   Report of His Majesty's Commission, 34.

16   *Economist*, "Division of Labour – The Allotment System," 2:65 (23 Nov. 1844): 441–2.

17   Culley, "Land for the Poor," *Annals* 36 (1800): 385–7.

18   Malthus, *An Essay on the Principles of Population*, 223.

19   *Poor Law Report*, 279–80.

20   "Extract from an Account of a Provision for Cottagers Keeping Cows at Humberston, the county of Lincoln," *Reports of the Society for Bettering ...* vol. 2, (1799): 133–8, esp. 136–7.

21   *Poor Law Report* (unpaginated).

22   Joan Thirsk, "Agricultural Innovations and their Diffusion," 533–89, esp. 585; Thirsk, "Agricultural Policy: Public Debate and Legislation," 298–388; Thick,

"Market Gardening in England and Wales," 503–32, esp. 511, 515; Thirsk, "The Southwest Midlands," 159–96, esp. 170–1.

23 Cited in Ian Dyck, *William Cobbett and Rural Popular Culture*, 30.

24 *Annals* 36 (1801): 145–7.

25 *Times*, 30 October 1830, p. 3.

26 *Times*, 22 March 1844, p. 5.

27 William Cobbett, "To the Bull-frog Farmers: On the Price of Corn and the Wages of Labour," 671–5.

28 John Bohstedt, "Devon 1795 and 1800–1," 116–18.

29 Thompson, "The Moral Economy of the English Crowd in the Eighteenth Century" was first published in *Past and Present* 50 (1971) and reprinted along with a chapter addressing some of the criticisms of the essay in his *Customs in Common*, 185–258. The quote comes from the latter, p. 188.

30 Roger Wells, *Wretched Faces*, 80–7, 165.

31 John Bohstedt, *The Politics of Provisions: Food Riots, Moral Economy and Market Transitions in England c 1550–1850*, 191.

32 Cited in Wells, *Wretched Faces*, 165.

33 *Times*, 4, 5 September 1800; all on p. 3.

34 *Times*, 3 April 1801, p. 3.

35 *Times*, 28 April 1801, p. 3.

36 *Times*, 3 April 1801, p. 3.

37 *Times*, 21, 23, 30 May 1816; Hammond, *The Village Labourer*, 178; Peacock, *Bread or Blood: A Study of Agrarian Riots in East Anglia*, 132.

38 William Cobbett, "Letter to the People of the United States of America," 720–1.

39 William Cobbett, "To Parson Malthus: On the Rights of the Poor; and on the cruelty recommended by him to be exercised towards the poor," 1019–47, esp. 1027.

40 William Cobbett, "To The Bull-frog Farmers," 675.

41 *Times*, 4 Sept. 1800, p. 3.

42 Cobbett, *Rural Rides*, 348, 297.

43 *Times*, 25 Dec. 1830, p. 4.

44 *Times*, 15 Nov.1831, p. 2.

45 *Times*, 25 Oct. 1830, p. 3; *Times*, 26 Nov. 1830, p. 3; *Times*, 3 Dec. 1832, p. 4.

46 *Times*, 18 Nov. 1830, p. 3.

47 Ibid.

48 *Times*, 26 Nov. 1830, p. 3.

49 *Times*, 27 Nov. 1830, p. 3.

50 Cobbett was charged with sedition for his supposed role in inspiring the unrest. He was able to turn his trial into a mocking denunciation of his accusers and, this time, escape prison.

51 *Times*, 25 Dec. 1830, p. 4.

52 *Times*, 12 Nov. 1830, p. 3.

53 William Cobbett, "To the Yeomanry Cavalry on the Fires," 104–7.

54 *Times*, 18 Nov. 1830, p. 3.
55 *Times*, 25 Nov. 1830, p. 2.
56 *Times*, 30 Oct. 1830, p. 3.
57 *Times*, 27 Nov. 1830, p. 3.
58 *Times*, 26 Dec. 1831, p. 3.
59 *Times*, 28 June 1831, p. 1.
60 Cobbett, "To the Yeomanry …," 102.
61 *Times*, 25 Nov. 1830, p. 2.
62 *Times*, 9 Feb. 1831, p. 1.
63 E. Hobsbaum and G. Rudé, *Captain Swing*; Barry Reay, *Rural Englands: Labouring Lives in the Nineteenth Century*, 146.
64 James Sambrook, *William Cobbett*, 175.
65 For a useful discussion of the limited beneficial effects of the Captain Swing protests, see Carl J. Griffin, *The Rural War: Captain Swing and the Politics of Protest*, 319–20.
66 Mingay, *A Social History of the English Countryside*, 119.
67 *Annals* 19 (1793): 314–17.
68 William Cobbett, "Letter to Lord John Russell," 289.
69 See for example, *Times*, 31 Oct. 1818, p. 3.
70 *Times*, 2 April 1832, p. 3; *Times*, 19 Oct. 1833, p. 4.
71 *Times*, 17 Oct. 1839, p. 3; *Times*, 18 Oct. 1839, p. 4; *Times*, 2 Nov. 1839, p. 5; The *Times*' gleeful pillorying of Radnor (who later bankrolled the *Economist* newspaper) helps explain the ongoing feud between the two papers through the 1840s.
72 *Times*, 16 Jan. 1819, p. 3; *Times*, 15 July 1819, p. 3.
73 *Times*, 14 August 1819, p. 2.
74 *Times*, 14 August 1819, p. 3.
75 Reported in *Times*, 27 Jan. 1832, p. 4.
76 For the fullest discussion of the struggle for allotments in the middle of the nineteenth century see Jeremy Burchart, *The Allotment Movement in England, 1793–1873*.
77 *Times*, 13 May 1944, p. 6; see also Burchardt, *Allotment* and Boaz Moselle, "Allotments, Enclosure, and Proletarianization in Nineteenth-Century Southern England," 482–500.
78 "Wales," *Economist* 1:12 (18 Nov. 1843): 207.
79 "Rebecca Riots," *Economist* 1:7 (14 Oct. 1843): 105.
80 "Movement of Troops," *Economist* 1:7 (14 Oct. 1843): 110.
81 "Incendiaries," *Economist* 2:43 (22 June 1844): 913.
82 Cited in "Provinces," *Economist* 2:57 (28 Sept. 1844): 1259.
83 "Incendiarism at Rampston," *Economist* 2:58 (5 Oct. 1844): 1278.
84 *Times*, 23 March 1844, p. 5; *Times*, 7 June 1844, p. 6; *Times*, 10 June 1844, p. 7; *Times*, 11 June 1844, p. 5; *Times*, 14 June 1844, p. 6.
85 "The Peasant's Friend," *Times* 6 Nov. 1830, p. 3.

86 *Times*, 19 March 1832, p. 4.
87 J.L. and Barbara Hammond, *The Village Labourer*, 207.

5 Political Economy and the Rural Poor

1 Young, "On the Application of the Principles of Population, to the Question of Assigning Land to Cottages," *Annals* 41 (1804): 208–31, esp. 213, 219–20, 226–7.
2 Young, *Travels in France*, 278.
3 *Political Economy Club: Vol. IV, Minutes and Proceedings, 1821–1882*, 38–9.
4 Donald Winch, *Riches and Poverty: An Intellectual History of Political Economy in Britain, 1750–1834*, 45.
5 Nicholas Phillipson, "Smith and the Scottish Enlightenment," 105–22, esp. 116.
6 R.I. Meek, D.D. Raphael, and Peter Stein (eds.), *The Glasgow Edition of the Works and Correspondence of Adam Smith, Vol. 5: Lectures on Jurisprudence* (hereafter *LJ*).
7 Adam Smith, *The Theory of Moral Sentiments*, 124. Hereafter, *TMS*.
8 Adam Smith, *An Inquiry into the Nature and Causes of the Wealth of Nations*, Book 1, ch ii.
9 See, for example, Gavin Kennedy, "Adam Smith: Some Popular Uses and Abuses," 461–77, esp. 470; Partatp Bhanu Mehta, "Self-Interest and other Interests," 246–69. David McNally, *Against the Market: Political Economy, Market Socialism and the Marxist*, 51. Winch, *Riches and Poverty*, 21, 105–6. Winch makes the logical case that one book dealt with moral issues, the other with political economy. It would be striking if they did not address different issues.
10 Smith, *TMS*, 3.
11 Bernard Mandeville, *The Fable of the Bees: or, Private Vices, Publick Benefits*, 352–3. Hereafter, *Fable*.
12 Mandeville, *Fable* I, 344, 357–9.
13 Ibid., 344.
14 Smith, *TMS*, 451.
15 Ibid., 167.
16 Ibid., 264–5.
17 Ibid., 70–1, 272–3, 262–5. In both *TMS* and *Lectures*, Smith had the most difficulty making an argument that people pursued wealth not because they really desired wealth. In *Lectures* he tries to explain an argument about confusing wealth with the harmony of the system that produces wealth with an example of a man desiring to place the chairs, left askew in a room, back into order before sitting down. Smith argued what he desired was not the ease of sitting, but the enjoyment of a well-ordered system that permitted him to sit. Based on student notes, we cannot know for certain that Smith's lecture presented this argument in quite this unconvincing manner.
18 Adam Smith, *An Inquiry into the Nature and Causes of the Wealth of Nations*, I.1. Hereafter *WN*. Though Smith suggests in *WN* that this example comes from

his own observation, in *Lectures* he provides a similar argument with different numbers: 18 workers make 36,000 pins. R.J. Meek, D.D. Raphael, and Peter Stein (eds.), *The Glasgow Edition of the Works and Correspondence of Adam Smith, Vol. 5: Lectures on Jurisprudence*, 342.

19 Smith, *WN*, I.i.
20 Ibid., II.iii.
21 Ibid., IV.ii.
22 Ibid., IV.ix.
23 Meek, Raphael, and Stein (eds.), *LJ*, 521–2.
24 Smith, *WN*, IV.ii.
25 Ibid.
26 Meek, Raphael, and Stein (eds.), *LJ*, 5.
27 Smith, *WN*, I.ii. A number of historians have argued that Smith recommended a much more active role for government than is often portrayed or is suggested here. Smith did envision a role for government in the provision of infrastructure and in education, though his experience at Oxford did lead him to caution against removing the stimulus of paying lecturers primarily through student fees. See for example the introduction by D.D. Raphael to the D.J. Campbell Publishers 1991 edition; and José Luis Cardoso, "The Political Economy of Rising Capitalism," 574–99; Winch, *Riches and Poverty*, 115–23.
28 Smith, *WN*, I.vii.
29 Ibid., I.viii.
30 Sir James Steuart, *An Inquiry into the Principles of Political Economy* (1767), cited in Robert Allen, *The British Industrial Revolution in Global Perspective*, 12.
31 Smith, *WN*, I.ix.
32 Ibid., I.x.
33 Meek, Raphael, and Stein (eds.), *LJ*, 184, 522.
34 McNally, *Against the Market*, 43.
35 Smith, *WN*, I.viii.
36 Ibid., V.i
37 D.D. Raphael, "Introduction," *The Wealth of Nations*, xiii.
38 "Introduction: The Coherence of Smith's Thought," 3; for a similar argument, see José Luis Cardoso, "The Political Economy of Rising Capitalism," 574. Cardoso somewhat awkwardly says, "The year of 1776 is generally considered to be the year that brought the good news of the birth of political economy as an autonomous scientific field."
39 William Petty, *Political Arithmetick*.
40 Salim Rashid, *The Myth of Adam Smith*, 26.
41 Joyce Appleby, *Economic Thought and Ideology in Seventeenth-Century England*, 94.
42 Rashid, *Myth*, 3, 172.
43 See also Winch, *Riches and Poverty*, 128.

44   Kirk Willis, "The Role in Parliament of the Economic Ideas of Adam Smith,"
     505–44.
45   Emma Rothschild, *Economic Sentiments: Adam Smith, Condorcet and the Enlight-
     enment*, 45.
46   Michael Perelman, *The Invention of Capitalism*, 175.
47   Rothschild, *Sentiments*, 52, 64.
48   Michael Shapiro, *Reading Adam Smith: Desire, History and Value*, 53.
49   McNally, *Against the Market*, 43; Gareth Stedman Jones, "Malthus,
     Nineteenth-Century Socialism, and Marx," 91–106.
50   *Political Economy Club: Vol. 1: Names of Members 1821–1860*, 10. Vol. 4 from
     1882 includes a discussion of the history of the club and the questions debated
     in the club from its founding in 1821 to 1833. Unfortunately, the Club Minutes
     only include the questions proposed and the name of the member who proposed
     it. No summary of the arguments is presented. Malthus and Ricardo attended
     the second meeting in 1821 and were considered original members of the Club.
     Other notable political economists who were members from this second meeting
     include James Mills, Colonel Torrens, and Thomas Tooke.
51   Gertrude Himmelfarb, *The Idea of Poverty: England in the Early Industrial Age*,
     101, 133.
52   James, *Population*, 98.
53   T.R. Malthus, *An Essay on the Principle of Population, as it effects the future im-
     provement of society*, Preface, i.
54   Godwin, *The Enquirer*, 158.
55   Godwin, *An Enquiry Concerning Political Justice and its influence on general virtue
     and happiness*, 33, 35–6.
56   Ibid., 341.
57   Ibid., 334–5, 347.
58   Ibid., 347–8, 375.
59   Godwin, *Political Justice*, 380–92.
60   Michael Turner, *English Parliamentary Enclosure*, 79.
61   Mayhew, *Malthus*, 62.
62   Cited in Robert Mayhew, *Malthus: The Life and Times of an Untimely Prophet*, 88.
63   Godwin, *Of Population: An Enquiry Concerning the Power of Increase in the Num-
     bers of Mankind* (1820), cited in Patricia James, *Population Malthus: His Life and
     Times*, 379. Cobbett, "To Parson Malthus," 1019–47.
64   Marx, *Capital Vol. 1*, 616, footnote 2.
65   Cited in James, *Population*, 265.
66   Winch, *Riches and Poverty*, 246.
67   In *London Magazine* (1823), cited in James, *Population*, 274–5.
68   Cited in Donald Winch, *Malthus* (Oxford: Oxford University Press, 1987), 106.
69   William Empson, "Review of T.R. Malthus, *Principles of Political Economy
     and memoir*," in *Edinburgh Review*, Jan. 1837; in Bernard Semmel, ed.,

Occasional Papers of T.R. Malthus on Ireland, Population and Political Economy, 246–7.

70 Malthus, *Essay*, 1798, i. (Malthus suggests here that the conversation was with a friend, though it was with his father.)

71 Cited in James, *Population*, 458.

72 Niall O'Flaherty, "Malthus and the End of Poverty," 74–104; Donald Winch, *Malthus*.

73 Malthus, *Essay* 1798, 12–13.

74 Ibid., 16.

75 Ibid., 30.

76 Ibid., 36.

77 Ibid., 74.

78 Ibid., 78.

79 Ibid., 88.

80 Ibid., 83.

81 Ibid., 86.

82 Ibid., 177.

83 Ibid., 179.

84 Ibid., 204.

85 Ibid., 207.

86 Malthus, *An Essay on the Principle of Population, 1803*. Preface to the 1803 edition, 3. This is the 1803 edition complete with the varioria of 1806, 1807, 1817, and 1826.

87 Ibid., I, xiii.

88 Ibid., II, 106.

89 Ibid., II, 139.

90 Ibid., II, 127–8.

91 James, *Population*, 114–15.

92 Malthus, *Essay* 1803, II, 152, ff. 10.

93 Malthus, *Essay,* Preface to the 1803 edition, I:3; see the appendix to the 1807 edition of *Essay* and Malthus, *A Letter to Samuel Whitbread, Esq. MP*, 16–18, for a discussion of a lack of cottages being what negated the expected population increase.

94 Malthus, *Essay*, 1803, II, 155.

95 Letter to Senior included in Nassau Senior, *Two Lectures on Population 1828*, esp. 64–5.

96 T.R. Malthus, *Principles of Political Economy*, xxviii. (Note: this is the 1820 edition, with edited changes for 1836 marked.)

97 Malthus, *Principles*, 81–2, 155, 176.

98 Ibid., 120.

99 Malthus, *Essay* 1803, II 108–9.

100 For example, the second question Malthus raised for discussion in the Political Economy Club a couple of months after its formation in 1821 was "Can there be a

glut of commodities?" (25 June 1821), *Minutes of the Political Economy Club* Vol. 4, 1882.

101 Malthus, *Principles*, 470.

102 Ibid., 470, 412–13.

103 Marx, *Capital* Vol. 1, 634, ff. 2.

104 Malthus, *Essay*, 1803, II, 193.

105 Malthus to Ricardo, 17 Aug. 1817, in *The Works and Correspondence of David Ricardo*, Vol. 7, 225; Ricardo to Malthus, 4 Sept. 1817, in Saffra, *The Works and Correspondence of David Ricardo*, Vol. 7, 228.

106 Malthus, *Principles*, 390–8.

107 Saffra (ed.), *Works and Correspondence Vol II*, "Notes on Malthus," Note 225.

108 Ricardo to Malthus, 13 Jan. 1815, cited in Semmel, *Occasional,* 260.

109 Senior, *Two Lectures on Population 1828*, frontpiece; Humphrey House, *The Dickens World*, cited in Robert Tombs, *The English and Their History*, 400. Balancing this, there has been significant arguments that it was the Ricardian view of political economy that predominated. A position held, and lamented, by John Maynard Keynes. See Mark Blaug, *Ricardian Economics: A Historical Study*, esp. 111–16.

110 Winch, *Riches and Poverty*, 318.

111 Malthus, *Letter*, 10–11.

6 Nassau Senior and the New Poor Laws

1 Cited in Roger Wells, "Resistance to the New Poor Law in the Rural South," 91–126, esp. 112.

2 *Second Annual Report of the Poor Law Commissioners*, 24.

3 *Second Annual Report*, 31.

4 S. Leon Levy, *Nassau Senior: The Prophet of Modern Capitalism.*

5 "Mr. Nassau Senior," *The Economist*, 22:1086 (18 June 1864): 770–1.

6 Marc Blaug, "The Myth of the Old Poor Law and the Making of the New," 151–84, esp. 153.

7 Piercy Ravenstone, *Doubts*, iv.

8 For Dorfman see Ravenstone, *Doubts*, 19–21; for the acceptance of Sraffa's argument about Richard Puller Jr. see Patricia James, *Population Malthus*, 157; Michael Perelman, *The Invention of Capitalism*, 135. Sraffa identified Richard Puller Jr. based on the inscription on a copy of *Doubts* which named him as the author. As Giancarlo de Vivo and Arnold Heertje pointed out, this is unlikely. The inscription was written in 1890, almost 70 years after the book was published; Ravenstone's description of himself in retirement in 1821 fits Richard Puller Sr. and not Jr.; Arnold Heertje, "An Essay on the Catalogue of the Library of Piero Sraffa, edited by G. de Vivo," 63–71.

9 Ravenstone, *Doubts*, 23–4.

10 It did garner some attention. Ricardo recommended it to Malthus as an interesting though flawed work. Malthus for obvious reasons did not welcome the

recommendation. See Jacob Viner, "An Unpublished Letter of Ricardo to Malthus," 117–20.

11   Ravenstone, *Doubts*, 5. (Ravenstone uses the term "industry" most often to mean useful labour.)

12   Ibid., 152–4; Marx, of course, would make much the same argument in very similar language in *Capital*.

13   Ibid., 156–7.

14   Ibid., 163.

15   Ibid., 170, 185, 187.

16   In this Ravenstone was following along the lines of a number of critics of liberal political economy, most closely, perhaps, Charles Hall. Hall, a poor country doctor, had argued in 1805 that increasing poverty and hunger were caused by the growing dominance of capital and its ability to direct labour to frivolous ends rather than feeding the population. He asserted, in contrast to Smith and Malthus, that increased consumption of wants rather than needs led only to increased poverty. Increased poverty would lead to more repression. As Hall warned, "To keep people that are cold, naked and hungry from taking fuel to warm themselves, clothes to cover themselves with, and food to satisfy their hunger" required a police capable of "imposing punishments greater than the suffering of the poor." For Hall, like Young, the remedy for this was to recognize the dramatic productivity of small-scale agriculture – "the produce of the land is proportionate to the labour bestowed on it" – and to provide every rural family with three to three and half acres. Charles Hall, *The Effects of Civilization on the People of the European States*, esp. 80, 181–2 (note at bottom), 230–9.

17   Ravenstone, *Doubts*, 203, 200, 471–2.

18   Ibid., 205, 201, 206.

19   Ibid., 289, 317–39.

20   Ibid., 292–4. Ravenstone produced one other, shorter, work in 1824 entitled *Thoughts on the Funding System and its Effects*. In this essay, Ravenstone went on at more length about the detrimental effects on labour of investment in machinery, questioning Smith's assertions about the positive outcomes of the primary benefit of the division of labour (45).

21   Ravenstone, *Doubts*, 207, 365.

22   Ibid., 470, 461–2, 156–7, 120.

23   It is quite remarkable how many of the early political economists, many of whom argued for a very limited role for government, enjoyed government salaries for much of their lives. The list would include Smith, Senior, James Wilson – the founding editor of *The Economist* – and William Rathbone Gregg – a longtime writer for the paper. Many others received incomes for much of their life from the East India Company, in many ways a government in all but name. This includes Malthus and James Mill, who both worked for the company most of their lives, and J.S. Mill, whose only regular paid employment in his life was with the EIC.

24 See, for example, his 1847 lectures, published as *Four Introductory Lectures on Political Economy*, which were both partly a rehashing of his first set of lectures in 1826 and remarkably lifeless. They ostensibly dealt with the question of whether political economy was an art or a science and, if a science, whether a material or moral one. In the hands of a skilled writer, this topic discussed in 1826 or 1847 could have been fascinating. These lectures were not. Nassau Senior, *Four Introductory Lectures on Political Economy*.

25 Senior, *An Introductory Lecture* 1826, 2, 7–8, 10; Senior, *Four Introductory Lectures* 1847, 10, 11–12.

26 Most of this pamphlet is reprinted in Levy, *Senior*, 98–109; esp. 108.

27 Senior, *Two Lectures on Population*, frontpiece.

28 One indication of the questioning of that most Malthusian of arguments was the proposition put forth for debate in the Political Economy Club in August 1835, a few months after Malthus's death was announced to the Club: "Is there any sufficient number of well-authenticated facts so far disproving the principle of the Essay on Population, as to show that Population has not a uniform tendency to increase faster than Subsistence …" Unfortunately, we do not have minutes of the debate. *Political Economy Club: Vol I* 39.

29 Nassau Senior, *Journals, Conversations and Essays Relating to Ireland Vol. II.*, 178.

30 Senior, *Industrial Efficiency*, 1, 233.

31 Senior, *An Introductory Lecture*, 15.

32 Cited in Levy, *Senior*, 158–9.

33 Nassau Senior, *Letters on the Factory Act as it Affects the Cotton Manufacture, to the President of the Board of Trade, March 28, April 2, April 4, 1837*, 4, 7–8, 13, 9–10. We can get a sense of the divisions among political economists around specific issues of the day by the questions put forward for debate in the Political Economy Club. In 1834, Senior nominated his friend from the Poor Law Commission, Edwin Chadwick. Chadwick's second question to the Club, in July 1838, was "Is it expedient that the legislature should in any, and what cases, interfere in contracts between the Employer and Labourer to regulate the hours and mode of labour?" *Political Economy Club, Vol. 1,* 66.

34 Nassau Senior, *Three Lectures on the Rate of Wages*, vi, x–xi. The slave comment would be repeated in the Poor Law Commission report; this time in relation to the provision of wages by the Poor Law.

35 Senior, *Three Lectures*, xiii. These comments are in the foreword to the published lectures. These few pages are in many ways the most vivid and lively of all of Senior's publications. They were not part of the lectures themselves, which contained none of this liveliness.

36 Report from His Majesty's Commissioners for inquiring into the Administration and Practical Operation of the Poor Laws *House of Commons Papers,* 44, 1834, p. 37.

37 Senior, *Three Lectures*, xix–xx.

38 Nassau Senior's views on the poor laws are most clearly put forward in Lecture 6, On the Corn Law, of his inaugural lectures to Oxford in 1826; his *Three Lectures on the Rate of Wages* in 1830; and his *Letter to Lord Howick* in 1831.

39 See for example the report from Cameron and Wrottesley on the 300 parishes they were assigned to cover in Buckinghamshire. *Report of his Majesty's ... 1834* Supplement No. 3 (158A).

40 Tawney cited in Marc Blaug, "The Myth of the Old Poor Law and the Making of the New," 151–84, esp. 152.

41 *Report from the Select Committee on the Poor Laws with the Evidence Taken Before the Committee*, 3.

42 *Report ... 1817*, 4.

43 See for example the examination of Reverend Richard Vivian, Rector of Bushy, 81.

44 *Report ... 1817*, 165–6.

45 The instructions are in Supplement No. 3, in *Report from His Majesty's Commissioners for Inquiring into the Administration and Practical Operation of the Poor Laws*, esp. 251–2.

46 Samantha Williams, "Malthus, Marriage, and Poor Allowances Revisited: A Bedfordshire Case Study, 1770–1834," 56–82; Henry French, "How Dependent were the 'Dependent Poor'? Poor Relief and Life-course in Terling, Essex, 1862–1834," 192–222.

47 All in Supplement No. 3, in *Report from His Majesty's Commissioners for Inquiring into the Administration and Practical Operation of the Poor Laws*, 248–55.

48 This argument is also made by Marc Blaug in "The Poor Law Report Revisited," 229–45.

49 *Report of His Majesty's ... 1834*, Supplement No. 1, 235–44.

50 Ibid., 207–23.

51 The letter is cited in full in Levy, *Senior*, 173–85.

52 *Report of His Majesty's ... 1834*, Appendix A, 158A.

53 Ibid., 298A; Stuart, Suffolk and Norfolk, 379A.

54 *Report of His Majesty's ... 1834* Appendix A., 15A.

55 Ibid., 170A.

56 Ibid., 255A.

57 Ibid., 268A.

58 Ibid., 15A.

59 Ibid., 102.

60 Ibid., Appendix A, 380A.

61 Ibid., 170A.

62 Ibid., 269A.

63 Ibid., 34, 41.

64 Ibid., 156, 27, 127.

65 Ibid., 146–7.

66 Ibid., 176–7.

67 The recommendations are all included in ibid., 146–202.

68 Ibid., 108.

69 Cited in Felix Driver, *Power and Pauperism: The Workhouse System, 1834–1884*, 18.

70 *Second Annual Report of the Poor Law Commissioners*, 3.

71 Snell, *Annals of the Labouring Poor*, 119.

72 "Mr. Nassau Senior," *The Economist* 22:1086 (18 June 1864): 770–1.

73 Felix Driver, *Power and Pauperism*, 71.

74 Norman Longmate, *The Workhouse*, 13.

75 Cited in Longmate, *The Workhouse*, 97.

76 *Second Annual Report of the Poor Law Commission*, 1836, 25–6.

77 *Third Annual Report of the Poor Law Commission*, 1837, 10, 26–7.

78 *Times* 15 June 1844; 4 July 1844; also in Snell, *Annals of the Labouring Poor*, 128.

79 *Report from the Select Committee on Andover Union and Minutes of Evidence*, vi, vii, 1001. The *Times* coverage of the Andover Union inquiry began 25 August 1845 and continued every day for more than a month.

80 *Report from the Select Committee on Andover Union*, v, vii.

81 25 Aug. 1845, 4.

7 The *Economist*: "The Most Elementary Truths"

1 *Economist* 1:1 (1 Aug. 1843): 3, 15.

2 *Economist* 3:109 (27 Sept. 1845), 918; the paper got a very valuable boost in circulation through the assistance of the Anti–Corn Law League. Wilson had consulted with its leaders, especially Richard Cobden, when contemplating founding the journal and they recommended it to the League's many adherents. The paper's fortunes improved dramatically when the Anti–Corn Law League ceased publication of its own weekly paper, *The League*, recommending to its readers the *Economist* instead. See Angel Arrese Reca, *La Identidad de The Economist*, 34, 38–9; Alexander Zevin, *Liberalism at Large: The World According to the Economist*, 62.

3 In comparison the *Times*, the leading English daily, had a circulation of over 18,000 in 1840. Zevin, *Liberalism*, 16.

4 *Economist* 1:169 (4 Nov. 1843).

5 *Economist*, "Remuneration of Labour – Rights and Duty of Property," 2:66 (30 Nov. 1844): 1475–6.

6 *Economist*, "New Means and New Maxims," 6:243 (22 April 1848): 451–2.

7 Indeed, Bagehot might have been an important part of the paper's diminished vigour. Bagehot was a banker, from a banking family, and refocused the paper on financial issues, adding a Banking supplement in 1861. Even Bagehot recognized that this meant the paper had little "to tell the public about." And, though he was less tied to the "pure principles" of political economy he also evidenced little sympathy for the poor, once suggesting that economic literature spent

too much time discussing the "sufferings of the working men" and not enough those of the capitalist who "being a higher and more thinking kind of man" suffers more as "pecuniary anxiety is a more racking thing than any physical pain short of extreme hunger." Zevin, *Liberalism*, 79–80; Donald Winch, *Wealth and Life: Essays on the Intellectual History of Political Economy in Britain, 1848–1914*, 387.

8 Much of this background is drawn from the "Memoir of the Right Honourable James Wilson," written by his son-in-law and soon to be editor of the *Economist*, Walter Bagehot. *Economist* 18:899 (17 Nov. 1860): 1287–1300; and Emilie Barrington, *Servant of All: Pages form the Family, Social, and Political Life of my Father James Wilson, Twenty Years of Mid-Victorian Life* in 2 vols.

9 Barrington, *Servant*, 1:167.

10 Mary Rose, *The Gregs of Quarry Bank Mill: The Rise and Decline of a Family Firm, 1750–1914*, 36, 54, 78.

11 Ibid., 20.

12 This is mentioned in Barrington, *Servant*, I-85 and repeated in Ruth Dudley Edwards, *The Pursuit of Reason: The Economist, 1843–1993*, 152–3.

13 Rose, *The Gregs*, 134.

14 S. Leon Levy, *Nassau Senior*, 241; Rose, *The Gregs*, 78.

15 *Economist*, "Sign of the Times: Colonial Improvement," 2:45 (6 July 1844), 963.

16 For Wilson on the franchise see his letter to Lord Radnor's son, Sir G.C. Lewis, of 15 July 1852 in Barrington, *Servant*, I-212.

17 Bagehot cited in Barrington, *Servant*, I-84; beginning in the 1850s Greg also published a series of books on religious topics. It is clear that as he became more involved in religious issues, he became increasingly radical in his anti-labour, anti-democratic views.

18 Martha Westwater, *The Wilson Sisters*, 161.

19 The most complete background on Hodgskin is a work in French first published in 1902: Elie Halèvy, *Thomas Hodgskin*, edited and translated by A.J. Taylor.

20 Thomas Hodgskin, *Labour Defended Against the Claims of Capital, Or the Unproductiveness of Capital*, 24–5.

21 Ibid., 19; compare this to Marx decades later, "He who was previously the money-owner now strides out in front as a capitalist; the possessor of labour-power follows as his worker. The one smirks self-importantly and is intent on business; the other is timid and holds back, like someone who has brought his own hide to the market and knows he has nothing else to expect but – a tanning." Marx, *Capital Vol I*, 173.

22 Halèvy, *Hodgskin*, 60–2.

23 Thomas Hodgskin, *The Natural and Artificial Right of Property Contrasted*, unpaginated.

24 Halèvy, *Hodgskin*, 165.

25 Herbert Spencer, *Social Statics*, 150–1.

26 David Wiltshire, *The Social and Political Thought of Herbert Spencer*, 48, 50.

27 See for example, M.W. Taylor, *Men Versus the State: Herbert Spencer and Late Victorian Individualism*.

28 Herbert Spencer, *An Autobiography* Vol I, 424. This is a most peculiar book. Spencer starts by saying, "It has seemed to me that a natural history of myself would be a useful accompaniment to the books" he has written. He goes on to provide a review of his own *Social Statics* because he says there was no review of the book at the time. This is not correct; Thomas Hodgskin wrote a glowing review of the book in the *Economist* 9:389 (8 Feb. 1851): 149–51.

29 *Economist*, "Feeding the Irish," 4:134 (21 March 1846): 369–70.

30 *Economist*, "Emigration from Europe – United States," 13:603 (17 March 1855): 281–2. The paper argues here that "limits to the progress of the population' were not caused by deficiency in the quantity of land ..., but the manner in which land was appropriated, owned, held, and used."

31 *Economist*, "Ireland Again – The Beginning of the End," 4:172 (12 Dec. 1846): 1609–10.

32 Letter from Wilson to his wife, Elizabeth Preston, reprinted in Emilie Barrington, *Servant of All*, I-77.

33 *Economist*, 2:20 (13 Jan. 1844): 385–7.

34 *Economist*, "Prospectus," 1:1 (1 August 1843): 7.

35 *Economist*, "Constituencies and their Duties at the Present Crisis," 1:7 (14 Oct. 1843): 98–9.

36 *Economist*, "The State of Ireland," 4:133 (14 March 1846): 325; *Economist*, "Agricultural Dangers and Agricultural Chances," 2:22 (27 Jan. 1844): 428; *Economist*, "Widow Biddle and the Poor Needle Women of the Metropolis," 1:10 (4 Nov. 1843): 153–4.

37 *Economist*, "The End of the Corn Laws," 7:284 (3 Feb. 1846): 116–17.

38 *Economist*, "The Earl of Radnor and the *Times*," 4:167 (7 Nov. 1846): 1451–2.

39 *Economist*, "Political Economy Won't Do," 3:72 (11 Jan. 1845): 23.

40 *Economist*, "Widow Biddle and the Poor Needle Women of the Metropolis," 1:10 (4 Nov. 1843): 153–4.

41 *Economist*, "Socialism in England," 8:349 (4 May 1850): 481.

42 *Economist*, "The Diffusion of Wealth," 8:363 (10 Aug. 1850): 873–4.

43 *Economist*, "Political," 1:13 (25 Nov. 1843): 233.

44 *Economist*, "Political," 2:30 (23 March 1844): 614.

45 *Economist*, "The Practical Consequences of the Ten-Hours Bill," 2:31 (30 March 1844): 628–9.

46 *Economist*, "Protection to Labour," 2:32 (6 April 1844): 650; *Economist*, "The Factory Bill," 2:33 (13 April 1844): 673–4.

47 *Economist*, "The Political Economy of Young England," 2:51 (17 Aug. 1844): 1109.

48 *Economist*, "Lord Ashley's New Fallacy – the Manufacturers New Danger," 4:128 (7 Feb. 1846): 167–8.

49 *Economist*, "The Factory System and Mortality," 2:36 (4 May 1844): 761.

50 John Komlos, "The Secular Trend in Biological Standard of Living in the United Kingdom, 1730–1860," 115–44; Stephen Nicolas and Richard Steckel, "Heights and Living Standards of English Workers During the Early Years of Industrialization," 937–57; Robert Woods, *The Demography of Victorian England and Wales*, esp. 364–71. The classic description of Manchester in this period comes from Friederich Engels, *The Condition of the Working Class in England*. Malthus had pointed out that the cities devoured men and needed to be constantly supplied by fresh migrants from the country.

51 *Economist*, "Lord Ashley's New Ten-Hours Bill," 8:342 (16 March 1850): 286.

52 *Economist*, "Government Protection for Children From Excessive Labour," 22:1082 (21 May 1864): 642–3. This certainly reflected the approach of Bagehot, less wedded than Wilson to "pure principles" of political economy. Bagehot wrote most of the paper's articles about slavery and the US civil war in the early 1860s.

53 *Economist*, "Extension of the Machinery of Government – Principle of Centralization," 3:107 (13 Sept. 1845): 862–3.

54 *Economist*, "New Means and Maxims," 6:243 (22 April 1848): 451–2.

55 *Economist*, "Should the Capitalists be Blamed?," 4:166 (31 Oct. 1846): 1419–20.

56 *Economist*, "Is the State to Blame?," 4:168 (14 Nov. 1846): 1483–4.

57 *Economist*, "Who is to Blame for the Condition of the People?," 4:169 (21 Nov. 1846): 1517–18.

58 *Economist*, "The Impossibility of Feeding and Employing the Irish," 5:181 (13 Feb. 1847): 171–2.

59 *Economist*, "The Railway Crisis – its Cause and its Cure," 6:269 (21 Oct. 1848): 1186–8; the same line was repeated in *Economist*, "Audit of Railways," 7:308 (21 July 1849): 794–5.

60 *Economist*, "The Social Lessons of the Day," 6:242 (15 April 1848): 421–4.

61 *Economist*, "The First Half of the Nineteenth Century – Progress of the Nation and Race," 9:386 (18 Jan. 1851): 57–8.

62 *Economist*, "The First Half of the Nineteenth-Century – Increase of National Well-Being," 9:387 (25 Jan. 1851): 81–3; *Economist*, "Scientific, Educational, and Moral Progress of the last Fifty Years," 9:388 (1 Feb. 1851): 109–11.

63 *Economist*, "Opening of the Exhibition," 9:401 (3 May 1851): 473–4.

64 *Economist*, "Some Moral Aspects of the Exhibition," 9:403 (17 May 1851): 531–2.

65 *Economist*, "The Multitude at the Exhibition," 9:405 (31 May 1851): 586–7.

66 *Economist*, "Review of *The History of Progress in Great Britain*," 17:843 (22 Oct. 1859): 1180–1.

8 Bad Farming – The Ghost of a Dead Monopoly

1 *Economist*, "Scientific Agriculture for Farmers," 1:2 (9 Sept. 1843): 27.

2 *Economist*, "Bad Farming and Feudalism," 9:388 (1 Feb. 1851): 116.

3 *Economist*, "Agriculture: The Ghost of a Dead Monopoly," 4:153 (1 Aug. 1846): 984–5.

4 *Economist*, "Land and Labourers," 4:171 (5 Dec. 1846): 1584–5.

5 *Economist*, "The Progress of our Principle," 2:26 (24 Feb. 1844): 507.

6 *Economist*, "The Dukes of Northumberland and Sutherland upon the Anti-League Movement," 1:26 (24 Feb. 1844): 509.

7 *Economist*, "The Progress of our Principle," 2:26 (24 Feb. 1844): 507.

8 *Economist*, "The Corn Market and the Corn Laws," 3:109 (27 Sept. 1845): 909–10.

9 Cited in Barrington, *Servant*, I: 82.

10 The *Economist* pushed for the elimination of the Corn Laws as the only sure means to afford relief in Ireland as well. "The Ministry and the Corn Laws," 3:113 (25 Oct. 1845): 1029.

11 *Economist*, "The Great Crisis – A Warning to the Aristocracy," 4:125 (17 Jan. 1846): 69.

12 *Economist*, "Political," 2:20 (13 Jan. 1844): 394.

13 *Economist*, "Mr. Disraeli's Political Philosophy," 4:143 (23 May 1846): 659–60.

14 *Economist*, "Agriculture: Land; its Uses and Abuses," 4:150 (11 July 1846): 893–4.

15 *Economist*, "Agriculture: The Ghost of a Dead Monopoly," 4:153 (11 Aug. 1846): 984–5.

16 *Economist*, "Land: A Commodity," 7:303 (16 June 1849): 659.

17 *Economist*, "The Capital Required in Farming," 8:356 (22 June 1850): 679–80.

18 *Economist*, "Tenant Right and Tenant Might," 5:200 (26 June 1847): 726–7.

19 *Economist*, "Small Farms – Peasant Proprietors," 5:211 (11 Sept. 1847): 1052–3.

20 *Economist*, "The Productiveness of Large and Small Farms," 6:274 (25 Nov. 1848): 1330–1.

21 *Economist*, "The State and Temper of Farmers: Relations of Landlords and Tenants," 7:293 (7 April 1849): 378–9.

22 "The Permanent Occupation of Farms," 10:448 (27 March 1852): 339–40.

23 *Return of the Owners of the Land*, 1875; John Bateman, *The Great Landowners of Great Britain and Ireland*, 12–13; F.M.L. Thompson, *English Landed Society in the Nineteenth Century*.

24 *Economist*, "Owning Land and Farming," 16:761 (27 March 1858): 338–9.

25 *Economist*, "Landowning a Business," 10:459 (12 June 1852): 645–6.

26 *Economist*, "What is High Farming," 7:282 (20 Jan. 1849): 65.

27 *Economist*, "Provinces," 2:57 (28 Sept. 1844): 1258.

28 *Economist*, "Rural Labour as Affected by Law," 5:187 (27 March 1847): 354–5.

29 *Economist*, "Free Trade in Land," 5:196 (29 May 1847): 605–60. Two years later, the paper asserted that two-thirds of the land in England "is held in life-long leases." Though the paper championed statistics in its arguments, it seemed not to worry overly about whether these were correct. *Economist*, "What Farmers Say and Do," 7:291 (24 March 1849): 321–2.

30 *Economist*, "Rents," 7:291 (24 March 1849): 322–3; *Economist*, "The Permanent Occupation of Farms," 10:448 (27 March 1852): 339–40.

31 *Economist*, "The Peril of Yearly Tenancies," 6:751 (16 Jan. 1858): 58.
32 *Economist*, "Rents and Profits in Husbandry," 8:334 (19 Jan. 1850): 65–6.
33 *Economist*, "Compulsory Employment of Labour in Husbandry," 5:175 (2 Jan. 1847): 8–9.
34 *Economist*, "Low Farming Fallacies," 8:335 (15 June 1850): 651–2.
35 *Economist*, "Agricultural Distress," 9:391 (22 Feb. 1851): 198–9.
36 *Economist*, "Rents and Re-adjustments," 9:421 (20 Sept. 1851): 1038–9. Landlords, of course, complained of the same difficulty in the 1830s. At that time, they blamed the costs of poor relief as the reason for not being able to find tenants for their estates. In the 1840s, they blamed rural unrest; in the 1850s, cheap imports.
37 *Economist*, "Help out of Rural Difficulties," 9:422 (27 Sept. 1851): 1067–8.
38 *Economist*, "Rents and Re-adjustments," 9:421 (20 Sept. 1851): 1038–9.
39 *Economist*, "Guano – Los Lobos and Mr. Webster," 10:473 (18 Sept. 1852): 1038–9.
40 *Economist*, "Guano-Adulteration," 9:419 (6 Sept. 1851): 980; *Economist*, "Substitutes for Guano," 12:544 (28 Jan. 1854): 87–8.
41 *Economist*, "Guano Monopoly," 10:470 (28 Aug. 1852): 956; *Economist*, "Guano Substitutes," 15:709 (28 March 1857): 336–7; *Economist*, "Scarcity of Guano," 15:706 (7 March 1857): 254. See also Gregory Cushman, *Guano and the Opening of the Pacific World: A Global Ecological History*.
42 *Economist*, "Apparent Decline of the Land Interests," 11:514 (2 July 1853): 728–9.
43 *Economist*, "The Capital Requisite for Farming," 19:942 (14 Sept. 1861): 1015–16; *Economist*, "Social and Commercial Status of Farmers," 18:876 (9 June 1860): 619–20.
44 *Times*, 23 March 1844, p. 6.
45 Ravenstone, *Some Doubts*, 365. (See chapter 6.)
46 *Economist*, "Incendiary Fires in the Country," 2:20 (13 Jan. 1844): 388.
47 *Economist*, "Postscript," 2:48 (27 July 1844): 1033.
48 *Economist*, "Agriculture: The Agricultural Labourers," 4:157 (29 Aug. 1846): 1126–7.
49 For example, *Economist*, "The Labourers in Husbandry," 4:162 (3 Oct. 1846): 1228–89.
50 *Economist*, "Land and Labourers," 4:171 (5 Dec. 1846): 1584–5.
51 *Economist*, "Compulsory Employment of Labour in Husbandry," 5:175 (2 Jan. 1847): 8–9.
52 Cited in *Economist*, "Incendiary Fires in the Country," 2:20 (23 Jan. 1844): 388.
53 *Economist*, "Future Improvement of the People," 8:371 (5 Oct. 1850): 1098–9.
54 *Economist*, "Apparent Decline of the Landed Interest," 11:514 (2 July 1853): 728–9.
55 *Economist*, "Scarcity of Labour," 13:628 (8 Sept. 1855): 979–80.
56 *Economist*, "Is There a Surplus of Labour: Agricultural Wages," 8:349 (4 May 1850): 481–2.
57 *Economist*, "Employment of Labour in Husbandry," 7:229 (19 May 1849): 547.
58 *Economist*, "Are the Landowners to Blame," 4:167 (7 Nov. 1846): 1452–3.

59 *Economist*, "The Question of Rent," 8:333 (12 Jan. 1850): 29–30; *Economist*, "Apparent Decline of the Landed Interest," 11:514 (2 July 1853): 728–9.

60 *Economist*, "Cheap Food and Rural Wages," 9:419 (6 Sept. 1851): 984.

61 *Economist*, "The Condition of Rural Labourers," 17:824 (11 June 1858): 648–9.

62 *Economist*, "Rural Labour as Affected by Law," 5:187 (27 March 1847): 354–5.

63 See for example, *Economist*, "Agriculture: The Agricultural Labourers," 4:157 (29 Aug. 1846): 1126–7; *Economist*, "Agricultural Wages," 11:494 (12 Feb. 1853): 169–70.

64 *Economist*, "The Poor Law and the Commissioners," 5:195 (22 May 1847): 577–8.

65 *Economist*, "Enclosure of Waste Lands – Parliamentary Evidence on the Subject," 3:17 (26 April 1845): 384–5.

66 *Economist*, "The Labourer's Panacea – The Allotment System," 2:62 (2 Nov. 1844): 1369–70.

67 *Economist*, "Allotments," 2:62 (2 Nov. 1844): 1380. In fact, by 1844 it was clear that the "emancipated negro" in Jamaica would only work for wages when compelled by various schemes to deny them access to land or to compel them through pseudo-apprenticeships. See chapter 10 below for further discussion.

68 *Economist*, "The Division of Labour – The Allotment System," 2:65 (23 Nov. 1844): 1441–2.

69 *Economist*, "Protest against the Second Reading of the Field Gardens Bill," 3:100 (26 July 1845): 695.

70 *Economist*, "Mr. Greg on Allotments," 2:65 (23 Nov. 1844): 1499–51.

71 *Economist*, "The Allotment System," 17:838 (17 Sept. 1859): 1039.

72 William Thomas Thornton, *Over-population and its Remedy*, 121, 140–4, 207–8, 211.

73 William Thomas Thornton, *A Plea for Peasant Proprietors, with the Outlines of a Plan for their Establishment in Ireland*, 1–2.

74 Ibid., 5.

75 Ibid., 54. The rift among political economists between those who newly supported peasant farming and those opposed to it can be seen in the minutes of the Political Economy Club. Thornton was elected to the club in 1848, joining J.S. Mill on the side arguing the benefits of peasant ownership. Opposed most staunchly were McCulloch, Senior, and Chadwick. The first two suggested questions by Thornton to the club, both in 1849, dealt with a debate about McCulloch's opposition to Irish peasant proprietorship and, the second, about the limits of the rights of property in the land. *Minutes of the Political Economy Club* Vol. 1, 81–2.

76 Thornton, *A Plea for Peasant Proprietors*, 21, 28, 40–1, 22.

77 Ibid., 175.

78 John Stuart Mill, *Principles of Political Economy*, 178–9.

79 Samuel Laing, *Notes of a Traveler*, 299–300; also cited in Mill, *Principles*, 184–5.

80 Mill, *Principles*, 204.

81 Ibid., 206.

82 *Economist*, "The Labourer's Panacea – The Allotment System," 2:62 (2 Nov. 1844): 1369–70.

83 *Economist*, "French Husbandry," 9:420 (13 Sept. 1851): 1012–13.

84 *Economist*, "Large or Small Farms," 6:233 (12 Feb. 1848): 173–4.

85 *Economist*, "The Productiveness of Large and Small Farms," 6:274 (25 Nov. 1848): 1330–1.

86 *Economist*, "Future Improvement of the People," 8:371 (5 Oct. 1850): 1098–9.

87 *Economist*, "Flemish Farming," 9:338 (1 Feb. 1851): 116.

88 See for example, *Economist*, "Collateral Evils of Peasant Proprietorship," 9:425 (18 Oct. 1851): 1150–1.

89 *Economist*, "French Husbandry," 13:606 (7 April 1855): 364–5.

90 *Economist*, "French Husbandry," 13:627 (1 Sept. 1855): 953.

91 *Economist*, "French Husbandry: The Valley of Isere – Grenoble," 13:633 (13 Oct. 1855): 1123–4.

92 *Economist*, "Good Farming: The Helps and Hindrances," 19:923 (4 May 1861): 484–5.

93 *Economist*, "The Agricultural Labourers," 7:326 (24 Nov. 1849): 1304–6.

94 Alan Armstrong and J.P. Huzel, "Labour II: Food, Shelter, and Self-help, the Poor Law and the Position of the Labourer in Rural Society," 729–835, esp. 748.

95 *Economist*, "The Food of the English Labourer," 22:1102 (8 Oct. 1864): 1252–3.

9 Ireland: "They Lie Beyond the Pale"

1 Emilie Barrington, *The Servant of All*, 1:84–129. She reprints a number of letters between her father and Lord Clarendon. One from Clarendon on 7 June 1848 thanked Wilson for the favourable articles about his rule. 1:140.

2 Tim Patt Coogan, *The Famine Plot*; Cecil Woodham-Smith, *The Great Hunger*.

3 S. Donnelly Jr., *The Great Irish Potato Famine*, 1–3; C. O'Grada, *Ireland: A New Economic History*.

4 J.G. Kohl, *Travels in Ireland*, esp. 86–7; Gustave de Beaumont, *Ireland: social, political, and religious vol. 1*.

5 Census figures reported in *Economist*, "Statistics from Ireland," 2:27 (2 March 1844): 537.

6 Cited in J. Killen et al., *The Famine Decade: Contemporary Accounts*, 32.

7 K.H. Connell, "Population" in *Social Life in Ireland*, 85–97.

8 C. O'Grada, "The Population of Ireland 1700–1900: A Survey," 281–99, esp. 283.

9 Malthus to Ricardo, 17 August 1817, David Saffra (ed.) *The Works and Correspondence of David Ricardo*, 225.

10 Cited in Redcliffe Salaman, *The History and Social Influence of the Potato*, 286. Curren exaggerates; Salaman estimated that a family of six needed 1.6 acres of land for subsistence.

11 J. Stanley, *Ireland and Her Evils*, 16.

12 Cited in C. O'Grada, *Ireland*, 4.

13 Arthur Young, *Tour in Ireland*, Vol. 2, 116, 118; see also Smith, *The Wealth of Nations*, book 1: ch. xi.

14 James Belich, *Replenishing the Earth*, 446; see also Brinley Thomas, "Feeding England during the Industrial Revolution: A View from the Celtic Fringe," 328–42; Salaman, *Potato*, 274.

15 Belich, *Replenishing*, 445–9.

16 Connell, "Population," 89.

17 According to the 1841 census, agricultural wages averaged 4d to 10d in the south and west, and 8d to 1s a day in the north. "Statistics from Ireland," 2:27 (2 March 1844): 537. This compares to the agricultural wage of about 2s a day in the north or England.

18 Young, *Tour* 2: 97–8.

19 "Letter from Senior to Russell," 12 May 1837 in *Abstract of the Final Report of the Commissioners of Irish Poor Inquiry*, 37–41.

20 Cited in S. Leon Levy, *Nassau Senior*, 238.

21 Sir George Nichol, "First Report" in Nichol, *A History of the Irish Poor Law*, 160–1.

22 The term "moral disagreeableness" comes from a letter from George Cornewall Lewis, who was also a commissioner. Ibid., 53.

23 *Digest of Evidence taken before Her Majesty's Commission of Inquiry*, Part II, 829–30.

24 "Untitled note," 2:52 (24 Aug. 1844): 1136.

25 Cited in J.O. Ranelagh, *A Short History of Ireland*, 117; and Killen, *Famine Decade*, 145–6.

26 Cited in *Economist*, "The Present Condition of the Irish Poor," 5:175 (2 Jan. 1847): 5–6.

27 James Donnelly Jr. *The Great Irish Potato Famine*; there is a huge literature on deaths during the famine, beginning perhaps with the "Tables of Deaths," Part V, of *Census of Ireland for the Year 1851*, British Parliamentary Papers. For more recent estimates and regional breakdowns see John Crowley, William J. Smith, and Mike Murphy (eds.) *Atlas of the Great Famine, 1845–52*; Joel Mokyr, *Why Ireland Starved*; C. O'Grada, *Ireland: A New Economic History*; also see S.H. Cousens, "Regional Death Rates in Ireland during the Great Famine, from 1846 to 1851," 55–74.

28 Cited in Killen, *The Famine Decade*, 182; Ranelagh, *A Short History*, 117.

29 *Economist*, "Measures for Ireland," 3:71 (4 Jan. 1845): 3–4.

30 *Economist*, "The Real Grievance of Ireland," 2:25 (17 Feb. 1844): 482.

31 *Economist*, "Letter to the Editor," 2:27 (2 March 1844): 540.

32 *Economist*, "The Repeal of the union against the repeal of the corn laws" 1:17 (23 Dec. 1843): 140.

33 *Economist*, "Picture of a Wretched Country – What can be done for it?," 3:26 (28 June 1845): 258.

34 *Economist*, "Ireland," 3:97 (5 July 1845): 628–9; *Economist*, "Epitome of News," 3:97 (5 July 1845): 630; *Economist*, "Ireland: State of Cavan," 3:98 (12 July 1845): 655.

35 *Economist*, "Ireland," 2:63 (9 Nov. 1844): 1401.

36 *Economist*, "Ireland: The Weather," 3:102 (9 Aug. 1845): 749.

37 *Economist*, "Legislation for Scarcity," 3:112 (18 Oct. 1845): 997–8.

38 *Economist*, "Ireland," 3:117 (22 Nov. 1845): 1163.

39 *Economist*, "Provinces – Ireland," 3:118 (29 Nov. 1845): 1196.

40 *Economist*, "The Potato Disease," 3:119 (6 Dec. 1845): 1226.

41 *Economist*, "Legislation for Scarcity," 3:112 (18 Oct. 1845): 997–8.

42 *Economist*, "The Ministry and the Corn Laws," 3:113 (25 Oct. 1845); *Economist*, "Provinces – Ireland," 3:119 (6 Dec. 1845): 1226; *Economist*, "The State of Ireland," 4:133 (14 March 1846): 325.

43 Reprinted in *Economist*, "Ireland," 4:162 (3 Oct. 1846): 1291–2.

44 *Economist*, "Protection – Lord B. Bentinck and Ireland," 4:162 (3 Oct. 1846): 1285–6.

45 *Economist*, "Bombay Famine in 1812," 3:118 (29 Nov. 1845): 1193–4. The account the *Economist* cites is Capt. Basil Hunt's *Fragments of Voyages and Travels* Vol. 111; *Gazetteer of the Bombay Presidency* Vol. 14, 60.

46 Cited in Killen, *Famine Decade*, 145–6.

47 *Economist*, "Landlord Agitation – Ireland," 7:331 (29 Dec. 1849): 1442–3.

48 *Economist*, "Should the State Employ the Irish?," 4:174 (26 Dec. 1846): 1674–5.

49 *Economist*, "Removal of Protection not the Cause of Agrarian Distress," 8:365 (24 Aug. 1850): 932–3.

50 *Economist*, "Measures for Ireland," 4:156 (22 Aug. 1846): 1082–3.

51 *Economist*, "Faith in Principles," 5:175 (2 January 1847): 3–5.

52 *Economist*, "Ireland," 5:183 (27 Feb. 1847): 225–8.

53 *Economist*, "Charity as a Remedy in Case of Famine," 3:118 (29 Nov. 1845): 1192–3.

54 *Economist*, "Feeding the Irish," 4:133 (21 March 1846): 370.

55 Cited in *Economist*, "Ireland," 4:138 (18 April 1846): 505; *Economist*, "Ireland," 4:160 (19 Sept. 1846): 1225.

56 *Economist*, "Medicines which will not cure Ireland," 4:140 (2 May 1846): 562–3.

57 *Economist*, "Effects of the Government Feeding the Irish," 4:155 (15 Aug. 1846): 1049–50.

58 *Economist*, "Relief for Ireland," 4:159 (12 Sept. 1846): 1186–8.

59 *Economist*, "The Puzzle of Ireland," 4:163 (10 Oct. 1846): 1316–17.

60 *Economist*, "Ireland-Past Measures and their Result," 5:177 (16 Jan. 1847): 58–60. (This article so closely resembles a subsequent warning by Trevelyan that it is difficult not to see the paper's influence on Trevelyan's opinions here. Similarly, in July 1847 Clarendon repeated the charge, arguing that parts of the country remained uncultivated because cottiers had waited for "somebody to do something for them." Barrington, *Servant*, 1: 123.)

61 *Economist,* "The Impossibility of Feeding the Irish," 5:181 (13 Feb. 1847): 171–2.
62 *Economist,* "The Condition of Ireland and its Cure" 5:226 (15 Dec. 1847): 1475–6.
63 *Economist,* "Ireland – Landlord Rights" 4:136 (4 April 1846): 435–6.
64 *Economist,* "Conflict of Peasantry and Landlords," 4:137 (11 April 1846): 467–8.
65 *Economist,* "A Possible Cure for Ireland," 4:141 (9 May 1846) 595–6.
66 *Economist,* "Ireland – its Permanent Evils and their Remedy," 4:160 (19 Sept. 1846): 1218–20.
67 *Economist,* "Ireland – Its Permanent Evils and their Remedy--#2," 4:161 (26 Sept. 1846): 1249–50; *Economist,* "Ireland – Its Permanent Evils … #3," 4:162 (3 Oct. 1846): 1282–4.
68 *Economist,* "Irish Prospects," 4:166 (31 Oct. 1846): 1419.
69 Barrington, *Servant* 1:129.
70 *Economist,* "The New Drug for Irish Maladies," 9:423 (4 Oct. 1851): 1092.
71 *Economist,* "Tenant-Right – Ireland," 5:213 (25 Sept. 1847): 1101.
72 *Economist,* "Ireland Again – The Beginning of the End," 4:172 (12 Dec. 1846): 1610.
73 "Clarendon to Wilson," 26 Sept. 1848 in Barrington, *Servant* 1:150.
74 "Clarendon to Wilson," 7 May 1850, Barrington, *Servant* 1:140.
75 *Economist,* "What the Irish Should Do," 5:224 (11 Dec. 1847): 1419–20; *Economist,* "The Irish Coercion Bill," 5:225 (18 Dec. 1847): 1445–6.
76 *Economist,* "The Saxon, the Celt, and the Gaul," 6:244 (29 April 1848): 477–8.
77 *Economist,* "The Question Still is – What is to be done with Ireland? The Incumbered Estates Bill," 7:321 (20 Oct. 1849): 1157–8.
78 *Economist,* "Progress in Ireland" 8: 362 (3 Aug. 1850): 841–4.
79 *Economist,* "Ireland and the Poor Laws" 7:284 (3 Feb. 1849): 113–15.
80 Barrington, *Servant,* 1:91.
81 *Economist,* "Ireland: Present Prosperity and Late Famine," 10:478 (23 Oct. 1852): 1177–8.
82 *Economist,* "The New Drug for Irish Maladies," 9:423 (4 Oct. 1851): 1090–2.
83 *Economist,* "Ireland – Population – Agriculture," 15:724 (11 July 1857): 755.
84 *Economist,* "The New Drug for Irish Maladies," 9:423 (4 Oct. 1851): 1090–2.
85 *Economist,* "Irish Crime and Irish Justice," 10:442 (14 Feb. 1852): 167–8.
86 *Economist,* "Ireland: Past and Present," 21:1032 (6 June 1863): 620–1.

10 Cooked Land, Cotton, and Slavery

1 *Economist,* "First Statistical Supplement," 1:10 (4 Nov. 1843): 170–2.
2 Robert Tombs *The English and Their History,* 483.
3 There is a very large literature concerning the living standards of urban, particularly textile, workers during this period, most focused on urban/rural wage differentials. In the 1980s, various works by Peter Lindert and Jeffrey Williamson employed a "quality of life" index meant to compensate for both dreary work

and deplorable living conditions in calculating wage differentials. Even with the addition of this index, they argued there was still substantial benefit in higher urban wages. See for example Lindhert and Williamson, "English Workers' Living Standards During the Industrial Revolution: A New Look," 1–25; and Williamson "Was the Industrial Revolution Worth It? Disamenities and Death in 19th Century British Towns," 221–45. Other works have disputed these claims, either for particular regions or for the country as a whole: see Richard Fleischman, *Conditions of Life Among the Cotton Workers of Southeastern Lancashire*; John Brown, "The Condition of England and the Standard of Living: Cotton Textiles in the Northwest, 1806–1850," 591–614. It is not clear that any of these works sufficiently address the decline in living standards evident in rural areas in the decades preceding the rise of cotton industrialization nor the economic compulsion that precipitated the need to choose migration to Lancashire and industrial labour. That is, urban wages in the 1840s might have been higher than the depressed wages and squalid living conditions in rural area, but only after more than seven decades of decline.

4 *Economist*, "First Statistical Supplement," 1:10 (4 Nov. 1843): 170–2.

5 Barrington, *Servant* 1:166; Arthur Silver, *Manchester Men and Indian Cotton, 1847–1872*, 5–6.

6 Zevin, *Liberalism*, 50.

7 *Economist*, "Debate on the Supply of Cotton," 15:722 (27 June 1857): 689–99.

8 *Economist*, "Present and Future Prospects of Great Britain Relative to the Supply and Consumption of Cotton," 7:327 (1 Dec. 1849): 1325–9; *Economist*, "The Cotton Trade of the United Kingdom and Trade with the United States," 9:420 (13 Sept. 1851): 1006–7.

9 E.J. Hobsbawm, *Industry and Empire*, 56. Some works have questioned the overall importance of cotton. See for example, C. Knick Harley, "British Industrialization Before 1841: Evidence of Slower Growth during the Industrial Revolution," 267–9. Kenneth Pomerantz has recently reasserted cotton's importance; see *The Great Divergence: China, Europe and the Making of the Modern World Economy*. See also Sven Beckert, *Empire of Cotton: A Global History*, esp. 41–82; Hameeda Hossain, *The Company Weavers of Bengal: The East India Company and the Organization of Textile Production in Bengal, 1750–1813*; Prasannan Parthasarathi, *The Transition to a Colonial Economy: Weavers, Merchants and Kings in South India, 1720–1800*.

10 Kenneth Morgan, *The Birth of Industrial Britain: Economic Change, 1750–1850*, 39–40.

11 Sir James Kay-Shuttleworth, *The Moral and Physical Condition of the Working Classes Employed in Cotton Manufacture in Manchester*, esp. 22–8.

12 Frederich Engels, *The Condition of the Working Class in England*, 4, 199, 312.

13 Alexis de Toqueville, *Journeys to England and Ireland*, 107–8.

14 *Economist*, "Present and Future Prospects," 7: 327 (1 Dec. 1849): 1325–9; see also John Briggs, *The Cotton Trade of India Part II*, 4, 11.

15 *Economist*, "The Supply of Cotton," 7:318 (29 Sept. 1849): 1073–5; *Economist*, "The Cotton Crop," 8:365 (24 Aug. 1850): 1092–3.

16 Edward Baptist, *The Half Has Never Been Told: Slavery and the Making of American Capitalism*, esp. 261; Sven Beckert, *Empire of Cotton*, 108.

17 *Economist*, "Slavery in the United States," 8:368 (14 Sept. 1850): 1013–14.

18 *Economist*, "Our Brazilian Trade and the Anti-Slavery Party," 1:3 (16 Sept. 1843): 33–4.

19 *Economist*, "The Slave Trade and Economical Laws," 16:777 (17 July 1858): 783–4.

20 *Economist*, "Free Trade and Slave Trade," 1:10 (4 Nov. 1843): 156; *Economist*, "The Slave Trade and Slavery – Mr. Hutt's Motion," 3:26 (28 June 1845): 597–8.

21 *Economist*, "The Slave Trade and Slavery," 6:235 (26 Feb. 1848): 227–9; *Economist*, "The Slave Trade," 6:255 (15 July 1848): 788–9.

22 *Economist*, "Can the Slave Trade be Suppressed," 6:262 (2 Sept. 1848): 993–5.

23 *Economist*, "The West Indies; Cotton Growing in Jamaica," 8:370 (28 Sept. 1850): 1069–70.

24 *Economist*, "The Deficiency of Labour in the West Indies," 17:829 (16 July 1859): 784–6.

25 Thomas Carlyle, *Occasional Discourse on the N[*****] Question*, esp. 427. It was first published in *Fraser Magazine* (Dec. 1849) as "Occasional Discourse on the Negro Question." Catherine Hall says this was the moment when it became acceptable for public men to argue for an "essential inferiority of black people." This may be true, but as we have seen the *Economist* had been ascribing distinct and inferior racial characteristics for both Black people and the Irish since the inception of the paper, though they became more rigid and damning between the 1840s and the 1860s. Hall, *Civilising Subjects: Metropole and Colony in the English Imagination, 1830–1867*, 48.

26 *Economist*, "The West Indies," 8:348 (27 April 1850): 455–6.

27 *Economist*, "Cotton Cultivation in Jamaica," 8:348 (27 April 1850): 456–7.

28 *Economist*, "Why we do not Despair of the West Indies," 6:253 (1 July 1848): 729–31.

29 See for example the Select Committee on the Condition of the West Indian Colonies, *House of Commons Papers* 479 (1842) Resolutions 5, 6, 7, and 8 from the Committee and testimony of T. MacComack, 340–4.

30 Cited in Thomas Holt, *The Problem of Freedom: Race, Labor, and Politics in Jamaica and Britain, 1832–1938*, esp. 167.

31 *Economist*, "Correspondence," 4:140 (2 May 1846): 566; 4:141 (9 May 1846); *Economist*, "Correspondence," 4:143 (23 May 1846): 663–4.

32 *Economist*, "The Sugar Debate in the House of Lords," 4:155 (15 Aug. 1846): 1050–1.

33 *Economist*, "The Deficiency of Labour in the West Indies," 17:829 (16 July 1859): 784–6.

34 *Economist*, "Labour in the West Indies," 19:937 (10 Aug. 1861): 875.

35 Holt, *Problem*, 302; Gad Hueman, *Killing Time: The Morant Bay Rebellion, Jamaica*. See also Jean Besson, "Land Tenure and the Free Villages of Trelawny, Jamaica: A Case Study in the Caribbean Peasant Response to Emancipation," 3–23. For a fuller discussion of the tension between peasant farming and efforts to force wage labour in Jamaica see Jim Handy, *Tiny Engines of Abundance: A History of Peasant Productivity and Repression*, ch. 3.

36 *Economist*, "Present and Future Prospects of Great Britain Relative to the Supply and Consumption of Cotton," 7:327 (1 Dec. 1849): 1325–9; *Economist*, "Cultivation of Cotton in India and Slavery in America," 17:807 (12 Feb. 1859): 166–7.

37 *Economist*, "Can Slavery be Abolished," 11:508 (21 May 1853): 561–2.

38 *Economist*, "United States – Slavery Debate," 8:343 (23 March 1850): 312–13; *Economist*, "Slavery in the United States," 7:285 (10 Feb. 1849): 145–6.

39 *Economist*, "United States – Slavery Debate," 8:343 (23 March 1850): 312–13.

40 *Economist*, "Slave-Labour, the Conditions of its Extinction," 15:737 (10 Oct. 1857): 1120–1; *Economist*, "The Sources of the Value of Slave-Labour, and Causes of Depreciation," 15:738 (17 Oct. 1857): 1149–50.

41 *Economist*, "The Impending Crisis in the Southern States of America," 17:852 (24 Dec. 1859): 1428–9.

42 *Economist*, "Latest from America," 14:682 (20 Sept. 1856): 1034.

43 *Economist*, "The Political Crisis in America," 18:856 (21 Jan. 1860): 58–9.

44 *Economist*, "The Disruption of the Union, as it Would Affect England," 19:908 (19 Jan. 1861): 556–9.

45 *Economist*, "English Feelings towards America," 19:944 (28 Sept. 1861): 1065–7.

46 *Economist*, "Civil War, The Price and the Profit," 19:926 (25 May 1861): 562–4.

47 *Economist*, "The New Feature in the American Civil War," 19:943 (21 Sept. 1861): 1041–2.

48 *Economist*, "The Emancipation Proclamation," 20:1000 (25 Oct. 1862): 1178–9.

49 Ibid.

50 *Economist*, "Cotton and the Civil War," 19:937 (10 Aug. 1861): 869–71.

51 By 1862, three-fifths of the cotton mill labour force in Lancashire was unemployed. Some of the literature argues that this was not solely the result of the cotton famine, but rather the outcome of an oversupply of cotton cloth and yarn. See Eugene Brady, "A Reconsideration of the Lancashire 'Cotton Famine,'" 156–62; Norman Longmate, *The Hungry Mills: The Story of the Lancashire Cotton Famine*.

52 *Economist*, "Cotton Producing Countries," 20:991 (23 Aug. 1862): 928–30.

53 *Economist*, "Lancashire and America," 22:1080 (7 May 1864): 574–5.

54 Janet Abu-Lughod, *Before European Hegemony: The World System, A.D. 1250–1350*; Kenneth Pomerantz and Steven Topik, *The World That Trade Created*.

55 Hameeda Hossain, *The Company Weavers of Bengal: The East India Company and the Organization of Textile Production in Bengal, 1750–1813*; Prasannan Parthasaradhi, *The Transition to a Colonial Economy: Weavers, Merchants and Kings in South India, 1720–1800*.

56 For background see H.V. Bowen, *The Business of Empire: The East India Company and Imperial Britain, 1756–1833*; Sudipta Sen, *Empire of Free Trade: The East India Company and the Making of the Colonial Marketplace*; C.A. Bayly, *Indian Society and the Making of the British Empire*.

57 Bowen, *Business*, 31–9; Philip Stern, *The Company-State: Corporate Sovereignty and the Early Modern Foundations of the British Empire in India*, esp. 207–14.

58 Julie Murray, "Company Rules: Burke, Hastings, and the Specter of the Modern Liberal State," 55–69.

59 "OverLand Mail," 1:12 (11 Nov. 1843): 197. There is an abundant literature on the apparent contradiction of liberalism and empire. See Karuna Mantena, *Alibis of Empire: Henry Maine and the Ends of Liberal Imperialism*; Jennifer Pitts, *A Turn to Empire: The Rise of Imperial Liberalism in Britain and France*; Singh Mehta, *Liberalism and Empire: A Study in Nineteenth Century British Liberal Thought*. Andrew Sartori, *Liberalism in Empire: An Alternative History*, argues that there was more convergence than contradiction in these two movements.

60 *Economist*, "The Annexation of the Punjaub [*sic*]," 7:300 (26 May 1849): 571–2; *Economist*, "The Great Commercial Consequences of Our Indian Conquests," 7:301 (2 June 1849): 597–8.

61 *Economist*, "Waste Land and Indian Revenue," 19: 954 (7 Dec. 1861): 1348–50; *Economist*, "Sir C. Wood's Despatch Recommending the Perpetual Settlement of the Land Revenue of India," 20:994 (13 Sept. 1862): 1009–11.

62 *Economist*, "Prospects of the West Indies – The Management of West Indian Estates," 2:61 (26 Oct. 1844): 1346–8.

63 *Economist*, "Cotton Culture in India," 5:209 (28 Aug. 1847): 982–4.

64 Arthur Silver, *Manchester Men*, esp. 30–5, 44–9.

65 Silver, *Manchester*, 35–41.

66 Briggs, *The Cotton Trade of India Part I*, esp. 3.

67 Briggs, *Cotton Trade Part II*, 54. Both the report to the House in 1848 and Mackay's evidence in 1853 also focused much attention on the problems with the land tax, and land tenure issues in general, as did most other reports. See, for example, *The Cotton Dearth*; J.A. Mann, "On the Cotton Trade of India," 346–87.

68 *Economist*, "East India Railways and East India Cotton," 4:171 (5 Dec. 1846): 1582–3; *Economist*, "Why Does not India Supply us With Cotton?," 5:178 (23 Jan. 1847): 89–90; Part II, 5:181 (13 Feb. 1847): 174; Part III, 5:182 (20 Feb. 1847): 201–2.

69 Ranajit Guha, *A Rule of Property for Bengal*, 3.

70 One example of that debate was a question proposed to the Political Economy Club by John McCulloch in 1840 on the advantages or disadvantages of the "Zemindary and Ryotwar system." *Minutes*, Vol. 1, 54.

71 Firoj High Sirwar, "A Comparative Study of Zamindari, Raiyatwair, and Mahalwari Land Revenue Settlements: The Colonial Mechanisms of Surplus Extraction in 19th Century British India," 16–26; Thomas Metcalf, *The Ideologies of the Raj: The New Cambridge History of India, Vol. 4*, esp. 25–36; Eric Stokes, *The Peasant*

Armed: The Indian Revolt of 1857, 108–15; P.J. Marshall, *Bengal: The British Bridgehead*, 142–58.

72 *Economist*, "Why Does not India Supply us With Cotton?," Part I, 5:178 (23 Jan. 1847): 89–90; Part II, 5:181 (13 Feb. 1847): 174; Part III, 5:182 (20 Feb. 1847): 201–2; Part IV, 5:184 (6 March 1847): 269–70; Part V, 5:186 (20 March 1847): 325–6.

73 *Economist*, "Land Tax and Cotton Cultivation," 5:210 (4 Sept. 1847): 1019–20.

74 *Economist*, "The India Committee," 10:452 (24 April 1852): 445–6.

75 Zevin, *Liberalism*, 50.

76 *Economist*, "Progress in India," 11:491 (22 Jan. 1853): 88.

77 *Economist*, "Railway Crisis in Britain," 6:269 (21 Oct. 1848): 1186–8; *Economist*, "Audit of Railways," 7:308 (21 July 1849): 794–5.

78 *Economist*, "East India Railways and East India Cotton," 4:171 (5 Dec. 1846): 1582–3.

79 Cited in Barrington, *Servant*, 2:182.

80 Ibid., 1:140. There is some evidence that Wilson had conversations with Manchester cotton interests about such a scheme before he was elected to Parliament. If that was the case, he may have in fact initiated the idea.

81 *Economist*, "East India Railways," 7:292 (31 March 1849): 352.

82 The original plan envisioned a 4 per cent return. This was increased to 5 per cent in return for the lines carrying Royal Mail free of charge.

83 W.J. McPherson, "Investment in Indian Railways, 1845–1875," 177–86; see also Bhariti Ray, "The Genesis of Railway Development in Hyderabad State: A Case Study of Nineteenth Century British Imperialism," 45–69.

84 *Economist*, "East India Railway Companies," 7:310 (4 Aug. 1849): 850–2.

85 *Economist*, "Cultivation of Cotton in India and Slavery in America," 17:807 (12 Feb. 1859): 166–7.

86 *Economist*, "Indian Railways and their Effect on the Money Market," 19:926 (25 May 1861): 566–7.

87 *Economist*, "Insurrection in India," 13:630 (22 Sept. 1855): 1036.

88 15:712 (18 April 1857): 426–7.

89 *Economist*, "The Indian Army," 15, 723 (4 July 1857): 725–6.

90 *Economist*, "The Forthcoming Debate on India," 15:726 (25 July 1857): 809–10; *Economist*, "Indian Railways," 15:726 (25 July 1857): 810–11.

91 *Economist*, "The Reflex Influence of the Indian Massacres on our Position in the East," 15:746 (12 Dec. 1857): 1371–2.

92 *Economist*, "The Indian Crisis and the Past Year," 16:749 (2 Jan. 1858): 4.

93 *Economist*, "Her Majesty's Proclamation and the Future of India," 16:798 (11 Dec. 1858): 1372–3. *Economist*, "Lord Canning and Talookers of Oude," 17:850 (10 Dec. 1859): 1373–4.

94 *Economist*, "Correspondence," 20:990; 20:991; 20:992; 20:993; 20:994; the quote comes from the last, 1014–15.

95 *Economist*, "How to Make India Take the Place of America as Our Cotton Field," 21:1024 (11 April 1863): 396–7.

96 *Economist*, "Indian versus American Cotton," 20:961 (25 Jan. 1862): 85–7; *Economist*, "African Cotton and Cotton Manufactures in Relation to the Slave Trade," 17:810 (5 March 1859): 251–3.

97 *Economist*, "English Feelings Toward America," 19:944 (28 Sept. 1861): 1065–7.

98 *Economist*, "The Economic Value of Justice to the Dark Races," 23:1163 (9 Dec. 1865): 1163–4.

99 Both the paper and Wilson argued that direct taxation – that is, a tax on sales – was not suitable for India because "Asiatics" simply reduced consumption. *Economist*, "Should the Income Tax be Increased?," 17:848 (26 Nov. 1859): 1314–15; *Economist*, "The Income Tax in England and in India," 18:868 (14 April 1860): 390–1; *Economist*, "Indian Finance and Revenue: The Conspiracy against the English Exchequer," 17:812 (19 March 1859): 309–10.

100 *Economist*, "Memoir of the Right Honourable James Wilson," 18:899 (17 Nov. 1860): 1287–1300.

101 *Economist*, "The Indian Schedule D," 17:840 (1 Oct. 1859): 1089–90.

102 "Wilson to Bagehot," 19 July 1860 in Barrington, *Servant*, 2:303.

103 "Albert to Wilson," 19 April 1860, in ibid., 2:237.

104 *Economist*, "Sir C. Trevelyan's Explanation," 18:903 (15 Dec. 1860): 1389–90.

105 *Economist*, "Sir Charles Trevelyan's Minute on Mr. Wilson's Budget," 18:872 (12 May 1860): 501–2; *Economist*, "Indian Finance and the Madres Protest," 18:875 (2 June 1860): 589–91.

106 Barrington, *Servant*, 2:252–311.

107 *Economist*, "The Death of the Right Honourable James Wilson," 18:890 (15 Sept. 1860): 1005. Though Trevelyan was briefly reprimanded and brought back to England, despite what the paper labelled as his "monstrous act of misjudgement and insubordination" within two years he returned to India, now as the new Finance Minister in the Council of India. *Economist*, "Sr. C. Trevelyan as Finance Minister for India," 20:1002 (8 Nov. 1862): 1233–4.

11 Conclusion: "The Home-made Civilization of the Rural English"

1 George Sturt, *Change in the Village,* 117–25. (Written under his pseudonym, George Bourne.)

2 Ibid., 29.

3 See the articles in Stephen King and Allanah Tomkins (eds.), *The Poor in England: An Economy of Makeshifts.*

4 Barry Reay points out that well into the mid-nineteenth century up to 50 per cent of the cottagers in Lancashire still did weaving. *Rural Englands*, 27–30.

5 Samantha Williams, *Poverty, Gender, and Life Cycle under the English Poor Law,* 156.

6 Leigh Shaw-Taylor, "Parliamentary Enclosure," 657.

7 Leigh Shaw-Taylor, "Labourers, Cows, Common-Rights," esp. 97–8.

8 Brenner, "Agrarian Class Structure."

9 Jane Humphries, "Enclosures, Common Rights, and Women"; R.W. Malcolmson, "Ways of Getting a Living in Eighteenth Century England"; Jeannette Neeson, "English Enclosures and British Peasants," 17–31.

10 Cobbett, *Autobiography*, 107–8.

11 S. Horrell and Jane Humphries, "Old Questions, New Data, and Alternative Perspectives: Families' Living Standards in the Industrial Revolution," 849–80; Samantha Williams, "Earnings, Poor Relief, and the Economy of Makeshifts: Bedfordshire in the Early Years of the New Poor Law," 21–52, esp. 39.

12 Reay, *Rural Englands*, 78.

13 For one example, see Arthur Young, "Cottager's Garden Calendar," *Annals*, Vol. 36 (1801): 145–7.

14 Shaw-Taylor, "Parliamentary Enclosure," 645.

15 Sir William Pulteney, "Accounts of Cottagers," *Annals*, Vol. 44 (1806): 97–101, esp. 101.

16 Cobbett, *Cottage Economy*, 139.

17 Walter Rose, *Good Neighbours: Some Recollections of an English Village and its People*, 65; cited in Verdon, *Rural Women Workers in Nineteenth Century England*, 187; also Reay, *Rural Englands*, 76.

18 Arthur Young, *An Inquiry into the Propriety of Applying Wastes to the Better Maintenance and Support of the Poor*, 11.

19 *Economist*, "Scarcity of Labour," 13:628 (8 Sept. 1855): 979–80. (See chapter 9 for fuller context.)

20 Snell, *Parish and Belonging: Community, Identity, and Welfare in England and Wales, 1700–1950*, 4.

21 *Autobiography of William Cobbett*, 9, 99.

22 Cited in Snell, *Parish*, preface.

23 Cited in *Economist*, "Incendiary Fires in the Country," 2:20 (23 Jan. 1844): 388. (See chapter 9 for context.)

24 Ravenstone, *A Few Doubts*, 207.

25 *Economist*, "French Husbandry," 9:420 (13 Sept. 1851): 1012–13; *Economist*, "The Labourer's Panacea – The Allotment System," 2:62 (2 Nov. 1844): 1369–70.

26 Letter from Wilson to his wife in Barrington, *Servant*, 1:77.

27 *Economist*, "English Feelings Toward America," 19:944 (28 Sept. 1861): 1065–7.

28 Karl Marx, *Capital: Volume I*, 642.

Bibliography

This book relies on contemporary writings through the period from the 1760s to the 1860s: letters, memoirs, pamphlets, books, government and other reports, journals, and accounts in various newspapers.

The first section on Arthur Young, agricultural improvement, and rural unrest explores primarily the *Annals of Agriculture and Other Useful Arts* and the other copious writings of Arthur Young listed in the bibliography. The *Annals*, begun in 1784 and ending in 1806 (except for one more edition of leftover material a decade later), consists of forty-six volumes of Young's writings and letters to Young or (after 1793) to the Board of Agriculture and Internal Improvement. Also of importance were the various *General Views* on counties prepared for the Board of Agriculture under the direction of Young, again listed in the bibliography. Many of these were included in *Annals*. Other contemporary sources important for this section include the writings of William Cobbett, including his newspaper *Political Register*. Newspaper accounts, especially the *Times* and the *Morning Chronicle*, were useful for chapter 4 on rural unrest.

The second section relies primarily on the writings of Adam Smith, the Reverend Thomas Robert Malthus, Nassau Senior, and some of their contemporaries and critics, most importantly Piercy Ravenstone. Their works are listed in the bibliography. Also useful were the various volumes of the *Minutes of the Political Economy Club* – perhaps it is a singular indication of an obsession that one might find these fascinating and wish they were more extensive. The second chapter in this section also draws heavily from the thousands of pages of the *Report from His Majesty's Commissioners for Inquiring into the Administration and Practical Operation of the Poor Laws* of 1834, the various annual reports of the Poor Law Commission in subsequent years, and the Report of the Select Committee on the Andover Union Workhouse.

The core of the third section comes from a close reading of the *Economist* newspaper from 1843 to 1865. Various other contemporary works were useful in each of the chapters in this section. In chapter 7, the writings of Thomas Hodgskin and Herbert Spencer were important; in chapter 8, the critiques of William Thomas Thornton and J.S. Mill. In chapter 10, contemporary travel accounts and discussions of agriculture in Ireland before the famine, the report of the Devon Commission, and the report of the Poor Law Commission were all useful, as were, more sporadically, the writings of Nassau Senior and the letters between Malthus and Ricardo. An extensive range of Select Committee Reports in the House of Commons Papers to do with the ending of slavery, the apprentice system in Jamaica, and Jamaican peasant agriculture were also used. They are listed in the bibliography as well.

I list in the bibliography articles in *Annals of Agriculture* which were identified by a specific author. I also list the articles cited from Cobbett's *Political Register*. I do not attempt to list separately here the articles from the *Economist* or from the *Times*.

Part of the pleasure in writing this book derived from the eloquence and, often, humour of many of these contemporary accounts. For anyone who appreciates the use of language Cobbett is a joy to read. Though often irritating, the articles in the *Economist* were usually carefully crafted and evocative.

I make no attempt in the bibliography to separate contemporary accounts from all of the useful and sophisticated secondary works that were consulted in writing this; one can easily see how indebted I am to many of them throughout.

Abstract of the Final Report of the Commissioners of the Irish Poor Inquiry. London: F.C. Westley, 1837.

Abu-Lughod, Janet. *Before European Hegemony: The World System, AD 1250–1350.* Oxford: Oxford University Press, 1989.

Allen, Robert. *The British Industrial Revolution in Global Perspective.* Cambridge: Cambridge University Press, 2009.

– *Enclosure and the Yeoman.* Cambridge: Cambridge University Press, 1992.

– "The Nitrogen Hypothesis and the English Agricultural Revolution: A Biological Analysis." *Journal of Economic History* 68 (2008): 182–210.

Allen, Robert, and Carmac O'Grada. "On the Road Again with Arthur Young: English, Irish and French Agriculture during the Industrial Revolution." *Journal of Economic History* 48 (1988): 93–116.

Appleby, Joyce Oldham. *Economic Thought and Ideology in Seventeenth-Century England.* Princeton: Princeton University Press, 1978.

Archer, John. *"By a Flash and a Scare": Arson, Animal Maiming, and Poaching in East Anglia, 1815–1870.* London: Breviary Stuff Publications, 2010.

– *Social Unrest and Popular Protest in England, 1740–1840.* Cambridge: Cambridge University Press, 2000.

Armstrong, Alan. *Farmworkers: A Social and Economic History, 1770–1980.* London: Batsworth, 1988.

- "Rural Population Growth, Systems of Employment and Incomes" 641–728. In *Agricultural History of England and Wales, Vol VI, 1750–1850*, ed. G.E. Mingay, 641–728. Cambridge: Cambridge University Press, 1985.

Armstrong, Alan, and J.P. Huzel. "Labour II: Food, Shelter and Self-help, the Poor Law and the Position of the Labourer in Rural Society" In *The Agrarian History of England and Wales Vol. VI, 1750–1850*, ed. G.E. Mingay, 729–835. Cambridge: Cambridge University Press, 1985.

Arrese Reca, Angel. *La Identidad de The Economist*. Pamplona: Ediciones Universidad de Navarra, 1995.

Avery, John. *Progress, Poverty and Population: Re-reading Condorcet, Godwin and Malthus*. London: Routledge, 1997.

Bailey, John, and George Culley. *General View of the Agriculture of the county of Cumberland drawn up for the consideration of the Board of Agriculture and internal improvement*. 1794, 1813.

- *General View of the Agriculture of the county of Northumberland drawn up for the consideration of the Board of Agriculture and internal improvement*. 1794, 1813.

Baptist, Edward. *The Half Has Never Been Told: Slavery and the Making of American Capitalism*. New York: Basic Books, 2014.

Barrington, Emilie. *Servant of All: Pages from the Family, Social, and Political Life of my Father James Wilson*. 2 vols. London: Longman, Green and Co. Ltd, 1927.

Bashford, Alison, Duncan Kelly, and Shailaja Fennell. "Malthusian Moments: Introduction." *The Historical Journal* 63, Special Issue 1 (2002): 1–13.

Bateman, John. *The Great Landowners of Great Britain and Ireland*. New York: Leicester University Press, 1971.First published in 1876.

Bayly, C.A. *Indian Society and the Making of the British Empire*. Cambridge: Cambridge University Press, 1987.

Beaumont, Gustave de. *Ireland: social, political and religious vol. I*. London: Richard Bentley, 1839.

Beckert, Sven. *The Empire of Cotton: A Global History*. New York: Knopf, 2014.

Belich, James. *Replenishing the Earth*. Oxford: Oxford University Press, 2009.

Bentham, Jeremy. "Situation and Relief of the Poor." *Annals of Agriculture* 29 (1797): 393–427.

Bernard, Trevor. "An Account of a Cottage and Garden." *Annals of Agriculture* 30 (1798): 1–9.

Besson, Jean. "Land Tenure and the Free Villages of Trelawny, Jamaica: A Case Study in Caribbean Peasant Response to Emancipation." *Slavery and Abolition* 5:1 (1984): 3–23.

- *Martha Brae's Two Histories*. Chapel Hill: University of North Carolina Press, 2002.

Bigelow, John. *Jamaica in 1850*. Chicago: University of Illinois Press, 2006. Originally published New York, 1851.

Billingsley, John. "Uselessness of Commons to the Poor" *Annals of Agriculture* 31 (1798): 27–32.

Blaug, Marc. "The Myth of the Old Poor Law and the Making of the New" *Journal of Economic History* 23:2 (1963): 151–84.
– "The Poor Law Report Revisited." *Journal of Economic History* 24:2 (1964): 229–45.
– *Ricardian Economics: A Historical Study* New Haven: Yale University Press, 1958
Bohstedt, John. *The Politics of Provisions: Food Riots, Moral Economy and Market Transitions in England, c, 1550–1850*. Farnham, Surrey: Ashgate Books, 2010.
Bowden, Peter. "Agricultural Prices, Wages, Farm Profits and Rents." In *The Agrarian History of England and Wales, Vol. V, 1640–1740*, ed. Joan Thirsk, 1–118. Cambridge: Cambridge University Press, 1985.
Bowen, H.V. *The Business of Empire: The East India Company and Imperial Britain, 1756–1833.* Cambridge: Cambridge University Press, 2005.
Boys, J. "Crops and Poor." *Annals of Agriculture* 36 (1800): 368–70.
Brady, Eugene. "A Reconsideration of the Lancashire Cotton Famine." *Agricultural History* 37:3 (1963): 156–62.
Brassely, Paul. "Northumberland and Durham," 30–58. In *The Agrarian History of England and Wales, Vol. I, Regional Farming Systems*, ed. Joan Thirsk, 30–58. Cambridge: Cambridge University Press, 1984.
Briggs, John. *The Cotton Trade of India Part I.* London: John W. Parker, 1839.
– *The Cotton Trade of India Part II.* London: John W. Parker, 1840.
Brown, John. "The Condition of England and the Standard of Living: Cotton Textiles in the Northwest, 1806–1850." *Journal of Economic History* 50:3 (1990): 591–614.
Brunt, Liam. "Rehabilitating Arthur Young." *Economic History Review* 56:2 (2003): 265–99.
Buchardt, Jeremy. *The Allotment Movement in England, 1793–1873.* Woodbridge, UK: Boydell Press, 2002.
Butler, Kathleen Mary. *The Economics of Emancipation, 1823–1843.* Chapel Hill: University of North Carolina Press, 1995.
Cardoso, José Luis. "The Political Economy of Rising Capitalism." In *The Cambridge History of Capitalism, Vol. I*, ed. Larry Neal and Jeffrey G. Williamson, 574–99. Cambridge: Cambridge University Press, 2014.
Carlyle, Thomas. *Occasional Discourse on the N[*****] Question.* London: n.p., 1853.
Census of Ireland for the Year 1851 Part V: The Table of Deaths. British Parliamentary Papers.
Chambers, J.D. "Enclosure and the Labour Supply in the Industrial Revolution." *Economic History Review* 5:3 (1953): 319–43.
Chambers, J.D., and G.E. Mingay. *The Agricultural Revolution.* London: Batsford, 1966.
Charlesworth, Andrew, ed. *An Atlas of Rural Protest in Britain, 1548–1900.* Philadelphia: University of Pennsylvania Press, 1983.
Checkland, S.G., and E.O.A., eds. *The Poor Law Report of 1834.* London: Penguin, 1974.
CIVIS. "Management of the Poor in Leeds" *Annals of Agriculture* 27 (1796): 408–29.

Claeys, Gregory. "Malthus and Godwin: Rights, Utility and Productivity." *The Historical Journal* 63 (2002): 52–73.

Clays, Christopher. "Landlords and Estate Management in England." In *The Agrarian History of England and Wales Vol. V, II*, ed. Joan Thirsk, 119–251. Cambridge: Cambridge University Press, 1985.

Cobbett, William. *The Autobiography of William Cobbett*. Edited by William Reitzell. London: Faber and Faber Ltd., 1962.

– *Cottage Economy*. London: n.p., 1823.

– "Letter to Lord John Russell." *Political Register*, 31 July 1824, 289.

– "Letter to the People of the United States of America." *Political Register*, 8 June 1816, 720–1.

– *Rural Rides in the Counties of Surrey, Kent, Hampshire, etc.* London: np, 1830.

– "To the Bull-frog Farmers: On the Price of Corn and the Wages of Labour." *Political Register*, 11 Sept. 1824, 671–5.

– "To Parson Malthus: On the Rights of the Poor; and on the cruelty recommended by him to be exercised towards the poor." *Political Register*, 8 May 1819, 1019–47.

– "To the Yeomanry Cavalry on the Fires." *Political Register*, 7 January 1832, 104–7.

Connell, K.H. "Population." In *Social Life in Ireland*, ed. R.B. McDowell, 85–97. Dublin: Three Candles, 1963.

Coogan, Tim Pat. *The Famine Plot: England's Role in Ireland's Great Tragedy*. New York: Palgrave MacMillan, 2012.

The Cotton Dearth. Bristol Selected Pamphlets, 1858.

Cousens, S.H. "Regional Death Rates in Ireland during the Great Famine, from 1846 to 1851." *Population Studies* 14:1 (1960): 55–74.

Crutchely, John. "On Management of the Poor in Rutlandshire." *Annals of Agriculture* 22 (1793): 416–26.

Culley, George. "Land for the Poor." *Annals of Agriculture* 36 (1800): 385–7.

Cushman, Gregory. *Guano and the Opening of the Pacific World: A Global Ecological History*. Cambridge: Cambridge University Press, 2013.

Davies, David. *The Case of Labourers in Husbandry Stated and Considered*. London: G.G. and J. Richardson, 1795.

Digest of Evidence Taken before Her Majesty's Commission of Inquiry (Devon Commission). Dublin: Alexander Thom, 1848.

Dinwiddy, J.R. "Charles Hall, Early English Socialist." *International Journal of Social History* 21:2 (1976): 256–76.

Donelly Jr., S. *The Great Irish Potato Famine*. Gloucestershire: Sutton, 2001.

Driver, Felix. *Power and Pauperism: The Workhouse System, 1834–1884*. Cambridge: Cambridge University Press, 1993.

Duncan, Colin. *The Centrality of Agriculture*. Montreal: McGill-Queens University Press, 1996.

Dyck, Ian. *Cobbett and Rural Popular Culture*. Cambridge: Cambridge University Press, 1992.

Edwards, Ruth Dudley. *The Pursuit of Reason: The Economist 1843–1993*. London: Hamish Hamilton, 1993.

Empson, William. "Review of T.R. Malthus, *Principles of Political Economy* and memoir." *Edinburgh Review,* Jan. 1837. Reprinted in B. Semmel, ed., *Occasional Papers of T.R. Malthus on Ireland, Population and Political Economy*. New York: Burt Franklin, 1963.

Engels, Friederich. *The Condition of the Working Class in England*. Moscow: Progress Publishers, 1972.

Fideler, Paul. *Social Welfare in Pre-Industrial England*. New York: Palgrave, 2006.

Finkelstein, A. *Harmony and Balance: An Intellectual History of Seventeenth-Century English Economic Thought*. Ann Arbor: University of Michigan Press, 2000.

Fitzpatrick, Barbara Laning. "Arthur Young and 'Ten or a Dozen Booksellers': The Publication of the *Universal Museum* in 1762." *Studies in Newspaper and Periodical History* 2:1 (1994): 35–43.

Fleischman, Richard. *Conditions of Life among the Cotton Workers of Southeastern Lancashire*. New York: Garland Publishing, 1985.

Foley, Duncan. *Adam's Fallacy: A Guide to Economic Theology*. Cambridge: Harvard University Press, 2006.

Fraser, Derek, ed. *The New Poor Law in the Nineteenth Century*. New York: St. Martin's Press, 1976.

French, Henry. "How Dependent were the 'Dependent Poor'? Poor Relief and the Life-course in Terling, Essex, 1762–1834." *Continuity and Change* 130 (2015): 192–222.

Fussell, G.E. "My Impressions of Arthur Young." *Agricultural History* 17 (1943): 135–44.

Gazetteer of the Bombay Presidency Vol. 14. Government of Ahmedabad, 1882.

Gazely, John G. *The Life of Arthur Young, 1741–1820*. Philadelphia, PA: American Philosophical Society, 1973.

"General Enclosures Act." *Annals of Agriculture* 35 (1800): 140–2.

Goddard, Nicolas. "The Development and Influence of Agricultural Periodicals and Newspapers, 1780–1870." *Agricultural History Review* 31 (1983): 116–21.

Godwin, William. *The Enquirer: Reflections on Education, Manners, and Literature in a Series of Essays*. London: G.G. and J. Robinson, 1797.

– *An Enquiry Concerning Political Justice and its Influence on General Virtue and Happiness*. London: G.G. and J. Robinson, 1793.

Griffin, Carl. *The Rural War: Captain Swing and the Politics of Protest*. Manchester: Manchester University Press, 2012.

Guha, Ranajit. *A Rule of Property for Bengal. 2nd Edition*. Durham, NC: Duke University Press, 1966.

Haakonssen, Knud, ed. *Cambridge Companion to Adam Smith*. Cambridge: Cambridge University Press, 2006.

Halévy, Elie. *Thomas Hodgskin*. Edited and translated by A.J. Taylor. London: Ernest Benn Ltd., 1956.

Hall, Catherine. *Civilising Subjects: Metropole and Colony in the English Imagination, 1830–1867*. Chicago: University of Chicago Press, 2002.

Hall, Charles. *The Effects of Civilization on the People of the European States*. London: John Minter Morgan, 1849.

Hall, Douglas. *Free Jamaica, 1838–1865*. New Haven: Yale University Press, 1959.

Hallett, Christine. "The Attempt to Understand Puerperal Fever in the Eighteenth and Early Nineteenth Centuries: The Influence of Inflammation Theory." *Medical History* 49:1 (2005): 1–28.

Hammond, J.L. and Barbara. *The Village Labourer, 1760–1820: A Study in the Government of England before the Reform Bill*. London: Longmans, 1911.

Handy, Jim. *Tiny Engines of Abundance: A History of Peasant Productivity and Repression* Winnipeg: Fernwood, 2022.

Hanley, Ryan Patrick, ed. *Adam Smith: His Life, Thought, and Legacy*. Princeton, NJ: Princeton University Press, 2016.

Harley, J. Knick. "British Industrialization Before 1841: Evidence of Slower Growth during the Industrial Revolution." *The Journal of Economic History* 42:2 (1982): 267–89.

Havinden, Michael. "Agricultural Progress in Open-Field Oxfordshire." *The Agricultural History Review* 9 (1961): 73–83.

Heertje, Arnold. "An Essay on the Catalogue of the Library of Piero Saffra, edited by G. de Vivo." *History of Economics Review* 66:1 (2017): 63–71.

Hey, David. "The Northwest Midlands." In *The Agrarian History of England and Wales, Vol. I, Regional Farming Systems*, ed. Joan Thirsk, 129–38. Cambridge: Cambridge University Press, 1984.

– "Yorkshire and Lancashire." In *The Agrarian History of England and Wales, Vol. I, Regional Farming Systems*, ed. Joan Thirsk, 59–88. Cambridge: Cambridge University Press, 1984.

Higgs, Henry. "Arthur Young (1741–1820)." In *Dictionary of National Biography* Vol. 63, ed. Sidney Lee. London: Elder Smith & Co., 1900.

Hill, Christopher. *The World Turned Upside Down*. London: Penguin Books, 1972.

Himmelfarb, Gertrude. *The Idea of Poverty: England in the Industrial Age*. New York: Alfred A. Knopf, 1984.

Hindle, Steve. *On the Parish? The Micro-Politics of Poor Relief in Rural England*. Oxford: Clarendon Press, 2004.

Hirschman, Albert O. *The Passions and the Interests: Political Arguments for Capitalism Before Its Triumph*. Princeton, NJ: Princeton University Press, 1977.

Hobsbawm, E. *Industry and Empire*. London: Penguin Books, 1969.

Hobsbawm, E., and G. Rudé. *Captain Swing*. London: Lawrence and Wishart, 1969.

Hodgskin, Thomas. *Labour Defended Against the Claims of Capital, or the Unproductiveness of Capital*. New York: Augustus M. Kelley, 1969.

– *The Natural and Artificial Rights of Property Contrasted*. London: B. Stell, Patermaster Row, 1832.

Holderness, B.A. "East Anglia and the Fens." In *The Agrarian History of England and Wales, Vol. I, Regional Farming Systems*, ed. Joan Thirsk, 197–328. Cambridge: Cambridge University Press, 1984.

Holt, Thomas. *The Problem of Freedom: Race, Labor, and Politics in Jamaica and Britain, 1832–1938*. Baltimore: Johns Hopkins University Press, 1992.

Horrell, S., and Jane Humphries. "Old Questions, New Data, and Alternative Perspectives: Families' Living Standards in the Industrial Revolution." *Journal of Economic History* 52:4 (1992): 849–80.

Hossain, Hameeda. *The Company Weavers of Bengal: The East India Company and the Organization of Textile Production in Bengal, 1750–1813*. Delhi: Oxford University Press, 1988.

Howlett, John. *Enclosures, A Cause of Improved Agriculture*. London: W. Richardson, 1787.

Hueman, Gad. *The Killing Time: The Morant Bay Rebellion, Jamaica*. Knoxville: University of Tennessee Press, 1995.

Humphries, Jane. "Enclosures, Common Rights, and Women: The Proletarianization of Families in the Late Eighteenth and Early Nineteenth Centuries." *The Journal of Economic History* 50:1 (1990): 17–42.

Hutchison, T.W. *Before Adam Smith: The Emergence of Political Economy, 1662–1776*. Oxford: Basil Blackwell, 1988.

James, Patricia. *Population Malthus: His Life and Times*. London: Routledge. 1979.

Jones, Gareth Stedman. "Malthus, Nineteenth-Century Socialism, and Marx." *The Historical Journal* 63 (2002): 91–106.

Jones, Peter. *Agricultural Enlightenment: Knowledge, Technology, and Nature*. Oxford: Oxford University Press, 2016.

– "Arthur Young, For and Against." *English Historical Review* 127: 528 (2012): 1100–20.

Kay-Shuttleworth, Sir James. *The Moral and Physical Condition of the Working Classes Employed in Cotton Manufacture in Manchester*. London: J. Ridgeway, 1832.

Kennedy, Gavin. "Adam Smith: Some Popular Uses and Abuses." In *Adam Smith: His Life, Thought and Legacy*, ed. Ryan Patrick Hanley, 461–77. Princeton: Princeton University Press, 2016.

Kerridge, Eric. *The Agricultural Revolution*. London: George Allen and Unwin, 1967.

– "The Agricultural Revolution Reconsidered." *Agricultural History* 43:4 (1969): 463–76.

Killen, J., et al. *The Famine Decade: Contemporary Accounts*. Belfast: Blackstaff Press, 1995.

King, Peter. "Gleaners, Farmers and Failure of Legal Sanctions, 1750–1850." *Past and Present* 125 (1988): 116–50.

King, Steven, and Allanah Tomkins, eds. *The Poor in England: An Economy of Makeshifts*. Manchester: Manchester University Press, 2003.

Kohl, J.G. *Travels in Ireland*. London: Bruce and Wyld, 1844.

Komlos, John. "The Secular Trend in the Biological Standard of Living in the United Kingdom, 1730–1860." *Economic History Review* 46:1 (1993): 115–44.

Laing, Samuel. *Notes of a Traveler.* London: Longman, Brown, Green and Longmans, 1842.

Lavrovksy, V.M. "Parliamentary Enclosures in the County of Suffolk (1797–1814)." *Economic History Review* 3:2 (1937): 186–206.

Lees, Lynn Hollen. *The Solidarity of Strangers: The English Poor Laws and the People, 1700–1948.* Cambridge: Cambridge University Press, 1998.

Levy, S. Leon. *Nassau Senior: The Prophet of Modern Capitalism.* Boston, MA: Bruce Humphries, 1943.

Lindert, Peter, and Jeffrey Williamson. "English Workers' Living Standards During the Industrial Revolution: A New Look." *Economic History Review* 36 (1983): 1–25.

Longmate, Norman. *The Hungry Mills: The Story of the Lancashire Cotton Famine.* London: Maurice Temple Smith, 1978.

– *The Workhouse.* London: Ashgate Publishing, 1974.

L'Orster, J. "Effects of Enclosures." *Annals of Agriculture* 36 (1800): 114–19.

Malcolmson, R.W. "Ways of Getting a Living in Eighteenth Century England." In *On Work*, ed. R. Phal, 48–60. Oxford: Oxford University Press, 1988.

Malthus, Reverend Thomas Robert. *Definitions in Political Economy.* London: John Murray, 1827.

– *An Essay on the Principle of Population.* Edited by Patricia James. Cambridge: Cambridge University Press, 1989.

– *An Essay on the Principle of Population as it Affects the Future Improvement of Society* … London: J. Johnson, 1798.

– *A Letter to Samuel Whitbread.* London: J. Johnson, 1807.

– *Principles of Political Economy.* Edited by John Pullen. Cambridge: Cambridge University Press, 1989.

Mandeville, Bernard. *The Fable of the Bees: or, Private Vices, Publick Benefits.* Oxford: Clarendon Press, 1957.

Mann, J.A. "On the Cotton Trade of India" *Journal of the Royal Asiatic Society* 17 (1860): 346–87.

Mantena, Karuna. *Alibis of Empire: Henry Maine and the Ends of Liberal Imperialism.* Princeton: Princeton University Press, 2010.

Marshall, P.J. *Bengal: The British Bridgehead.* Cambridge: Cambridge University Press, 1988.

Marx, Karl. *Capital.* Vol. I. New York: International Publishers, 1967.

Mayhew, Robert. *Malthus: The Life and Times of an Unlikely Prophet.* Cambridge: Belknap Press, 2014.

– ed. *New Perspectives on Malthus.* Cambridge: Cambridge University Press, 2016.

McDowell, R.B., ed. *Social Life in Ireland.* Dublin: Three Candles, 1963.

McNally, David. *Against the Market: Political Economy, Market Socialism and other Marxist Critique.* London: Verso, 1993.

McPherson, W.J. "Investment in Indian Railways, 1845–1875." *The Economic History Review* 8:2 (1955): 177–86.

Meek, R.I., D.D. Raphael, and Peter Stein, eds. *The Glasgow Edition of the Works and Correspondence of Adam Smith, Vol 5: Lectures on Jurisprudence.* Oxford Scholarly Editions Online.

Mehta, Partatp Bhanu. "Self-Interest and other Interests," In *Cambridge Companion to Adam Smith*, ed. Knud Haakonssen, 246–9. Cambridge: Cambridge University Press, 2006.

Mehta, Singh. *Liberalism and Empire: A Study in Nineteenth Century British Liberal Thought.* Chicago: Chicago University Press, 1999.

Metcalfe, Thomas. *The Ideologies of the Raj: The New Cambridge History of India, Vol. 3.* Cambridge: Cambridge University Press, 1994.

Mill, John Stuart. *Principles of Political Economy.* London: George Routledge and Sons Ltd., 1848.

Mills, Reverend. "Account of a Hundred Houses of Industry." *Annals of Agriculture* 6 (1786): 331–50.

Mingay, G.E., ed. *The Agrarian History of England and Wales Vol. VI, 1750–1850.* Cambridge: Cambridge University Press, 1985.

– ed. *Arthur Young and His Times.* London: Macmillan, 1975.

– "The Course of Rents in the Age of Malthus," In *Malthus in His Time*, ed. Michael Turner, 85–95. London: Palgrave Macmillan, 1986.

– "The East Midlands." In *The Agrarian History of England Wales Vol I, Regional Farming Systems*, ed. Joan Thirsk, 89–128. Cambridge: Cambridge University Press, 1984.

– *A Social History of the English Countryside.* London: Routledge, 1990.

Mitchison, Rosalind. *Agricultural Sir John: The Life of Sir John Sinclair of Ulbster, 1754–1835.* London: Geffrey Bles, 1962.

Mokyr, Joel. *The Enlightened Economy.* New Haven: Yale University Press, 2009.

– *Why Ireland Starved.* London: George Allen and Unwin, 1983.

Moncure, James. "James Wilson and *The Economist*, 1805–1860." PhD dissertation, Columbia University, 1960.

Morgan, Kenneth. *The Birth of Industrial Britain: Economic Change, 1750–1850.* Oxford: Routledge, 2013.

Moselle, Boaz. "Allotments, Enclosure, and Proletarianization in Nineteenth-Century Southern England." *Economic History Review* 48:3 (1995): 482–500.

Murray, Julie. "Company Rules: Burke, Hastings and the Specter of the Modern Liberal State." *Eighteenth Century Studies* 41:1 (2007): 55–69.

Neal, Larry, and Jeffrey G. Williamson, eds. *The Cambridge History of Capitalism, Vol. I.* Cambridge: Cambridge University Press, 2014.

Neeson, J.M. *Commoners: Common Right, Enclosure and Social Change in England, 1700–1820.* Cambridge: Cambridge University Press, 1993.

– "English Enclosures and British Peasants: Current Debates about Rural Social Structure in Britain, c.1750–1870." *Economic History Yearbook* 41:2 (2000): 17–31.

Nichol, Sir George. *A History of the Irish Poor Law.* London: John Murray, 1856.

Nicolas, Stephen, and Richard Steckel. "Heights and Living Standards of English Workers during the Early Years of Industrialization." *The Journal of Economic History* 51:4 (1991): 937–57.

O'Flaherty, Niall. "Malthus and the End of Poverty." In *New Perspectives on Malthus,* ed. Robert Mayhew, 74–104. Cambridge: Cambridge University Press, 2016.

O'Grada, C. *Ireland: A New Economic History.* Oxford: Clarendon Press, 1994.

– "The Population of Ireland, 1700–1900." *Annales de Démographie Historique* (1979): 281–99.

Overton, Mark. *Agricultural Revolution in England: The Transformation of the Agrarian Economy, 1500–1850.* Cambridge: Cambridge University Press, 1996.

– "Re-establishing the English Agricultural Revolution." *Agricultural History Review* 44 (1996): 1–20.

Parkinson, John. "Cottagers' Lands." *Annals of Agriculture* 36 (1800): 360–3.

Parthasarthi, Prasannan. *The Transition to a Colonial Economy: Weavers, Merchants, and Kings in South India, 1720–1800.* Cambridge: Cambridge University Press, 2001.

Patriquin, Larry. "Agrarian Capitalism and Poor Relief in England, c. 1500–1790." In *The Capitalist State and Its Economy,* ed. Paul Zarembka, 3–50. Amsterdam: Elsevier B.V., 2005.

Peacock, A.J. *Bread or Blood: A Study of Agrarian Riots in East Anglia.* London: Victor Gollanz, 1965.

Perelman, Michael. *The Invention of Capitalism.* Durham, NC: University of North Carolina Press, 2000.

Petty, William. *Political Arithmetick.* London: n.p., 1690.

Phelps Brown, H., and S.V. Hopkins. "Seven Centuries of Building Wages." *Economica* 24 (1955): 296–314.

Phillipson, Nicholas. "Smith and the Scottish Enlightenment." In *Adam Smith: His Life, Thought, and Legacy,* ed. Ryan Patrick Hanley, 105–22. Princeton, NJ: Princeton University Press, 2016.

Pitt, William. *General View of the Agriculture of the county of Leicestershire drawn up for the consideration of the Board of Agriculture and internal improvement.* 1809.

– *General View of the Agriculture of the county of Northampton drawn up for the consideration of the Board of Agriculture and internal improvement.* 1813.

– *General View of the Agriculture of the county of Stafford drawn up for the consideration of the Board of Agriculture and internal improvement.* 1794.

– *General View of the Agriculture of the county of Worcestershire drawn up for the consideration of the Board of Agriculture and internal improvement.* 1813.

Pitts, Jennifer. *A Turn to Empire: The Rise of Liberal Imperialism in Britain and France.* Princeton: Princeton University Press, 2010.

Political Economy Club: Vol I London: n.p., 1860.

Political Economy Club: Vol. IV, Minutes and Proceedings, 1821–1882 London: np. 1882.

Pomerantz, Kenneth. *The Great Divergence: China, Europe and the Making of the Modern World Economy.* Princeton: Princeton University Press, 2000.

Pomerantz, Kenneth, and Steve Topick. *The World That Trade Created.* New York: M.E. Sharpe, 2000.

Poor Law Commissioners' Report, 1834. London: H.M. Stationary Office, 1905.

Pulteney, Sir William. "Accounts of Cottagers." *Annals of Agriculture* 44 (1806): 97–111.

Ranelagh, J.O. *A Short History of Ireland.* Cambridge: Cambridge University Press, 1994.

Raphael, D.D., and A.L. Macfie, eds. *The Theory of Moral Sentiments.* Oxford: Oxford University Press, 1976.

Rashid, Salim. *The Myth of Adam Smith.* Cheltenham, UK: Edward Elgar Publishers, 1998.

Ravenstone, Piercy. *A Few Doubts as to the Correctness of Some Opinions Generally Entertained on the Subjects of Population and Political Economy.* New York: Augustus M. Kelly, 1966.

– *Thoughts on the Funding System and its Effects.* London: J. Murray, 1824.

Ray, Bhariti. "The Genesis of Railway Development in Hyderabad State: A Case Study of Nineteenth Century British Imperialism." *Indian Economic and Social History Review* 21:45 (1984): 45–69.

Reay, Barry. *Rural Englands: Labouring Lives in the Nineteenth Century.* New York: Palgrave MacMillan, 2004.

Reed, Mick, and Roger Wells, eds. *Class, Conflict and Protest in the English Countryside, 1700–1880.* London: Frank Cass, 1990.

Rees, Joan. *Matilda Betham-Edwards: Novelist, Travel-Writer and Francophile.* Hastings: The Hastings Press, 2006.

Report from His Majesty's Commissioners for Inquiring into the Administration and Practical Operations of the Poor Laws, *House of Commons Papers*, 44, 1834.

Report on the Poor Laws of this Kingdom, *House of Commons Papers*, 485, 1816.

Report from The Select Committee on Andover Union, *House of Commons, Select Committee on Andover Union*, 1847.

Report of the Select Committee Appointed to take into Consideration the Means of Promoting the Cultivation and Improvement of the Waste, Uninclosed, and Unproductive Lands of the Kingdom. *House of Commons Papers*, 9, 1795–6.

Report of the Select Committee on the Extinction of Slavery throughout the British Dominions, *House of Commons Papers*, 721, 1831–2.

Report from the Select Committee on the Poor Laws, *House of Commons Papers* 462, B, 1817.

Report of the Select Committee on the West Indian Colonies, *House of Commons Papers*, 479, 1842.

Report of the Society for Bettering the Condition and Increasing the Comforts of the Poor London, 1798.

Return of Owners of the Land, 1873 … presented to both Houses of Parliament. London, 1875.

Ricardo, David. *Principles of Political Economy and Taxation*. New York: Prometheus Books, 1966.

Rose, Mary. *The Gregs of Quarry Bank Mill: The Rise and Decline of a Family Firm, 1750–1914*. Cambridge: Cambridge University Press, 1986.

Rose, Michael. "Settlement, Removal and the New Poor Law." In *The New Poor Law in the Nineteenth Century*, ed. Derek Fraser, 25–42. New York: St. Martin's Press, 1976.

Rose, Walter. *Good Neighbours: Some Reflections on an English Village and its People*. Cambridge: Cambridge University Press, 1964.

Rothschild, Emma. *Economic Sentiments: Adam Smith, Condorcet and the Enlightenment*. Cambridge: Harvard University Press, 2001.

Ruggles, Thomas. *A History of the Poor: Their Rights, duties and laws respecting them*. London: W. Richardson, 1797.

– "Land for the Poor" *Annals of Agriculture* 36 (1800): 354–5.

Rule, John, and Roger Wells, eds. *Crime, Protest and Popular Politics in Southern England, 1740–1850*. London: Hambledon Press, 1997.

Saffra, Piero, ed. *The Works and Correspondence of David Ricardo, Vol. 7, 1816–1818*. Indianapolis: Liberty Fund, 2005.

Salaman, Redcliffe. *The History and Social Influence of the Potato*. Cambridge: Cambridge University Press, 1985.

Sandbrook James. *William Cobbett*. London: Routledge and Kegan Paul, 1973.

Sartori, Andrew. *Liberalism in Empire: An Alternative History*. Oakland: University of California Press, 2014.

Scott, Joseph. "Crops, Markets, etc." *Annals of Agriculture* 36 (1800): 376–8.

Second Annual Report of the Poor Law Commissioners, 1836.

Semmel, B., ed. *Occasional Papers of T.R. Malthus on Ireland, Population and Political Economy*. New York: Burt Franklin, 1963.

Sen, Sudipta. *Empire of Free Trade: The East India Company and the Making of the Colonial Marketplace*. Philadelphia: University of Pennsylvania Press, 1998.

Senior, Nassau. *Four Introductory Lectures on Political Economy*. London: J. Murray, 1852.

– *An Introductory Lecture on Political Economy*. London: J. Murray, 1831.

– *Industrial Efficiency and Social Economy*. Edited by S. Leon Levy. New York: Holt, 1928.

– *Journals, Conversations and Essays Relating to Ireland, Vol II*. London: Longmans, Green and Co., 1868.

– *A Letter to Lord Howick on a Legal Provision for the Irish Poor*. London: J. Murray, 1831.

– *Letters on the Factory Act as it Affects the Cotton Manufacture*. London: B. Fellows, 1844.

– *Three Lectures on the Rate of Wages*. London: J. Murray, 1830.

– *Two Lectures on Population*. London: Saunders and Otley, 1828.

Shapiro, Michael. *Reading Adam Smith: Desire, History and Value*. Newbury Park, CA: Rowen and Little Publishers, 1993.

Shaw-Taylor, Leigh. "Labourers, Cows, Common-Rights and Parliamentary Enclosure: The Evidence of Contemporary Comment c. 1760–1810." *Past and Present* 171 (2001): 95–126.

– "Parliamentary Enclosure and the Emergence of an English Agricultural Proletariat." *Journal of Economic History* 61:3 (2001): 640–62.

Silver, Arthur. *Manchester Men and Indian Cotton, 1847–1872*. Manchester: Manchester University Press, 1966.

Sinclair, John. *Essays on Miscellaneous Subjects*. London: W. Strahan, 1802.

– "General Enclosure Bill." *Annals of Agriculture* 26 (1796): 85.

– "Observations on the Means of Enabling a Cottager to Keep a Cow by the Produce of a Small Portion of Arable Land." *Annals of Agriculture* 36 (1801): 231–48.

Sirwar, Firoj High. "A Comparative Study of Zamindari, Raiyatwair, and Mahalwari Land Revenue Settlements; The Colonial Mechanism of Surplus Extraction in 19th Century British India." *Journal of Humanities and Social Sciences* 2:4 (2012): 16–26.

Smith, Adam. *An Inquiry into the Nature and Causes of the Wealth of Nations*. London: W. Strahan, 1776.

– *The Theory of Moral Sentiments*. Amherst, NY: Prometheus Books, 2000.

Smith, Will, and Mike Murphy, eds. *Atlas of the Great Famine, 1845–52*. Cork: Cork University Press, 2012.

Snell, K.D.M. "Agricultural Seasonal Employment: The Standard of Living and Women's Work in the South and East, 1690–1860." *Economic History Review* 34 (1981): 407–37.

– *Annals of the Labouring Poor*. Cambridge: Cambridge University Press, 1985.

– *Parish and Belonging: Community, Identity and Welfare in England and Wales, 1700–1950*. Cambridge: Cambridge University Press, 2006.

– "Pauper Settlement and the Right to Poor Relief in England and Wales." *Continuity and Change* 6:3 (1991): 375–415.

Spencer, Herbert. *An Autobiography Vol I*. London: Williams and Northgate, 1904.

– *Social Statics: or, The Conditions Essential to Human Happiness Specified, and the First of them Developed*. New York: Appleton and Company, 1915.

Stanley, J. *Ireland and Her Evils: Poor Laws Fully Considered*. Dublin: Milliken and Sons, 1836.

Stern, Phillip. *The Company State: Corporate Sovereignty and the Early Modern Foundations of the British Empire in India*. Oxford: Oxford University Press, 2011.

Stokes, Eric. *The Peasant Armed: The Indian Revolt of 1857*. Edited by C.A. Bayly. Oxford: Clarendon Press, 1987.

Sturt, George [George Bourne]. *Change in the Village*. London: Duckworth & Co., 1912.

Tate, W.E. *The English Village Community and the Enclosure Movements*. London: Gollanz, 1967.

Taylor, W.W. *Men Versus the State: Herbert Spencer and Late Victorian Individualism*. Oxford: Clarendon Press, 1992.

Thick, Malcolm. "Market Gardening in England and Wales." In *The Agricultural History of England and Wales, Vol V: II Agrarian Change*, ed. Joan Thirsk, 502–32. Cambridge: Cambridge University Press, 1985.

Third Annual Report of the Poor Law Commissioners, 1837.

Thirsk, Joan. "Agricultural Innovations and Their Diffusion." In *The Agrarian History of England and Wales, Vol V, 1640–1740*, ed. Joan Thirsk, 533–89. Cambridge: Cambridge University Press, 1985.

– "Agricultural Policy: Public Debates and Legislation." In *The Agrarian History of England and Wales, Vol V:II Agrarian Change*, ed. Joan Thirsk, 298–388. Cambridge: Cambridge University Press, 1985.

– *Alternative Agriculture: A History from the Black Death to the Present Day*. Oxford: Oxford University Press, 1997.

– ed. *Chapters from the Agrarian History of England and Wales, 1500–1750: Vol. 3*. Cambridge: Cambridge University Press, 1990.

– "Enclosing and Engrossing." In *Chapters from the Agrarian History of England and Wales, 1500–1750: Vol. 3*, 54–109. Cambridge: Cambridge University Press, 1990.

– "The South Midlands." In *The Agrarian History of England and Wales Vol 1, Regional Farming Systems*, ed. Joan Thirsk, 159–96. Cambridge: Cambridge University Press, 1984.

Thomas, Brinley. "Feeding England during the Industrial Revolution: A View from the Celtic Fringe." *Agricultural History* 56 (1982): 328–42.

Thompson, E.P. *Customs in Common*. New York: The New Press, 1993.

– *The Making of the English Working Class*. London: Penguin Books, 1991.

Thompson, F.M.L. *English Landed Society in the Nineteenth Century*. London: Routledge & Kegan Paul, 1966.

– "The Social Distribution of Landed Property in England since the 16th Century." *Economic History Review* 19 (1966): 505–17.

Thompson, Thomas. "Extract from an Account of a Provision for Keeping Cows at Humberston, the county of Lincoln." *Reports of the Society for Bettering the Condition and Increasing the Comforts of the Poor*. Vol. 2 (1799): 133–8.

Thornton, William Thomas. *Over-population and its Remedy*. London: Longman, Brown, Green and Longmans, 1846.

– *A Plea for Peasant Proprietors, with the Outlines of a Plan for their Establishment in Ireland*. London: MacMillan and Co., 1874.

Tocqueville, Alexis de. *Journeys to England and Ireland*. New Haven: Yale University Press, 1958.

Tombs, Robert. *The English and Their History*. New York: Vintage Books, 2014.

Townsend, Joseph. *A Dissertation on the Poor Laws*. Berkeley: University of California Press, 1971.

Turner, Michael. *Enclosures in Britain, 1750–1830*. London: Macmillan, 1984.

– *English Parliamentary Enclosure: Its Historical, Geographical and Economic History*. Folkestone, Kent: Wm. Dawson and Sons, 1980.

– ed. *Malthus in His Time.* London: Palgrave Macmillan, 1986.

Turner, M.E., J.V. Beckett, and B. Afton. *Farm Production in England, 1700–1914.* Oxford: Oxford University Press, 2001.

Vancouver, Charles. *General View of the Agriculture of the county of Cambridge drawn up for the consideration of the Board of Agriculture and internal improvement.* 1794.

– *General View of the Agriculture of the county of Devon drawn up for the consideration of the Board of Agriculture and internal improvement.* 1808.

– *General View of the Agriculture of the county of Essex drawn up for the consideration of the Board of Agriculture and internal improvement.* 1795.

– *General View of the Agriculture of the county of Hampshire drawn up for the consideration of the Board of Agriculture and internal improvement.* 1810.

Verdon, Nicola. *Rural Women Workers in Nineteenth Century England: Gender, Work, and Wages.* Woodbridge, Suffolk: Boydell Press, 2002.

Viner, Jacob. "An Unpublished Letter of Ricardo to Malthus." *Journal of Political Economy* 41:1 (1933): 117–20.

Wells, Roger. "Resistance to the New Poor Law in the Rural South." In *Crime, Protest and Popular Politics in Southern England, 1740–1850,* ed. John Rule and Roger Wells, 91–126. London: Hambledon Press, 1997.

– "Social Protest, Class Conflict and Consciousness in the English Countryside, 1700–1880." In *Class, Conflict and Protest in the English Countryside, 1700–1880,* ed. Mick Reed and Roger Wells, 121–4. London: Frank Cass, 1990.

– *Wretched Faces: Famine in Wartime England, 1793–1801.* New York: St. Martin's Press, 1988.

Westwater, Martha. *The Wilson Sisters.* Athens, OH: Ohio University Press, 1984.

Wilberforce, William. *Practical View of the Prevailing System of Professed Christians of the Higher and Middle Ranks of this Country, Contrasted with Real Christianity.* London: n.p., 1797.

Williams, Samantha. "Earnings, Poor Relief, and the Economy of Makeshifts: Bedfordshire in the Early Years of the New Poor Law." *Rural History* 16:1 (2005): 21–52.

– "Malthus, Marriage, and Poor Allowances Revisited: A Bedfordshire Case Study, 1770–1834." *Agricultural History Review* 52 (2004): 56–82.

– *Poverty, Gender and Life Cycle under the English Poor Law, 1760–1834.* Woodbridge, Suffolk: Boydell Press, 2011.

Williamson, Jeffrey. "Was the Industrial Revolution Worth It? Disamenities and Death in 19th Century British Towns." *Explorations in Economic History* 19 (1982): 221–45.

Willis, Kirk. "The Role in Parliament of the Economic Ideas of Adam Smith." *History of Political Economy* 11 (1979): 505–44.

Wiltshire, David. *The Social and Political Thought of Herbert Spencer.* Oxford: Oxford University Press, 1958.

Winch, Donald. *Malthus.* Oxford: Oxford University Press, 1987.

– *Riches and Plenty.* Cambridge: Cambridge University Press, 1996.

– *Wealth and Life*. Cambridge: Cambridge University Press, 2009.
Winchilsea, Earl of. "On the Advantages of Cottagers Renting Land." *Annals of Agriculture* 26 (1796): 227–46.
– "Extract from An Account of the Advantages of Cottagers Renting Land." *Reports of the Society for Bettering the Condition and Increasing the Comforts of the Poor* 1: (1798): 93–101.
Wood, Neal. *John Locke and Agrarian Capitalism*. Berkeley: University of California Press, 1984.
Woodham-Smith, Cecil. *The Great Hunger*. London: Hamish Hamilton, 1962.
Woods, Robert. *The Demography of Victorian England and Wales*. Cambridge: Cambridge University Press, 2000.
Wrightson, Keith. *Earthly Necessities: Economic Lives in Early Modern Britain*. New Haven: Yale University Press, 2000.
Wrigley, E.A. *Continuity, Chance, Change: The Character of the Industrial Revolution in England*. Cambridge: Cambridge University Press, 2004.
– "Country and Town: The Primary, Secondary, and Tertiary Peopling of England in the Early Modern Period." In *The People of Britain*, ed. Paul Slack and Ryk Ward, 217–42. Oxford: Oxford University Press, 2002.
– *Energy and the English Industrial Revolution*. Cambridge: Cambridge University Press, 2010.
Wrigley, E.A., and Richard Smith. "Malthus and the Poor Law." *The Historical Journal* 63 (2002): 33–62.
Wyndham, Hugh. *A Family History, 1688–1837*. Oxford: Oxford University Press, 1950.
Young, Arthur. *Autobiography of Arthur Young*. Edited by Matilda Betham-Edwards. London: Smith, Elder and Co, 1898.
– "Conduct of the Workhouses." *Annals of Agriculture* 31 (1798): 382–8.
– "Cottagers' Garden Calendar." *Annals of Agriculture* 36 (1801): 145–7.
– *The Example of France: A Warning to Britain*. London: W. Strahan, 1793.
– "A Farmer's Letter to the Yeomanry of England." *Annals of Agriculture* 27 (1796): 49–54.
– "A Farmer's Letter to the Yeomanry of England." *Annals of Agriculture* 28 (1797): 177–87.
– *The Farmer's Letters to the People of England containing the Sentiments of a Practical Husbandmen*. 2nd Edition. London: W. Nicholl, 1768.
– *A Farmer's Tour Through the East of England*. London: W. Strahan, 1771.
– "French Events Applicable to British Agriculture." *Annals of Agriculture* 18 (1792): 486–95.
– *General Report on Enclosures*. London: M. McMillan, 1808.
– *General View of the Agriculture of Essex drawn up for the consideration of the Board of Agriculture and internal improvement*. 1813.
– *General View of the Agriculture of Hertfordshire drawn up for the consideration of the Board of Agriculture and internal improvement*. 1804.

- *General View of the Agriculture of Lincoln drawn up for the consideration of the Board of Agriculture and internal improvement.* 1813.
- *General View of the Agriculture of Oxfordshire drawn up for the consideration of the Board of Agriculture and internal improvement.* 1813.
- *General View of the Agriculture of Suffolk drawn up for the consideration of the Board of Agriculture and internal improvement.* 1794.
- *General View of the Agriculture of Sussex drawn up for the consideration of the Board of Agriculture and internal improvement.* 1813
- *An Inquiry into the Propriety of Applying Wastes to the Better Maintenance and Support of the Poor.* Bury: J. Rackman, 1801.
- "Means of National Tranquility." *Annals of Agriculture* 18 (1792): 144–50.
- "Memoirs of the last Thirty Years of a Farming Life." *Annals of Agriculture* 15 (1791): 152–82.
- "Minutes Concerning Parliamentary Inclosures in the County of Bedford." *Annals of Agriculture* 42 (1804): 22–58, 479–501.
- "A Month's Tour of Northamptonshire, Leicesterschire, etc." *Annals of Agriculture* 16 (1791): 480–607.
- *Observations on the Present State of Waste Lands of Great Britain.* London: W. Nichol, 1773.
- "On the Application of the Principle of Population to the Question of Assigning Land to Cottages." *Annals of Agriculture* 41 (1804): 208–31.
- "On the Price of Corn: and the Situation of the Poor in the Ensuing Winter" *Annals of Agriculture* 33 (1799): 621–9.
- "On the State of the Poor." *Annals of Agriculture* 34 (1800): 186–91.
- *Political Arithmetic.* New York: Augustus M. Kelley, 1967.
- *A Six Months' Tour through the North of England.* London: W. Strahan, 1771.
- *Travels in France during the Years 1787, 1788, and 1789.* Edited by Constancia Maxwell. Cambridge: Cambridge University Press, 1950.
- *Tour in Ireland, 2 Vols.* London: G. Goldney, 1780.
- "Tour to the West." *Annals of Agriculture* 6 (1786): 17–151.
- "A Week in Essex." *Annals of Agriculture* 18 (1792): 391–444.
- "Yeomanry Corps." *Annals of Agriculture* 38 (1802): 148–51.
Zevin, Alexander. *Liberalism at Large: The World According to the Economist.* London: Verso, 2019.

Index

Milton Keynes UK
Ingram Content Group UK Ltd.
UKHW011255210424
441408UK00003B/86/J